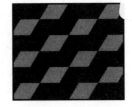

READINGS &

ISSUES IN $\boxed{cost}$

MANAGEMENT

Edited by James M. Reeve, Ph.D, C.P.A.

Professor of Accounting, University of Tennessee, Knoxville

Collection of articles from the *Journal of Cost Management*, the *Handbook of Cost Management*, and other sources.

WARREN, GORHAM & LAMONT

SOUTH-WESTERN College Publishing

An International Thomson Publishing Company

Acquisitions Editor: David L. Shaut
Developmental Editor: Ken Martin
Production Editor: Marci Dechter
Cover Design: Michael H. Stratton

AE65AA
Copyright ©1995
by South-Western College ·Publishing
and Warren, Gorham & Lamont

1 2 3 4 5 6 7 8 9 MA 2 1 0 9 8 7 6 5 4

Printed in the United States of America

Readings and issues in cost management / contributing editor, James M.
  Reeve.
      p.   cm.
   Includes bibliographical references.
   ISBN 0-538-84248-2
   1. Activity-based costing. 2. Managerial accounting. 3. Cost
control. I. Reeve, James M.
   HF5686.c8R3648   1995
   658.15'52--dc20
                                                  94-11412
                                                  CIP

International Thomson Publishing
South-Western and Warren, Gorham & Lamont are ITP Companies. The ITP
trademark is used under license.

PREFACE

Over the past decade, business enterprises have had to respond to increasing domestic and international competition with newer and better approaches to managing their organizations. These new approaches are being implemented in organizations under names such as: total quality management, employee involvement and empowerment, business process re-engineering, continuous process improvement, and short-cycle management. These philosophies require firms to be responsive, agile, and flexible in profitably providing value-added products and services to customers at competitive prices. Thus, firms are now discovering that they must be able to manage complex and changing environments without the significant costs that traditionally have attended these characteristics.

Within this changing environment, businesses have witnessed a significant rebirth of cost management. By "cost management," we mean a set of techniques and methods for:

(1) identifying and focusing upon strategic options, and
(2) planning, measuring, and improving a company's products and processes.

The first objective relates to strategic improvement, while the second objective relates to operational improvement. Note that these two purposes are necessarily interlinked. The strategy of the firm will dictate product and process improvement priorities.

Thus, cost management is much more than just cost accounting. Cost accounting is concerned with the proper accumulation of cost for inventory valuation in GAAP-based financial statements. Cost management is far more concerned with management's use of cost information for decision making. In this way cost management is much more similar to managerial accounting, yet it incorporates a number of new approaches that can be thought of as additions to the traditional discipline of management accounting.

This book provides a sampling of readings that reflect these dual purposes. There are 16 articles that have been published between 1987 and 1993 and reprinted in this book. The book is divided into five chapters as follows:

Strategic Cost Management
1. Cost Management and Strategy
2. The Design of Activity-Based Cost Systems
3. Applications in Activity-Based Costing

Operational Cost Management
4. Improving Performance
5. Japanese Cost Management Approaches

The first three chapters refer to the role of cost management in strategy, while the last two chapters refer to the operational role of cost management. The articles within these five chapters provide a broad overview of contemporary practices in cost management.

I have preceded each chapter with some opening comments about each of the readings. In many instances these opening comments provide some additional material beyond what is discussed in the articles.

HOW TO USE THIS BOOK—A MESSAGE TO STUDENTS

Cost management is one of the few areas in accounting that does not "follow the rules." By this I mean that cost management practices are not constrained by a set of codified rules promulgated by the SEC, IRS, FASB, or AICPA. Do not look for Generally Accepted Accounting Principles when studying managerial accounting, but instead open your mind to various alternatives for reporting to management. Cost management is an area that is open to good ideas and innovation. New practices that work will be employed, while those that do not will be discarded. The basic charge in cost management is: "Will this idea benefit decision making?" In other words, does the information add value to the firm? The emerging practices discussed by the authors in this book are new ideas that are being tested by a variety of firms all around the world. Thus, these readings give you a glimpse into the exciting changes and innovations that are occurring in this field.

The readings in this book provide primary source material that has been influential in advancing emerging practices in cost management. By "primary source material" I mean articles written by the individuals who have contributed directly to inventing or applying the innovative practice. In this sense, primary literature goes directly to the source, before it has been synthesized by a textbook author prior to your reading it. When you read primary source literature, the job of synthesis is yours!

You will update and improve your skills after you graduate by reading professional journals. Professional journals will provide you a window to the newest ideas and practices. Ideas that you glean from reading professional articles will spark innovation within your own professional life. Thus, this book of readings is designed to provide you an opportunity to begin learning how to read about and interpret new practices that have not yet been synthesized within a textbook.

HOW TO USE THIS BOOK—A MESSAGE TO INSTRUCTORS

Why should you use supplemental readings in your course? We are all faced with more material than we have time to fit into our courses. Yet, even so, it is important to expose students to primary source literature, since this will become a primary method of advancing professional skills once a student leaves with a degree in hand. Thus, we should be helping our students read and digest primary source material before it has been massaged by textbook authors. Students need to realize that the world of the textbook is one that will be left behind once they become professionals. The latest offerings of any field will be found in professional journals, and the student who builds habits of reading professional literature will be more able to adapt to changing professional requirements.

With these thoughts in mind, this book is intended to provide supplemental readings to either a managerial or cost accounting course, or a sourcebook for an advanced topics course. The topics covered in these readings will generally be covered at a greater depth here than would be found in textbooks. The various articles have been chosen for their relevance to emerging cost management practices and for their readability. Thus, my intent was to select readings that your students would be able to understand without great difficulty. However, I would recommend using this book as a supplement to upper division or graduate-level classes. The authors of these articles assume a working vocabulary of managerial accounting.

What I have provided in this book is topical breadth yet flexibility to instructors. Each chapter stands on its own. Thus, it is not necessary to assign every chapter, and you can emphasize the chapters that are important to you. At the very minimum I would stress both the strategic and operational roles of cost management to some degree. Secondly, it is not necessary to assign all the readings within a chapter, yet the readings within a chapter are not redundant. If you wish to assign more readings within a particular chapter area, the end of the chapter provides a more in-depth bibliography.

In addition, I have provided some opening material for each chapter. The opening material provides some of my additional thoughts related to the reading topic. You can either assign these openings in addition to the readings, or use them for yourselves for additional class discussion.

Contents

OPERATIONAL COST MANAGEMENT

STRATEGIC COST MANAGEMENT

CHAPTER ONE

Cost Management and Strategy

INTRODUCTION

In this chapter, three articles will introduce you to the role of cost management in strategy. The three articles each reflect a somewhat different theme. The three basic themes can be identified as:

1. Cost improvement is a strategic endeavor.
2. The value chain is a critical component in evaluating strategy for a strategic business unit.
3. The strategy of the firm will impact the design of a control system.

All three themes begin with the premise that the strategy of a firm consists of the long-range plans of the organization to profitably deliver value-added goods and services to customers. The strategy of the firm impacts how this is to be accomplished. Cost management information provides key information to help formulate strategies and monitor strategies once they have been implemented.

Reading 1.1   Strategic Cost Reduction

Michael D. Shields and S. Mark Young, "Effective Long-Term Cost Reduction: A Strategic Perspective," *Journal of Cost Management* **(Spring 1992), pp. 16–30.**

Shields and Young (SY) suggest that the conventional "slash and burn" response to impending profit squeezes is neither strategic nor effective. Likewise, a firm cannot naively rely on technology to drive cost reduction. In fact, it will likely be just the opposite. For example, Federal Mogul, an automobile parts supplier, invested in robots, production line computers, and automated material movement systems in order to regain a cost advantage they had lost to the Japanese. Unfortunately, this automation not only failed to lower costs, but caused the plant to become much less flexible than required by customers. As one manager stated, "Very clearly we made some poor decisions. One of them was that high-tech was the answer."[1] SY advocate a firm's taking a much different view of cost reduction —one that is based upon seeking root causes, rather than merely attempting to manage the end results. In SY's view, cost reduction should not just focus on the symptoms, much like losing weight must focus on underlying causes (eating habits, exercise regimen) rather than merely demanding that the pounds be shed.

The root causes are the "why" an organization is incurring cost. These causes are termed *cost drivers*.[2] For example, poor quality is a cost driver. If the firm improves quality, then the cost may go down. Thus, high quality equals low cost. How can this be? To illustrate, if a firm has unreliable quality, then the following costs may be incurred as a result:

scrap (throwing the problem away)

rework (fixing the problem)

rescheduling production (due to unpredictable good output)

paperwork (to record the problem and its likely causes)

inspecting (to make sure problems are detected)

inventory (to protect against uncertain production quantities)

inventory management (the support costs associated with inventories)

If the firm improves the quality of its products and processes, then these sources of cost can be eliminated. Thus, high quality is a source for improved cost (and market) effectiveness. In SY's view, the strategic firm realizes that quality, dependability, and speed lead to strategic advantages as well as to lower costs. Improved costs are a by-product of these activities.

SY go further to suggest that there are a number of organizational cost drivers associated with both structure and processes. These cost drivers are directly related to the strategy of the organization. Firms that poorly match their organizational systems with their strategies will experience a declining profit position. For example, a firm that wishes to maintain a low cost position, but at the same time attempts to provide differentiated service by carrying a broad product line may find itself requiring organizational resources to accomplish the latter and simultaneously dooming the former strategy.

An important point by SY is that organizations are changing from vertical structures with narrow spans of control to more horizontal structures organized around products and customers. These latter structures have a very favorable impact on organizational cost drivers and lie at the heart of organizational re-engineering efforts.[3] Exhibit 1 provides some additional perspective on the difference between vertical and horizontal organizations.

As you can see in the exhibit, the horizontal organization requires a very different organizational culture than does the traditional vertical, functionally based organization.

The vertical organization is characterized by functional organizations that are arranged within a multi-layered hierarchy with narrow spans of control. The information and control system mirrors this structure. Therefore, the organizational participants are measured on their ability to meet functional objectives, which may not be consistent at all with the requirements of the external customer. The horizontal organization arranges tasks around products or customers

EXHIBIT 1.

Vertical vs. Horizontal Organizations

Theme	Vertical Organization	Horizontal Organization
Customer	My boss	The external customer
Principle of organization	Tasks (functions)	Products or customers
Focus of economies	Scale economies	Scope economies
Control	Top/down — formal	Local — informal
Role of management	Coordinating	Leading
Role of work force	Entitled	Accountable
Role of information	Assign blame	Support organizational learning

in order to align participants, information flow, and feedback along dimensions that are important to customers.

The vertical organizational structure is designed for a stable environment where "one size fits all" (scale economies). In contrast, the horizontal organization is designed to learn and adapt to changing circumstances. In this organization, one size need not fit all, but can lead to what some have termed "mass customization," or an ability to provide wide product/service scope at low cost (scope economies). In the horizontal organization, participants don't exclusively wait for directives from above, but are empowered to make changes. Employees are accountable for continuous improvement of the processes in which they participate. The senior management does not coordinate disparate functions, but provides leadership in the overall strategic direction of the firm. Without leadership from the top, an organization will be unable to adapt quickly enough to new market realities. Note that this is one of SY's major points for a cost-conscious organizational culture.

Reading 1.2   Value Chain Strategic Cost Management

John K. Shank and Vijay Govindarajan, "Strategic Cost Management and the Value Chain," in *Handbook of Cost Management*, edited by Barry Brinker (New York: Warren Gorham and Lamont), D1, 1993.

Shank and Govindarajan (SG) have been the major proponents of value chain strategic cost management. This article provides a concise overview of their thoughts in this area, as well as some examples to illustrate their points. A *value chain* is a linked set of value-adding activities that link product/service creation to final customer product/service consumption. The concept was originally developed by Michael Porter.[4] SG use Porter's strategic model to provide management guidance in identifying strategic options and opportunities.

5

A key aspect of SG's approach is that the firm must look beyond its own four walls in order to appreciate its strategic environment. All firms are part of a value chain. Vertically integrated firms control greater portions of the value chain than do non-vertically integrated firms. However, few firms control the complete value chain. To illustrate a value chain, consider Exhibit 2, which is a value chain for men's slacks.

The value chain in Exhibit 2 incorporates a number of different organizations. For example, a textile company spins and weaves the cotton into fabric. An apparel manufacturer purchases the fabric and manufactures the slacks. A trucking company transports the slacks into a retailer's distribution center, and the slacks are then transported to the individual stores and sold to final consumers.

Value chain cost management asks the following questions about the value chain:

Where are the profits in this value chain?

Which firm holds the economic power?

How can the value chain be improved to serve customers better and lower overall value chain costs?

Are there superior value chain configurations, and how will this impact value chain participants?

All of these questions are strategically important and can begin to be answered by analyzing the profitability of the value chain segments. SG would argue that each element of the value chain can be evaluated with respect to (1) revenues and costs and (2) structural cost drivers. Thus, the value chain elements can be evaluated with respect to their individual contributions to the overall profits that can be earned across the complete chain.

In the example in Exhibit 2, the textile company could evaluate the profits in spinning and weaving (separately), the apparel manufacturer could evaluate the profits of manufacturing slacks (or cutting and sewing separately), and the retailer can evaluate the profitability of distributing and retailing slacks. This information would provide any one of the value chain participants insights as to their position in the chain. Low profitability would imply low economic power within the chain, while high profits would indicate high power, but vulnerability to competing value chain strategies. For example, in the Exhibit 2 value chain the retailer currently has a great deal of power and profitability (especially if the men's slacks are private label and not branded). However, the retailer now must compete with alternative value chain configurations, such as catalog sales that bypass the retailer entirely. In this alternative configuration the catalog merchandiser captures the retailer's profit in the value chain.

SG stress that a particular company should "develop sustainable competitive advantage by either controlling cost drivers or reconfiguring the value chain." SG go on to say that a firm should consider reconfiguring the value chain outside of its

EXHIBIT 2.

Value Chain for Men's Slacks

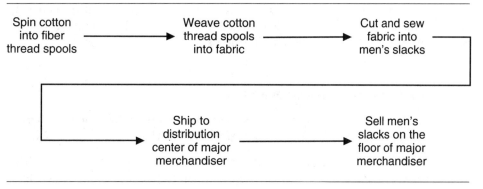

own organization "box" by looking upstream to vendor relations and downstream to customer relations. For example, the apparel manufacturer could look to the customer's activities in the distribution center and re-engineer its own processes to increase value to the chain. This could be done by separately boxing all merchandise with bar coded advance shipping labels (to retail stores). The advance shipping labels allow the retailer's distribution center to effectively unload the apparel manufacturer's shipment and immediately "cross dock" the boxes into trucks that will go to the individual retail store. By using advance shipping labels, the apparel manufacturer saves the retailer from having to store and sort merchandise in the distribution center. The distribution center becomes a regional switching station rather than a storing and sorting location. However, this can only be accomplished if the manufacturer provides the necessary pre-packaging and bar code information. There will be some cost to providing this activity, for which the manufacturer receives some price premium, but the total cost to the chain will drop, since the manufacturer's cost of providing this value-added service is less than the distribution center performing the same activities across all product lines.

SG also point out that the value chain for different products of the same company may be different. A strategic company will outline major product categories and identify value chain opportunities or competitive threats. For example, one of British Air's most frequently traveled routes is London to Paris. The value chain for this "product" includes all the items identified in the SG article. However, what is on the horizon that will significantly alter this value chain? The answer is a tunnel under the English Channel. The new tunnel will allow passengers to take a train from central London to central Paris in less time and cost than it would take to commute to and from airports and fly to Paris. This particular British Air value chain, the London to Paris route, will undergo a major competitive threat. How should British Air respond? There are any number of choices, but one might be to expand into the commuter rail business or partner with commuter railroads to provide seamless transportation between rails and air in other routes (value chains).

The SG article represents a new area wherein cost information can help guide firm strategy. There are few actual examples in the literature of this approach, but it appears to be one that holds much future promise.

Reading 1.3   Control Systems and Strategy

Vijay Govindarajan and John K. Shank, "Strategic Cost Management: Tailoring Controls to Strategies," *Journal of Cost Management* **(Fall 1992), pp. 14-24.**

The Govindarajan and Shank (GS) article is the second in this series by these authors. The topic discussed in this article is much different than the value chain considerations in the previous article. In this article, GS address an element of contingency theory. *Contingency theory* states that accounting performance and control system designs will be contingent upon the nature of the firm (its strategy, industry, capital intensity, competition, regulatory requirements, structure, power, and culture). The GS paper focuses upon one aspect of the firm, its *strategy*, and its impact on accounting control systems.

One of the important learnings from contingency theory is that there is no such thing as the single "right" accounting and control system. Although textbooks provide a number of approaches, the "correct" accounting and control system is the one that fits the firm. Thus, we should not be surprised to see a variety of different accounting and control system designs in practice, combined with some degree of clustering of systems around firms with common characteristics. This is the basic point of GS.

GS point out that the firm's mission can be on a continuum that goes from aggressive growth and market share development (build stage) to maximizing short-term profit and cash flow (harvest stage). To illustrate, Microsoft would be said to be in a "build" stage of its product life cycles, while the Philip Morris tobacco units would be in a "harvest" stage of product life cycles. GS suggest that the accounting and control systems for the firm in the build stage will need greater flexibility and less cost precision than would be found in the "harvest" mode. The article provides specific expectations of what should be found for each stage.

Although this article does not provide the necessary case evidence to validate the hypotheses empirically, a more extensive set of case study findings that are supportive are listed in footnote 8 of the article.

Notes

1. Quoted from *Wall Street Journal*, May 7, 1993, pA6.

2. We will see that managing cost drivers is a common theme identified in the readings in this book.

3. A bestselling book that is a "must read" is M. Hammer and J. Champy, *Reengineering the Corporation* (New York: HarperBusiness, 1993).

4. M.E. Porter, *Competitive Advantage: Creating and Sustaining Superior Performance* (New York: The Free Press, 1985).

Additional Readings

Archer, S., and D. Otley. "Strategy, Structure, Planning and Control Systems," *Management Accounting Research*, (December 1991): 263–303.

Govindarajan, Vijay, and John K. Shank. "Strategic Cost Analysis: The Crown Cork and Seal Case." *Journal of Cost Management,* (Winter 1989): 5–15.

McGaughey, Nick, and Claire Starry. "Cost/Value Analysis: A Strategic Tool." *Journal of Cost Management,* (Summer 1989): 32–38.

Richardson, Peter R. "Managing Costs Strategically." *Journal of Cost Management,* (Summer 1987): 11–20.

Shank, John K. "Strategic Cost Management: New Wine, or Just Different Bottles?" *Journal of Management Accounting Research,* (Fall 1989): 47–65.

———. "Strategic Cost Management and the Value Chain," *Journal of Cost Management,* (Winter 1992): 5–21.

Shank, John K. Vijay Govindarajan, and Eric Spiegel. "Strategic Cost Analysis: A Case Study." *Journal of Cost Management,* (Fall 1988): 25–33.

Shields, Michael P., and S. Mark Young. "Managing Product Life Cycle Costs: an Organizational Model," *Journal of Cost Management,* (Fall 1991): 39–52.

Effective Long-Term Cost Reduction: A Strategic Perspective

MICHAEL D. SHIELDS

Michael D. Shields is professor of accounting at San Diego State University in San Diego, California.

S. MARK YOUNG

S. Mark Young is KPMG Peat Marwick Faculty Fellow at the University of Colorado-Boulder in Boulder, Colorado.

Effective long-term cost reduction is a continuous activity that must be a strategic and cultural priority. In contrast to traditional cost reduction, with its emphasis on expedient and quick reductions in short-term costs because of immediate crises, strategic cost reduction must be part of a competitive strategy that integrates technological and human resource management strategies to provide a coordinated, broad-based, and long-term approach to reducing costs. Long-term competitive cost advantage depends on establishing a culture of continuous improvement of quality, time, and cost through innovation. Long-term cost reduction is most effectively accomplished by continuously learning about target core competencies faster than competitors can and by establishing long-term employment relationships with innovative, multiskilled employees who are paid above-average compensation.

Between the recessions of the late 1970s and early 1990s, several million U.S. managers and workers received significant pay cuts or were laid off because of cost reduction programs.[1] These programs were intended primarily to increase cost competitiveness. The business press described these cost reduction programs in phrases such as "slash and burn," "retrenching," "meat axing," "cutting and slicing," "repositioning," "restructuring," "demassing" and "downsizing." In an attempt to justify the overall approach to cost reduction, the term "rightsizing" was coined. It is still unclear whether firms that engaged in these cost reduction programs will experience long-term success, since little systematic empirical evidence exists. Nonetheless, as articles in the business press show, cost reduction programs aimed at reducing the work force are still being implemented.[2] This article first describes and evaluates the cost reduction programs employed in the late 1970s and throughout the 1980s, then sets forth a more viable basis for effective long-term cost reduction. The ultimate conclusion is that long-term controllable costs are caused (i.e., both increased and decreased) by employees, individually and in groupings that range from small teams to entire organizations. As a consequence, the key to successful long-term cost reduction is to make cost reduction part of organizational culture — i.e., part of a competitive strategy based on the integration of human resources and technological strategies.

TRADITIONAL COST REDUCTION PROGRAMS

Starting in the late 1970s and throughout the 1980s, most firms relied on traditional cost reduction, which means a collection of crash programs that focus on cutting costs by reducing payrolls and eliminating jobs.[3] The key features of traditional cost reduction are identified in Exhibit 1.

A traditional cost reduction program is typically a distress tactic targeted at all employees. It is triggered in reaction to an immediate threat, such as poor performance, losses of contracts, or price reductions. Some of these programs

EXHIBIT 1.

Differences Between Traditional and Strategic Cost Reduction

Attribute	Traditional	Strategic
Goals	Specific	Competitive advantage
Scope	Narrow	Broad
Time frame	Short-term	Long-term
Frequency	Periodic	Continuous
Trigger	Reaction	Proaction
Target	Labor	Entire value chain

(especially offshore retreat and diversification, both of which are explained below), are employed in the hope of escaping to places where labor and facilities costs are cheaper. While these traditional approaches often reduce costs immediately, the associated reduction in the value of human assets sets the stage for potential long-term failure. Five frequently used traditional cost reduction programs are described in the sections below; their effectiveness is also analyzed.[4]

THE TECHNOLOGY APPROACH

The technology approach focuses on replacing direct labor with technology to increase operating efficiency and to reduce the influence of unions. This approach is usually adopted or intensified after performance measures indicate poor performance. But the successful implementation of this approach requires money, time, an effective innovation process, and highly skilled employees—all of which, in firms that are performing poorly, are in short supply.

It is doubtful whether this labor-focused cost reduction—with its emphasis on immediate improvements in direct labor efficiency—can provide sustainable competitive advantage.[5] Its effectiveness is questionable since, in many manufacturing settings, a product's cost of direct labor is typically no more than 10 percent of its sales price. This means, for example, that a 100 percent increase in direct labor efficiency can only reduce a product's total cost as a percentage of its sales by 5 percent. Alternatively, the complete elimination of direct labor can only reduce the product's total cost as a percent of its sales by 10 percent (*assuming* that the substitute for this labor is costless).

Thus, attempts to gain or sustain competitive advantage by reducing labor cost would appear to be weak foundations for a successful cost reduction program. As Hamel and Prahalad[6] point out, the *cost* of labor is rarely a source of sustainable competitive advantage. First, labor is a small percentage of total cost. Second, when the labor force is the key to a firm's competitive advantage, that advantage stems from labor's ability to be innovative through work methods (e.g., through total quality management) and flexibility. Moreover, many firms adopt technology-intensive strategies (e.g., computer integrated manufacturing, or CIM) when they reduce their work force. Importantly, the success of these strategies requires having highly skilled employees who can design, implement, operate, and service these advanced technologies. Unfortunately, these critical human resource issues are ignored or receive only lip service because of short-term cost considerations. Ironically, however, long-term success with technology is determined by how employees work with the technology.

Another important consideration in achieving good performance from a technology-intensive strategy is knowing when and how much should be spent on technological innovation. Evidence indicates that the relationship follows an elongated S-shape, with spending related to technology on the X-axis and techno-logical performance on the Y-axis.[7] This elongated S-relationship indicates that initial spending on technology results in little, if any, increase in performance. At some point, as spending continues to increase, there are dramatic increases in the performance of the technology. Finally, a point is reached at which further increases in spending result in only small (or no) increases in performance as the limits of the technology are hit (e.g., conventional washing machines can get clothes only so clean).

The implication for cost management is that a firm will achieve a better payoff from its spending on technology if it knows where it is on the S-curve. For example, when a new technology is first introduced, a firm may decide to stop spending for the new technology when only a negligible increase in performance is obtained. At the other extreme, a firm at the far end of its S-curve may fail to realize that it has moved beyond the point at which increased spending will lead to worthwhile increases in performance. The result could be wasted spending as the technology hits its performance limit.

"LEAN AND MEAN"

The "lean and mean" approach has been a popular cost reduction program since the 1980s. Firms that follow this approach apply tough policies and controls to reduce the number of employees. A common approach is to employ across-the-board cost cuts through layoffs and reductions in pay and benefits.[8]

An appropriate depiction of the effects of a lean and mean program is a roller coaster traveling through time. The end of the ride can be—and frequently is—a long-term failure, despite short-term thrills and success. Exhibit 2 illustrates the interaction of lean and mean cost reduction efforts and the state of the economy. As shown in Exhibit 2, a firm's costs—total and unit—rise when the economy is "good" and fall when the economy is "bad." We define a good (or bad) economy as one in which there is low (high) unemployment and a growing (shrinking) GNP.

EXHIBIT 2.

Cost Reduction Roller Coaster

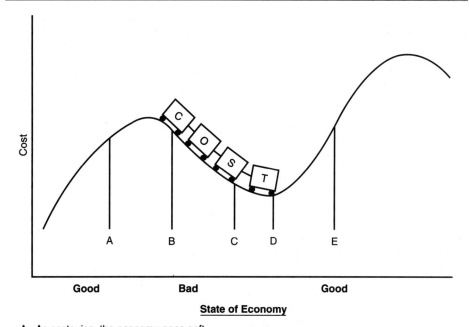

A: As costs rise, the economy goes soft.
B: To reduce costs, cut discretionary programs, reduce work force, etc.
C: Problems develop: moral, motivation, conflict, shortages, delays.
D: To reduce problems and to react to the expanding economy, hire new employees.
E: Incur extra costs to train new employees and to cover learning curve effects.

When the economy is good, the lean and mean approach is not employed; as a result, costs creep up as inefficiency increases and new programs are initiated or expanded. As costs rise across firms, the economy begins to soften as prices become inflated. In response, firms begin to implement lean and mean programs to cut costs by reducing and eliminating discretionary programs and employees. While there is an immediate cost decrease, adverse effects become noticeable shortly thereafter.[9] The morale, motivation, and commitment of remaining employees begins to decrease. Their stress increases because they worry about being the next ones who will be laid off, and also because they are overworked due to the layoffs.[10] Having fewer employees also leads to coordination problems (e.g., production delays and missed schedules), which can cause decreases in quality and increases in delivery time. Another bad consequence is that the creative and motivated employees leave for better employment opportunities.

In time, the economy begins to expand again as firms' products regain their competitiveness as a result of their cost reduction program. In response, firms abandon their lean and mean programs; they begin to hire employees again and to reestablish or expand programs to reduce the adverse effects of the previous cost reduction programs. As the economy expands, firms continue to hire new employees and to incur associated training and learning-curve costs.[11] The net result is that costs begin to increase again. This cycle keeps repeating, but as time goes on, each new cost peak becomes higher than the previous cost peaks.

How Effective Are Traditional Cost Reduction Programs?

Recent surveys suggest that traditional cost reduction programs do not meet their objectives.* One survey found that—out of 350 senior managers in 275 companies that, together, make up 26 percent of the U.S. gross national product—half responded that the cost-cutting or restructuring programs at their companies had failed to achieve what had been hoped.

Results of the other survey (this one of managers from 1,005 corporations) found as follows:

- Less than one-half of the companies had met their cost reduction targets;
- Only 32 percent had raised profits to an acceptable level;
- Only 21 percent had improved return on investment appreciably;
- 58 percent reported that employee morale was battered;
- 37 percent were having trouble persuading the survivors to remain; and
- 87 percent reported that early retirement programs let to decisions by star employees to leave.

* Surveys by the Cresap division of the consulting firm Towers Perrin and by consultant Wyatt Co. cited in Anne Fisher, "Morale Crisis," *Fortune*, November 18, 1991, pp. 71–72.

Lean and mean is not effective in the long term because it attempts to reduce costs by reducing workers, but it does *not* reduce the work that needs to be done to make and sell products. While cutting workers, but not work, is a popular approach to traditional cost reduction, it causes an immediate decrease in costs that is usually followed by an increase because the work still needs to be done.[12] The long-term effects of lean and mean programs are like the roller coaster ride shown in Exhibit 2.

OFFSHORE RETREAT

Many firms have tried to reduce costs by escaping to places (e.g., Asia) that offer the promise of lower labor costs used offshore retreat efforts to reduce direct labor costs. Many of these firms have found, however, that startup costs of offshore retreats are higher than expected, while quality and delivery performance are lower.[13] The success of this cost reduction approach often depends on how employees at home are treated and on the vagaries of exchange rates and currency fluctuations. Employee morale at home can be hurt if domestic or local employees are laid off when the firm moves jobs offshore.

MERGERS

Mergers purport to create economies of scale by eliminating overlapping employees, products, plants and overhead. The idea is to build on the strengths of each merging entity, but the result is often that the worst aspects of each firm survive.[14] Problems often occur in assimilating diverse or incompatible management styles, corporate cultures, product lines, and technologies. Frequently, these mergers result in layoffs and compensation reductions, with the result that morale and motivation decrease. Ultimately, the hoped-for-economies of scale from the merger are not realized as hidden or unexpected costs arise.

DIVERSIFICATION

Diversification into new industries is an approach that firms often use when they are searching for cheaper operating environments. If a firm expands beyond its core competency, however, it is likely to experience difficulties in developing and implementing new products, technologies, or distribution systems, with the result that costs are higher than expected.[15] The increasing diversity also increases the cost of complexity, which in many cases exceeds the incremental revenue.

WHEN CAN TRADITIONAL COST REDUCTION APPROACHES SUCCEED?

Given these five approaches to traditional cost reduction, the question arises, "Are there situations when traditional cost reduction can be effective?" Some managers have found that traditional cost reduction is effective in only the following three situations:

1. When "dressing up" a business for divestiture;
2. When implementing a harvest strategy; and
3. When reducing operating costs—but only when a firm's overall strategic position is good.[16]

While traditional approaches to cost reduction may be effective in these special situations, in general, traditional approaches do not appear to provide a basis for long-term competitive success.

STRATEGIC COST REDUCTION

In contrast to the traditional approach, this article advocates strategic cost reduction as an approach that can provide companies with better opportunities for creating and sustaining long-term competitive advantage. Strategic cost reduction is a long-term approach that integrates competitive strategy, technological strategies, human resource management strategies, and organizational design considerations to provide a focused and coordinated basis for sustaining competitive advantage. Exhibit 1 compares traditional and strategic cost reduction strategies.

The importance of viewing cost reduction as part of a long-term competitive strategy is reinforced by evidence that Ferdows and DeMeyer provide.[17] Their analysis of 187 European manufacturers indicates that cost reduction is the result of having achieved success with other manufacturing strategies. Specifically, they argue and empirically show that long-term cost improvement is the result of having first achieved improvement in quality, then dependability, and finally speed. There is a cumulative effect by which prior gains influence current gains, a process that can illustrated as a pile of sand with four layers: quality at the bottom and cost at the top (see Exhibit 3). Increases in quality help increase dependability; then gains in both quality and dependability spur gains in speed. Finally, the cumulative effects of these prior gains result in cost efficiency gains.

Ferdows and DeMeyer also point out that, due to the shape of the pile of sand, achieving a small gain in cost requires successively larger gains for these other aspects of performance (e.g., a 10 percent cost gain may require a 15 percent gain in speed, a 25 percent gain in dependability, and a 40 percent gain in quality). The implication is that long-term successful cost reduction is achieved indirectly—through gains made in other strategically important areas. Thus, cost reduction strategy should be deeply embedded in the firm's competitive strategy.

Strategic cost reduction occurs continuously and is intertwined with competitive strategy.[18] Ideally, competitive strategies and also cost reduction strategies are derived from analyses of a firm's own value chains and of the value chains of its competitors to identify key activities that offer the best competitive alternatives. Strategic cost reduction is part of a competitive strategy that is focused on improving the performance of key activities and their cost drivers in a firm's value chain.

EXHIBIT 3.

The Sand Cone Model of Cost Reduction

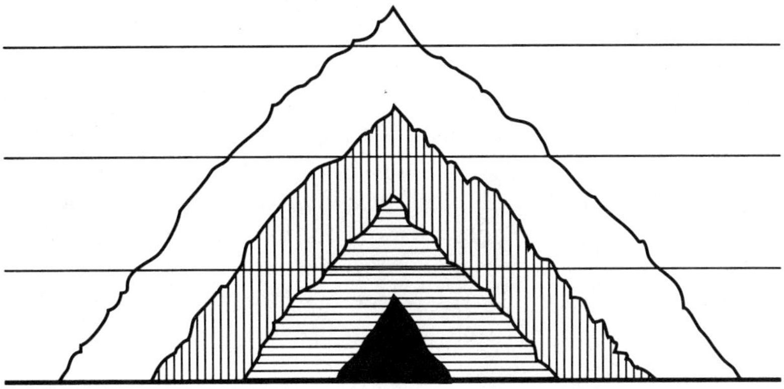

Cost efficiency

Speed

Dependability

Quality

Source: K. Ferdows and A. DeMeyer, "Lasting Improvements in Manufacturing Performance: In Search of a New Theory," 9 *The Journal of Operations Management* 168–184 (No. 2, 1991)

FOCUS

Two critical aspects of developing a strategic cost reduction program involve deciding where to focus the program and the mix of methods to use to reduce strategically important costs. Many manufacturing firms achieve competitive advantage from activities that occur before (e.g., R&D) or after (e.g., distribution) manufacturing, rather than in manufacturing itself. For many manufacturers, the most effective strategy to reduce a product's total life cycle cost is to focus cost reduction efforts on those activities that occur before manufacturing begins.[19] For instance, many Japanese manufacturing firms focus their cost reduction efforts on activities that occur before manufacturing begins, because they have found that this gives them the most and the quickest reductions in costs.[20] Quickly reducing costs significantly is crucial to maximizing market share and achieving target cost strategies.[21] Thus, for most firms, initial efforts at cost reduction should be focused on those activities that occur before manufacturing ever begins—i.e., conception, development, design.

SET OF METHODS

While manufacturing firms use many methods to reduce costs, there is only limited evidence that they are used in coordinated ways to achieve synergistic gains.[22] Thus, an important aspect of developing an effective cost reduction strategy is to identify a set of cost reduction methods that can be used in concert to continuously reduce strategically important costs. The methods selected should be compatible with—and should reinforce—a firm's competitive strategy, culture, and human resource management strategy.[23]

For instance, the implementation of a cost reduction strategy may coincide with the adoption of a competitive strategy and a corporate culture of continuous improvement. A set of methods can be employed to achieve continuous improvement, including activity-based management (ABM), value analysis and engineering, just-in-time manufacturing methods (JIT), total quality management (TQM), cross-functional teamwork, employee involvement, and employee skill enhancement.[24] Rappaport[25] provides a list of coordinated ways by which a firm can reduce its long-term costs if it is pursuing a cost leadership strategy or a differentiation competitive strategy. Hayes, Wheelwright and Clark[26] provide examples of how manufacturing firms can use a set of cost reduction methods to achieve synergistic gains in performance.

TRADE-OFFS

In some cases, the strategically important issue is to *increase* cost to achieve other competitive gains. For example, a study by McKinsey and Company found that being six months late to market but meeting the developmental cost budget resulted in actual profits that were one-third lower than budgeted profits.[27] In contrast, bringing a product to market on time but 50 percent over the developmental budget resulted in a profit loss of only four percent. The important point of this example is that sometimes it is strategically advantageous to increase costs if doing so can help achieve other competitive gains.

EMPLOYEES ARE THE ULTIMATE LONG-TERM COST DRIVER

Effective cost reduction (especially in the long term) requires changing employees' behavior. In the long-term, the decisions and actions of employees cause costs; only employees can make decisions and take actions to reduce costs. Thus, the key to effective long-term cost is employees—their beliefs, values, and goals. This means that successful cost reduction depends on establishing and nurturing an appropriate organizational culture, such as one based on continuous improvement and cost consciousness.[28] In the long term, successful cost reduction depends on how well a cost reduction strategy fits with a firm's competitive strategy, culture, and human resource management strategy.

The major reason that traditional cost reduction fails to have a positive long-term strategic impact is that it excludes the value of having employees who are broadly and deeply skilled—employees who work together and are committed to the long-term success of a firm. This human resource management approach is one of the most important reasons for the comparative success of Japanese firms. For example, one key to the success of Japanese firms has been their treatment of human resource management as long-term and strategic; human resource management is an important, if not *the* most important, part of their competitive strategy.[29]

The importance of employees as long-term cost drivers can be illustrated based on a discussion of quality improvement. Many firms have adopted the approach of trying to improve quality and reduce the cost of quality by substituting technology for people. But, behind all this technology are employees who design, operate, and service it. Technology can produce products that are only as good as the employees who develop and operate the technology—software programmers, machine technologists, design engineers, and others.

In the long term, the way to improve product quality and reduce the cost of quality through technology is to use technology to supplement high-quality employees. Technology will work better if it is complemented by employees who are highly educated, highly skilled, highly motivated, and committed to continuous improvement. All the innovation that is necessary for technology to be effective comes from humans. Having creative employees is important because, when trying to sustain competitive advantage through technology, technology does not stand still. Technology-intensive firms must continuously innovate to improve existing technology or to introduce new technology; otherwise, they will fall behind their technology-intensive competitors.

Three prerequisites to realizing the maximum benefits to be derived from long-term cost reduction efforts of employees are having good top management, having a cost culture, and offering long-term employment. Each provides an important and necessary contribution to the establishment of an organizational setting in which employees are willing and able to make strategic cost reductions. The next sections discuss how top management, cost culture, and long-term employment affect long-term costs. Later sections explain how organizational cost drivers affect strategic cost reduction.

TOP MANAGEMENT

Top management must take the initiative in decision making and action to demonstrate to other employees and stakeholders that they are serious about improving the competitive position of the firm.[30] Top management should be prepared to set examples by taking tough action (e.g., taking a bigger reduction in pay than do the workers, laying off senior executives before laying off line workers, and eliminating executive perks) and getting involved with all employees. Top managers should take these actions to show that they are aware of the problems other employees face and that top management cares about employees and their fate during tough times.

One important determinant of success is the ability of top management to establish *strategic intent*, which means that they must provide *leadership* to achieve a *vision* by exploiting *core competencies*.[31] Top management must provide the leadership that makes all employees committed to achieving this strategic intent.[32] Top management must discuss strategic problems, challenges, and opportunities with employees. Finally, top management must set a steady course of action, set clear targets, and establish review mechanisms.

Top management must establish strategic goals for cost reduction. These goals should be based on supporting or reinforcing the firm's core competencies and competitive strategy. For example, top management may decide that the best way to reduce cost and to increase both quality and flexibility in the long-term is by exploiting the firm's competence in mechanical, manufacturing, and software engineering by implementing CIM. Accompanying this introduction would be a change in the human resource management strategy to increase employees' knowledge of how to use the new technology. For example, direct labor employees could be retrained to become machine technologists and monitors.

COST CULTURE

Top management must also develop a cost-conscious culture. The goal of a cost-conscious culture is continuous improvement of cost, quality, and time through innovation. Achieving this goal can be aided by redesigning the organization to focus attention on key factors that have to do with sustaining continuous improvement strategies. The acid test of a cost-conscious culture is whether employees are motivated to take actions that reduce long-term costs but expose them to short-term risk. An example is a culture in which workers are willing to be innovative enough to eliminate their own jobs because they believe that they will then be assigned to more challenging and rewarding jobs.

Eight ways to develop a cost culture. Eight key ways to develop a cost culture are as follows:[33]

1. Having top management demonstrate daily to employees the importance of reducing costs to the firm's success.
2. Hiring the best-qualified employees. These employees can then develop high-quality activities and products, because long-term total cost with high quality is less than long-term total cost with low quality.
3. Empowering employees through participation, involvement, and autonomous, cross-functional work teams.

4. Increasing the levels of education, training, retraining, and cross-training provided to employees to increase and broaden their skills, commitment, and innovation.

5. Motivating employees to break existing paradigms (e.g., eliminating existing constraints rather than optimizing within them).

6. Communicating horizontally more than vertically; eliminating conflicting bureaucratic messages; focusing all employees' communication on two or three keys to success; reducing the number of rules, policies and standard operating procedures; and providing scoreboards for continuous feedback.

7. Linking compensation to cost reduction (such as gains in productivity and efficiency, achievement of target costs, and improvement over previous period's costs).

8. Providing all employees with continuous feedback about competitors' costs, their own performance, and the performance of other teams.

Train[34] provides an interesting description of a firm with cost problems that is struggling—philosophically and politically—with whether to implement a traditional cost reduction program (i.e., deep across-the-board cuts). Analysis of this case by senior executives and consultants illustrates why and how such situations should be a strategic cultural priority that is dealt with by methods like the eight outlined above.

LONG-TERM EMPLOYMENT

Many firms have found that the best way to realize the maximum potential from all employees to reduce long-term costs is to establish a long-term employment relationship in which both employees and the employer can adjust to changing circumstances.

For example, a human resource strategy that is based on long-term employment, cross-training of employees, continuous education, job rotation, and work teams creates an organizational skill set that provides a firm with the flexibility to adapt quickly to changes, opportunities, and threats. Having broadly skilled employees also increases flexibility when product and activity volume decrease and it becomes necessary to rearrange employee work assignments. The bottom line is that if firms want employees to be committed to long-term cost reduction, they must make long-term commitments to their employees. An employee's commitment will extend only as far into the future as his expected employment benefit horizon (e.g, including pension benefits).

Avoiding layoffs. Many firms have found that it is in their best interest not to lay off workers as a means of cutting costs.[35] Over a period of time, it is cheaper to keep excess employees. For example, the employees can be put to work on

23

projects that will improve efficiency or eliminate non-value-added activities; alternatively, they can be provided with additional training. Some firms have used excess workers to lay the groundwork for an expected expansion in business by having them prepare the firm to use new technologies. This proactive approach can help a firm adapt faster when the business environment improves.

Laying off employees causes motivational problems for the remaining employees and, when business improves, the firm must incur the cost of hiring and training new employees who will probably not be as effective and efficient as were the employees who were laid off. Thus, while laying off employees may bring about an immediate reduction in cost, over a period of several years it could become the more costly alternative because of the roller coaster effect.

When a company must lay off employees, a program should be implemented that to maintain (if not increase) the morale of the remaining employees. Imberman[36] suggests a three-step program:

1. Define the sources of the firm's competitive problems. In many cases, this requires changing the corporate culture to accept the problems for what they really are. Changing the culture will help the survivors establish a shared vision of what is required for success, which usually requires communication and innovation.
2. Initiate action to solve the problem. This requires realistic challenges and experiments. It is critical that employees believe that to solve these problems they must work smarter, not harder or longer.
3. Increase employees' skills through education, training, retraining, and cross-training.

ORGANIZATIONAL COST DRIVERS

An organization is a collection of people. Based on the view that employees are the ultimate long-term cost driver, it is a natural extension to see an organization as an important long-term cost driver. If an employee causes and reduces costs, then groups of employees will also cause and reduce costs.

Organizations group employees into teams, departments, divisions, and similar groupings to efficiently and effectively accomplish activities. The way in which employees are organized affects the long-term cost structure. The diversity of operating units and their boundaries (e.g., functional or geographical boundaries) affect a firm's complexity (e.g., its number of parts and their interrelationships), which, in turn, affects long-term costs. Some have offered ABM as a solution to reducing the cost of complexity, because ABM focuses on eliminating non-value-added activities and reducing the number and frequency of cost drivers.[37] Gingrich and Metz[38] provide examples of how to reduce the cost of organi-

EXHIBIT 4.

Organizational Cost Drivers

Structure	Process
Number of work units	Planning and control processes
Number of functional departments/ horizontal layer	Employee involvement and participation
Number of profit centers	Total quality management
Number of distribution channels	Capacity utilization
Number of product lines	Plant layout and its efficiency
Number of vertical levels in organization	Product configuration
Number of operating facilities	Linkages between suppliers and/or customers
Number of products produced at more than one facility	Education and training programs
Number of employees	Activity-process sequence (linear, concurrent)
	Management style
	Number of internal transactions
	Number of external transactions
	Number of meetings
	Number of trips
	Number of memos sent or received
	New product sales/total sales
	[Number of new employees + number of exited employees]/ total employees

zationally induced complexity by making changes in organizational structures and processes.

Organizational cost drivers include organizational structure, organizational process, and organizational learning. Examples of organizational cost drivers include vertical structure, horizontal structure, work units (e.g., individuals vs. teams), educational programs, process sequence (e.g., linear vs. concurrent), culture and management style (e.g., decentralization, a vertical chain of command or entrepreneurial); see Exhibit 4.

Firms adapt their organizational structure and processes over time in response to various challenges and opportunities. Many of the contemporary changes to these organizational cost drivers are intended to increase a firm's speed, flexibility, quality, and innovation. Organizational structure and process significantly affect what and how fast an organization learns.

Organizational cost drivers determine a significant percentage of a firm's long-term cost structure and its competitive position. It is difficult to identify any one of these cost drivers as being the most significant. Nonetheless, they act in concert to determine long-run costs. Thus, organizational cost drivers should be the focus of a cost reduction strategy.

A specific example of how these cost drivers affect long-term costs can be seen in the case of a large aerospace firm whose cost structure was analyzed by a well-known strategic consulting firm. This consulting study predicted that unit operating costs could be reduced by 47 percent if the aerospace firm changed its cost drivers as follows:

- A 17 percent reduction could be achieved if the firm adopted a focused manufacturing strategy and flattened the organizational structure;
- A 6 percent reduction could be achieved if the firm implemented efficient cross-functional communication; and
- A 24 percent reduction could be achieved if the firm switched product design structures (e.g., by implementing concurrent engineering) and emphasized throughput time (e.g., by adopting JIT and cycle time management).

A more general example is based on Skinner's argument[39] that a manufacturing firm's cost reduction efforts are most effective when they focus on the firm's manufacturing structure and process. Skinner advances the view that manufacturing cost reduction and productivity improvement is based on a "40-40-20" rule about the sources of competitive advantage through manufacturing. That is, about 40 percent of the possible advantage stems from long-term manufacturing structure (e.g., number, size, location, and capacity of facilities) and basic approaches to materials and work force management. Another 40 percent comes from equipment and process technology (e.g., JIT, TQM, and flexible manufacturing systems). Only about 20 percent is derived from traditional approaches to productivity improvement (e.g., those that focus on labor). The implication of this argument is that the key to successful long-term manufacturing cost reduction is to focus on improving organizational cost drivers.

ORGANIZATIONAL STRUCTURE

Organizational structure is how responsibility for activities is differentiated horizontally and vertically. These structures evolve over time in response to changing opportunities and challenges.

For example, throughout the 1970s, most firms were structured like a pyramid with many vertical layers (see the left-hand side of Exhibit 5). This structure was used to transmit information vertically between the top and the bottom layers of the firm. Humans were the key communicators, and an extensive verti-

EXHIBIT 5.

Temporal Changes in Vertical Organizational Structures

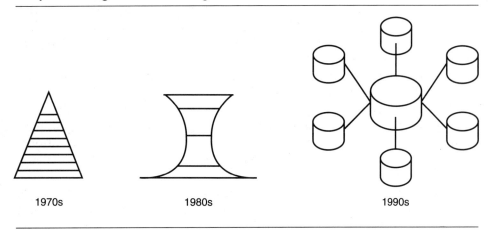

| 1970s | 1980s | 1990s |

cal hierarchy was needed to increase the probability that effective and efficient communication occurred. The limiting factor was the horizontal span of control within a vertical layer. For example, assuming a horizontal span of control of ten, if there are 1,000 workers at the bottom level of a pyramid, then the firm's vertical structure would consist of at least three additional vertical levels with 100 first-level supervisors, ten second-level supervisors, and one third-level supervisor (e.g., the CEO). Extrapolating this analysis to firms with 100,000 workers indicates that they will have at least six vertical layers with at least 11,110 employees between the top and bottom vertical layers. An important detrimental consequence of these pyramidal structures was slow and distorted vertical communications, which reduced the quality of outputs and increased their time-to-market and cost.

A significant change began in the 1980s. The introduction of new information processing and communication technologies (e.g., personal computers, facsimile machines, and local area networks) allowed the tops and bottoms of pyramids to communicate more directly. This greatly reduced the need for middle managers. Firms therefore began to transition their vertical structures from the pyramid form to the hourglass form (see the middle figure in Exhibit 5). This change is continuing in the 1990s. Now it is predicted that in the future companies will be organized like flat networks, as the figure on the right-hand side of Exhibit 5 illustrates.[40] While these flatter vertical structures reduce costs because fewer managers are needed, that is not their primary strategic benefit. These flatter structures speed up and increase the quality of information exchange, which (in turn) results in getting products of higher quality and lower cost more quickly to customers.

Horizontal structure. A significant portion of the cost of complexity arises from how firms are horizontally structured. Many firms are organized horizontally by product, geography, or function. This creates a firm that is fragmented and has a series of narrow goals or visions (e.g., one for each horizontal unit). One result is myopic, short-term management. This fragmentation also reduces a firm's speed and flexibility.

The most common organizational structures consist of many horizontal layers. These can create functional barriers, especially if information is intended to flow vertically rather than horizontally. One way to reduce the cost of this horizontally induced complexity and rigidity is to design the firm so that the primary organizational structure is horizontal. The intention of this organizational approach is to break down the functional barriers that impede the horizontal flows of information.

It is important that information flow horizontally at the lowest level possible (i.e., rather than up to a high level in the organization, where senior managers make decisions that are then channeled back down to the functional areas). The importance of keeping the information down at the local level is highlighted by the fact that it is employees in the field or on the shop floor who are most aware of problems and how to resolve them. Thus, firms should consider organizing so that the various functional employees can regularly meet to exchange information, quickly solve problems, and coordinate action.

Another way to reduce the cost of horizontal complexity is to tear down the functional lines and horizontally reorganize the firm into cross-functional teams that have broad responsibility for all aspects of a product.[41] These local employees are better able to deal with product diversity and process complexity. A firm is better off not transmitting this complexity upward to seniors managers, who are often not as intimately familiar with the details as local employees. Besides, transmitting information vertically increases time and hence cost. The goal is to reduce the cost of horizontal communication which could also increase quality, speed, learning, and flexibility by breaking down functional barriers (e.g., through concurrent engineering). The result of this change in horizontal structure is an expected decrease in long-term costs.

Firms can also reduce their long-term costs by organizing horizontally based on groups of activities.[42] For example, Prahalad and Hamel[43] argue that to achieve global competitive advantage, an effective basis for horizontal structuring is to organize based on core competencies. Core competencies are activities or knowledge that a firm has that make it a world-class performer.

Appropriate groupings of activities into horizontal units can reduce the costs of coordinating across diverse functions; they can also focus each grouping of activities on a customer (whether the customer is internal or external). An example of this is a Navy supply center that, after introducing ABC, found that its previous functional structure resulted in processes that were cost inefficient.[44] In response, the supply center changed its organizational structure so that it was based on groupings of activities that were required to deliver completed services to customers. The supply center also increased employees' training in team building and statistical quality control. Within two years, the supply center found that its operating costs had decreased, that delivery performance had increased, and that no layoffs were necessary. Using an ABM approach to organizational design also allows a firm to analyze how expected long-term costs vary depending on how the various activities are aggregated and linked together to form linear and parallel processes. A further advantage of an ABM approach to organizational design is that the activity representation of a firm fits nicely with value chain analysis.[45]

Some Japanese firms are now designing their organizational structures and management accounting systems based on horizontal relationships. Accounting systems are being designed primarily by product line rather than by functional areas.[46] The basic unit of design is a product line, with functional areas nested within each product line. These firms have decentralized responsibility for costs and defined cost centers based on product lines. The advantage of this horizontal organization is that it clearly divides responsibility for products, activities, and costs. Since the organization and its accounting system are designed based on products rather than functional areas, most costs are direct to products, which significantly reduces the amount of costs that are allocated to products. To reduce costs, these Japanese firms have a continuous improvement strategy for each product line.

ORGANIZATIONAL PROCESSES

Organizational design also includes developing processes to accomplish and coordinate activities. In the strategic consulting literature, *executional cost drivers* are thought to affect the ability of a firm to implement action successfully.[47] These cost drivers include work force involvement (which means participation, culture, and commitment to continuous improvement), total quality management, capacity utilization, plant layout efficiency, product configuration, and exploiting linkages with suppliers and customers (e.g., through JIT and electronic data interchange). As discussed above, how activities and employees are linked determines the basic processes within an organization and, hence, how—and how much—they drive organizational costs.

ORGANIZATIONAL LEARNING

Exhibit 6 provides a general example of how organizational cost drivers affect long-term costs. The idea behind this example is that the rate of organizational learning determines whether a firm can sustain a competitive cost advantage. To

EXHIBIT 6.

An Example of How Organizational Cost Drivers Can Reduce Long-Term Costs

do so requires that the firm learn about a core competency (e.g., new product technology or manufacturing process technology) faster than its competitors.[48] Important sources of organizational learning are educational programs, R&D, information systems, budgeting and performance evaluation systems, and cross-functional teams.

Organizational learning occurs when a firm learns about its environment and how to make it better. Organizational learning also deals with how this learning is stored in organizational memory for future use.[49] Much of management accounting can be interpreted as strategies for organizational learning. For example, budgeting is a process organizations use to solve problems (i.e., to learn better ways to manufacture and market products to achieve desirable financial outcomes), to share this information across vertical and horizontal levels, and to serve as an organizational memory for storing this information.

Organizational cost drivers (e.g., vertical and horizontal structures and processes, culture, and education programs) determine the type and rate of organizational learning because they affect the type and extent of communications and problem solving by various parts of a firm (Exhibit 6). For instance, a firm learns faster about product and process interactions when it is structured by concurrent engineering rather than functionally (e.g., according to design, engineering, and manufacturing). Organizational learning affects the rate of managerial innovation (e.g., learning about total quality management), which then serves to promote process and product innovation (e.g., product designs with no quality defects and manufacturing processes that minimize the occurrence of errors).[50] The result is a sustainable source of competitive advantage that derives from learning faster and better than competitors can about core competencies and about process and product innovation. Thus, an important source of long-term cost reduction is organizational learning, which (in turn) is determined by how an organization is structured and the processes that occur within the structure.

CONCLUSION

The central idea that this article develops is that effective long-term cost reduction is a continuous activity that is a strategic and cultural priority. In contrast to traditional cost reduction, with its emphasis on expedient and quick reductions in short-term costs in response to immediate crises, strategic cost reduction is part of a competitive strategy that integrates technology and human resource management strategies to provide a coordinated, broad-based, and long-term approach to reducing costs.

Firms will be better long-term performers if they can get off the short-term cost-reduction roller coaster. Long-term competitive cost advantage depends on establishing a culture of continuous improvement of quality, time, and cost through innovation. Long-term cost reduction is most effectively accomplished by continuously learning about target core competencies faster than competitors can and by establishing long-term employment relationships with innovative, multiskilled employees who are paid above-average compensation.

Notes

1. R.M. Tomasko, *Downsizing — Reshaping the Corporation for the Future* (New York: AMACOM, 1987).

2. "The New Executive Unemployed," *Fortune* (April 8, 1991): 36–48.

3. P. Richardson, *Cost Containment: The Ultimate Advantage* (New York: The Free Press, 1988).

4. *Id.*

5. W. Skinner, *Manufacturing: The Formidable Competitive Weapon* (New York: John Wiley & Sons, 1985); also G. Hamel and C. Prahalad, "Strategic Intent," *Harvard Business Review* (May–June 1989): 63–76.

6. Hamel and Prahalad, "Strategic Intent," *supra* note 5.

7. R. Foster, *Innovation — The Attacker's Advantage* (New York: Summit Books, 1986).

8. R. Henkoff, "Cost Cutting: How To Do It Right," *Fortune* (April 9, 1990): 40–49.

9. Business International Research Report, *Strategic Cost Reduction: How International Companies Achieve Cost Leadership* (Geneva: Business International S.A., 1987); Henkoff, "Cost Cutting," *supra* note 8.

10. T. Jick, "The Stressful Effects of Budget Cuts in Organizations," in L. Rosen, *Topics in Managerial Accounting* (New York: McGraw-Hill Ryerson Limited, 3d ed., 1984): 267–280.

11. B.C. Ames and J.D. Hlavacek, "Vital Truths About Managing Your Costs," *Harvard Business Review* (January–February 1990): 140–147.

12. Henkoff, "Cost Cutting," *supra* note 8.

13. Richardson, *Cost Containment: The Ultimate Advantage, supra* note 3.

14. *Id.*

15. C. Prahalad and G. Hamel, "The Core Competence of the Corporation," *Harvard Business Review* (May–June, 1990): 79–91.

16. Business International Research Report, *Strategic Cost Reduction, supra* note 9.

17. K. Ferdows and A. DeMeyer, "Lasting Improvements in Manufacturing Performance: In Search of a New Theory," 9 *The Journal of Operations Management* (No. 2 1991): 168–184.

18. Business International Research Report, *Strategic Cost Reduction, supra* note 9.

19. M.D. Shields and S.M. Young, "Managing Product Life Cycle Costs: An Organizational Model," *Journal of Cost Management* (Fall 1991): 39–52.

20. T. Makido, "Recent Trends in Japan's Cost Management Practices," in *Japanese Management Accounting*, Y. Monden and M. Sakurai, eds. (Cambridge, Mass.: Productivity Press, 1989); M. Tanaka, "Cost Planning and Control Systems in the Design Phase of a New Product," in *Japanese Management Accounting*.

21. C. Berliner and J. Brimson, *Cost Management for Today's Advanced Manufacturing: The CAM-I Conceptual Design* (Boston: Harvard Business School Press, 1988); Makido, "Recent Trends," *supra* note 20; R. Cooper and M. Sakurai, "How the Japanese Manage Overhead" (unpublished paper, Harvard Business School, 1990); Toshiro Hiromoto, "Another Hidden Edge—Japanese Management Accounting," *Harvard Business Review* (July–August 1988): 22–27; M. Sakurai, "Target Costing and How to Use It," *Journal of Cost Management* (Summer 1989): 39–50; Tanaka, "Cost Planning" *supra* note 20; F. Worthy, "Japan's Smart Secret Weapon," *Fortune* (August 12, 1991): 72–75.

22. Shields and Young, "Managing Product Life Cycle Costs," *supra* note 19.

23. A. Majchrzak and M. Rahimi, "Transitioning to CIM Systems: Effects of Human Factors and Resources Management," in *Success Factors for Implementing Change: A Manufacturing Viewpoint*, K. Blanche, ed. (Dearborn, Mich.: Society of Manufacturing Engineers, 1988); D. Opalka and J. Williams, "Employee Obsolescence and Retraining: An Approach to Human Resource Restructuring," *The Journal of Business Strategy* (Spring 1987): 90–96; H. Thompson and R. Scalpone, "Managing the Human Resource in the Factory of the Future," 5 *Human Systems Management* (1985): 221–230; R. Hayes, S. Wheelwright, and K. Clark, *Dynamic Manufacturing* (New York: The Free Press, 1988); R. Schuler and I. MacMillan, "Gaining Competitive Advantage Through Human Resource Management Practices," *Human Resource Management* (Fall 1984): 244–255.

24. Shields and Young, "Managing Product Life Cycle Costs," *supra* note 19.

25. A. Rappaport, *Creating Shareholder Value* (New York: The Free Press, 1986): Chapter 4.

26. Hayes, Wheelwright, and Clark, *Dynamic Manufacturing, supra* note 23.

27. "A Smarter Way to Manufacture," *Business Week* (April 30, 1990): 110–117.

28. M.D. Shields and S.M. Young, "A Behavioral Model for Implementing Cost Management Systems," *Journal of Cost Management* (Winter 1989): 17–27; Shields and Young, "Managing Product Life Cycle Costs, *supra* note 19.

29. V. Pucik and N. Hatvany, "Management Practices in Japan and Their Impact on Business Strategy," in *Advances in Strategic Management*, Vol. 1 (Greenwich, Conn.: Jai Press, 1983): 103–131.

30. Business International Research Report, *Strategic Cost Reduction,"* *supra* note 9; Richardson, *Cost Containment, supra* note 3.

31. Hamel and Prahalad, "Strategic Intent," *supra* note 5; Prahalad and Hamel, "The Core Competence," *supra* note 15.

32. R. Walton and G. Susman, "People Policies for the New Machines," *Harvard Business Review* (March–April 1987): 98–106; Shields and Young, "Managing Product Life Cycle Costs," *supra* note 19.

33. Richardson, *Cost Containment, supra* note 3; Shields and Young, "A Behavioral Model," *supra* note 28; Henkoff, "Cost Cutting," *supra* note 8; E. Lawler, G. Ledford, and S. Mohrman, *Employee Involvement in America: A Study of Contemporary Practice* (Houston: American Productivity and Quality Center, 1989); E. Lawler, *High-Involvement Management: Participative Strategies for Improving Organizational Performance* (San Francisco: Jossey-Bass Publishers, 1986).

34. A. Train, "The Case of the Downsizing Decision," *Harvard Business Review* (March–April 1991): 14–30.

35. B. Saporito, "Cutting Costs Without Cutting People," *Fortune* (May 25, 1987): 26–32; Schuler and MacMillan, "Gaining Competitive Advantage," *supra* note 23.

36. W. Imberman, "Managers and Downsizing," *Business Horizons* (September–October, 1989): 28–33.

37. Berliner and Brimson, *Cost Management for Today's Advanced Manufacturing, supra* note 21; P. Turney, "How Activity-Based Costing Helps Reduce Cost," *Journal of Cost Management* (Winter 1991): 29–35.

38. J. Gingrich and H. Metz, "Conquering the Costs of Complexity," *Business Horizons* (May–June 1990): 64–71.

39. W. Skinner, "The Productivity Paradox," *Harvard Business Review* (July–August 1986): 55–59.

40. P. Drucker, "The Coming of the New Organization," *Harvard Business Review* (January–February 1988): 45–53; R. Miles and C. Snow, "Organizations: Concepts for New Forms," *California Management Review* (Spring 1986): 62–73; J.B. Quinn, T. Doorley, and P. Paquette, "Beyond Products: Services-Based Strategy," *Harvard Business Review* (March–April 1990): 58–67; H. Thorelli, "Networks: Between Markets and Hierarchies," 7 *Strategic Management Journal* (1986): 37–51.

41. Shields and Young, "Managing Product Life Cycle Costs," *supra* note 19.

42. C.J. McNair, "Interdependence and Control: Traditional vs. Activity-Based Responsibility Accounting," *Journal of Cost Management* (Summer 1990): 15–24; M. Hammer, "Reengineering Work: Don't Automate, Obliterate," *Harvard Business Review* (July–August 1990): 104–112.

43. Prahalad and Hamel, "The Core Competence," *supra* note 15.

44. D. Harr, "How Activity Accounting Works in Government," *Management Accounting* (September 1990): 36–40.

45. J. Shank and V. Govindarajan, *Strategic Cost Analysis* (Homewood, Ill.: Richard D. Irwin, 1989); M. Hergert and D. Morris, "Accounting Data for Value Chain Analysis," 10 *Strategic Management Journal* (1989): 175–188.

46. Cooper and Sakurai, "How the Japanese Manage Overhead," *supra* note 21.

47. D. Riley, "Competitive Cost-Based Investment Strategies for Industrial Companies," *Manufacturing Issues* (New York: Booz, Allen & Hamilton Inc., 1987).

48. R. Stata, "Organizational Learning — The Key to Management Innovation," *Sloan Management Review* (Spring 1989): 63–74; P. Senge, "The Leader's New Work: Building Learning Organizations," *Sloan Management Review* (Fall 1990): 7–23.

49. C. Fiol and M. Lyles, "Organizational Learning," *Academy of Management Review* (1985): 803–813; B. Levitt and J. March, "Organizational Learning," 10 *Annual Review of Sociology* (No. 4 1988): 319–340.

50. C. Fine, "Quality Improvement and Learning in Productive Systems," *Management Science* (October 1986): 1301–1315.

Strategic Cost Management and the Value Chain

JOHN K. SHANK

Noble Professor of Managerial Accounting and Management Control, Amos Tuck School of Business Administration, Dartmouth College, Hanover, New Hampshire

VIJAY GOVINDARAJAN

Professor of Strategy and Control, Amos Tuck School of Business Administration, Dartmouth College, Hanover, New Hampshire

INTRODUCTION

The *value chain* for any firm in any business is the linked set of value-creating activities—from basic raw material sources to the ultimate product or service that is delivered to consumers. This chapter explains how to construct and use value chains. It uses real-world case studies from the airline industry and the packaging industry to highlight the fact that the strategic cost management (SCM) insights that emerge from value chain analysis are different from—and better than—the insights available from traditional management accounting approaches.

The first part of the chapter defines the value chain concept, contrasts it with the value-added notion, and demonstrates its power. Next, the methodology for constructing and using a value chain is introduced. Two case studies are then presented to illustrate the power of value chain analysis. The final part of the chapter explains how the value chain concept is the overarching framework for SCM and how activity-based costing (ABC) and similar cost management tools can be usefully accommodated within the value chain concept.

THE VALUE CHAIN

One of the major themes in SCM concerns the focus of cost management efforts: How does a firm organize its thinking about cost management? In the SCM framework, managing costs effectively requires a broad focus that Michael Porter calls the "value chain"—that is, the linked set of value-creating activities defined earlier.[1] This focus is external to the firm, with each firm viewed in the context of the overall chain of value-creating activities of which it is only a part, from basic raw material to end-use consumers.

In contrast, traditional management accounting adopts a focus that is largely internal to the firm, with each firm viewed in the context of its purchases, its processes, its functions, its products, and its customers. In other words, management accounting takes a "value-added" perspective that starts with payments to suppliers (purchases) and stops with charges to customers (sales). The key theme is to maximize the difference (i.e., *the value added*) between purchases and sales. The strategic insights yielded by value chain analysis, however, differ significantly from—and are superior to—those suggested by value-added analysis.

THE CONCEPT

Michael Porter notes that a business can develop a sustainable competitive advantage by following one of two strategies:[2]

- A low-cost strategy; or
- A differentiation strategy.

Low-Cost Strategy

The primary focus of a low-cost strategy is to achieve low cost relative to competitors (i.e., cost leadership). Cost leadership can be achieved through such approaches as:

1. Economies of scale in production;
2. Experience curve effects;
3. Tight cost control; and
4. Cost minimization in such areas as research and development (R&D), service, sales force, or advertising.

Firms that have followed this strategy include Texas Instruments in consumer electronics, Emerson Electric in electric motors, Hyundai in automobiles, Briggs and Stratton in gasoline engines, Black and Decker in machine tools, Commodore in business machines, K Mart in retailing, BIC in pens, and Timex in wrist watches.

Differentiation Strategy

The primary focus of a differentiation strategy is to create something that customers perceive as being unique. Product uniqueness can be achieved through such approaches as brand loyalty (Coca Cola in soft drinks), superior customer service (IBM in computers), dealer network (Caterpillar Tractors in construction equipment), product design and product features (Hewlett-Packard in electronics), or technology (Coleman in camping equipment). Some firms that have followed a differentiation strategy include Mercedes Benz in automobiles, Stouffer's in frozen foods, Neiman-Marcus in retailing, Cross in pens, and Rolex in wrist watches.

Whether or not a firm can develop and sustain cost leadership or differentiation depends fundamentally on how the firm manages its own value chain relative to those of its competitors. Both intuitively and theoretically, competitive advantage in the marketplace ultimately derives from providing better customer value for equivalent cost or equivalent customer value for a lower cost. Thus, value chain analysis is essential to determine exactly where in the firm's segment of the chain—from design to distribution—costs can be lowered or customer value enhanced.

The value chain framework is a method for breaking down the chain—from basic raw materials to end-use customers—into strategically relevant activities to understand the behavior of costs and the sources of differentiation. As noted earlier, a firm is typically only one part of the larger set of activities in the value delivery system. Suppliers not only produce and deliver inputs used in a firm's value activities, they profoundly influence the firm's cost or differentiation position as well. Similarly, distribution channels have a significant impact on a firm's value activities.

As is discussed more fully below, gaining and sustaining a competitive advantage require a firm to understand the *entire* value delivery system, not just the portion of the value chain in which it participates. Suppliers and distribution channels have profit margins that are important to identify in understanding a firm's cost or differentiation positioning, because end-use customers ultimately pay for all the profit margins throughout the value chain.

Strategic Implications

Exhibit D1.1 provides a conceptual value chain for the paper industry. The distinct value activities, such as timber, logging, pulp mills, paper mills, and conversion plants are the building blocks by which this industry creates a product of value to buyers. It is possible to quantify the economic value created at each stage by identifying the costs, revenues, and assets for each activity. What is argued here is that every firm in Exhibit D1.1—A, B, C, D, E, F, and G—must construct a value chain for the total paper industry, breaking the total value in the chain into its fundamental sources of economic value. Such an analysis has potential strategic implications for every competitor in this industry:

- If competitor A (a fully integrated company) calculates the return on assets (ROA) at each stage of the chain by adjusting all transfer prices to competitive market levels, it could highlight potential areas where the firm could more economically buy from the outside instead of "making" (which is the strategic choice of make or buy). For example, most "fully integrated"

EXHIBIT D1.1

Value Chain in the Paper Products Industry

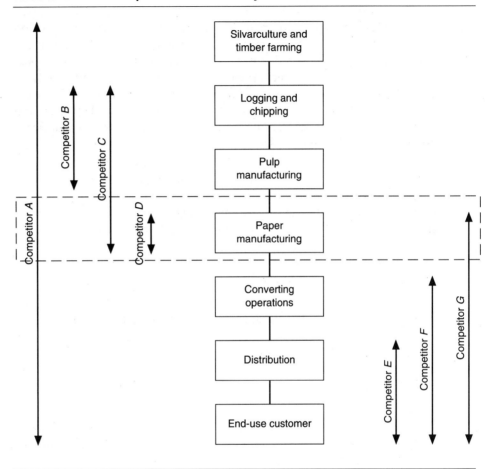

forest product companies still use independent loggers to cut their trees on the way to their mills.

- With a complete value chain, competitors *B, C, D, E, F,* and *G* might be able to identify possibilities to integrate forward or backward into areas that can enhance their performance. Westvaco, for example, has stopped manufacturing envelope paper, although it still owns a large envelope converter. Champion International has sold its envelope-converting business but still produces envelope paper.
- Each value activity has a set of unique cost drivers that explain variations in costs in that activity.[3] Thus, each value activity has its unique sources of

competitive advantage. Companies are likely to face a different set of competitors at each stage: Some of these competitors would be fully integrated companies, and some of them would be more narrowly focused specialists. For example, company *D* in Exhibit D1.1 faces competition from *A, C,* and *G* in the paper manufacturing stage. Yet *A, C,* and *G* bring very different competitive advantage to this stage of the value chain vis-à-vis *D*. It is possible for *D* to compete effectively with *A, C,* and *G* only by understanding the total value chain and the cost drivers that regulate each activity. For example, if "scope" (vertical integration) is a key structural driver of paper mill cost, *A* has a significant advantage, and *D* a significant disadvantage in this marketplace.

• The value chain analysis helps to quantify buyer power (for *B, C,* and *D*) and supplier power (for *E, F,* and *G*) by calculating the percentage of total profits that can be attributed to each stage in that chain. This calculation can help firms identify ways to exploit linkages with both their suppliers and their customers to reduce costs, enhance differentiation, or both.

Value Chain vs. Value-Added Analysis

The value chain concept can be contrasted with the internal focus that typically is adopted in management accounting. Management accounting usually takes a value-added perspective, as noted earlier. From a strategic perspective, the value-added concept has two big disadvantages:

1. It starts too late; and
2. It stops too soon.

Starting cost analysis with purchases misses all the opportunities for exploiting linkages with the firm's suppliers. Such opportunities can be dramatically important to a firm.

Supplier Linkages

The differences between a value chain perspective and a value-added perspective can be seen clearly in the context of scheduling problems that can arise if a firm ignores the complete value chain. The automobile industry provides a good example.

A few years ago, a major U.S. automobile manufacturer began to implement just-in-time (JIT) management concepts in its assembly plants. Assembly costs represented 30 percent of sales. The company reasoned that use of JIT would eliminate 20 percent of these costs, because assembly costs in Japanese automobile plants were known to be more than 20 percent below those in U.S. plants. As the firm began to manage its factories differently to eliminate inventory buffers and waste, its assembly costs did begin to drop noticeably. But the firm experienced dramatic problems with its major suppliers, who began to demand price increases that more than offset the savings in the assembly plants. The automobile firm's first response was to chide its suppliers and tell them that they, too, needed to embrace JIT concepts for their own operations.

A value chain perspective revealed a much different picture of the overall situation. Of the automobile company's sales, 50 percent was purchases from parts suppliers. Of this amount, 37 percent was purchases by the parts suppliers, and the remaining 63 percent was value added by the suppliers. Thus, suppliers actually were *adding* more manufacturing value to the automobile than the assembly plants (63 percent × 50 percent = 31.5 percent). By reducing buffer inventory and requiring JIT deliveries by suppliers, the company had placed major strains on its suppliers. As a result, the suppliers' aggregate manufacturing costs went up more than the company's assembly costs went down.

The reason, once identified, was very simple. The assembly plants experienced huge and uncertain variability in their production schedules. One week ahead of actual production, the master schedule was more than 25 percent wrong 95 percent of the time. When inventory buffers are stripped away from a highly unpredictable production process, the manufacturing activities of the suppliers become a nightmare. For every dollar of manufacturing cost that the assembly plants saved by moving toward JIT management concepts, the suppliers' plants spent much more than one dollar extra because of the schedule instability.

Because of its narrow, value-added perspective, the automobile company had overlooked the ramifications its scheduling changes had on its suppliers' costs. Management had ignored the fact that JIT requires a partnership with suppliers. A major factor in the success of JIT at a Japanese automobile assembly plant is stable scheduling for suppliers. Whereas the U.S. plant regularly missed schedules only one week in the future by 25 percent or more, Japanese plants vary by one percent—or less—from schedules that are planned four weeks in advance.

A failure to adopt a value chain perspective doomed this major effort to failure; ignorance of supply chain cost analysis concepts on the part of the automobile company's management accountants proved very costly. These scheduling ramifications might have been handled better if management accountants in the automobile industry had been taught value chain concepts somewhere in their accounting education.

Beneficial linkages (i.e., linkages with suppliers and customers that are managed in such a way that all parties benefit) can also be tracked more accurately with value chain analysis than with value-added analysis. For example, when bulk chocolate began to be delivered as a liquid form in tank cars instead of as 10-pound, molded bars of chocolate, industrial chocolate companies (i.e., the suppliers) eliminated the cost of molding bars and packing them, but they also saved candy makers the cost and trouble of unpacking and melting the solid bars of chocolate.[4]

Customer Linkages

In addition to starting too late, value-added analysis has another major flaw: It stops too soon. Customer linkages can be just as important as supplier linkages; stopping cost analysis at the point of sale eliminates all opportunities for exploiting linkages with customers.

Exploiting customer linkages is the key idea behind the concept of life cycle costing. *Life cycle costing* is a costing concept that argues for including all the costs incurred for a product—from the time when a product is conceived until it is abandoned—as part of the product cost. Life cycle costing thus deals explicitly with the relationship between what a customer pays for a product and the total cost the customer incurs over the life of the product. A life cycle costing perspective on the customer linkage in the value chain can lead to enhanced profitability. Explicit attention to postpurchase costs by the customer can lead to more effective market segmentation and product positioning. Designing a product to reduce postpurchase costs of the customer can be a major weapon in capturing competitive advantage. In many ways, the lower life cycle cost of imported Japanese automobiles helps to explain their success in the U.S. market.

There are other examples where the linkage between a firm and its customer is designed to be mutually beneficial and where the relationship with the customer is viewed not as a zero-sum game but as a mutually beneficial one. A case in point is the container industry. Some container producers have constructed manufacturing facilities near beer breweries and deliver the containers through overhead conveyers directly onto the customers' assembly line. This practice results in significant cost reductions for both the container producers and their customers by expediting the transport of empty containers, which are bulky and heavy.[5]

Missed Opportunities

Just as many cost management problems are misunderstood because of failure to see the impact on the overall value chain, many management opportunities are missed in the same way. The paper industry again provides an example of these missed opportunities when a value-added, rather than a value chain, analysis is applied.

In the late 1980s, U.S. suppliers of paper to envelope converters lost profits because they were caught unawares by a significant change in the value chain of the envelope converter. The shift from sheet-fed to roll-fed envelope finishing machines had dramatically changed the raw material specifications for envelope paper.

Although roll-fed machines were not introduced in the United States until around 1980, today they produce more than 60 percent of all domestic envelopes. Roll-fed machines—which are far more expensive to buy but much less expensive to operate than sheet-fed machines—can bring substantial overall savings for envelope converters, especially when large volumes of envelopes are produced.

With sheet-fed machines, an envelope company buys large rolls of paper 40–60 inches wide, which are cut into sheets, cut into blanks in die-cutting machines, and finally fed by hand into folding-and-gluing machines. With roll-fed machines, however, the envelope company buys narrow rolls of paper 5–11 inches wide, which are converted directly into envelopes in one combined operation.

Paper manufacturers do not want to complicate their primary manufacturing process by producing the narrow rolls directly on the paper machines. Instead, they use secondary machines called "rewinder slitters" to convert the large rolls of paper from the paper machines into the narrower rolls the converters who use roll-fed machines now want. Thus, the transition from selling wide rolls to selling narrow rolls has added an additional processing step for the paper manufacturers. The business issue, therefore, is how the change in the customers' (i.e., the envelope company's) value chain should be reflected in paper prices now that manufacturing costs along the value chain have increased because of the envelope company's changed requirements.

Management accounting in the paper industry takes neither value chain analysis nor life cycle costing into account. Consequently, the additional costs for the rewinder slitter machines are considered just a small part of mill overhead, which is assigned to all paper production on a per-ton basis. For a large, modern paper mill, rewinder slitter cost ranges from 1 to 7 percent of total cost. The impact on total average cost per ton is less than $10. Little of this cost is variable with incremental production, because the mill always keeps excess capacity in such a small department. (It is only common sense to make sure that $300 million paper machines are never slowed down by a bottleneck at a $2 million rewinder slitter machine.)

The industry norm is to charge $11 per ton extra if the customer wants the rolls slit to the narrow widths (i.e., 11 inches or less). The savings to the envelope converter from roll-fed machines far exceed this extra charge. Unfortunately, the full cost to the paper mill of providing the incremental rewinder slitting service also far exceeds this extra charge. It can cost more than $100 per ton to have an outside subcontractor slit rolls to narrow widths. An external value chain perspective would look at the savings from narrow rolls for the customer and the extra costs to the paper mill and set a price differential somewhere in between. An internal mill costing perspective, however, sees no cost issue at all.

The lack of a value chain perspective contributes to the lack of concern about product costing issues. The $11 surcharge looks like pure extra contribution to profit. The result is an uneconomic price, the impact of which is buried in a mill management accounting system that ignores value chain issues. The opportunity to more accurately price might not have been missed if the management accountants in the paper companies (like their colleagues in the automobile and candy industries) had been exposed to value chain concepts somewhere in their management accounting education.

A Framework of Interdependence

The value chain framework highlights how a firm's products fit into the buyer's value chain. Under this framework, for example, it is readily apparent what percentage the firm's product costs are in relation to the ultimate buyer's total costs. The fact that paper constitutes over 40 percent of the total costs of a magazine is very useful in encouraging the paper mill and the publisher to cooperate on cost-reduction activities.

Unlike the value-added concept, value chain analysis explicitly recognizes the fact that the various activities within a firm are not independent but, rather, interdependent. At McDonald's, for example, the timing of promotional campaigns (one value activity) significantly influences capacity utilization in "production" (another value activity). These linked activities must be coordinated if the full effect of a promotion is to be realized. As another example, Japanese VCR producers were able to reduce prices from $1,300 in 1977 to $298 in 1984 by emphasizing the impact of an early step in the chain (product design) on a later step (production): They drastically reduced the number of parts in VCRs.[6]

Conventional management accounting approaches tend to emphasize across-the-board cost reductions. By recognizing interdependencies, however, value chain analysis admits to the possibility that deliberately increasing costs in one value activity can bring about a reduction in total costs. The expense that Procter & Gamble incurred to place order-entry computers directly in Wal-Mart stores, for example, significantly reduced overall order-entry and processing costs for both firms.

THE METHODOLOGY

The value chain concept just described has a unique methodology. Its methodology involves the following steps:

1. Identify the industry's value chain and then assign costs, revenues, and assets to value activities.
2. Diagnose the cost drivers regulating each value activity.
3. Develop sustainable competitive advantage, either through controlling cost drivers better than competitors or by reconfiguring the value chain.

These steps are considered in greater detail in the following sections.

Identifying the Value Chain

The first step in constructing and using a value chain is to identify the industry's value chain. This step must be executed with the idea of gaining competitive advantage, for competitive advantage cannot be meaningfully examined at the level of the industry as a whole.

A value chain disaggregates an industry into its distinct strategic activities. Therefore, the starting point for cost analysis is to define an industry's value chain, then to assign costs, revenues, and assets to the various value activities. These activities are the building blocks with which firms in the industry create a product that buyers find valuable.

Activities should be isolated and separated if they satisfy any or all of the following conditions:

- They represent a significant percentage of operating costs;
- The cost behavior of the activities (or the cost drivers) is different;
- They are performed by competitors in different ways; and
- They are likely to create differentiation.

Each value activity incurs costs, generates revenues, and ties up assets in the process.

After identifying the value chain, operating costs, revenues, and assets must be assigned to individual value activities. For intermediate value activities, revenues should be assigned by adjusting internal transfer prices to competitive market prices. With this information, it should be possible to calculate ROA for each value activity.

Diagnosing Cost Drivers

The second step in constructing and using a value chain is to diagnose the cost drivers that explain variations in costs in each value activity.

In conventional management accounting, cost is primarily a function of only one cost driver: output volume. Cost concepts related to output volume permeate the thinking and the writing about cost: fixed versus variable cost, average cost versus marginal cost, cost-volume-profit analysis, break-even analysis, flexible budgets, and contribution margin, to name a few.

In the value chain framework, by contrast, output volume per se is seen to capture little of the richness of cost behavior. Rather, multiple cost drivers are usually at work. Further, cost drivers differ across value activities. For example, number of orders received is the cost driver for the receiving activity, number of setups is the cost driver for the production control activity, and number of orders shipped is the cost driver for the shipping activity.

Attempts have been made to create a comprehensive list of cost drivers.[7] In the strategic management literature, in particular, good lists of cost drivers exist.[8] In line with these lists, the following list of cost drivers is divided into two categories:

- Structural cost drivers; and
- Executional cost drivers.

These two categories are discussed in the sections below. An attempt is also made below to define which drivers in these two categories can be considered "fundamental" cost drivers.

Structural Cost Drivers

The first category of cost drivers, structural cost drivers, draws on industrial organization literature.[9] *Structural cost drivers* derive from a company's choices about its underlying economic structure. These choices drive cost positions for any given product group. There are at least five strategic choices that a firm must make about its underlying economic structure:

1. *Scale:* What is the size of the investment to be made in manufacturing, R&D, and marketing resources?
2. *Scope:* What is the degree of vertical integration? (Horizontal integration is more related to scale.)
3. *Experience:* How many times in the past has the firm already done what it is doing again?
4. *Technology:* What process technologies are used in each step of the firm's value chain?
5. *Complexity:* How wide a line of products or services is being offered to customers?

Each structural driver involves choices that drive product cost. Given certain assumptions, the cost calculus of each structural driver can be specified.[10]

Recently, much interest has arisen over activity-based costing (ABC).[11] The ABC analysis is largely a framework to operationalize complexity, which is a fundamental cost driver.

Executional Cost Drivers

The second category of cost drivers, *executional cost drivers,* are those determinants of a firm's cost position that hinge on its ability to "execute" successfully.

Whereas structural cost drivers are not monotonically scaled with performance, executional drivers are. That is, for each of the structural drivers, more is not always better. Thus, for example, there are diseconomies of scale or of scope: A more complex product line is not necessarily better or necessarily worse than a less complex line. Too much experience can be as bad as too little in a dynamic environment. Texas Instruments, for example, emphasized the learning curve and became the world's lowest-cost producer of obsolete microchips. Technological leadership versus "followership" is a legitimate choice for most firms.

In contrast, for each one of the executional cost drivers, more is *always* better. The list of basic executional cost drivers includes at least the following:

- *Work force involvement ("participation"):* Is the work force committed to continuous improvement (*kaizen* in Japanese)?
- *Total quality management (TQM):* Is the work force committed to total product quality?
- *Capacity utilization:* What are the scale choices on maximum plant construction?
- *Plant layout efficiency:* How efficient, against current norms, is the plant's layout?
- *Product configuration:* Is the design or formulation of the product effective?
- *Linkages with suppliers or customers:* Is the linkage with suppliers or customers exploited, according to the firm's value chain?

Quantifying the effects of each of these drivers also involves specific cost analysis issues. Many strategic planners maintain that SCM is moving quickly away from structural drivers and toward executional drivers because the insights from analyses based on structural drivers are too often obsolete and hence ineffective.

Fundamental Cost Drivers

No consensus currently exists on what constitutes "fundamental" cost drivers. One source, for example, offers two different lists of fundamental cost drivers.[12] Those who see cost behavior in strategic terms, however, agree that output volume alone cannot catch all aspects of cost behavior. Ultimately, how unit costs change because of changes in output volume in the short run is seen as a less interesting question than how a company's cost position is influenced by the firm's comparative position on the various drivers that are relevant in its competitive situation.

Whatever items are on the list of "fundamental" cost drivers, the key ideas behind it are as follows:

1. *Value chain as the broader framework.* The concept of cost drivers is a way to understand cost behavior in each activity in the value chain. Thus, ideas such as ABC are only a subset of the value chain framework.
2. *Volume not a sufficient factor.* For strategic analysis, volume is usually not the most useful way to explain cost behavior.
3. *Structural choices and executional skills.* What is more useful in a strategic sense is to explain cost position in terms of the structural choices and executional skills that shape the firm's competitive position. For example, Michael Porter[13] analyzes the classic confrontation in 1962 between General Electric and Westinghouse over steam turbines in terms of the structural and executional cost drivers for each firm.
4. *Relevant strategic drivers.* Not all strategic drivers are equally important all the time, though several are probably important in every case. For example, Porter[14] develops a strategic assessment of du Pont's position in titanium dioxide, based primarily on scale and capacity utilization issues.
5. *Cost analysis framework.* For each cost driver, a particular cost analysis framework is critical to understanding the positioning of a firm.
6. *Cost drivers specific to activities.* Different activities in the value chain are usually influenced by different cost drivers. For example, the relevant cost driver for advertising is market share, whereas promotional costs are usually variable. For example, Coca Cola can realize economies of scale in advertising because of its large market share. A price-off, by contrast (an example of a sales promotion activity), is strictly a variable cost per unit.

Developing Sustainable Competitive Advantage

The third step in constructing and using a value chain is to develop sustainable competitive advantage. Once a firm has identified the industry's value chain and diagnosed the cost drivers of each value activity, sustainable competitive advantage can be gained either by controlling those drivers better than competitors or by reconfiguring the value chain.

For each value activity, the key questions to ask about developing sustainable competitive advantage are:

1. Can costs in this activity be reduced, holding value (revenues) constant?
2. Can value (revenue) be increased in this activity, holding costs constant?

Cost Reduction

By systematically analyzing costs, revenues, and assets in each activity, a firm can achieve both differentiation and low cost. An effective way to accomplish this goal is to compare the firm's value chain with the value chains of one or two of its major competitors and then identify the actions needed to manage the firm's value chain better than competitors manage their value chains.

Value Increase

While continuing the focus on managing the existing value chain better than competitors, a company should devote more effort toward identifying where in the value chain payoffs could be significant. For example, in the mature and highly competitive meatpacking industry, Iowa Beef Processors has performed exceptionally well by controlling its processing, distribution, and labor costs. It accomplished these cost reductions by redefining the traditional value chain in this industry:

> Earnings per share [of Iowa Beef Processors] have soared at a compound annual rate of over 23 percent since 1973. The company has achieved this remarkable record by never wavering from its strategy and obsession—to be the low-cost producer of beef.
>
> To that end, it rewrote the rules for killing, chilling, and shipping beef. It built plants on a grand scale, automated them to a fare-thee-well, and now spends up to $20 million a year on renovation to keep them operating efficiently. The old-line packers shipped live animals to the abattoirs at such rail centers as Chicago, but Iowa Beef brought the plant to the cattle in the sprawling feedlots of the High Plains and Southwest. This saved on transportation and avoided the weight loss that commonly occurs when live animals are shipped. Iowa Beef also led the industry in cleaving and trimming carcasses into loins, ribs, and other cuts, and boxing the pieces at the plant, which further reduced transport charges by removing excess weight.
>
> The company has fought tenaciously to hold down labor costs. Though some of its plants are unionized, it refused to pay the wages called for in the United Food & Commercial Workers' expensive master agreement, which the elders of the industry have been tied to for 40 years. Iowa Beef's wages and benefits average half those of less hard-nosed competitors.[15]

It is not suggested here that constructing a value chain for a firm is easy, as the above details demonstrate. There are several thorny problems to confront: calculating value for intermediate products, isolating cost drivers, identifying linkages across activities, and computing supplier and channel margins, for example. Despite these problems, it is in every firm's self-interest to construct its value chain. The very process of performing the value chain analysis can be quite instructive. Such an exercise forces managers to ask: "How does my activity add value to the chain of customers who use my product or service?"

THE POWER OF VALUE CHAIN ANALYSIS: CASE STUDIES

Two case studies are now presented to illustrate the value chain concept and methodology. These case studies also demonstrate how value chain analysis differs from conventional management accounting analysis. The case studies are as follows:

- *An airline industry case study.* In the first case study, the cost and differentiation positioning of two firms from the airlines industry is contrasted by comparing the cost per seat mile of these two airlines in the different components of their value chains. Again, the analysis offered is based on the published financial statements of the firms discussed.
- *A packaging industry case study.* In the second case study, the methodology for constructing a full-blown value chain for a packaging industry firm is detailed, along with the strategic insights derived from such an analysis.

While the first case study about the airline industry is based on published financial statements, the analysis for the packaging industry case study is based on field research.

An Airline Industry Case Study

In the following case study about the airline industry, the value chains of airline competitors are described in both qualitative and quantitative terms.

Generally, it can be said that all commercial airlines provide value to customers at the following three stages:

1. By providing reservation information and ticketing services;
2. By operating the aircraft from point A to point B; and
3. By providing other services to passengers before a flight, during a flight, and after a flight arrives.

Each element in the value chain utilizes specific assets and has a specific cost function. Overall return on investment is a result of value added at all three linked stages.

Conventional financial reports reveal nothing about the separate value-creating activities in which the airline is engaged. Exhibit D1.2 shows a disguised and condensed version of the published income statements and balance sheets of one of the major trunk airlines (which here is fictitiously called Ajax Airlines). The statements clearly reveal much that is interesting about the company—but nothing about the value chain. Combining the financial statements with a du

EXHIBIT D1.2

Ajax Airlines: Financial Data

	1988	1987
Statements of income		
Sales	$8,800	$7,200
Expenses		
Salaries and benefits	2,900	2,400
Aircraft fuel	1,100	1,000
Fleet operations cost (leases and depreciation)	3,900	3,200
Total operating expense	7,900	6,600
Operating income	900	600
Interest expense	230	200
Tax	335	200
Net income	$ 335	$ 200
Balance sheets		
Current assets	$2,600	$2,100
Property and equipment	7,000	6,300
Total assets	$9,600	$8,400
Current liabilities	$2,700	$2,000
Long-term debt	3,000	3,000
Equity	3,900	3,400
Total liabilities	$9,600	$8,400

Pont analysis (as shown in Exhibit D1.3) can yield conventional insights, but not much about business strategy.

Profit Margins

The du Pont analysis reveals (for one thing) that profit margins at Ajax Airlines improved along with sales. That is, the airline was able to sell more tickets, while operating expense declined per dollar of sales. Asset utilization—a critical factor in the airline industry—also improved, as the improved asset turnover (from 0.857 to 0.917 in Exhibit D1.3) shows. All the while, financial leverage remained constant. So it appears that Ajax Airlines was able to improve both margins and asset utilization, while holding financial risk constant. It would appear that management has done a good job and should continue with its apparently successful growth strategy.

But *how* has Ajax Airlines grown? And *how* has the company been able to

EXHIBIT D1.3

Ajax Airlines: du Pont Analysis

	$\dfrac{\text{Net income}}{\text{Sales}}$	×	$\dfrac{\text{Sales}}{\text{Assets}}$	×	$\dfrac{\text{Assets}}{\text{Equity}}$	=	$\dfrac{\text{Net income}}{\text{Equity}}$
1988	$\dfrac{\$335}{\$8,800}$	×	$\dfrac{\$8,800}{\$9,600}$	×	$\dfrac{\$9,600}{\$3,900}$	=	$\dfrac{\$335}{\$3,900}$
	0.038	×	0.917	×	2.46	=	0.086
1987	$\dfrac{\$200}{\$7,200}$	×	$\dfrac{\$7,200}{\$8,400}$	×	$\dfrac{\$8,400}{\$3,400}$	=	$\dfrac{\$200}{\$3,400}$
	0.028	×	0.857	×	2.47	=	0.059

earn greater margins at a higher level of sales? Where has Ajax Airlines added capacity to improve asset utilization? And, finally, what strategy is Ajax Airlines pursuing? Financial statement analysis provides no answers to these questions.

Traditional Management Accounting Analysis

Traditional management accounting provides additional information about Ajax Airlines, though it also ignores a value chain perspective. Traditional cost accounting would suggest that, in an industry, such as the airline industry, with high fixed costs, contribution analysis is the key. The argument would be that, since fleet cost and compensation for pilots, flight attendants, and ground personnel do not depend on volume in the short run, the airline strategy should be to fill up capacity by aggressive pricing. Once the break-even point is met, most of every incremental dollar of revenue goes straight to the bottom line, because incremental variable cost is probably confined mainly to fuel and food.

Given additional information that is usually supplied in the annual report of most major airline companies, the traditional contribution analysis for a firm can be constructed. Exhibit D1.4 shows that analysis for Ajax Airlines, using seat miles flown as the per-unit metric.

Since incremental cost in the short run is very low, traditional management accountants would recommend filling up the unused capacity (as shown in Exhibit D1.4) at almost any price. But the supplementary financial data show that Ajax Airlines did not pursue this objective. Ajax Airlines was able to charge significantly more for each seat mile flown without improving utilization of the available seat miles, because seat miles flown capacity utilization stayed constant at 64 percent. This conflicts, moreover, with conclusions drawn from the du Pont analysis in Exhibit D1.3. That analysis shows that asset utilization improved, while traditional management accounting concludes that it remained constant. This conflict resurfaces when other factors are analyzed, as is discussed next.

EXHIBIT D1.4

Ajax Airlines: Contribution Analysis

	1988	1987
Additional information		
Seat miles flown	65,000	57,000
Available seat miles	102,000	89,000
Asset utilization (load factor realized)	64%	64%
Revenue per seat mile flown	$0.135	$0.126
Compensation per seat mile flown	$0.045	$0.042
Fuel per seat mile flown	0.017	0.018
Fleet operations cost per seat mile flown	0.060	0.056
Total	$0.122	$0.116
Operating profit per seat mile flown	$0.013	$0.010
Contribution margin per seat mile flown	$0.118	$0.108
Break-even level	$6,800	$5,600
	$0.118	$0.108
	= 57,600	= 51,900
Break-even percent of available capacity	56.5%	58.3%

Further Management Accounting Analysis

The management accounting analysis in Exhibit D1.4 reveals that, for the same capacity utilization, Ajax Airlines was able to charge a higher price per seat mile flown while paying more for compensation and equipment (compensation per seat mile flown rose from $0.042 to $0.045, while fleet operations cost per seat mile flown rose from $0.056 to $0.06). This suggests reasoning that would conclude that, by improving the quality of service and the quality of equipment used, Ajax Airlines was able to charge higher prices. Although this conclusion may correspond to what happened, there is no way to be sure that this was the strategy that Ajax actually pursued. (In fact, it probably is not what happened.) Moreover, how can the contradictory conclusions about asset utilization from the two different analyses be explained? Also, should the extra revenue from the unused seats flow straight to the bottom line (as both analyses would seem to suggest)?

In an attempt to understand these problems, quite different insights can be gleaned from a value chain analysis. Exhibit D1.5 yields these insights. Clearly, Ajax Airlines invested heavily in ticketing and reservations (T&R), probably to improve its computerized reservations system. And—despite a 14 percent increase in seat miles flown (i.e., from 57,000 in 1987 to 65,000 in 1988, as

EXHIBIT D1.5

Ajax Airlines: A Value Chain Analysis

	1988	1987
Sales	$8,800	$7,200
Ticketing and reservations	320	300
Aircraft operations	4,980	3,900
Customer service	2,600	2,400
Total expenses	$7,900	$6,600

Identifiable property, plant, and equipment (PPE) assets

	1988	1987
Ticketing and reservations	$2,000	$1,000
Aircraft operations	5,000	5,300
Customer service	0	0
Total	$7,000	$6,300

	Per seat mile flown		Per available mile	
	1988	1987	1988	1987
Costs				
Ticketing and reservations	$0.005	$0.005	$0.003	$0.003
Aircraft operations	0.077	0.069	0.049	0.044
Customer service	0.040	0.042	0.025	0.027
Total	$0.122	$0.116	$0.077	$0.074
Assets				
Ticketing and reservations	$0.031	$0.018	$0.020	$0.011
Aircraft operations	0.077	0.093	0.049	0.060
Customer service	0	0	0	0
Total	$0.108	$0.111	$0.069	$0.071

Exhibit D1.4 shows)—T&R cost per seat mile flown held constant at $0.005 (see the "Costs" section near the bottom of Exhibit D1.5), though T&R cost is hardly a fixed cost. Presumably, Ajax Airlines is willing to increase T&R costs and assets as a strategic investment in better service.

A value chain analysis also shows that operating an aircraft is not purely a fixed cost, as traditional management accounting suggests. While the number of seat miles flown increased 14 percent, operating expenses increased 28 percent (i.e., from $3,900 to $4,980, as the first line item labeled "Aircraft operations" in Exhibit D1.5 shows), so this figure is obviously not a fixed cost. Clearly, therefore, cost drivers other than capacity utilization are at work here, and management evidently does not control them.

The reduction in the asset base (see the line item "Aircraft operations" in Exhibit D1.5 under the category "Identifiable property, plant, and equipment assets") is presumed to reflect one more year's depreciation on the aging fleet rather than a strategic change in fleet configuration. Also, it is interesting that cost per seat mile flown has risen about 12 percent (i.e., from $0.069 to $0.077—see the line item "Aircraft operations" in Exhibit D1.5 under the category "Costs" near the bottom of the exhibit). This is an element in the value chain that seems not to translate easily into value to the customer—the part, that is, that simply involves getting from point *A* to point *B*. Apparently, Ajax Airlines has raised the price per seat mile flown mostly to compensate for an increase in fleet operating expenses that has no clear strategic justification.

Customer service expense per seat mile flown has dropped from $0.042 to $0.040. As a straight fixed cost, this expense should have dropped to $0.037 (0.042 ÷ 1.14, where 1.14 adjusts for the 14 percent increase in seat miles flown), so Ajax Airlines is spending a little more on this activity, as adjusted for volume.

Strategically, Ajax Airlines seems to be hoping that a small increase in aggregate (but not per-unit) customer service expenditures and a better T&R system will justify higher prices in an aging fleet. But increased aircraft operations costs offset most of the profit impact of the increase in revenue per seat mile flown from $0.126 in 1987 to $0.135 in 1988 (see "Revenue per seat mile flown" in Exhibit D1.4). This result hardly seems to fit the "success story" told by the traditional management accounting analysis. Value chain analysis, however, can yield different insights. The linking of traditional financial analysis with strategic positioning in this way is a critical element in effective financial analysis.

Comparative Analysis

It should be noted that the ability to present value chain analyses that are comparative across competing firms increases the value of the technique. Exhibit D1.6 shows a simple example of the comparative value chain perspective. The exhibit shows a chart that was prepared from publicly available information for two very different major airlines: United Airlines and People Express (in its heyday).

Structured in this way, the difference in strategies between the two airlines becomes obvious. The "no frills" concept of People Express is readily apparent. Specifically, strategic decisions in the five areas listed in the "Value chain elements" column of Exhibit D1.7 account for the $13,500 difference in the cost per 10,000 seat miles flown between these two airlines.

A Packaging Industry Case Study

Exhibit D1.7 shows a value chain analysis for the airline industry that confirms what is already known about United Airlines and People Express. But the real

EXHIBIT D1.6

Value Chain Configurations: A Comparison Between People Express and United Airlines

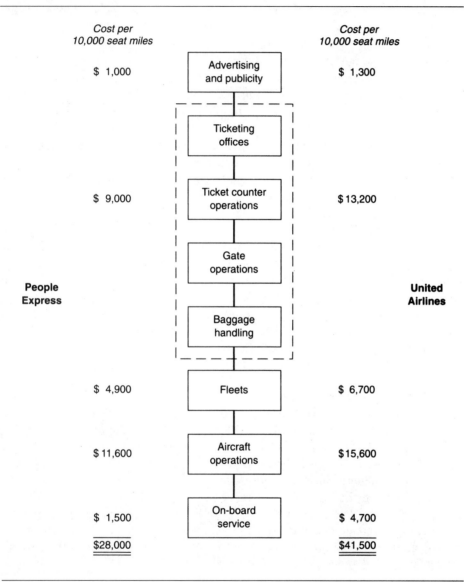

People Express Cost per 10,000 seat miles		United Airlines Cost per 10,000 seat miles
$ 1,000	Advertising and publicity	$ 1,300
	Ticketing offices	
$ 9,000	Ticket counter operations	$13,200
	Gate operations	
	Baggage handling	
$ 4,900	Fleets	$ 6,700
$ 11,600	Aircraft operations	$15,600
$ 1,500	On-board service	$ 4,700
$28,000		$41,500

EXHIBIT D1.7

Strategic Inferences From the Value Chains of People Express and United Airlines

Value chain elements	People Express less than United Airlines (cost per 10,000 seat miles)	Strategic differences	
		People Express	**United Airlines**
Advertising and publicity	$ 300	Heavy promotion to tout low price/no frills airline	Heavy promotion of full service airline
Ticketing and reservations	$4,200	No ticket offices No separate computer reservation system	Ticket offices in downtown locations Extensive computer reservation system
		Secondary airports and terminals No ticket counters (check-in only) Tickets purchased on board the aircraft or from machines No interline tickets Few fare options	Full service
		First-come, first-serve seating No ticketing at gates	Full service
		Carry-on space provided Charge for checked baggage No interline baggage	Free baggage checking
Fleet costs	$1,800	Used aircraft ("budget" airplanes)	New aircraft
Flight operations	$4,000	High-density seating Nonunion pilots Smaller crews and more flying hours per day Flight crews paid on dramatically lower scale Flight crews double on ground duties	Union pilots Bigger crews Crews paid on higher scale
Cabin operations	$3,200	Nonunion flight attendants Lower pay scale No first class No meals Charge for snacks and drinks served	Full service

power of value chain analysis comes from applying it to situations that have not already been analyzed and understood.

The case study from field research that is presented in this section presents such a situation. It shows how to construct a value chain for a particular firm. (As in the case of Ajax Airlines, the name of the company presented here— NorthAm Packaging Co.—and the financial data presented are disguised.) This case study highlights how to use the value chain to derive strategic insights.

NorthAm Packaging Co. produced 180,000 tons of coated paperboard in 1989. This paperboard was sold to consumer product firms, which formed, filled, and sealed the paperboard as cartons. NorthAm Packaging served two market segments: The bulk of the company's output (140,000 tons) went to commodity product firms, but a significant share (the remaining 40,000 tons) went to differentiated processors.

NorthAm Packaging's 140,000 tons of output to the commodity processors represented a 40 percent market share in this segment. These processors' products were considered commodities, because they could not charge a price premium for a brand name. The processors were also typically small. NorthAm Packaging sold to over 300 customers in this segment. Although aggregate sales in this segment had declined 3 percent per year over the last five years, it was believed to have stabilized in 1989.

The second customer segment to which NorthAm Packaging sold paperboard was high-quality, differentiated processors. The company currently had a 15 percent market share in this segment. These processors were typically larger in size. This segment, which had been expanding at a rate of approximately 10 percent per year, was a fast-growing area in packaging and was projected to grow even faster in the future. The quality of the packaging material (i.e., its strength, durability, and printability) was particularly important for this segment, because the carton was a point-of-sale merchandising aid for the differentiated products. NorthAm Packaging's market share in this segment had declined over time because it had not been able to produce the consistently high-quality paperboard that this segment demands.

NorthAm Packaging was one of four major competitors in the coated paperboard industry. Because of the scale, technology, and integrated economies of these firms, new entrants were effectively shut out.

Substitutes

Plastic was the major threat to manufacturers of coated paperboard. Shell Chemical and Hoover International (now Johnson Controls) had changed the consumer packaging industry overnight in 1965 when they combined to introduce the plastic resin pellet and the blow molding machine to manufacture plastic cartons. At first, the polyethylene pellets, which were supplied by Shell

Chemical, were quite expensive. But the blow molding machine was so easy to use that plastic had made steady inroads into the consumer packaging industry. However, coated paperboard continued to be used for several reasons:

- Although plastic was more economical when the price of plastic resin was low, when the input price increased, coated paperboard became a better choice. Guessing future levels of ethylene gas prices (the basic driver of polyethylene price) was a notoriously difficult task.
- Processors did not want to be at the total mercy of oil companies. By using dual suppliers, processors created a hedge against the volatile price of plastic resin. For example, in 1988, a Shell Chemical refinery in Louisiana suffered a major fire that destroyed 30 percent of the plastic polyethylene pellet supply in the United States overnight. This forced many processors that had largely converted to plastic back to coated paperboard.
- As new uses of the plastic resin were created (industrial and consumer uses of plastic containers), the input price was bound to go up.
- Since plastic was just a by-product for the oil companies, there was no real assurance of supply.
- Finally, "environmental indignation" over plastic jugs was heating up. They were being outlawed in many states because of the problem of burning them or dumping them into landfills. (The most populous county in the United States (Suffolk County, New York, on Long Island) passed legislation in 1987 banning plastic cartons from its landfills.)

Cost Structure

One way to understand NorthAm Packaging's position was to study the process flow from basic raw material sources through to the ultimate end-use product delivered into the final customers' hands. (In the interest of brevity, the discussion here focuses on the paper mill and conversion stages of the chain. The timber, logging, chipping, and pulp mill stages are not stressed because they are not critical to the issues addressed here. Obviously, the full value chain would consider these stages as well.)

NorthAm Packaging's primary manufacturing facility bought raw stock (pulp) for $319 per ton and converted the raw stock into uncoated paperboard by incurring additional costs of $105 per ton. The uncoated paperboard was then shuttled to an extruding plant at a cost of $3 per ton. Polyethylene was applied to both sides of the board by two extruders at a cost of $94 per ton. The company also sold some uncoated board to other converters at an average price of $483 per ton, net of freight to the customer.

After extrusion, the coated paperboard traveled to NorthAm Packaging's carton converting plant, at an average freight cost of $35 per ton. Coated paperboard currently was sold in the market for an average price of $605, net of freight. In the first stage of the converting operation, rolls of coated paperboard were spliced together to form a long, continuous web. Next, each particular processor's name, logo, and design were printed on one side. Then, the carton blanks were stamped out and stacked for loading on shipping pallets. The total cost of the conversion operation was $231 per ton, plus $10 per ton for freight to the end-use customers. Industry statistics showed that one ton of board yielded an average of 14,400 containers.

The blank cartons were set up, filled, and then sealed in the processor's factory. The processors delivered their products to convenience stores and supermarkets. Without recycling, the cycle was complete when consumers purchased the products and eventually threw away the disposable cartons. The processors who produced an undifferentiated product usually paid $0.08 per carton.

The other costs of such processors were:

- Product cost of $0.75 per carton; and
- Conversion, distribution, and shrinkage cost of $0.12 per carton.

NorthAm Packaging sold a carton of the commodity product for an average of $1.04 to the supermarket.

The branded processors, on the other hand, had very different economics. Their cost structure was as follows:

- Average container cost of $0.07;
- Product cost of $0.64 per carton;
- Conversion, distribution, and shrinkage cost of $0.11 per carton; and
- National selling and advertising cost of 25 percent of the $1.42 per carton wholesale price to supermarkets.

A typical supermarket sold the undifferentiated product for $1.16 and the branded product for $1.89.

The assets tied up at each stage of the process were estimated as follows:

	Current market value of assets per ton of paperboard
Mill	$2,800
Extruder	190
Converter	830
Commodity processor	5,400
Differentiated processor (lower because of scale economies)	2,890
Store	1,800

Strategic Options

NorthAm Packaging had some major decisions to make. Specifically, the company had to decide:

- Which market segments to emphasize; and
- Where it should invest capital dollars.

The strategic positioning and capital spending decisions facing NorthAm as of 1989 would shape its future for many years to come.

On the choice of market segments, NorthAm Packaging had several options:

1. NorthAm could continue to emphasize the commodity processors. Although this market had been declining by 3 percent per year, its customers had always been the company's main market.
2. NorthAm could try to aggressively build market share with differentiated processors, which was a market that was growing at 10 percent or more. This market would pay top dollar for paperboard, but it demanded a consistently high-quality product.

In analyzing these questions, NorthAm Packaging recognized its weaknesses vis-à-vis the differentiated segment:

- NorthAm Packaging's primary manufacturing was technologically obsolescent, because most of the plant and equipment had been bought in the 1960s. As a result, the company experienced nagging problems with the quality of its paperboard because of the lack of up-to-date machinery.
- NorthAm Packaging had limited extrusion capacity.
- NorthAm Packaging lacked high-quality printing—which would have been very expensive to acquire—in the conversion plant.

NorthAm Packaging's existing 15 percent market share in the differentiated segment simply reflected the company's status as largely a "backup" supplier. Major capital investments had to be made if NorthAm decided to build market share in this fast-growing segment. Three specific areas for this investment would be as follows:

- About $43 million would be needed to upgrade its primary manufacturing facility to improve board strength, printability, and smoothness.
- About $17 million would be required to add a state-of-the-art extruder to compete in multilayered polymer coating applications. Differentiated processors required multiple coatings to extend shelf life and to hold difficult products (e.g., liquids).

- About $1.5 million would be needed to purchase a rotogravure printing press. Currently, NorthAm Packaging used flexography, which printed from a raised image on rubber printing rolls. This method was inexpensive. After the initial capital investment, the rubber plates were about $150 each, and six were needed for a standard six-color process. The quality was not as good as with rotogravure printing, but high-quality printing had never been required by the commodity processors. Rotogravure gave an extremely precise and high-quality finish—but it was expensive. After the initial capital expense, each etched metal printing plate cost $2,500. With a six-color process, $15,000 must be spent for only one run. And once that run was complete, those etched cylinders would probably never be used again.

NorthAm Packaging's senior management had to evaluate the marketing and investment options open to them. Conventional capital expenditure requests using discounted cash flow analyses had been prepared to justify the proposed investments. These focused solely on projected "value added" for NorthAm. A Boston Consulting Group grid[16] would be another way to address these options. Exhibit D1.8 displays NorthAm Packaging's strategic options on the familiar portfolio grid, using the dimensions of market attractiveness and market share.

NorthAm Packaging historically has emphasized the commodity processor segment. Even though volume in this market had shrunk at the rate of 3 percent per year over the preceding five years, the firm has maintained a market share of 40 percent in this large segment (350,000 tons per year). This segment appears to be the classic "cash cow" in the Boston Consulting Group terminology: the high-market-share, low-growth segment. The strategic inference from the Boston Consulting Group grid in Exhibit D1.8 would be that NorthAm Packaging should "harvest" this commodity segment.

On the other hand, NorthAm Packaging has a relatively modest 15 percent of the market in the differentiated package segment. The overall market in this segment has been growing at 10 percent per year and is projected to grow even faster in the future. NorthAm Packaging has a low market share in this smaller (267,000 tons) but fast-growing segment. The strategic inference from the Boston Consulting Group grid would be that NorthAm Packaging should aggressively "build" market share in this segment by making the $61.5 million investment. This strategy was, in fact, the prevailing sentiment within NorthAm Packaging when the value chain analysis was undertaken.

A Value Chain Perspective

An alternative way of organizing the information—the value chain framework—provides a fundamentally different view of the marketing and investment options facing NorthAm Packaging. Exhibits D1.9–D1.12 contain the relevant calculations using the value chain framework:

EXHIBIT D1.8

Boston Consulting Group Grid

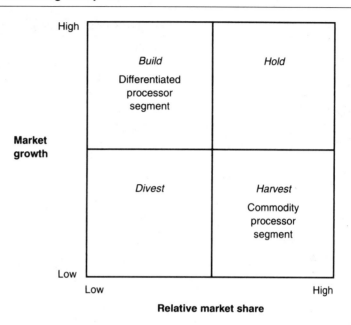

- The mill, extruder, converter, processor, and supermarket are identified as the key building blocks in the value chain. (Note that a conventional management accounting system, with its emphasis on value added, will ignore the value created by the processors and supermarkets.)
- Since the value chain analysis was done to draw inferences about the strategically distinct market segments, separate value chains were prepared for the commodity and differentiated processor segments.
- After identifying the value activities, the next step was to assign operating costs and revenues to these activities and to perform a profit analysis, as shown in Exhibits D1.9 and D1.10, respectively. All costs and revenues have been calculated for one ton of paperboard.
- NorthAm's converting operations have a "true" market price for sales to the processors. But how can "value" for intermediate products be approximated? Uncoated paperboard is transferred internally from the mill to the extruder, and coated paperboard is transferred from the extruder to the converter. Since uncoated and coated paperboard are traded on external markets, the competitive market prices were used for the intermediate products. Calculating profit per ton for each value activity based on com-

EXHIBIT D1.9

NorthAm Packaging Co.: A Process Flow Value Chain Per Ton of Paperboard

	Commodity segment	Differentiated segment
Consumer pays	$16,704	$27,216
Store profit (from merged carton and product value chains)	**1,728**	**6,768**
Store pays	14,976	20,448
Processor profit	**1,296**	**3,456**
Processor cost	12,528	15,984
Price to processor	1,152	1,008
Converter profit	**268**	**124**
Freight to processor	10	10
Converter cost	231	231
Price to converter	643[a]	643[a]
Extruder profit	**28**	**28**
Freight to converter	35	35
Extruder cost	94	94
Price to extruder	486[b]	486[b]
Mill profit	**59**	**59**
Freight to extruder	3	3
Mill cost		
Raw material	319	319
Other	105	105

[a]Outside market price (net of freight) $605 + freight to extruder $3 + freight to converter $35 = $643.
[b]Outside market price (net of freight) $483 + freight to extruder $3 = $486.

petitive market price, as opposed to arbitrary accounting transfer prices, helps to identify the fundamental sources of economic value and allows each stage to be evaluated independently.

- The assets per ton of board at each value activity were estimated, assuming full utilization of capacity and current replacement costs. With profit and assets, ROA was calculated for each value stage, as shown in Exhibit D1.11.
- The computations in Exhibits D1.9–D1.12 do not, it must be emphasized, involve the level of precision that one is likely to encounter in audited financial statements. In fact, margins for processors and stores are based on estimates that average out the continual, day-to-day volatility in net prices. As the analysis proceeds and particular activities become critical in answering strategic questions, greater effort at precision can be made.

EXHIBIT D1.10

NorthAm Packaging Co.: Profit Per Ton of Paperboard

	Commodity segment	Differentiated segment
Store	$1,728	$ 6,768
Processor	1,296	3,456
Converter	268	124
Extruder	28	28
Mill	59	59
Total	$3,379	$10,435
NorthAm Packaging (%)	10.5%	2.0%

EXHIBIT D1.11

Return on Assets Per Ton of Paperboard

	Commodity segment			Differentiated segment		
	Profit	Assets	ROA	Profit	Assets	ROA
Store	$1,728	$ 1,800	96%	$ 6,768	$1,800	376%
Processor	1,296	5,400	24	3,456	2,890	120
Converter	268	830	32	124	830	15
Extruder	28	190	15	28	190	15
Mill	59	2,800	2	59	2,800	2
Total	$3,379	$11,020	31%	$10,435	$8,510	123%

The information based on value chain analysis does, in fact, lead to new insights about NorthAm Packaging. Dramatically different strategic insights emerge when one considers the value chain analysis, as summarized in Exhibit D1.12.

Of the total profit of $3,379 per ton of paperboard created in the commodity processor segment, NorthAm Packaging realized $355, or 10.5 percent of the total value. In sharp contrast, in the differentiated processor segment, the company's share of the total profit in the chain is only $211 per ton, which is a mere 2 percent of the total value.

The buyer power in the differentiated segment is extremely strong. As noted earlier, the customers in the differentiated segment tend to be much larger than the customers in the commodity segment. Even though the carton is much more a marketing tool in the differentiated segment, volume discounts and overall buyer power hold unit prices below those for the commodity carton.

EXHIBIT D1.12

NorthAm Packaging Co.: A Value Chain Perspective

Commodity segment				Differentiated segment		
Profit	Percent of the total profit	ROA		Profit	Percent of the total profit	ROA
$ 59	2%	2%	Mill	$ 59	0.56%	2%
28	1	15	Extruder	28	0.27	15
268	8	32	Converter	124	1.19	15
1,296	38	24	Food processor	3,456	33.12	120
1,728	51	96	Supermarket	6,768	64.86	376
$3,379	100%			$10,435	100.00%	

Note that there is no particular reason to believe that 10.5 percent of the overall profit is a "reasonable" or an "unreasonable" share for the carton manufacturer versus the contents manufacturer or the retailer. But whatever the share is for the carton manufacturer in the commodity segment, it should be higher in the differentiated segment where the carton is much more important as a point-of-sale marketing tool. For the share to drop from 10.5 percent to 2 percent is dramatic evidence for NorthAm Packaging of the lack of seller power in the higher-value segment.

As Exhibit D1.11 shows, NorthAm Packaging's ROAs in the commodity segment are 2 percent at the mill, 15 percent at the extruder, and 32 percent at the converter. In the differentiated segment, by contrast, the ROAs are 2 percent, 15 percent, and 15 percent for the mill, extruder, and converter, respectively. These ROAs further reinforce the unattractiveness of the differentiated segment.

From the Boston Consulting Group grid in Exhibit D1.8, the branded processor segment looked extremely attractive. But based on the value chain analysis, this market looks much less attractive. The differentiated processors realize enormous leverage. Why invest over $60 million to build market share in the differentiated segment where NorthAm Packaging currently is able to extract only 2 percent of the total value created in the chain? This insight is apparent neither from the Boston Consulting Group strategic analysis nor from the conventional value-added approach. The value-added concept does not help at all in quantifying buyer power because it ignores the total value created in the chain.

Due to the buyers' tremendous bargaining power in the differentiated segment, it is highly unlikely that NorthAm Packaging will be able to extract any more than 2 percent of the total value even after it matches its leading competitor's investment. The reasons are as follows:

- There are very few buyers in the differentiated segment—less than a dozen versus more than 1,000 in the commodity segment.
- Buyers are large in size.
- The average order size tends to be quite large.
- Customers in the differentiated segment typically keep two or more sources of supply. Poor service, poor quality, or uncompetitive prices are punished by cuts in order size.
- Plastic has several attractive features as a packaging material, including break resistance, design versatility, eye appeal, and printability. Plastic, therefore, poses a more significant threat to coated paperboard in the differentiated segment, since this segment values more highly the marketing appeal of the package. This substitution threat sets a cap on paperboard carton prices.

Overall, this value chain analysis gives a much different picture of this industry. It appears to be an industry in which the closer the value activity is to the final customer and the more product differentiation created, the more money there is to be made, as shown in Exhibit D1.12.

NorthAm Packaging seems to lose on both counts. For one thing, it lacks the ability to forward integrate into the processor and supermarket segments. Moreover (as mentioned previously), NorthAm Packaging currently lacks the product quality required to compete successfully as a supplier to the differentiated processor segment.

What should the company do? NorthAm Packaging's position is reminiscent of drawing in a poker game, yet failing to improve the hand. Does it put more money in the pot, even though it knows it has a bad hand? Does it fold? Or should it stay in the game as long as possible without adding more to the pot?

A value chain analysis would suggest the following strategy: Instead of deemphasizing the commodity segment (as the Boston Consulting Group analysis would suggest), NorthAm Packaging should find ways to effectively compete in the commodity segment by being the low-cost producer. Here again, the value chain framework can provide important insights. NorthAm Packaging needs to understand the structural and executional drivers of cost behavior for the major cost items in the mill, extruder, and converter operations.[17] The company then needs to manage these drivers better than its competitors.

Staying in the commodity segment is the only logical choice that NorthAm Packaging has. The attractiveness of this option is further enhanced by significant continuing growth in commodity carton demand in export markets. NorthAm Packaging's reputation has been made in this market, and its manufacturing system is already geared to serve this market. Also, NorthAm Packaging currently has a low investment base to support this business, since most of the plant and equipment were bought before 1970. No major investments are required to compete.

Looking at the economics of the mill, extruder, and converting operations, NorthAm Packaging currently is destroying value (rather than creating value) by selling in the differentiated segment. The profitability at the mill is well below satisfactory levels. A cost driver analysis at the mill and extruder stages, which is beyond the scope of this chapter, might go a long way in identifying opportunities for improving profits.

A STRATEGY FOR COMPETITIVE ADVANTAGE

Traditional cost analysis focuses on the notion of value added (i.e., selling price less the cost of purchased raw materials) under the mistaken impression that this is the only area where a firm can influence costs. This chapter argues that value chain analysis provides a more meaningful way to explore competitive advantage.

Value added could be quite misleading for at least three reasons:

1. It arbitrarily distinguishes between raw materials and many other purchased inputs. Purchased services, such as maintenance or professional consulting services, are treated differently than raw materials purchased.

2. It does not point out the potential to exploit linkages (whether between a firm and its suppliers or between a firm and its customers) with a view to reducing costs or enhancing product differentiation.

3. Competitive advantage cannot be fully explored without considering the interaction between purchased raw materials and other cost elements (e.g., purchasing higher-quality and higher-priced raw material can reduce scrap costs and thus could lower total costs).

The focus of the value chain analysis is external to the firm. Each firm is seen in the context of the overall chain of value-creating activities, of which the firm is likely to be only a small part. (There apparently are no firms that span the entire value chain in which they operate.)

In summary, the methodology for constructing and using a value chain involves the following steps:

1. Identify the industry's value chain, then assign costs, revenues, and assets to each activity.

2. Identify the cost drivers that regulate each value activity.

3. Build sustainable competitive advantage, either by controlling cost drivers better than competitors or by reconfiguring the value chain.

Efforts at simultaneously reducing costs and enhancing differentiation are possible by carefully considering costs, revenues, and assets at each value activity vis-à-vis competitors.

Cost driver analysis (of which ABC is a subset) is a part of value chain analysis. In SCM, therefore, the value chain provides the overall framework; topics such as ABC are components of constructing and using value chains.

The case studies provided in this chapter illustrate that the insights derived from value chain analysis are much different from those suggested by more conventional management accounting tools. Exhibit D1.13 summarizes the key differences between value chain and conventional management accounting.

The value chain perspective can be used to derive the following insights:

- Since virtually no two companies compete in exactly the same set of value activities, value chain analysis is a critical first step in understanding how a firm is positioned in its industry. Building sustainable competitive advantage requires a knowledge of the full, linked set of value activities of which the firm and its competitors are a part.

- Once a value chain is fully articulated, critical strategic decisions (e.g., make-or-buy decisions or forward versus backward integration) become clearer. Investment decisions can be viewed from the perspective of their impact on the overall chain and the firm's position within it.

- The value chain analysis helps to quantify supplier power by calculating the percentage of total profits that can be attributed to suppliers. This activity could help the firm to identify ways to exploit linkages with suppliers.

- The value chain framework highlights how a firm's product fits into the buyer's value chain. Given this framework, it is readily apparent what percentage the firm's product costs comprise of the buyer's total costs. This information could be useful in encouraging the firm and buyers to work together in cost reduction activities.

- In the final analysis, the simultaneous pursuit of low cost and differentiation depends on a sophisticated understanding of the drivers of costs, revenues, and assets at each value activity and the interdependencies between value activities.

EXHIBIT D1.13

Value Chain vs. Conventional Management Accounting — A Summary

	Traditional management accounting	Value chain analysis in the SCM framework
Focus	Internal	External
Perspective	Value-added	Entire set of linked activities from suppliers to end-use customers
Cost driver concept	Single driver ("volume")	Multiple cost drivers • Structural drivers (e.g., scale, scope, experience, technology, and complexity) • Executional drivers (e.g., participative management, total quality management, and plant layout)
	Application at the overall firm level (cost-volume-profit analysis)	A set of unique cost drivers for each value activity
Cost containment philosophy	"Across the board" cost reductions	View cost containment as a function of the cost driver(s) regulating each value activity Exploit linkages with suppliers Exploit linkages with customers "Spend to save"
Insights for strategic decisions	None readily apparent (this is a large reason why the strategic consulting firms always discard the conventional reports as they begin their cost analyses)	Identify cost drivers at the individual activity level, and develop cost/differentiation advantage either by controlling those drivers better than competitors or by reconfiguring the value chain (e.g., Federal Express in mail delivery, and MCI in long-distance telephone) For each value activity, ask strategic questions pertaining to • Make versus buy • Forward/backward integration Quantify and assess "supplier power" and "buyer power," and exploit linkages with suppliers and buyers

Notes

1. Michael E. Porter, *Competitive Advantage: Creating and Sustaining Superior Performance* (New York: The Free Press, 1985): 62–67.

2. *Ibid.*: 34–44.

3. John K. Shank, "Strategic Cost Management: New Wine, or Just New Bottles?" *Journal of Management Accounting Research* (Fall 1989): 47–65.

4. Michael E. Porter, *Competitive Advantage:* 88.

5. M. Hergert and D. Morris, "Accounting Data for Value Chain Analysis," *Strategic Management Journal* (June 1989): 175–188.

6. *Ibid.*

7. Michael E. Porter, *Competitive Advantage:* 70–87.

8. Daniel Riley, "Competitive Cost Based Investment Strategies for Industrial Companies," in *Manufacturing Issues* (New York: Booz, Allen and Hamilton, 1987): 27–34.

9. F.M. Scherer, *Industrial Market Structure and Economic Performance, 2nd ed.* (New York: Rand McNally, 1980).

10. Pankaj Ghemawat, *The Arithmetic of Strategic Cost Analysis* (Boston: Harvard Business School Press, 1986).

11. Robin Cooper, "You Need a New Cost System When . . . ," *Harvard Business Review* (January–February 1989): 38–49; Robin Cooper and Robert S. Kaplan, "Measure Costs Right: Make the Right Decisions," *Harvard Business Review* (September–October 1988): 72–91; Robert S. Kaplan and H. Thomas Johnson, *Relevance Lost: The Rise and Fall of Management Accounting* (Boston: Harvard Business School Press, 1987).

12. *Manufacturing Issues* (New York: Booz, Allen and Hamilton, 1987): 16–31.

13. M.E. Porter, *Du Pont in Titanium Dioxide* (Boston: Harvard Business School Press, 1986).

14. Michael E. Porter, "GE vs. Westinghouse in Large Turbine Generators," *Harvard Business School Case Series 930–128* (1986).

15. A. Stuart, "Meatpackers in Stampede," *Fortune* (July 29, 1981): 67–73.

16. B.D. Henderson, *Corporate Strategy* (Cambridge, MA: ABT Books, 1979).

17. John K. Shank, "Strategic Cost Management": 34.

Strategic Cost Management: Tailoring Controls to Strategies

Vijay Govindarajan

Professor of Strategy and Control, Amos Tuck School of Business Administration, Dartmouth College, Hanover, New Hampshire.[20]

John K. Shank

Noble Professor of Managerial Accounting and Management Control, Amos Tuck School of Business Administration, Dartmouth College, Hanover, New Hampshire.[20]

Strategic cost management can be defined as the use of cost information to do the following: help formulate and communicate strategies; carry out tactics that implement those strategies; and then develop and implement controls that monitor success at achieving strategic objectives. Management control systems are, ultimately, tools to implement strategies. Since strategies differ in different types of organizations, management controls should be tailored to the requirements of specific strategies. This article explains how.

One important role of internal accounting information in a business is to facilitate the *development and implementation* of business strategies. Under this view, business management is a continuously cycling process consisting of the following four stages:

1. Formulating strategies;
2. Communicating those strategies throughout the organization;
3. Developing and carrying out tactics to implement the strategies; and
4. Developing and implementing controls to monitor the success of the implementation steps, and hence the success in meeting the strategic objectives.

Cost information plays a role at each of these stages. From this perspective, strategic cost management (SCM) can be thought of as the managerial use of cost information *explicitly* directed at one or more of the four stages of the strategic management cycle. Giving explicit attention to the strategic management *context* distinguishes SCM from managerial accounting.

Previous articles have explained value chain analysis and cost driver analysis —tools that are designed to help in the *formulation* of strategies.[1] This article discusses the role of control systems in the *implementation* of strategies.

MANAGEMENT CONTROL SYSTEMS

Management control systems are tools to implement strategies. Since strategies differ in different types of organizations, controls should be tailored to the requirements of specific strategies. The logic for linking controls to strategy is based on the following line of thinking:

- For effective execution, different strategies require different task priorities, different key success factors, and different skills, perspectives, and behaviors.
- Control systems are measurement systems that influence the behavior of those people whose activities are being measured.
- Thus, a continuing concern in the design of control systems should be whether behavior induced by the system is consistent with the strategy.

The first part of this article defines the concept of strategy and describes "generic" strategies that business units can adopt. The second part of the article discusses how to vary the form and structure of control systems in accordance with variations in generic business-level strategies. The final part of the article contrasts the view of controls given with conventional management accounting practices.

CONCEPT OF STRATEGY

Strategy has been conceptualized as the process by which managers, using a time horizon of three to five years, evaluate external environmental opportunities and also internal strengths and resources to decide on *goals* as well as *a set of action plans* to accomplish these goals.[2] Thus, a business unit's strategy depends on two interrelated aspects:

1. Its mission or goals; and
2. The way the business unit chooses to compete in its industry to accomplish its goals—i.e., the business unit's competitive advantage.

Mission. Turning first to the mission, consulting firms (e.g., Boston Consulting Group,[3] Arthur D. Little,[4] and A.T. Kearney[5]) and also academic researchers[6] have proposed the following three missions that a business unit can adopt:

- *Build.* This mission implies a goal of increased market share, even at the expense of short-term earnings and cash flow. A business unit that follows this mission is expected to be a net user of cash: that is, the cash flow from its current operations would usually be insufficient to meet its capital investment needs. Business units with "low market share" in "high growth industries" typically pursue a "build" mission (e.g., Apple Computer's Macintosh business and Monsanto's biotechnology business).
- *Hold.* This strategic mission is geared to the protection of the business unit's market share and competitive position. The cash outflows for a business unit that follows this mission generally equal the cash inflows. Businesses with "high market share" in "high growth industries" typically pursue a "hold" mission (e.g., IBM in mainframe computers).
- *Harvest.* The harvest mission implies a goal of maximizing short-term earnings and cash flow, even at the expense of market share. A business unit that follows the harvest mission is a net supplier of cash. Businesses with "high market share" in "low growth industries" typically pursue a "harvest" mission (e.g., American Brands in tobacco products).

Competitive advantage. In terms of competitive advantage, Porter[7] has proposed the following two generic ways in which businesses can develop sustainable competitive advantage:

- *Low cost.* The primary focus of this strategy is to achieve low cost relative to competitors. Cost leadership can be achieved through approaches such as economies of scale in production, learning curve effects, tight cost control, and cost minimization in areas such as R&D, service, sales force, or advertising. Firms that follow this strategy include Texas Instruments (in consumer electronics), Emerson Electric (in electric motors), Chevrolet (in automobiles), Briggs and Stratton (in gasoline engines), Black and Decker (in machine tools), and Commodore (in business machines).
- *Differentiation.* The primary focus of this strategy is to differentiate the product offering to create something that customers perceive as unique. Approaches to product differentiation include: brand loyalty (Coca Cola in soft drinks), superior customer service (IBM in computers), dealer network (Caterpillar Tractors in construction equipment), product design and product features (Hewlett-Packard in electronics), or product technology (Coleman in camping equipment).

BUSINESS UNIT MISSION

The planning and control requirements of business units differ according to the strategies they pursue. This section discusses how control systems should be designed to achieve the various missions of business units.

As noted earlier, the mission for ongoing business units could be to build, hold, or harvest. These missions constitute a continuum, with "pure build" at one end and "pure harvest" at the other end. For effective implementation there should be congruence between the mission chosen and the types of controls used. The control-mission "fit" is developed using the following line of reasoning:[8]

- The mission of a business unit influences the uncertainties that its general manager faces and the short-term versus long-term trade-offs that the manager makes.
- Management control systems can be systematically varied to help motivate managers to cope effectively with uncertainty and make appropriate short-term versus long-term trade-offs.
- Thus, different missions often require systematically different management control systems.

MISSION AND UNCERTAINTY

Build units tend to face greater environmental uncertainty than harvest units for several reasons:

- Build strategies are typically undertaken in the growth stage of a product life cycle, whereas harvest strategies are typically undertaken in the mature/decline stage of the product life cycle. Factors such as the following change more rapidly and are more unpredictable in the growth stage than the mature/decline stage of the product life cycle: manufacturing process; product technology; market demand; relations with suppliers, buyers, and distribution channels; number of competitors; and competitive structure.
- An objective of a build business unit is to increase market share. Since the total market share of all firms in any industry is 100 percent, the battle for market share is a zero-sum game; thus, a build strategy pits a business unit into greater conflict with its competitors than does a harvest strategy. Since competitors' actions are likely to be unpredictable, this contributes to the uncertainty faced by build business units.
- Both on the input side and on the output side, build managers tend to experience greater dependencies with external individuals and organizations that do harvest managers. For example, a build mission signifies additional capital investment (greater dependence on capital markets), expansion of capacity (greater dependence on the technological environment), increase in market share (greater dependence on customers and competitors), increase in production volume (greater dependence on raw material suppliers and labor market), and so on. The greater the external dependencies that a business unit faces, the greater the uncertainty it confronts.
- Since build business units are often in new and evolving industries, the experience of build managers in their industries is likely to be less. This also contributes to the greater uncertainty faced by managers of build units in dealing with external constituencies.

MISSION AND TIME SPAN

The choice of build versus harvest strategies has implications for short-term versus long-term profit trade-offs. The share-building strategy includes:

- Price cutting;
- Major R&D expenditures (to introduce new products); and
- Major market development expenditures.

These actions are aimed at establishing market leadership, but they depress short-term profits. Thus, many decisions that a manager of a build unit makes

EXHIBIT 1.

Different Strategic Missions: Implications for Strategic Planning

	Build	Hold	Harvest
Importance of strategic planning	Relatively high	⟶	Relatively low
Formalization of capital expenditure decisions	Less formal DCF analysis; longer payback	⟶	More formalized DCF analysis; shorter payback
Capital expenditure evaluation criteria	More emphasis on nonfinancial data (market share, efficient use of R&D dollars, etc.)	⟶	More emphasis on financial data (cost efficiency; straight cash on cash incremental return)
Hurdle rates	Relatively low	⟶	Relatively high
Capital investment analysis	More subjective and qualitative	⟶	More quantitative and financial
Project approval limits at business unit level	Relatively high	⟶	Relatively low

today may not result in profits until some future period. A harvest strategy, on the other hand, entails maximizing short-term profits.

The following sections discuss how the form and structure of control systems might differ across business units with different missions.

STRATEGIC PLANNING

Several design issues need to be addressed for a strategic planning process. There are no hard and fast answers about these design choices; instead, the answers tend to depend on the mission that the business unit is pursuing (see Exhibit 1).

When the environment is uncertain, the strategic planning process is especially important. Management must think about how to cope with uncertainties, which usually requires a longer-range view of planning than is possible in an annual budget. If the environment is stable, there may be no strategic planning process at all, or only a broad-brush strategic plan. Thus, strategic planning is more critical for build business units than it is for harvest business units. Nevertheless, strategic plans may still be necessary for harvest business units, because a company's overall strategic plan must encompass all its businesses to effectively balance cash flows.

Capital deployment. In screening capital investments and allocating resources, the systems may be more quantitative and financial for harvest units. A harvest business unit operates in a mature industry and does not offer tremendous new investment possibilities. Hence, the required earnings rate for such a business unit may be set relatively high to motivate managers to search for projects with truly exceptional returns.

Since harvest units tend to experience stable environments (with predictable products, technologies, competitors, and customers), discounted cash flow (DCF) analysis often can be used with confidence. The required information used to evaluate investments from harvest units is primarily financial.

A build unit, on the other hand, is positioned on the growth stage of the product life cycle. The corporate office wants to take advantage of the opportunities in a growing market, so the corporate officers may set a relatively low discount rate to motivate managers to forward more investment ideas to the corporate office. Given the product and market uncertainties, the financial analysis of some projects from build units may be unreliable. For such projects, nonfinancial data are more important.

BUDGETING

Implications for designing budgeting systems to support varied missions are contained in Exhibit 2.

A key issue is how much importance should be attached to meeting the budget in evaluations of a business unit manager's performance. The greater the uncertainty, the more difficult it is for superiors to regard subordinates' budget targets as firm commitments and to consider unfavorable budget variances as clear indicators of poor performance.[9] There are several reasons for this, as the following sections explain.

Predictability of profit targets. First, performance evaluation presupposes establishment of accurate profit targets. Targets that can serve as valid standards for subsequent performance appraisal require the ability to predict the conditions that will exist during the coming year. If these predictions are incorrect, the profit objective will also be incorrect. Obviously, these conditions can be predicted more accurately under stable conditions than under changing conditions. The basic effect of uncertainty is to limit the ability of managers to plan or make decisions about activities in advance of their occurrence. Thus, the greater the uncertainty, the more difficult it is to prepare targets that can become the basis for performance evaluation.

Knowledge about cause-effect relationships. Second, since efficiency refers to the amount of output per unit of input, evaluations of a manager's efficiency depend on a detailed knowledge of the outcomes associated with given management

EXHIBIT 2.

Different Strategic Missions: Implications for Budgeting

	Build	Hold	Harvest
Role of the budget	More a short-term planning tool	→	More a control tool ("document of restraint")
Business unit manager's influence in preparing the annual budget	Relatively high	→	Relatively low
Revisions to the budget during the year	Relatively easy	→	Relatively difficult
Roles of standard costs in assessing performance	Relatively low	→	Relatively high
Importance of such concepts as flexible budgeting for manufacturing cost control	Relatively low	→	Relatively high
Frequency of informal reporting and contacts with superiors	More frequent on policy issues; less frequent on operating issues	→	Less frequent on policy issues; more frequent on operating issues
Frequency of feedback from superiors on actual performance versus the budget	Less often	→	More often
"Control limit" used in periodic evaluation against the budget	Relatively high (i.e., more flexible)	→	Relatively low (i.e., more flexible)
Importance attached to meeting the budget	Relatively low	→	Relatively high
Output versus behavior control	Behavior control	→	Output control

actions—that is, knowledge about cause-effect relationships. Better knowledge about cause-effect relationships exists under stable conditions than under uncertain conditions. Therefore, judgments about efficiency are more difficult under uncertain conditions.

Use of financial performance indicators. Third, the emphasis of financial performance indicators is on outcomes rather than on process. Managers control their own actions, but they cannot control the states of nature that combine with their actions to produce outcomes. In a situation with high uncertainty, therefore, financial information does not adequately reflect managerial performance.

LESS RELIANCE ON BUDGETS IN BUILD UNITS

Since build units tend to face higher uncertainly than harvest units, less reliance is usually placed on budgets in build units than in harvest units.

Example. In the late 1970s, the SCM Corporation adopted a two-dimensional yardstick to evaluate business units: bottom-line performance against budget was one dimension, and performance against specific objectives was another. The ratios of the two were made to vary according to the mission of the business unit. For instance, evaluations of pure harvest units were based 100 percent on budget performance. Evaluations of "pure hold" units were based 50 percent on budget performance and 50 percent on completion of objectives. Finally, evaluations of pure build units were based 100 percent on completion of objectives.[10]

Other differences in the budget process. The following additional differences in the budget process are likely to exist between build and harvest units:

- In contrast to harvest units, budget revisions are likely to be more frequent for build units because of the more frequent changes in the product or market environment.
- Managers of build units may have relatively more input and influence in the formulation of budgets than managers of harvest units. This occurs because build managers operate in rapidly changing environments and have better knowledge of these changes than senior management. The stable environments of harvest units make the knowledge of the manager less important.

INCENTIVE COMPENSATION SYSTEM

In designing an incentive compensation package for business unit managers, questions such as these need to be resolved:

1. What should the size of incentive bonus payments be relative to the base salary of general managers? Should the incentive bonus payments have upper limits?
2. What measures of performance (e.g., profit, return on investment, sales volume, market share, or product development) should be employed as

EXHIBIT 3.

Different Strategic Missions: Implications for Incentive Compensation

	Build	Hold	Harvest
Percent compensation as bonus	Relatively high	⟶	Relatively low
Bonus criteria	More emphasis on nonfinancial criteria	⟶	More emphasis on financial criteria
Bonus determination approach	More subjective	⟶	More formula based
Frequency of bonus payment	Less frequent	⟶	More frequent

the basis for determining a general manager's incentive bonus awards? If multiple performance measures are employed, how should they be weighted?

3. How much reliance should be placed on subjective judgments in deciding on the bonus amount?

4. How often (e.g., semiannually, annually, biennially) should incentive awards be made?

Decisions about these design variables are influenced by the mission of the business unit (see Exhibit 3).

Bonus-to-base salary ratio. As for the first question, many firms follow the principle that the riskier the strategy, the greater the proportion of the general manager's compensation in bonus compared to salary (the "risk/return" principle). They maintain that since managers in charge of more uncertain situations should be willing to take greater risks, those managers should receive a higher percentage of their remuneration in the form of incentive bonuses. Thus, reliance on bonuses is likely to be higher for building managers than for harvest managers.

Which performance measures to use. As for the second question, when an individual's rewards are tied to performance according to certain criteria, his behavior is influenced by the desire to optimize performance with the respect to those criteria.

Some performance criteria (e.g., cost control, operating profits, cash flow from operations, and return on investment) focus on short-term performance, whereas other performance criteria (e.g., market share, new product development, market development, and people development) focus on long-term profitability. Thus, linking incentive bonus to the former set of criteria tends to promote a short-term focus on the part of general managers, whereas linking incentive bonus to the latter set of performance criteria is likely to promote a long-term focus.

Given the differences in the time horizons of build and harvest managers, it may be inappropriate to use a single, uniform financial criterion (such as return on investment) to evaluate the performance of every business unit. Rather, it may be preferable to use multiple performance criteria, with differential weights applied for each criterion depending on the mission of the business unit.

Example. "General Electric Company and Westinghouse Electric Corporation, for example, are tailoring compensation packages to the different 'missions' of their individual businesses.

Both GE and Westinghouse have mature as well as young businesses. In the mature businesses, short-term incentives might dominate the compensation packages of managers, who are charged with maximizing cash flow, achieving high profit margins, and retaining market share. In the younger businesses, where developing products and establishing marketing strategies are most important, non-financial measures geared to the execution of long-term performance might dictate the major portion of managers' remuneration."[11]

Use of subjective judgments. As for the third question, in addition to varying the importance of different criteria, superiors must also decide on the approach to take in determining a specific bonus amount.

At one extreme, a manager's bonus might be a strict formula-based plan with the bonus tied to performance on quantifiable criteria (e.g., X percent bonus on actual profits in excess of budgeted profits). At the other extreme, a manager's incentive bonus might be based solely on the superior's subjective judgment or discretion. Alternatively, incentive bonuses might be based on a combination of formula-based and subjective approaches.

Performance on most long-run criteria (e.g., market development, new product development, and people development) is clearly less amenable to objective measurement than performance on most short-run criteria (e.g., operating profits, cash flow from operations, and return on investment). Since, as already noted, build managers—in contrast to harvest managers—should focus more on the long run than on the short run, build managers are typically evaluated more subjectively than harvest managers.

Frequency of bonuses. Finally, the frequency with which bonuses are paid influences the time horizon of managers. More frequent bonus awards encourage concentration on short-term performance, since they have the effect of motivating managers to focus on those facets of the business that they can affect in the short run. Less frequent calculation and payment of bonuses encourage managers to take a long-term perspective. Thus, build managers tend to receive bonuses less frequently than harvest managers.

Example. Premark International (which was formed in 1986 in a spin-off from Dart & Kraft, Inc.) adopted the design of an incentive bonus plan for the general manager of its Tupperware division, whose mission was to build market share: "[If you award the bonus annually,] Tupperware could reduce advertising and promotional activities and you can look good in profits that year. Then the franchise starts to go to hell. If you're shooting for an award after three years, there's less tendency to do things short term."[12]

BUSINESS UNIT COMPETITIVE ADVANTAGE

A business unit can choose to compete either as a differentiated player or as a low-cost player. The choice of a differentiation approach rather than a low-cost approach increases uncertainty in a business unit's task environment for three reasons.

First, product innovation is likely to be more critical for differentiation business units than for low-cost business units. This is partly because of the fact that a low-cost business unit, with its primary emphasis on cost reduction, typically prefers to keep its product offerings stable over time, whereas a differentiation business unit, with its primary focus on uniqueness and exclusivity, is likely to engage in greater product innovation. a business unit with greater emphasis on new product activities tends to face greater uncertainty since the business unit is betting on unproven products.

Second, low-cost business units tend to have narrow product lines to minimize inventory carrying costs and to benefit from economies of scale. Differentiation business units, on the other hand, tend to have a broader set of products to create uniqueness. Product breadth creates high environmental complexity and consequently, higher uncertainty.

Third, low-cost business units typically produce no-frill, commodity products—these products succeed primarily because they have lower prices than competing products. By contrast, products of differentiation business units succeed if customers perceive that the products have advantages over competing products. Since customer perception is difficult to learn about and since customer loyalty is subject to change because of actions by competitors or for other reasons, the demand for differentiated products is typically more difficult to predict than the demand for commodities.

The specifics of the control systems for low-cost and differentiation business units are similar to the ones described earlier for harvest and build business units. This is so because the uncertainty facing low-cost and differentiation business units is similar to the uncertainty facing harvest and build business units.

Examples. Digital Equipment Corporation (DEC) followed a differentiation strategy, whereas Data General followed a low-cost strategy. The control systems in these companies differed accordingly. DEC's product managers were evaluated primarily on the basis of the quality of their interaction with their customers (a subjective measure), whereas Data General's product managers were evaluated on the basis of results, or profits. Further, DEC's sales representatives were on straight salary, while Date General's salesmen received 50 percent of their pay on a commission basis. Salaried compensation indicates behavior control, and commission compensation, outcome control.[13]

A broad-based chemicals manufacturer used differentiated management controls focusing on the differing key success factors for its yellow dye unit (which followed a cost leadership strategy) and its red dye unit (which followed a differentiation strategy). The performance of the manager in charge of yellow dye was evaluated closely according to *theoretical* standard costs rather than currently achievable standard costs. The results of this tight financial control were remarkable: Within two years, actual cost for yellow dye decreased from $5.72 per pound to $3.84 per pound, thus giving the yellow dye unit a major cost advantage. By contrast, since the key strategic issue for red dye was product differentiation rather than cost leadership, the management control reports for the red dye unit focused on product leadership variables (e.g., milestone reporting on the development project for hot spray dyeing) rather than on cost control variables.[14]

ADDITIONAL CONSIDERATIONS

Although tailoring controls to strategies has a sound logic, designers of control systems need to be cognizant of several potential problems.

The changing environment. First, a business unit's external environment inevitably changes over time, and a change in the operating environment might imply the need for a shift in strategy. This raises an interesting issue. Success at any task requires commitment. The strategy-control "fit" is expected to foster such a commitment to the current strategy. However, if the control system is too closely related to the current strategy, it could result in overcommitment, thereby inhibiting managers from shifting to a new strategy when they should.

Examples of declining industries that have been transformed into growth industries include the major growth of Arm & Hammer baking soda, which was once in the decline stage of the product life cycle, and the surge in demand during the 1980s for fountain pens, which were once considered an obsolete product.

The following examples in the radio, musical instrument, and motorcycle industries illustrate the problems of overcommitment when there is a close fit between strategy and controls:

Examples. "Financially oriented U.S. manufacturers once treated the radio as essentially a dot on the product portfolio matrix. Convinced that every product has a life cycle, they viewed the radio as having passed its peak and being a prime candidate for 'milking.' Starved for investment funds and resources and being subject to tight financial controls, the radio died in a self-fulfilling prophecy. On the other hand, Japanese radio manufacturers such as Matsushita (Panasonic) and Sony—ignoring or unaware of product life cycle and portfolio theories— obstinately believed in their product's value. The division heads of these firms had no option but to extend the life of the product since to do otherwise would mean dissolving their divisions, which was an untenable option. So they pressed their engineers, component manufacturers, and marketing people for new ideas . . . Today the portable radio-cassette and Sony Walkman stories are part of business folklore."[15]

Yamaha in the musical instrument market in the United States and Honda, Kawasaki, Suzuki, and Yamaha in the motorcycle market in the United States and in Europe have successfully destroyed the dominance of incumbent manufacturers that concentrated on milking their products for profit in a stagnant market.[16]

Thus, there is an ongoing dilemma: How to design control systems that can simultaneously maintain a high degree of commitment to—as well as a healthy skepticism regarding—current strategies.

Mission and competitive advantage. Second, we have discussed mission and competitive advantage as separate characteristics. However, business units have both a mission and a competitive advantage that, in some combinations, may result in a conflict regarding the type of controls to be used. As Exhibit 4 demonstrates, the ordinal classification of mission and competitive advantage yields four distinct combinations. There is an unconflicting design in cells 2 and 3.

Both of these cells have a similar level of uncertainty, which suggests a similar control system design. Cells 1 and 4, however, have conflicting demands; designing a control system that fits both is difficult. Several possibilities exist. It might be possible to change the mission or competitive advantage so that they do not conflict from the standpoint of systems design (i.e., move the business unit to cell 2 or cell 3). If this is not feasible, perhaps either mission or competitive advantage is more critical for implementation and would, therefore, dominate the choice of the appropriate type of control. If mission and competitive advantage are equally important, control system design becomes especially difficult. Here, control systems cannot be designed for the mission or competitive advantage in isolation without incurring costs.

Administrative problems and dysfunctional effects. Third, explicitly differentiated controls across business units might create administrative awkwardness and dysfunctional effects, especially for managers in charge of harvest units.

EXHIBIT 4.

Fits and Misfits in Control System Design

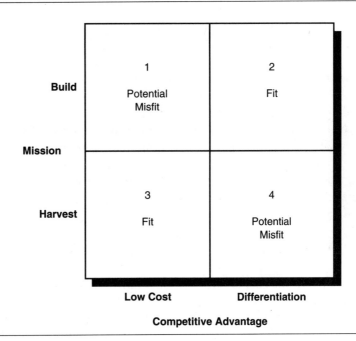

Many harvest managers believe that their career prospects within their companies are somewhat limited. While corporate managers in most diversified firms may find it rational to harvest one or more of their businesses, every company wants to grow at the overall firm level. Thus, as one goes higher in the corporate hierarchy, skills at successfully executing a build strategy become more important than those of successfully executing a harvest strategy. From a career perspective, this likelihood tends to favor managers currently in charge of build businesses.

Example. The following speculation regarding who might succeed Walter Wriston as the next CEO of Citicorp appeared in *The Wall Street Journal* nearly three years *before* the actual announcement of his successor: "Ironically, Mr. Theobald may not get to the top precisely because he runs a division that has always been a big money maker for Citicorp, its institutional division. Unlike his two competitors, who are charting new courses for Citicorp, Mr. Theobald is simply carrying forward a tradition of profiting handsomely from making loans to corporations and governments, domestically and abroad."[17] Subsequent events confirmed these speculations.

Given these possibilities, harvest managers may perceive their roles as being less important. Explicitly designing tight controls over harvest strategies compounds this problem.

System designers might consider two possibilities to mitigate this problem. First, as part of the planning process, they might avoid using such harshly graphic and negative terms as "cash cow," "dog," "question mark," and "star" and instead use terms such as "build," "hold," and "harvest." The former are "static" terms that do not convey missions as well as do "dynamic," action-oriented terms such as "build," "hold," and "harvest."

Second, to the extent possible, a harvest manager should be given one or more products with high growth potential. Doing this should prevent managers from becoming typecast solely as "harvesters." Corning Glass Works follows this policy of assigning a growth-oriented product to a manager who is in charge of a harvest business.[18]

SUMMARY

This article argues that the role of management control depends on the strategy being followed and that effective control systems are differentiated depending on strategy. For example, carefully engineered product standard costs are likely to be a very important ongoing management control tool for a firm that follows a cost leadership strategy in a mature, commodity business. But for a firm that follows a product differentiation strategy in a market-driven, rapidly growing, fast-changing business, carefully engineered standard manufacturing costs may well be much less important.

It is not surprising that monitoring R&D productivity is much more important to a company like Merck than manufacturing cost control. On the other hand, a better system for monitoring R&D costs would not gain much attention in a company like International Paper, which employs many accountants to track manufacturing cost variances on a regular monthly basis. Although cost information is important in all companies in one form or another, different strategies demand different control perspectives.

It is interesting to compare the SCM perspective about the role of cost information with the perspective that is more prevalent in management accounting today. The theme in management accounting texts today has been the same for thirty years. That theme was first articulated by Simon and others,[19] who coined three phrases to capture the essence of management accounting:

- Scorekeeping;
- Problem solving; and
- Attention directing.

Although these specific words are not always preserved, these three objectives still come through frequently in today's textbooks—as they also clearly did when the Controllers Institute (which now is the Financial Executive Institute) commissioned a team of faculty from Carnegie Tech (which now is Carnegie Mellon) to study the elements of effective controllership.

The point is not to deprecate per se this long-standing common starting point, but rather to emphasize how much our conception of *what* we do starts with our consensus about *why* we do it. Each of the three well-known roles involves a set of concepts and tehniques that are implicitly assumed to apply to all firms, if perhaps in varying degrees. For example, standard cost variances are a key tool for "attention directing," and contribution margin analysis is a key tool for "problem solving."

Because the three roles are not seen as varying across firms depending on strategic context, the relevance of the related tool concepts also is not seen to vary across firms. If agreement could be reached that *why* we do management accounting differs in important ways depending on the basic strategic thrust of the firm, it would be a much easier transition to see that *how* we do management accounting should also reflect the basic strategic thrust.

Even if management accounting in most companies today is still heavily involved with conventional tasks, this need not be true in the future. Management accounting as it is reflected in management control systems can and should be redirected to explicitly consider the strategic issues that a firm faces.

Notes

1. John Shank & Vijay Govindarajan, *Strategic Cost Analysis* (Chicago: Richard D. Irwin 1989); and John Shank & Vijay Govindarajan, "Strategic Cost Management and the Value Chain," *Journal of Cost Management* (Winter 1992): 5–21.

2. See, e.g., K.R. Andrews, *The Concept of Corporate Strategy* (Homewood, Ill.: Dow-Jones Irwin 1971); H.I. Ansoff, *Corporate Strategy* (New York: McGraw-Hill 1965); Alfred A. Chandler, *Strategy and Structure: Chapters in the History of American Industrial Enterprise* (Cambridge, Mass.: The MIT Press 1962); C.W. Hofer & D.E. Schendel, *Strategy Formulation: Analytical Concepts* (St. Paul, Minn.: West Publishing Co. 1978); and R.E. Miles & C.C. Snow, *Organizational Strategy, Structure and Process* (New York: McGraw-Hill 1978).

3. B.D. Henderson, *Henderson on Corporate Strategy* (Cambridge, Mass.: ABT Books 1979).

4. R.V.L. Wright, *A System for Managing Diversity* (Cambridge, Mass.: Arthur D. Little, Inc. 1975).

5. C.W. Hofer & M.J. Davoust, *Successful Strategic Management* (Chicago, Ill.: A.T. Kearney, Inc. 1977).

6. R.D. Buzzell & F.D. Wiersema, "Modeling Changes in Market Share: A Cross-Sectional Analysis," *Strategic Management Journal* (January–February 1981): 27–42; and Hofer & Schendel, *Strategy Formulation*.

7. Michael E. Porter, *Competitive Strategy* (New York: The Free Press 1980).

8. This section draws from an extensive body of research that has focused on strategy implementation issues at the business-unit level. Some of the key references are: V. Govindarajan, "A

Contingency Approach to Strategy Implementation at the Business Unit Level: Integrating Management Systems With Strategy," *Academy of Management Journal* (September 1988): 4, 31, 828–853; V. Govindarajan, "Implementing Competitive Strategies at the Business Unit Level: Implications of Matching Managers to Strategies," *Strategic Management Journal* 10 (1989): 251–269; V. Govindarajan & Joseph Fisher, "The Interaction Between Strategy and Controls: Implications for Managerial Job Satisfaction" (working paper, The Amos Tuck School of Business Administration, Dartmouth College 1989); V. Govindarajan & J. Fisher, "Impact of Output Versus Behavior Controls and Resource Sharing on Performance Strategy as a Mediating Variable," *Academy of Management Journal* (June 1990): 259–285; V. Govindarajan & J. Fisher, "Incentive Compensation, Strategic Business Unit Mission, and Competitive Strategy" (working paper, The Amos Tuck School of Business Administration, Dartmouth College 1991); V. Govindarajan & A.K. Gupta, "Linking Control Systems to Business Unit Strategy: Impact on Performance," *Accounting Organizations and Society* 9, No. 4 (1985): 51–66; A.K. Gupta & V. Govindarajan, "Business Unit Strategy, Managerial Characteristics, and Business Unit Effectiveness at Strategy Implementation," *Academy of Management Journal* 27 (1984): 25–41; A.K. Gupta & V. Govindarajan, "Build, Hold, Harvest: Converting Strategic Intentions into Reality," *Journal of Business Strategy* 4, no. 3 (1984): 34–47; G.E. Hall, "Reflections on Running a Diversified Company," *Harv. Bus. Rev.* (January–February 1987); R. Sata & M.A. Maidique, "Bonus System for a Balanced Strategy," *Harv. Bus. Rev.* (November–December 1980); John K. Shank & V. Govindarajan, *Strategic Cost Analysis* (Homewood, Ill.: Irwin 1989): chs. 6, 7; J.K. Shank & V. Govindarajan, "Profit Variance Analysis: A Strategic Focus," *Issues in Accounting Education* 4, No. 2 (Fall 1989); Robert Simons, "The Relationship Between Business Strategy and Accounting Control Systems: An Empirical Analysis," *Accounting Organizations and Society* (July 1987): 357–374.

9. See V. Govindarajan, "Appropriateness of Accounting Data in Performance Evaluation: An Empirical Evaluation of Environmental Uncertainty as an Intervening Variable," *Accounting Organizations and Society* 9, no. 2 (1984): 125–135.

10. Hall, "Reflections on Running a Diversified Company," at 88–89.

11. "Executive Compensation: Looking to the Long Term Again," *Business Week* (May 9, 1983): 81.

12. L. Reibstein, "Firms Trim Annual Pay Increase and Focus on Long Term: More Employers Link Incentives to Unit Results," *The Wall Street Journal* (April 10, 1987): 25.

13. B. Uttal, "The Gentlemen and the Upstarts Meet in a Great Mini-battle," *Fortune* (April 23, 1979): 98–108.

14. Shank & Govindarajan, *Strategic Cost Analysis,* at 114–130.

15. K. Ohmae, "The Long and Short of Japanese Planning," *The Wall Street Journal* (January 18, 1982): 28.

16. B.G. James, "Strategic Planning Under Fire," *Sloan Management Review* (Summer 1984): 57–61.

17. J. Salamon, "Challenges Lie Ahead for Dynamic Citicorp After the Wriston Era," *The Wall Street Journal* (December 18, 1981): 1.

18. Richard F. Vancil, "Corning Glass Works: Tom MacAvoy," in F.F. Vancil, *Implementing Strategy* (Boston: Division of Research, Harvard Business School 1982): 21–36.

19. Herbert Simon, et al., *Centralization Versus Decentralization in Organizing the Controller's Department* (New York: The Controllership Foundation, Inc. 1954).

20. A modified version of this article will appear in the forthcoming book by the authors, *Strategic Cost Management* (New York: The Free Press 1993).

CHAPTER TWO

The Design of Activity-Based Cost Systems

This chapter provides three articles on the design concepts behind activity-based costing. *Activity-based costing* is a methodology that measures the cost and performance of activities, resources, and cost objects. Resources are assigned to activities, and then activities are assigned to cost objects (such as products or customers), based on their use by the cost object.[1] Activity-based costing has emerged in the literature and in practice within the last decade, so is still considered a new approach by many firms.

Activity-based costing provides management with strategic information about product and customer profitability. This information can be used by management to guide product and market segment strategies.

The articles that follow show how activity-based costing can provide product cost information superior to that which has been available from conventional systems. There are three important insights that have evolved from this literature represented in the selected articles. They are:

1. The concept of activity hierarchies;
2. The activity-based management cross model;
3. The distinction between consumption models and spending models.

Reading 2.1   Hierarchies of Activities and ABC Design Concepts

R. Cooper, "Activity-Based Costing for Improved Product Costing," in *Handbook of Cost Management*, edited by Barry Brinker (New York: Warren Gorham and Lamont), B1, 1993.

Robin Cooper is one of the seminal contributors to the literature in activity-based costing. His articles and case studies (many co-authored with Robert Kaplan) have provided a rich resource for activity-based costing practitioners. This article is an abbreviated summary of his work in this field.

A major contribution reflected in this article is the concept of activity hierarchies. Cooper introduces the concept of unit-level, batch-level, product-sustaining level, and facility-level activities. Cooper then demonstrates how conventional cost systems typically assume that overhead is consumed proportionally by every unit produced (e.g., allocating by direct labor or machine hours), possibly leading to systematic product cost distortions when there are batch- and product-level activities present.

Specifically, Cooper demonstrates that there are two major conditions that can lead to distortions under the conventional unit-based allocation approach. Under either of these conditions, an activity-based allocation approach will provide more accurate product costs.

These conditions are:

Condition 1. Significant batch activities and batch size differences across the different products.

or

Condition 2. Significant product-sustaining activities and product-attribute differences across the different product lines.

In the first condition, *batch activities* refer to activities performed to benefit a group, or batch, of product.[2] Batch activities are not performed for every unit of production; thus, they are non-volume activities. Examples of batch activities include:

Setting up

Moving

Order taking

Order processing

Production scheduling

Inspecting

Purchasing

For example, setup is an activity performed to prepare the machine for the next product run. The setup is not performed for every unit manufactured in the run. Therefore, the setup effort required for a production run of 10 units could be the same as the setup effort for a production run of 100 units. Thus, the effort is related to the number of production runs, not the volume of units.

Products will exhibit *batch size differences* if some products are processed in small batches, while others are processed in large batches. Typically, batch size differences will occur in companies that have "commodity" products and "custom" products. The commodity products are popular among customers and are made in large batches (long runs). In contrast, the specialty products are not required by customers in large numbers and are produced in smaller batches (small runs).

EXHIBIT 1

Batch Activity Product Cost Distortion

	A	B	C	D
			Allocated	Unit Cost
Conventional	Activity	Driver ×	Cost	(Col. C ÷
Allocation	Driver	Rate[1]	(from Col. B)	1,000 units)
Product X	1,000 dlh.	1,000 × $1	$1,000	$1.00
Product Y	1,000	1,000 × $1	$1,000	$1.00
Total	2,000 dlh.			

[1]Set up cost ÷ Direct labor hrs. $2,000 ÷ 2,000 = $1 per direct labor hour

	A	B	C	D
			Allocated	Unit Cost
Activity-Based	Activity	Driver ×	Cost	(Col. C ÷
Allocation	Driver	Rate[2]	(from Col. B)	1,000 units)
Product X	200 setups	200 × $8	$1,600	$1.60
Product Y	50	50 × $8	$400	$0.40
Total	250 setups			

[2]Setup cost ÷ Number of setups: $2,000 ÷ 250 = $8 per setup

When a company has significant batch activities and batch size differences across the product line, then the conventional unit-based allocation approach will distort costs in such a way as to penalize the large batch product with an artificially high cost and benefit the short batch product with an artificially low cost. To illustrate distortion caused by batch activities more closely, assume that two products (X and Y) each require one direct labor hour to produce and have a demand of 1,000 units each. Product X is produced in batches of 5, while Product Y is produced in batches of 20. Thus, Product X will be set up for 200 production runs (1,000 units ÷ 5) and Product Y will be set up for 50 production runs (1,000 units ÷ 20). Assume that factory overhead includes only setup, which has a cost of $2,000. Exhibit 1 shows the conventional unit-based allocation approach compared to an activity-based approach for the setup batch activity.

Under the conventional approach the unit costs are equal. However, the activity-based approach assigns more cost to Product X, because Product X consumes more setup activity, due to the shorter production runs (more setups), than does Product Y.

In the second condition, *product-sustaining activities* refer to activities that are performed to support a product line or family. Product-sustaining activities are *not* performed for every unit of production nor for a batch of production, but

EXHIBIT 2

Examples of Product Attribute Diversity and Effect on Activities

Product-Sustaining Activity	Attribute Associated with High Product Cost	Attribute Associated with Low Product Cost
Customer return processing and problem resolution activities	The product has low quality	The product has high quality
Engineering changes and process change activity	The product is new or recently modified	The product is older — mature
Procurement effort	The product has many special features requiring many unique purchased parts	The product is an "off-the-shelf" commodity product with no special features requiring unique parts
Design effort	The product has a complex or unfamiliar design	The product has a simple and familiar design
Advertising and promotion effort	The product requires heavy promotional support	The product requires no promotional support
Expediting and rework effort	The product is difficult to manufacture	The product is easy to manufacture

are instead performed on routine occasions for the benefit of the product line as a whole. Thus, product-sustaining activities are non-volume activities. Examples of product-sustaining activities include:

Engineering changes

Advertising and promotion

Design engineering

Maintaining product specifications

Customer return processing

Rework effort

Expediting (special instructions to speed up the completion of a product)

Environmental and regulatory activities

For example, an engineering change is an activity that is performed to improve the design of product or production process. Frequently, new products will incur greater engineering change activity from "working the bugs out" than will more mature products.

A *product attribute* is a characteristic of a product, such as product quality. Products will exhibit *attribute differences* when some products have different characteristics than others. Product attributes causing product families to consume different levels of product-sustaining activities are illustrated in Exhibit 2.

EXHIBIT 3

Product-Sustaining Product Cost Distortion

	A	B	C	D
			Allocated	Unit Cost
Conventional	Activity	Driver ×	Cost	(Col. C ÷
Allocation	Driver	Rate[1]	(from Col. B)	1,000 units)
Product P	1,000 dlh.	1,000 × $3	$3,000	$3.00
Product Q	1,000	1,000 × $3	$3,000	$3.00
Total	2,000 dlh.			

[1]Return Processing ÷ Direct labor hrs.: $6,000 ÷ 2,000 = $3 per direct labor hour

			Allocated	Unit Cost
Activity-Based	Activity	Driver ×	Cost	(Col. C ÷
Allocation	Driver	Rate[2]	(from Col. B)	1,000 units)
Product P	100 customer returns	100 × $50	$5,000	$5.00
Product Q	20	20 × $50	$1,000	$1.00
Total	120 customer returns			

[2]Return Processing ÷ Number of customer returns: $6,000 ÷ 120 = $50 per customer return

When a company has significant product-sustaining activities and product attribute differences, then the conventional unit-based approach will likely distort product costs. To illustrate distortion caused by product-sustaining activities more closely, assume that Products P and Q each require one direct labor hour to produce and have a demand of 1,000 units each. Product P has had some quality problems that have resulted in processing 100 customer returns. Product Q has satisfied customers and has processed only 20 returns. Assume that the cost of processing all customer returns is $6,000 and that this activity is the only factory overhead. Exhibit 3 shows the conventional allocation approach compared to an activity-based approach for a product-sustaining activity.

Under the conventional approach the unit costs are equal. However, the activity-based approach assigns more cost to Product P, because Product P consumes more customer return processing, due to the lower quality, than does Product Q.

The examples in the Cooper article capture similar themes.

Reading 2.2   The Activity-Based Management Cross Model

P.B.B. Turney, "Second-Generation Architecture" in *Handbook of Cost Management*, edited by Barry Brinker (New York: Warren Gorham and Lamont), B3, 1993.

This article by Peter Turney, the author of the widely acknowledged book *Common Cents*,[3] provides additional design considerations in an activity-based costing system. A very important contribution in this article is the activity-based management (ABM) cross model. *Activity-based management* refers to a discipline that focuses on the management of activities as a route to improving the value received by the customer and the profit achieved by providing this value. The discipline includes cost driver analysis, activity analysis, and performance measurement. Activity-based management draws upon activity-based costing as its major source of information.[4] The ABM cross model suggests that there are two important views to using activity cost information. The cost assignment view is the vertical view that assigns resources to activities and activities to cost objects (e.g., products, customers, and vendors). The cost assignment view is used for strategic decision making and is the view that was used by Cooper in the prior reading (2-1). In addition to the cost assignment view, there is also the process view, which is the horizontal part of the ABM model. In this view, cost drivers cause linked activities (processes) to be activated. For example, field failures is a cost driver that causes activities to be activated with respect to processing customer returns. The performance measures are output measures of process performance with respect to time, cost and quality. The process view is mostly concerned with operational cost management as discussed in greater detail in Chapter 3.

Turney also demonstrates that activities can be placed into a database so that various types of activities can be sorted according to predefined criteria. Thus, for example, activities can be coded as value-added or non-value-added and sorted along this dimension. Additionally, activities can be hierarchically arranged. Macro activities are high-level aggregations that can be used for cost assignment, while the micro activities can be used for operational management considerations. The rationale is that cost assignment does not require a high degree of activity precision, while operational management within processes of the organization does require cost resolution. This design characteristic allows the user to "drill down" the activity hierarchy to a level that meets decision needs.

Reading 2.3 Consumption vs. Spending and the Cost of Excess Capacity

R. Cooper and R. Kaplan, "Activity-Based Systems: Measuring the Cost of Resource Usage," *Accounting Horizons* (September 1992), pp. 1–13.

Cooper and Kaplan (CK) suggest that there are many costs that are incurred in "lumps" prior to their use. In other words, managers must commit to spending the resources prior to actually using the resource. Most resources are acquired in this lumpy pattern. Very few resources, except for materials and energy, are truly variable to the units of activity consumption. Thus, managers are constantly

EXHIBIT 4

Cost Allocation vs. Cost Estimation Schemas

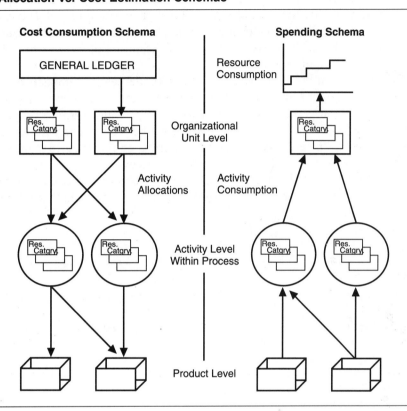

faced with attempting to match the acquired capacity with the demand for activities and resources. The more flexible the resources, whether labor or capital, the more able this match can be made. If, however, the resources are not flexible, then the firm must often deal with the cost consequences of unused capacity. CK suggest that excess capacity costs should be reported separately so that management is able to discern how much resource is underdeployed. CK also suggest that activity-based product costs give managers a long-term view of how resources are committed for a given product mix, and thus can aid in relevant costing (make-buy, pricing, abandonment-type decisions).

Moreover, CK imply a distinction between the consumption and spending perspectives of activity-based costing. The two perspectives can be illustrated as shown in Exhibit 4.[5]

The cost consumption schema is concerned with assigning resources to activities, and activities to cost objects along the vertical dimension of the ABM model. However, firms often wish to make decisions about the impact of changes in product mix or activities on resource spending. The nature of the spending question is in the direction opposite from the consumption model. It is not how costs are consumed by products, but rather how resources are influenced by decisions in the firm. These are much more of the nature of short-term "what-if" and budgeting-type questions.

CK suggest that the analyst may be able to model selected impacts of activity and product mix change on activities, and then activity changes on resources. From this the firm can determine the *cash flow consequences* of a decision. By necessity the cash flow consequences will not likely be linear with changes in activity volume, since the resources are incurred or removed in "lumps." An example of this is provided in Greenwood and Reeve.[6]

It should be pointed out that the CK view of the world is still controversial. There are many that believe that the only relevant costs are the "variable costs" of the organization.[7]

Notes

1. N. Raffish and P.B.B. Turney, "Glossary of Activity-Based Management," *Journal of Cost Management* (Fall 1991): 57.

2. The concept of batch and product activities was introduced by Robin Cooper, "Cost Classification in Unit-Based and Activity-Based Manufacturing Cost Systems," *Journal of Cost Management* (Fall 1990): 4–13.

3. P.B.B. Turney, *Common Cents: The ABC Performance Breakthrough* (Portland, Ore.: Cost Technology), 1992.

4. N. Raffish and P.B.B. Turney, p. 57.

5. T. Greenwood and J. Reeve, "Activity-Based Costing for Continuous Improvement: A Process Design Framework," *Journal of Cost Management* (Winter 1992): 22–40.

6. T. Greenwood and J. Reeve, "Process Cost Management" *Journal of Cost Management* (Winter 1993): 4–19.

7. For an interesting panel discussion of this controversy, see R. Kaplan, J. Shank, C. Horngren, G. Boer, W. Ferrara, and M. Robinson, "Contribution Margin Analysis: No Longer Relevant/ Strategic Cost Management: The New Paradigm," *Journal of Management Accounting Research* (Fall 1990): 1–32.

Additional Readings

Bakke, Nils Arne, and Roland Hellberg. "Relevance Lost? A Critical Discussion of Different Cost Accounting Principles in Connection with Decision Making for Both Short and Long Term Production Scheduling," *International Journal of Production Economics* (November 1991): 1–18.

Berliner, Callie, and James A. Brimson, eds. *Cost Management for Today's Advanced Manufacturing: The CAM-I Conceptual Design* (Boston: Harvard Business School Press, 1988).

Brimson, James A. *Activity Accounting* (New York: John Wiley and Sons, 1991).

Brinker, Barry J., ed. *Emerging Practices in Cost Management* (Boston: Warren Gorham and Lamont, 1991).

_____. *Handbook of Cost Management* (Boston: Warren, Gorham and Lamont, 1991).

Bruns, William J., and Robert S. Kaplan, eds. *Accounting and Management: Field Study Perspectives* (Boston: Harvard Business School Press, 1987).

Cooper, Robin. "Does Your Company Need a New Cost System?" *Journal of Cost Management* (Spring 1987): 45–49.

_____. "The Two-Stage Procedure in Cost Accounting—Part One," *Journal of Cost Management* (Summer 1987): 43–51.

_____. "The Two-Stage Procedure in Cost Accounting—Part Two," *Journal of Cost Management* (Fall 1987): 39–45.

_____. "When Should You Use Machine-Hour Costing?" *Journal of Cost Management* (Spring 1988): 33–39.

_____. "The Rise of Activity-Based Costing—Part One: What Is an Activity-Based Cost System?" *Journal of Cost Management* (Summer 1988): 45–54.

_____. "The Rise of Activity-Based Costing—Part Two: When Do I Need an Activity-Based Cost System?" *Journal of Cost Management* (Fall 1988): 41–48.

_____. "The Rise of Activity-Based Costing—Part Three: How Many Cost Drivers Do You Need, and How Do You Select Them?" *Journal of Cost Management* (Winter 1989): 34–46.

_____. "You Need a New Cost System When . . . " *Harvard Business Review* (January–February 1989): 77–82.

_____. "Cost Classification in Unit-Based and Activity-Based Manufacturing Cost Systems," *Journal of Cost Management* (Fall 1990): 4–14.

Cooper, Robin, and Robert S. Kaplan. "How Cost Accounting Systematically Distorts Product Costs," in *Accounting and Management: Field Study Perspectives*, William S. Bruns, Jr. and Robert S. Kaplan, eds. (Boston: Harvard Business School Press, 1987).

_____. "Measure Costs Right: Make the Right Decisions," *Harvard Business Review* (September–October 1988): 96–103.

_____. "Profit Priorities From Activity-Based Costing," *Harvard Business Review* (May-June 1991): 130–135.

Cooper, Robin, Robert S. Kaplan, Lawrence S. Maisel, Eileen Morrissey, and Robert M. Oehm. "From ABC to ABM," *Management Accounting* (November 1992): 54–57.

Cooper, Robin, and Peter B.B. Turney. "Internally-Focused Activity-Based Cost Systems," in *Measures for Manufacturing Excellence*, edited by R.S. Kaplan (Boston: Harvard Business School Press. 1991): 291–308.

Drury, Colin. "Product Costing in the 1990s," *Accountancy* (May 1990): 122–126.

Ferrara, William L. "The New Cost/Management Accounting—More Questions Than Answers," *Management Accounting* (October 1990): 48–52.

Hall, Robert W., H. Thomas Johnson, and Peter B.B. Turney. *Measuring Up: Charting Pathways to Manufacturing Excellence* (Homewood, Ill.: Business One Irwin, 1991).

Hirsch, Maurice L., Jr., and Michael C. Nibbelin. "Incremental, Separable, and Common Costs in Activity-Based Costing," *Journal of Cost Management* (Spring 1992): 39–47.

Johnson, H. Thomas. "Activity-Based Information: A Blueprint for World-Class Information," *Management Accounting* (June 1988): 23–30.

_____. "Reviewing the Past and Future of Cost Management," *Journal of Cost Management* (Winter 1990): 4–7.

———. "Beyond Product Costing: A Challenge to Cost Management's Conventional Wisdom," *Journal of Cost Management* (Fall 1990): 15–21.

Johnson, H. Thomas, and Robert S. Kaplan. *Relevance Lost: The Rise and Fall of Management Accounting* (Boston: Harvard Business School Press, 1987).

Kaplan, Robert S. "Accounting Lag—The Obsolescence of Cost Accounting Systems," in *The Uneasy Alliance: Managing the Productivity-Technology Dilemma*, Kim B. Clark, Robert H. Hayes, and Christopher Lorenz, eds. (Boston: Harvard Business School Press, 1985).

———. "One Cost System Isn't Enough," *Harvard Business Review* (January–February 1988): 61–66.

———. "Management Accounting for Advanced Manufacturing Environments," *Science* (Aug. 1989): 819–823.

———. "The Four-Stage Model of Cost Systems Design," *Management Accounting* (February 1990): 22–26.

Kaplan, Robert S. "In Defense of Activity-Based Cost Management," *Management Accounting* (November 1992): 58–63.

———. ed. Measures for Manufacturing Excellence. (Boston: Harvard Business School Press, 1990).

King, Alfred. "The Current Status of Activity-Based Costing: An Interview with Robin Cooper and Robert S. Kaplan," *Management Accounting* (September 1991): 22–26.

King, Alfred M. "Cost Management Concepts and Principles: Green Dollars and Blue Dollars: The Paradox of Cost Reduction," *Journal of Cost Management* (Fall 1993).

Kingcott, Timothy. "Opportunity Based Accounting—Better Than ABC," *Management Accounting* (UK) (October 1991): 36–37, 48.

Kleinsorge, Ilene K., and Ray D. Tanner. "Activity-Based Costing: Eight Questions to Answer Before You Implement," *Journal of Cost Management* (Fall 1991): 84–88.

MacArthur, John B. "Activity-Based Costing: How Many Cost Drivers Do You Want?" *Journal of Cost Management* (Fall 1992): 37–41.

Maskell, Brian. "Management Accounting: Relevance Regained—An Interview with Professor Robert S. Kaplan," *Management Accounting* (UK) (September 1988): 38–42.

Miller, Jeffrey G., and Thomas Vollman. "The Hidden Factory," *Harvard Business Review* (September–October 1985): 142–150.

Nanni, Alfred J., Jeffrey G. Miller, and Thomas E. Vollman. "What Shall We Account For?" *Management Accounting* (January 1988): 42–48.

Noreen, Eric. "Conditions Under Which Activity-Based Cost Systems Provide Relevant Costs," *Journal of Management Accounting Research* (Fall 1991): 159–168.

Roth, Harold, and A. Faye Borthick. "Getting Closer to Real Product Costs," *Management Accounting* (May 1989): 28–33.

———. "Are You Distorting Costs by Violating ABC Assumptions?" *Management Accounting* (November 1991): 39–42.

Schnoebelen, Steven C. "Lurking Issues in Cost Management," *Journal of Cost Management* (Summer 1991): 3–6.

Shank, John K., and Vijay Govindarajan. *Strategic Cost Analysis: The Evolution from Managerial to Strategic Accounting* (Homewood, Ill.: Richard D. Irwin, 1989).

———. *Strategic Cost Management; The New Tool for Competitive Advantage* (New York: The Free Press, 1993).

———. "The Perils of Cost Allocations Based on Production Volumes," *Accounting Horizons* (December 1988): 71–79.

Spicer, B.H., "The Resurgence of Cost and Management Accounting: A Review of Some Recent Developments in Practice, Theories, and Case Research Methods," *Management Accounting Research* (March 1992): 1–38.

Turney, Peter B.B. *Common Cents: The ABC Performance Breakthrough* (Hillsboro, Oregon: Cost Technology, 1991).

_____. "What an Activity-Based Cost Model Looks Like," *Journal of Cost Management* (Winter 1992): 54–60.

_____. "What Is the Scope of Activity-Based Costing?" *Journal of Cost Management* (Winter 1990): 40–42.

Turney, Peter B.B., and James M. Reeve. "The Impact of Continuous Improvement on the Design of Activity-Based Cost Systems," *Journal of Cost Management* (Summer 1990): 43–50.

Activity-Based Costing for Improved Product Costing

ROBIN COOPER

Professor of Management, Claremont Graduate School
Peter F. Drucker Graduate Management Center, Claremont, California

INTRODUCTION

The use of activity-based costing (ABC) for improved product costing has attracted much attention in recent years. (Note that this chapter uses the abbreviation "ABC" to refer to "activity-based costing" in general and also to replace the phrase "activity-based cost," as in "ABC systems.") Viewed strictly from a cost accounting viewpoint, ABC can be considered an evolutionary extension of the two-stage allocation procedure that underlies most modern cost accounting systems.[1]

THE STRUCTURE OF ACTIVITY-BASED COSTING SYSTEMS

The first stage of this procedure assigns indirect resource expenses to cost pools, and the second stage assigns the expenses accumulated in the cost pools to products. The first-stage assignment is typically used to evaluate the performance of the manager responsible for the cost pool. The second stage is used to cost products. In the second stage, a cost system designer must choose a measure for assigning expenses to products. This measure is called an *allocation base* if the assignment is an arbitrary allocation, and an *activity driver* if a causal attribution is being attempted. Dividing the total expenses in the cost pool by the total budgeted quantity of the allocation base or cost driver for that pool gives the burden or activity driver rate. Overhead expenses are assigned to products by multiplying the burden or driver rate of each pool by the allocation base or cost driver quality consumed by each product.

Conventional, unit-based cost accounting systems focus on *units* of particular products. Costs are allocated to the product unit because only products are assumed to consume resources. Conventional allocation bases thus measure attributes of the product unit (e.g., the number of direct labor hours, machine hours, or material dollars consumed in making each unit).

Hierarchies of Activities

By contrast, ABC systems focus on the *activities* performed to produce products in the manufacturing process. The costs of activities are attributed to products based on each product's consumption of those activities.

A manufacturing ABC system recognizes up to four different categories of activities:

1. *Unit-level* activities, which are performed each time a unit is produced;
2. *Batch-level* activities, which are performed each time a batch of goods is produced;
3. *Product-sustaining* activities, which are performed as needed to support the production of each different type of product; and

4. *Facility-sustaining* activities, which support a facility's general manufacturing process.

The last two categories of the manufacturing hierarchy are called sustaining activities, because the number of times these activities are performed is not strictly proportional to the number of products or facilities. For example, while the number of engineering changes will increase with the number of products produced, there is no guarantee that doubling the number of products will lead to a doubling of the number of engineering changes. In contrast, unit-level and batch-level activities are strictly proportional to the number of units or batches produced.

The number of times unit-level activities (such as drilling holes, machining surfaces, and inspecting every part) are performed varies according to the number of units produced. The costs of these activities can be assigned to the individual units upon which they are performed. The number of times batch-level activities (such as setting up a machine or ordering a group of parts) are performed varies according to the number of batches made. The costs of these activities can be assigned to individual batches but they are common (or fixed) regardless of the number of units in the batch.

Product-sustaining activities are performed to support different products in a company's product line. Examples of product-sustaining activities include maintaining product specifications (such as the bill of materials and routing information), performing engineering change notices, developing special testing routines, and expediting products. The costs of these activities can be assigned to individual products, but the costs are independent; i.e., they are fixed regardless of the number of batches or the number of units of each product produced.

Arbitrary Allocation of Facility-Sustaining Costs

The first three categories of activities used by manufacturing ABC systems deal with costs that can be directly attributed to individual products. However, the fourth category—facility-sustaining activities—contains costs that are common to a variety of products and can only be allocated to products arbitrarily.

Examples of facility-sustaining activities include lighting and cleaning the facility, facility security, and managing the facility. Facility-sustaining activities can be further broken down by changing the focus of analysis from the product to aggregations of products. For example, facility-sustaining activities can be split into product line-sustaining activities—that is, activities performed to sustain a particular product line (such as prototype development) and the residual facility-sustaining activities that cannot be associated with products or product lines. Such additional analyses provide insights into the economics of producing and supporting product lines or other aggregations of products.

ACTIVITY-BASED COSTING FULL-ABSORPTION COSTING

The majority of ABC systems described in the literature compute full-absorption costs. That is, the product costs are reported for the individual unit and contain all of the costs associated with manufacturing. These costs are obtained by:

- Dividing batch-level costs by the number of units in the batch;
- Dividing product and facility costs by the number of product units produced; and
- Adding the results to the unit-level costs.

These ABC costs are not numerically the same as the full-absorption costs reported by conventional cost systems. They differ because ABC systems use different cost assignment procedures that take advantage of the hierarchical view of activities. The advantage of the different procedures that ABC systems use is reduced distortion of product costs.

Apparent Variability of Unit Costs

ABC unit costs do suggest, however, an inappropriate degree of variability, namely, that all manufacturing costs vary with the number of units produced. In reality, batch-related costs can be reduced only by decreasing the number of batches (or by performing the batch-level activity more efficiently), not simply by reducing the number of units produced. The inappropriate suggestion of variability is introduced by allocation of facility-sustaining costs to product units. From an ABC perspective, only the allocation of *facility-sustaining* costs to products is arbitrary. Theoretically, facility-sustaining costs should not be assigned to products in an ABC system, because the arbitrary allocation of facility-sustaining costs to products adds no information about the economics of production.

Some ABC systems that report full-absorption unit costs overcome the inappropriate appearance of variability by reporting product costs separately for unit-level, batch-level, and product-sustaining activities. They achieve this result by separately reporting the cost assigned by each allocation base or activity driver. Exhibit B1.1 illustrates this approach.

The fundamental difference between ABC and conventional cost systems can be seen by comparing how conventional cost systems allocate the costs of facility-sustaining, product-sustaining, and batch-level activities to products through the use of a unit-level allocation base. Exhibit B1.2 shows the use of a unit-level allocation base.

The Nature of Activity Drivers

ABC systems differ from conventional cost systems in the *nature* of activity drivers used to attribute costs. Conventional cost systems use only second-stage

EXHIBIT B1.1

The Activity-Based Perspective: Product Profitability

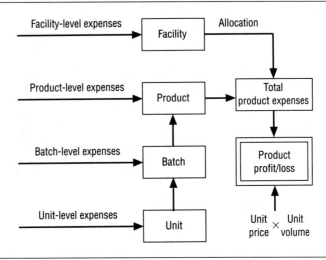

allocation bases, which are based on unit-level characteristics of the product (typically, direct labor hours is the allocation base used). An ABC system, on the other hand, may use activity drivers that are not related to unit-level characteristics, including:

1. *Batch-level drivers,* which assume that certain resources are consumed in direct proportion to the number of batches of each type of product produced; and
2. *Product-sustaining drivers,* which assume that certain resources are consumed to develop or permit production of different products.

Well-designed ABC systems take advantage of these extra types of drivers by matching the level of the activity and the driver chosen to attribute its costs to products. For example, in a well-designed ABC system, the costs of batch-level activities are attributed to products using batch-level drivers.

A DEFINITION OF AN ACTIVITY-BASED COSTING SYSTEM

The four-category hierarchy of activities leads to the following definition of a manufacturing ABC system:

EXHIBIT B1.2

The Traditional Perspective: Traditional, Unit-Based Product

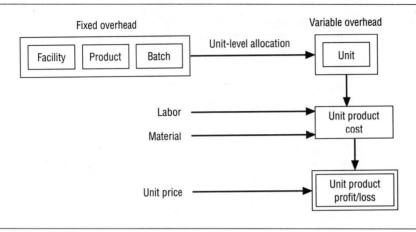

A manufacturing ABC system identifies and then classifies the major activities of a facility's production process into one of the following four categories: unit-level, batch-level, product-sustaining, and facility-sustaining activities. Costs in the first three categories of activities are assigned to products using activity drivers that capture the underlying behavior of the costs that are being assigned. The costs of facility-sustaining activities, however, are treated as period costs or allocated to products in some arbitrary manner.

Excluded Systems

The above definition excludes many systems that are currently described as ABC systems. In particular, it excludes systems that contain only two of the three types of activity driver. There are several possible explanations for a design team's choosing not to use all three types of drivers:

- First, the designers of the cost system may not have understood that three different categories of drivers exist.
- Second, in some production processes, two of the categories of activities became indistinguishable. For example, if production batches contain only one unit, then the unit-level and batch-level categories are identical.
- Third, the benefit of reporting one of the categories of activities separately may be small.
- Fourth, even if the designers were aware that three different categories of activity drivers exist, they might choose for reasons of simplicity and ease of understanding to use only two of them.

Cost systems that use only two types of drivers can be considered partial ABC systems. According to this classification scheme, cost systems fall somewhere in a continuum that starts with conventional, unit-based systems (which use only unit-level drivers) and ends with full-fledged ABC systems (which use all three types).

A MODEL FOR CONSUMPTION OF RESOURCES[2]

ABC is properly viewed as a model of how an organization's resources are consumed, not as a model of organizational spending. This distinction is important because changes in resource consumption and spending are often non synchronous.

If a company drops a single product, for example, a decrease in the consumption of product-sustaining activities will occur. There will be one less bill of materials to maintain, but there will typically be no equivalent decrease in spending on these activities. Typically, the resources freed by dropping a single product will not be sufficient to reduce spending. For example, a single individual might be able to maintain fifty bills of materials. The 1/50 of that person's time that is freed by dropping one product will typically be consumed elsewhere. However, if the company drops fifty products, not only will there be a decrease in consumption for product-sustaining activities but (assuming management takes appropriate action) a matching decrease in spending will occur.

By reporting changes in consumption, an ABC system allows managers to estimate the changes in spending that might occur. For example, the potential benefits of dropping fifty products are observable. In contrast, if a spending model were adopted, the cost of the product-sustaining activities would be ignored for the first forty-nine products. It would be acknowledged only when the fiftieth product was dropped and the individual reassigned to perform other activities. Thus, a spending model provides no early signals of the potential savings associated with dropping many products. In addition, the savings from the reassignment of the individual are contingent on management action. No cost system can be designed a priori to capture this type of contingency.

A Guide to Action

ABC helps managers estimate the changes in resources that will be consumed as a consequence of particular decisions. If a proposed decision reduces the number of batch-level activities required or increases the efficiency of performing batch-level activities (e.g., by reducing setup times), the decision maker can estimate the future reduction in demands for resources used to perform these activities, and how these reduced demands translate into reduced levels of spending. If a proposed decision increases the number of products in the plant, the increased number of product-sustaining activities can be estimated and linked to subsequent demands for increased spending.

Taking Actions to Enhance Profitability

An ABC system thus provides managers with new insights into how consumption—and thus spending—can be better managed. The cost information provided by an ABC system must not be used naively to close plants or eliminate products merely because an activity-based analysis shows them to be unprofitable. Instead, an ABC analysis should capture the attention of managers and prompt them to take one of three types of actions to enhance profitability:

1. When market conditions permit, managers can reprice products (or customer transactions) so that revenues are better aligned with the expenses of products and customer orders. This action is perhaps the simplest, since it involves no fundamental changes internal to the company.

2. Managers can take actions designed to alter the company's product or customer mix so that fewer demands are made on the organization's resources. This goal can be accomplished, for example, by designing products with fewer parts or more common parts. Similarly, product customization can be delayed until the last possible production stage. A company can also impose minimum order sizes, encourage customers to use standard products rather than custom products, and gradually eliminate products and customers that cannot be made profitable. Finally, factories can be focused so that low-volume, customized products do not interrupt the production of high-volume standard items.

3. A company can attempt to perform its activities more efficiently. Thus, the company can encourage employees to implement continuous improvement concepts to enhance quality, reduce setup times, and improve factory layouts. Advanced information technology can be installed to facilitate processing of batches, products, and customer orders. These actions enable the same number of activities to be performed with fewer resources.

Converting Reduced Consumption to Increased Profits

As managers reduce the demands on organizational resources by reducing the number of redundant activities and performing the remaining activities more efficiently, a second set of actions should be taken if the company is to capture the benefits from the ABC analysis:

1. The company can produce and sell more output, thus leading to increased revenues without requiring increased operating expenses.

2. Alternatively, managers can redeploy or eliminate what have become excess resources, thus enabling the same revenue to be earned with reduced operating expenses.

Either action will lead to higher profitability. But if managers do not increase throughput or eliminate excess resources, they create excess capacity, not increased profits. Managers may conclude erroneously from this experience that operating expenses were indeed "fixed." This is not the case, however: The operating expenses only seem fixed because managers failed to take the actions required to make the costs variable.

Expenses are not intrinsically either fixed or variable. ABC analysis permits managers to understand the causes of variability and reveals actions they can take to reduce demands on their organizational resources. But managers must be prepared to take the second set of actions (i.e., to increase throughput or reduce resource spending) if their companies are to realize increased profits signaled by ABC profitability analysis.

ILLUSTRATING ACTIVITY-BASED COSTING SYSTEMS: FIVE SIMPLE EXAMPLES

The following series of related examples demonstrates when an ABC system reports more accurate product costs than a conventional cost system that uses direct labor hours as the allocation base.[3] The examples explore the effect that different production volumes and physical sizes of products have on the costs reported by conventional versus ABC systems.

Example 1

Company A manufactures four products: $P1$, $P2$, $P3$, and $P4$. All are produced on the same equipment using similar processes. The products differ according to their physical size (either large or small) and also according to their production volumes (i.e., whether they are high-volume or low-volume products).

The production of the four products requires the performance of seven activities. The expenses associated with these activities are assigned to the products indirectly. Note that the only issue is how *overhead* is assigned to products: In other words, direct product costs (i.e., direct material costs and direct labor costs) are not the issue here.

The seven activities and their costs are:

- Procuring material (10 percent of direct material costs);
- Supervising direct labor ($10 per direct labor hour);

EXHIBIT B1.3

Activities Categorized by Hierarchy

Activity	Activity category
Procuring material	Unit-level
Supervising labor	Unit-level
Running the machines	Unit-level
Performing setups	Batch-level
Fulfilling orders	Batch-level
Handling material	Batch-level
Administering parts	Product-sustaining

- Running machines ($15 per machine hour);
- Performing setups ($120 per setup);
- Fulfilling orders ($125 per order);
- Handling material ($25 per batch handled); and
- Administering parts ($500 per part).

Exhibit B1.3 shows that these activities can be categorized into three unit-level activities, three batch-level activities, and one product-sustaining activity. The top of Exhibit B1.4 shows the quantities and dollar values of these resources for each product.

Exhibit B1.5 shows that A employs a cost accounting system that consists of one cost center — the entire facility. The system allocates overhead expenses to the products by means of direct labor hours.

The shaded box entitled "Reported unit cost" near the top of Exhibit B1.4 shows the overhead costs reported by A's conventional cost system. Note that the overhead costs reported by the conventional cost system in this example would be the same whether direct labor hours, direct material dollars, or machine hours were used as the allocation base since all three alternatives are strictly proportional.[4]

An analysis of the overhead costs that the conventional cost accounting system allocates to the four products leads to two conclusions — both of them (as it turns out) wrong:

- The high-volume products ($P2$ and $P4$) cost the same per unit to manufacture as their low-volume counterparts ($P1$ and $P3$); and
- The large products ($P3$ and $P4$) cost three times more per unit to produce than their small counterparts ($P1$ and $P2$).

Varying Consumption of Resources

As the "direct labor hours" column near the top of Exhibit B1.4 shows, the two high-volume products (*P2* and *P4*) consume ten times more direct labor hours than their low-volume counterparts (*P1* and *P3*). As a result, the conventional cost system allocates ten times more overhead to *P2* and *P4*. Since the number of high-volume products (*P2* and *P4*) manufactured is ten times higher than the number of corresponding low-volume products (*P1* and *P3*), the reported unit costs are the same for the products that are the same size (i.e., $22.56 for the small products *P1* and *P2*, and $67.67 for the large products *P3* and *P4*).

The large products (*P3* and *P4*) consume three times more direct labor hours than their small counterparts (*P1* and *P2*). Therefore, the cost system allocates three times more overhead to *P3* and *P4*. Consequently, their reported unit costs are three times higher than the unit costs reported for *P1* and *P2*.

Questionable Reported Overhead Costs of the Conventional Cost System

Intuitively, the overhead costs reported by *A*'s cost accounting system seem questionable. Most managers would probably be comfortable with the general relationship between the reported overhead costs of the large versus the small products. However, many managers would raise an eyebrow at the fact that the reported unit costs of the high-volume products exactly equal the reported unit costs of their low-volume counterparts, because most managers expect to see economies of scale come into play.

In fact, all the costs reported by the conventional accounting system are highly distorted. The source of this distortion lies in the choice of a single, unit-level allocation base (direct labor hours in this example) to allocate *all* overhead to the products. The implicit assumption is that when unit volume doubles, so does the quantity of all indirect resources consumed by a product.

Using only unit-level allocation bases to allocate overhead to products invariably distorts reported product costs if some of the manufacturing activities are unrelated to production volume.

Product Costing Using Activity-Based Costing

The reported cost of a product in an ABC system equals the sum of the costs of all activities that must be performed to manufacture the product. As Example 1 shows, four of the activities are not unit-level: that is, setups, fulfilling orders, and material handling are batch-level activities, while the fourth activity—parts administration—is a product-sustaining activity. Since these activities are not performed at the unit level, their costs should be attributed to the products using non-unit level drivers. For example, setups can be costed by dividing all setup-related costs by total setup hours to yield an hourly setup cost. This figure can

EXHIBIT B1.4
Example 1 (Company A)

Consumption patterns by product

| Product | Size | Volume | Unit-level activities | | | Batch-level activities | | | Product-sustaining activities | Total overhead costs |
			Material costs	Direct labor hours	Machine hours	Number of setups	Number of orders	Times handled	Number of parts	
P1	Small	Low	$ 60	5	5	1	1	1	1	
P2	Small	High	600	50	50	3	3	3	1	
P3	Large	Low	180	15	15	1	1	1	1	
P4	Large	High	1,800	150	150	3	3	3	1	
Amounts consumed			$2,640	220	220	8	8	8	4	
Activity cost (overhead)			$ 264	$2,200	$3,300	$960	$1,000	$ 200	$2,000	
Aggregated activity cost			—	—	$5,764	—	—	$2,160	$2,000	$9,924

Overhead costs reported by a conventional cost system

Product	Size	Volume	Units produced	Direct labor hours consumed	Overhead rate	Costs allocated	Reported unit cost
P1	Small	Low	10	5	$45.11	$ 225.55	$22.56
P2	Small	High	100	50	45.11	2,255.50	22.56
P3	Large	Low	10	15	45.11	676.65	67.67
P4	Large	High	100	150	45.11	6,766.50	67.67
			220	220		$9,924.20	

Calculation of overhead rate

Total overhead costs	$9,924.00
Total direct labor hours	÷ 220.00
Overhead rate	$ 45.11

Overhead costs reported by an ABC system

	Unit-level activities	Batch-level activities	Product-sustaining activities	Total overhead costs
Total overhead costs	$5,764.00	$2,160.00	$2,000.00	$9,924.00
Total cost driver units	220	8	4	
Consumption intensity	$ 26.20	$ 270.00	$ 500.00	

	Unit-level activities			Batch-level activities			Product-sustaining activities		
Product	Direct labor hours	Consumption intensity	Costs traced	Setups	Consumption intensity	Costs traced	Part numbers	Consumption intensity	Costs traced
P1	5	$26.20	$ 131.00	1	$270.00	$270.00	1	$500.00	$500.00
P2	50	26.20	1,310.00	3	270.00	810.00	1	500.00	500.00
P3	15	26.20	393.00	1	270.00	270.00	1	500.00	500.00
P4	150	26.20	3,930.00	3	270.00	810.00	1	500.00	500.00
			$5,764.00			$2,160.00			$2,000.00

Total overhead costs reported by ABC system

Product	Unit-level activities	Batch-level activities	Product-sustaining activities	Total costs traced	Reported unit cost	Difference from conventional cost systems
P1	$ 131.00	$ 270.00	$ 500.00	$ 901.00	$ 90.10	-299%
P2	1,310.00	810.00	500.00	2,620.00	26.20	-16%
P3	393.00	270.00	500.00	1,163.00	116.30	-72%
P4	3,930.00	810.00	500.00	5,240.00	52.40	23%
	$5,764.00	$2,160.00	$2,000.00	$9,924.00		

EXHIBIT B1.5

Example 1: The Traditional Cost System at Company _A_

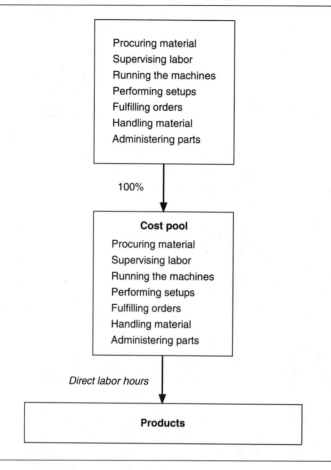

then be used in conjunction with the cost driver "setup hours" to attribute setup costs to products.

Note that ABC systems are necessarily more complex than conventional, unit-based cost accounting systems. Capturing the economics of production processes and the way in which products consume activities requires the use of cost drivers that measure the activities performed on products. This process generally means that multiple cost drivers are needed to report accurate product costs.

An ABC system for _A_ would (like a conventional cost system) use a unit-level activity driver (such as direct labor hours) to attribute unit-level expenses in Example 1. These expenses would include procuring materials, supervising labor, and running the machines.

Note that, in practice, three different unit-level activity drivers (e.g., material dollars, direct labor hours, and machine hours) might be required. However, the perfect correlation of these three activity drivers in this example makes it possible to use a single activity driver without distorting the reported product costs.

As the top of Exhibit B1.4 shows, the three possible batch-level activity drivers (the number of setups, the number of orders, and the number of times handled) are also strictly proportional. Consequently, only one batch-level activity driver is required to attribute these expenses accurately to the products. The final activity, parts administration, requires the same effort for each product. Therefore, the activity driver "number of parts" (one per product) is appropriate. Exhibit B1.6 shows the completed ABC system for A.

The bottom section of Exhibit B1.4 shows the unit overhead costs reported by an ABC system for A. Analyzing the differences between the overhead costs reported by the conventional cost accounting system compared with the costs reported by the ABC system gives insight into the effect that differing batch sizes and physical sizes can have on product costs reported by conventional cost systems.

Sources of Bias in Product Costs

To pinpoint the sources of the biases in the differing product costs reported in Exhibit B1.4, a series of related examples is given. The first set of examples (Examples 2A and 2B) isolates the effect of *batch size* (batch size diversity) on reported product costs. The second set (Examples 3A and 3B) isolates the effect of *physical size* (physical size diversity) on reported product costs.

For all four examples that follow, the products that are discussed are identical to the products having the same names in Example 1; the names, basic assumptions, and data for the products are consistent throughout.

Examples 2A and 2B

To analyze the effect that differing batch sizes have on product costs, consider the following two examples: Examples 2A and 2B.

Batch Size Diversity

Company A's conventional cost system indicates that $P2$ and $P4$ consume *ten* times more overhead in total than $P1$ and $P3$, their low-volume counterparts. Actually, however (as Exhibit B1.4 shows), the high-volume products

EXHIBIT B1.6

Example 1: The ABC System at Company *A*

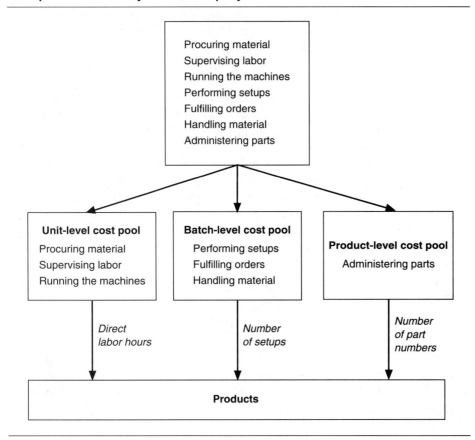

Procuring material
Supervising labor
Running the machines
Performing setups
Fulfilling orders
Handling material
Administering parts

Unit-level cost pool

Procuring material
Supervising labor
Running the machines

Batch-level cost pool

Performing setups
Fulfilling orders
Handling material

Product-level cost pool

Administering parts

*Direct
labor hours*

*Number
of setups*

*Number
of part
numbers*

Products

are set up, ordered, and handled only *three* times as often, and they have the same number of part numbers to administer. The conventional cost system ignores these differences in relative consumption. The ABC system, however, takes these differences into account and attributes appropriate amounts to each product.

Now assume that two new companies exist. Company *B* manufactures two products: *P1* and *P2*. As in the previous example, *P1* is small, low-volume product. *P2*, on the other hand, is a small, high-volume product. Exhibit B1.7 shows the cost data for the two products. Company *C* is identical to *B* except that it manufactures two different products: *P3*, which is a large, low-volume product, and *P4*, which is a large, high-volume product. Exhibit B1.8 shows the cost data for these two products.

As the shaded box near the top of Exhibit B1.7 shows, *B*'s conventional cost system reports the same $32.01 overhead cost per unit for both of the small products (*P*1 and *P*2) even though *P*1 is a low-volume product and *P*2 is a high-volume product. Similarly, *C*'s conventional cost system (see the shaded box near the top of Exhibit B1.8) reports the same overhead cost of $58.21 per unit for both of the large products (*P*3 and *P*4) even though *P*3 is a low-volume product and *P*4 is a high-volume product.

Analysis of the Effects of Batch Size Diversity

Contrast these results with the overhead costs reported by the ABC systems. As the shaded box at the bottom of Exhibit B1.7 shows, the ABC system reports overhead costs of $90.10 for the small, low-volume product (*P*1) versus $26.20 for *P*2, the small, high-volume product. Similarly, *C*'s ABC system (see the shaded box at the bottom of Exhibit B1.8) reports unit costs of $116.30 for *P*3 (the large, low-volume product) and $52.40 for *P*4 (the large, high-volume product).

These costs more accurately reflect the different consumption of resources by the two products manufactured in each company. The low-volume products (*P*1 and *P*3) incur higher reported overhead costs under the ABC system because they consume more of the batch-level and product-sustaining resources for every unit produced than their high-volume counterparts.

Two important observations can now be made:

1. Although the products in *B* and *C* are identical to the products manufactured in *A*, note that the conventional cost systems of *A, B,* and *C* all report different overhead costs (see the shaded boxes near the top of Exhibits B1.4, B1.7, and B1.8).
2. The ABC systems for *A, B,* and *C*—by contrast—report identical overhead costs for products *P*1, *P*2, *P*3, and *P*4.

Examples 3A and 3B

Examples 2A and 2B point out the effect that batch size diversity can have on reported product costs. Examples 3A and 3B point out the effect that differing physical sizes can have on reported product costs.

Physical Size Diversity

Now assume that two additional companies exist. Company *D* manufactures two products: *P*1 and *P*3. As before, *P*1 is a small, low-volume product, and *P*3 is a large, low-volume product. Exhibit B1.9 shows the activities at *D*. Company *E* also manufactures two products: *P2* and *P4*. *P2* is a small, high-volume product, and *P4* is a large, high-volume product. Exhibit B1.10 shows the activities at *E*.

Analysis of the Effects of Physical Size Diversity

Examples 3A and 3B illustrate how conventional cost systems can systematically overcost large products and undercost small products. The reason for this cross-subsidy again lies in the relative quantities of resources consumed. As Exhibit B1.4 shows, the large products (*P3* and *P4*) consume three times more direct labor hours than their small counterparts (*P1* and *P2*). A cost system that relies solely on the unit-level allocation basis, therefore, automatically allocates three times more overhead to the large products.

An analysis of *actual* consumption patterns, however, shows that—even though the large products consume three times more of the unit-based resources (i.e., overhead related to direct material, direct labor, and machine hours)—they consume the *same* level of batch-level and product-sustaining activities. Consequently, conventional cost systems systematically overcost larger products. ABC systems, however, take the differences in relative consumption of resources into account and thus attribute appropriate amounts of the resources consumed to each product.

The conventional cost system for *D* in the shaded box near the top of Exhibit B1.9 illustrates this bias: It reports unit overhead costs of $51.60 for *P1* (the small, low-volume product) and $154.80 for *P3* (the large, low-volume product). These unit costs contrast markedly with the corresponding unit costs of $90.10 for *P1* and $116.30 for *P3* reported by the ABC system (see the shaded box at the bottom of Exhibit B1.9).

Similarly, the conventional cost system for *E* (see the shaded box near the top of Exhibit B1.10) reports unit overhead costs of $19.65 for *P2* (the small, high-volume product) and $58.95 for *P4* (the large, high-volume product). Again, these unit costs differ markedly from the corresponding unit costs reported by the ABC system of $26.20 for *P2* and $52.40 for *P4* (see the shaded box at the bottom of Exhibit B1.10).

Finally, note that—throughout all the examples given above—the overhead costs reported by the ABC systems are the same regardless of the company. By contrast, the product costs reported by the conventional cost systems differ from one company to the other, even though the products and production processes are economically identical.

Overview of the Examples: The Interaction of Production Volume and Physical Size Diversity

Examples 2A and 2B demonstrate the bias of batch size diversity, and Examples 3A and 3B demonstrate the bias of physical size diversity. Example 1 demonstrates the interaction of these two biases. Exhibit B1.11 summarizes the product costs calculated and shown in all of the examples. As the columns for Example 1 in Exhibit B1.11 show, *P*1 (the small, low-volume product) is doubly *under*costed: While its ABC reported overhead costs per unit are $90.10, the costs reported by the conventional system are $22.56. Product *P*4, on the other hand (the large, high-volume product), is doubly *over*costed: While its ABC reported costs are $52.40, the costs reported by the conventional system are $67.67.

These batch size and physical size biases reinforce each other, but they are not additive. In other words, the errors in the reported product costs in Examples 2A and 2B (which result from batch size diversity) cannot simply be added to the errors in Examples 3A and 3B (which result from physical size diversity) to obtain the error in reported product costs caused by the interaction of batch size and physical size diversity.

Estimating the Bias

Although conventional cost systems systematically undercost small, low-volume products and overcost large, high-volume products, estimating whether products of *intermediate* batch size or physical size will be overcosted or undercosted (and, if so, by how much) is no easy task.

In the simple examples given that use only four products, some educated guesses can be made: Note that the conventional cost system overcosts *P*4 (the large, high-volume product) by $15.27 per unit (i.e., $67.67 − $52.40) and undercosts *P*1 (the small, low-volume product) by $67.54 per unit (i.e., $90.10 − $22.56). It can reasonably be concluded, therefore, that—between the two of them—*P*2 and *P*3 must be undercosted by $52.27 (i.e., $67.54 − $15.27).

Even in this simplistic example, however, it is difficult to predict either the direction or the magnitude of the bias in product costs for either product *P*2 or *P*3 (though, as it turns out, both intermediate products are undercosted). In a more realistic setting (e.g., in a company that has hundreds or even thousands of products and multiple sources of bias), therefore, managers cannot possibly predict the direction—let alone the magnitude—of biases in reported product costs.

A SAMPLE ACTIVITY-BASED COSTING SYSTEM

The simple examples used in this chapter to illustrate ABC theory were taken from a real-world example—the ABC system at John Deere Component Works (JDCW).[5] This ABC system contains eight distinct cost pools. Exhibit B1.12 shows these cost pools. The first three relate to unit-level activities, the second

EXHIBIT B1.7
Example 2A (Company B)

Consumption patterns by product

			Unit-level activities			Batch-level activities			Product-sustaining activities	Total overhead costs
Product	Size	Volume	Material costs	Direct labor hours	Machine hours	Number of setups	Number of orders	Times handled	Number of parts	
P1	Small	Low	$ 60	5	5	1	1	1	1	
P2	Small	High	600	50	50	3	3	3	1	
Amounts consumed			$660	55	55	4	4	4	2	
Activity cost (overhead)			$ 66	$550	$ 825	$480	$500	$ 100	$1,000	
Aggregated activity cost			—	—	$1,441	—	—	$1,080	$1,000	$3,521

Overhead costs reported by a conventional cost system

Product	Size	Volume	Units produced	Direct labor hours consumed	Overhead rate	Costs allocated	Reported unit cost
P1	Small	Low	10	5	$64.02	$ 320.09	$32.01
P2	Small	High	100	50	64.02	3,200.91	32.01
			110	55		$3,521.00	

Calculation of overhead rate

Total overhead costs	$3,521.00
Total direct labor hours	÷ 55
Overhead rate	$ 64.02

Overhead costs reported by an ABC system

	Unit-level activities	Batch-level activities	Product-sustaining activities	Total overhead costs
Total overhead costs	$1,441.00	$1,080.00	$1,000.00	$3,521.00
Total cost driver units	55	4	2	
Consumption intensity	$ 26.20	$ 270.00	$ 500.00	

	Unit-level activities			Batch-level activities			Product-sustaining activities		
Product	Direct labor hours	Consumption intensity	Costs traced	Setups	Consumption intensity	Costs traced	Part numbers	Consumption intensity	Costs traced
P1	5	$26.20	$ 131.00	1	$270.00	$270.00	1	$500.00	$500.00
P2	50	26.20	1,310.00	3	270.00	810.00	1	500.00	500.00
			$1,441.00			$1,080.00			$1,000.00

Total overhead costs reported by ABC system

Product	Unit-level activities	Batch-level activities	Product-sustaining activities	Total costs traced	Reported unit cost	Difference from conventional cost system
P1	$ 131.00	$ 270.00	$ 500.00	$ 901.00	$90.10	−181%
P2	1,310.00	810.00	500.00	2,620.00	26.20	18%
	$1,441.00	$1,080.00	$1,000.00	$3,521.00		

EXHIBIT B1.8
Example 2B (Company C)

Consumption patterns by product

Product	Size	Volume	Unit-level activities			Batch-level activities			Product-sustaining activities	Total overhead costs
			Material costs	Direct labor hours	Machine hours	Number of setups	Number of orders	Times handled	Number of parts	
P3	Large	Low	$ 180	15	15	1	1	1	1	
P4	Large	High	1,800	150	150	3	3	3	1	
Amounts consumed			$1,980	165	165	4	4	4	2	
Activity cost (overhead)			$ 198	$1,650	$2,475	$480	$500	$ 100	$1,000	
Aggregated activity cost			—	—	$4,323	—	—	$1,080	$1,000	$6,403

Overhead costs reported by a conventional cost system

Product	Size	Volume	Units produced	Direct labor hours consumed	Overhead rate	Costs allocated	Reported unit cost
P3	Large	Low	10	15	$38.81	$ 582.09	$58.21
P4	Large	High	100	150	38.81	5,820.91	58.21
			110	165		$6,403.00	

Calculation of overhead rate

Total overhead costs	$6,403.00
Total direct labor hours	÷ 165
Overhead rate	$ 38.81

Overhead costs reported by an ABC system

	Unit-level activities	Batch-level activities	Product-sustaining activities	Total overhead costs
Total overhead costs	$4,323.00	$1,080.00	$1,000.00	$6,403.00
Total cost driver units	÷ 165	÷ 4	÷ 2	
Consumption intensity	$ 26.20	$ 270.00	$ 500.00	

Unit-level activities

Product	Direct labor hours	Consumption intensity	Costs traced
P3	15	$26.20	$ 393.00
P4	150	26.20	3,930.00
			$4,323.00

Batch-level activities

	Setups	Consumption intensity	Costs traced
P3	1	$270.00	$270.00
P4	3	270.00	810.00
			$1,080.00

Product-sustaining activities

	Part numbers	Consumption intensity	Costs traced
P3	1	$500.00	$500.00
P4	1	500.00	500.00
			$1,000.00

Total overhead costs reported by ABC system

Product	Unit-level activities	Batch-level activities	Product-sustaining activities	Total costs traced	Reported unit cost	Difference from conventional cost system
P3	$ 393.00	$ 270.00	$ 500.00	$1,163.00	$116.30	-100%
P4	3,930.00	810.00	500.00	5,240.00	52.40	-10%
	$4,323.00	$1,080.00	$1,000.00	$6,403.00		

EXHIBIT B1.9

Example 3A (Company D)

Consumption patterns by product

Product	Size	Volume	Unit-level activities			Batch-level activities			Product-sustaining activities	Total overhead costs
			Material costs	Direct labor hours	Machine hours	Number of setups	Number of orders	Times handled	Number of parts	
P1	Small	Low	$ 60	5	5	1	1	1	1	
P3	Large	Low	180	15	15	1	1	1	1	
Amounts consumed			$240	20	20	2	2	2	2	
Activity cost (overhead)			$ 24	$200	$300	$240	$250	$ 50	$1,000	
Aggregated activity cost			—	—	$524	—	—	$540	$1,000	$2,064

Overhead costs reported by a conventional cost system

Product	Size	Volume	Units produced	Direct labor hours consumed	Overhead rate	Costs allocated	Reported unit cost
P1	Small	Low	10	5	$103.20	$ 516.00	$ 51.60
P3	Large	Low	10	15	103.20	1,548.00	154.80
			20	20		$2,064.00	

Calculation of overhead rate

Total overhead costs	$2,064.00
Total direct labor hours ÷	20
Overhead rate	$ 103.20

Overhead costs reported by an ABC system

	Unit-level activities	Batch-level activities	Product-sustaining activities	Total overhead costs
Total overhead costs	$524.00	$540.00	$1,000.00	$2,064.00
Total cost driver units	÷ 20	÷ 2	÷ 2	
Consumption intensity	$ 26.20	$270.00	$ 500.00	

	Unit-level activities			Batch-level activities			Product-sustaining activities		
Product	Direct labor hours	Consumption intensity	Costs traced	Setups	Consumption intensity	Costs traced	Part numbers	Consumption intensity	Costs traced
P1	5	$26.20	$131.00	1	$270.00	$270.00	1	$500.00	$500.00
P3	15	26.20	393.00	1	270.00	270.00	1	500.00	500.00

Total overhead costs reported by ABC system

Product	Unit-level activities	Batch-level activities	Product-sustaining activities	Total costs traced	Reported unit cost	Difference from conventional cost system
P1	$131.00	$270.00	$ 500.00	$ 901.00	$ 90.10	–75%
P3	393.00	270.00	500.00	1,163.00	116.30	25%
	$524.00	$540.00	$1,000.00	$2,064.00		

EXHIBIT B1.10

Example 3B (Company E)

Consumption patterns by product

Product	Size	Volume	Unit-level activities			Batch-level activities			Product-sustaining activities	Total overhead costs
			Material costs	Direct labor hours	Machine hours	Number of setups	Number of orders	Times handled	Number of parts	
P2	Small	High	$ 600	50	50	3	3	3	1	
P4	Large	High	1,800	150	150	3	3	3	1	
Amounts consumed			$2,400	200	200	6	6	6	2	
Activity cost (overhead)			$ 240	$2,000	$3,000	$720	$750	$ 150	$1,000	
Aggregated activity cost			—		$5,240	—		$1,620	$1,000	$7,860

Overhead costs reported by a conventional cost system

Product	Size	Volume	Units produced	Total output per year	Overhead rate	Direct labor hours consumed	Costs allocated	Reported unit cost
P2	Small	High	100	100	$39.30	50	$1,965.00	$19.65
P4	Large	High	100	100	39.30	150	5,895.00	58.95
			200	200		200	$7,860.00	

Calculation of overhead rate

Total overhead costs	$7,860.00
Total direct labor hours ÷	200
Overhead rate	$ 39.30

Overhead costs reported by an ABC system

	Unit-level activities	Batch-level activities	Product-sustaining activities	Total overhead costs
Total overhead costs	$5,240.00	$1,620.00	$1,000.00	$7,860.00
Total cost driver units	÷ 200	÷ 6	÷ 2	
Consumption intensity	$ 26.20	$ 270.00	$ 500.00	

Unit-level activities

Product	Direct labor hours	Consumption intensity	Costs traced
P2	50	$26.20	$1,310.00
P4	150	26.20	3,930.00

Batch-level activities

Setups	Consumption intensity	Costs traced
3	$270.00	$810.00
3	270.00	810.00

Product-sustaining activities

Part numbers	Consumption intensity	Costs traced
1	$500.00	$500.00
1	500.00	500.00

Total overhead costs reported by ABC system

Product	Unit-level activities	Batch-level activities	Product-sustaining activities	Total costs traced	Reported unit cost	Difference from conventional cost system
P2	$1,310.00	$ 810.00	$ 500.00	$2,620.00	$26.20	-33%
P4	3,930.00	810.00	500.00	5,240.00	52.40	11%
	$5,240.00	$1,620.00	$1,000.00	$7,860.00		

EXHIBIT B1.11
Summary Comparison of Unit Costs

Product	Size	Volume	Example 1: Company A Conventional	Example 1: Company A ABC	Example 2A: Company B Conventional	Example 2A: Company B ABC	Example 2B: Company C Conventional	Example 2B: Company C ABC	Example 3A: Company D Conventional	Example 3A: Company D ABC	Example 3B: Company E Conventional	Example 3B: Company E ABC
P1	Small	Low	$22.56	$ 90.10	$32.01	$90.10			$ 51.60	$ 90.10	$19.65	$26.20
P2	Small	High	22.56	26.20	32.01	26.20						
P3	Large	Low	67.67	116.30			$58.21	$116.30	154.80	116.30		
P4	Large	High	67.67	52.40			58.21	52.40			58.95	52.40

Production Volume Diversity

Physical Size Diversity

EXHIBIT B1.12

John Deere Component Works: Activity-Based Cost System

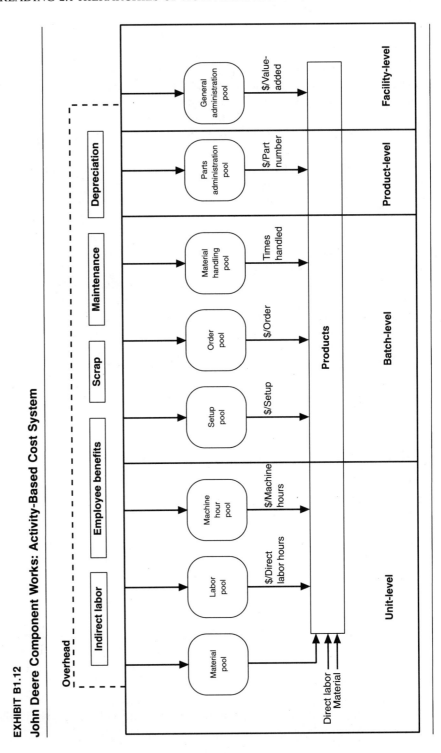

three to batch-level activities, the seventh to product-sustaining activities, and the last to facility-sustaining activities.

Three unit-level cost pools were required because the products were diverse in the way they consumed unit-level activities. The system designers determined that creating cost pools for direct material, direct labor, and machine-related expenses would be adequate for their purposes.

Three batch-level cost pools were required because the products displayed three different kinds of batch diversity. Since setups for the various products varied in duration, setup-related costs were attributed to products using setup hours rather than the number of setups (as in the examples given in this chapter). Costs related to the activity "fulfilling orders" were assigned to products using the number of orders as the activity driver. This activity driver, like number of setups and unlike setup hours, assigns a flat rate to each batch. Material handling was separated out because the large batches were broken into "loads" and thus handled more frequently than batches.

Administering parts, the next cost pool, is identical to the one used in the simplified examples given previously; it captures the cost of the product-sustaining activities. The designers of the system decided that product-sustaining diversity was sufficiently small that it could be ignored. The eighth and final cost pool in the JDCW ABC system contains the costs of the facility-sustaining activities. In the JDCW system, these costs are allocated arbitrarily to products using a value-added measure that includes all costs except material costs. These costs were omitted in the simple examples.

DESIGNING AN ACTIVITY-BASED COSTING SYSTEM

The overall objective that designers of an ABC system should set for themselves is to provide the most benefit possible at the lowest overall cost. To achieve that goal, four design steps should be taken:

1. Aggregate activities;
2. Report the cost of activities;
3. Identify the activity centers; and
4. Select the drivers (both first- and second-stage).

The complexity of an ABC system depends on many factors, including management's objectives for the cost system and the diversity of the company's product mix.[6] If a single management objective dominates, only a few activity drivers may be required to achieve that objective. However, as design objectives become more complex, multiple drivers may be required.

Each of the decisions or steps in the design process listed above is discussed in the sections that follow.

Aggregating Activities

The number of activities performed in a typical facility is so large that it is economically unfeasible to use a different activity driver for each of them. (The trade-off between the accuracy of a cost system and measurement costs is discussed later.) Ordinarily, therefore, many distinct activities must be aggregated into each activity cost pool. A single driver is then used to attribute the costs of those aggregated activities to products.

The first design decision for an ABC system, therefore, involves aggregating activities. Note that as more and more activities are aggregated, the ability of a single activity driver to accurately attribute the cost of resources to products decreases.

For example, if the activities "material movement" and "setup" are aggregated into a single activity and then attributed to products using the activity driver "setup hours," the implicit assumption is that the distance that material is moved varies directly according to the length of time required for the setup, which is obviously not necessarily true. If, alternatively, the activity driver "number of setups" is used, the implicit assumption is that the distance moved is the same regardless of how long the setup takes, which is a fairly reasonable assumption.

But consider the results if, instead, the cost system identifies two distinct activities—"setup" and "material movement"—and uses two separate activity drivers (e.g., "setup hours" and "distance moved" or "number of setups") to attribute the costs of these activities to the products. A cost system that attributes costs in this way makes no implicit assumptions about the relationship between setup time and distance moved. As a result, this cost system reports more accurate product costs than its one-activity counterpart. However, its measurement costs will be higher, because two sets of measurements must be made per product (i.e., both setup hours consumed and distance moved) instead of only one (i.e., only setup hours consumed).

Reporting the Cost of Activities

Once the activities of an ABC system are selected, the next issue is the *level of aggregation* used in reporting the resources consumed by each activity. For example, the cost of resources consumed by the activity "setup" can be reported separately or collectively. Reported product costs are not affected by this design choice: Only the level of reporting detail is affected.

For example, the system might report "setup" costs of $6 for product X, an amount that might include both setup and material movement costs. Alternatively, the system might break the costs down and report a "machine setup" cost of $4 and a separate "material movement" cost of $2.

Identifying the Activity Centers

The third design choice is to identify the activity centers. An activity center is a segment of the production process (possibly a support department) for which management wants to report the cost of the activities separately.

For example, the receiving department might be treated as the activity center "receiving." The product costs reported by the system are not affected by this design choice—the only effect is how those product costs are reported. The system might in this scenario report a total cost of $50. Alternatively, this total cost could be broken down and reported as $30 for manufacturing and $20 for receiving. Having the ability to report costs by activity center gives managers the ability to control activities better.

Selecting the Drivers

The advantage of a two-stage allocation procedure over a single-stage allocation procedure is that different measures of resource consumption can be used at each stage. For example, the resource driver "number of setup hours" can be used in the first stage and "number of setups" in the second stage. Having two stages is frequently beneficial, because the information available about the consumption of resources at the activity center level is often superior to that available at the product level.

Resource Drivers

ABC systems assign the costs of resources into cost pools in each activity center. Consequently, these drivers are called resource drivers. Each cost pool represents an activity or aggregation of activities performed in that center. The resource drivers used to trace costs into the cost pools determine the dollars traced to each pool and therefore the accuracy of reported costs.

For example, if the driver "inspection hours" is used, more inspection-related costs will be traced into activity centers with long inspections than if the resource driver "number of inspections" is used. In many cases, costs are *directly* charged (i.e., traced) to avoid introducing any distortion.

Activity Drivers

Once the cost of resources consumed by all the activities performed in each activity center has been assigned to the activity cost pools, activity drivers can be selected. This is the final design choice.

For the activity "setup," for example, the drivers "number of setup hours" or "number of setups" might be considered. The activity driver "number of setups" assumes that each setup consumes the same amount of resources regardless of the product being manufactured. The activity driver "number of setup hours" assumes that the consumption of resources varies by product, depending on the time needed to set up the machines. Again, the choice of activity driver determines the level of distortion introduced into reported product costs.

The Importance of Activity Drivers

Of the four design decisions listed previously, perhaps the most important is the selection of activity drivers. Selecting activity drivers requires answering two separate but interrelated decisions:

1. How many activity drivers to use; and
2. Which activity drivers to use.

These decisions are interrelated because the type of activity drivers selected affects the number of drivers needed to achieve a desired level of accuracy.

The complexity of a modern manufacturing process is virtually endless. For example, every time that a new batch is run in a metal-cutting operation, new tools have to be drawn from the tool room, inserted, and qualified. The feeds and speeds of the machine must be altered, parts must be moved from inventory storage to the shop floor, the first part must be inspected, and the batch must be scheduled, for example. Despite this complexity, a well-designed ABC system might use only one or two activity drivers to attribute the costs of setup-related activities to the products. For example, an ABC system might use the activity drivers "number of setups" or "number of feet moved."

Using only two drivers to attribute the costs of so many different activities generally introduces distortions into reported product costs. Consequently, the difficulty of designing good cost systems lies in achieving a system that is economical to maintain yet does not introduce excessive distortions in production costs (see the discussion of optimal cost systems later in this chapter).

THE NUMBER OF ACTIVITY DRIVERS REQUIRED

The minimum number of activity drivers that an ABC system uses depends on the desired accuracy of product costs and on the complexity of the product mix.

Desired *accuracy* plays an obvious role: as the number of activity drivers increases, the accuracy of product costs also increases. In other words, the more accurate a company wants its reported costs to be, the more activity drivers the company will need to achieve that accuracy.

The *complexity* of the product mix plays a more subtle role in determining whether the costs of two activities can be aggregated without introducing unacceptable levels of distortion. Three factors determine if a single driver is acceptable:

1. Product diversity;
2. The relative costs of the activities aggregated; and
3. Batch size diversity.

Each of these factors is discussed below.

Product Diversity

Whenever the unit-level resources that a product consumes do not vary in direct proportion to the other resources that it consumes, conventional unit-based cost systems report distorted product costs.

Among the many causes of this distortion are the following:

- Batch size diversity (as illustrated in Examples 2A and 2B);
- Physical size diversity (as illustrated by Examples 3A and 3B);
- Complexity diversity (i.e., complex products may consume more unit-level resources, but not necessarily more non-unit-level resources); and
- Material diversity (i.e., materials that take longer to machine may consume disproportionate shares of unit-level resources).

These many types of product diversity can be accounted for correctly only by use of an ABC system. Each class of diversity requires at least one activity driver if it is to be captured by the cost system.

In general, the greater the difference in how two different products consume manufacturing resources, the greater the distortion caused by using only one activity driver to attribute the costs of those resources to products.

The Relative Costs of the Activities Aggregated

The relative cost of the various activities is a measure of how much each activity costs as a percentage of the total cost of the production process. In general, the higher the relative cost of any given activity, the greater the distortion caused by using an imperfectly correlated activity driver to attribute the costs of the activity to products.

Batch Size Diversity

Batch size diversity occurs (as the examples given earlier in this chapter illustrate) when products are manufactured in different-sized batches. If the production volume of two products differs by a factor of 1,000 (which is not uncommon), the production, order, and shipping batch sizes will differ significantly. ABC systems use activity drivers that adjust for the effect of different production volumes; conventional cost systems do not.

The Role of Judgment and Analysis

In practice, identifying how many activity drivers to use in an ABC system calls for both judgment and analysis. The first step is to identify the resources having large dollar values. The second step is to consider how diverse the products are and in what batch sizes they are produced.

Isolating highly diverse products allows the designer of a cost system to identify which of the major resources can be aggregated without introducing excessive distortion into reported costs. The designer of a cost system can then analyze the smaller-dollar-value resources to see which of them can be aggregated with major resources and which need to be treated as separate activities to achieve the desired objectives.

Factors for Selecting Activity Drivers

Once the minimum number of required activity drivers is determined, appropriate activity drivers can be selected. Three factors should be taken into account when selecting an activity driver:

1. Measurement costs—how easy it is to obtain the data required by the driver;
2. Correlation—how actual consumption of the activity correlates with the consumption implied by the driver; and
3. Behavioral effects—what behavior the driver induces.

Each of these factors is discussed next.

Measurement Costs

ABC systems achieve increased accuracy by using different activity drivers than conventional cost accounting systems. To reduce the measurement costs associated with these drivers, designers of ABC systems should select drivers that use information and data that are relatively easy to obtain.

This objective can often be achieved by substituting drivers that *indirectly* capture the consumption of activities by products. For example, the driver "number of inspections" can be used instead of the driver "inspection hours." This replacement is acceptable if the duration of each inspection is about the same.

Substituting activity drivers that capture the *number of transactions generated* by an activity for ones that capture the actual *duration* of the activity is an important technique for reducing measurement costs. Many transaction-based activity drivers can be used. Examples include the following:

- Number of orders processed;
- Number of shipments processed; and
- Number of inspections performed.

The information required for these activity drivers is often readily available, because a transaction is generated every time the activity is performed. For example, a material requisition is required every time material moves from inventory to the shop floor.

Correlation

The use of activity drivers that only indirectly capture actual consumption entails the risk of introducing distortions into reported product costs. For example, if inspections take varying amounts of time for different products (inspection time diversity), using "number of inspections" as the activity driver instead of "inspection hours" will result in distorted product costs. As a result, a product that required much inspection time would be undercosted, whereas a product that required little inspection time would be overcosted.

How well a given activity driver captures the actual consumption of an activity by a particular product is measured by the *correlation* of the quantities traced to the products as compared with the *actual* quantities consumed by the product.[7]

Behavioral Effects

The effect that the use of a particular driver has on people's behavior must also be considered when choosing activity drivers. A driver affects behavior if individuals feel that their performance is evaluated in some way based on it (e.g., if their performance is evaluated based on price per unit or based on the costs attributed by the activity driver in question). The importance of behavioral effects—which can be either beneficial or harmful—should not be underestimated. For certain companies, the decision to implement an ABC system can be justified on behavioral grounds alone.

For example, a firm that wants to reduce the number of unique parts used in its products in order to simplify activities such as incoming inspection, bill of materials maintenance, and vendor qualification might decide to allocate the costs of these activities using "number of part numbers" as the activity driver. Thus, product engineers who are rewarded based on their ability to design low-cost products will be induced to design products that contain fewer part numbers.

But care must be taken if activity drivers are used to modify behavior. If too many costs are assigned using the same activity driver, the result could be too much of a good thing. Too much "beneficial" behavior might be induced, for example, if reducing the number of part numbers causes product engineers to sacrifice functionality that the marketplace requires simply to reduce part numbers.

An activity driver that induces beneficial behavior but is expensive and has a relatively low correlation might still be selected if the perceived benefit of the desirable behavior exceeds the drawbacks. For example, if the behavioral objective is to reduce throughput time, throughput time could be used as an activity driver for tracing even the cost of activities that are not strictly related to throughput time. In contrast, an activity driver that is expensive to measure *and* induces harmful behavior yet has a high degree of correlation might be selected if the potential cost of errors dominates the decision making. This could be the case, for example, if competition is fierce and knowing accurate product costs is strategically vital.

Determining When Activity-Based Costing Systems Are Appropriate

As explained previously, ABC systems typically use a number of different activity drivers to attribute costs to products. Unfortunately, every driver requires measuring some unique attribute of each product. For example, the driver "setup hours" requires measuring the number of setup hours consumed by each product.

Measuring these attributes can be expensive, and there is no guarantee that the additional measurement costs required by an ABC system will be justified by the benefits. Consequently, the following sections discuss three factors to consider in determining whether the benefits of an ABC system will exceed its implementation and operating costs:

1. The sophistication of the firm's information systems;
2. The cost of errors; and
3. The diversity of the firm's products.

THE OPTIMAL COST SYSTEM

To understand the role that these three factors play in the justification of an ABC system, consider an "ideal," or *optimal*, cost system—that is, a system that minimizes the sum of the following:

- Measurement costs required by the system; plus

- The cost of errors (i.e., costs associated with making poor decisions because of inaccurate product costs).

When a company's products are diverse, measurement costs and the cost of errors are inversely related. Thus, a simple cost system might have low measurement costs, but the product costs that it reported would likely cause managers to make poor (i.e., costly) decisions. Although the measurement costs would be much higher for more complex systems, the product costs should be more reliable, which means that managers should make better decisions—that is, fewer wrong (and thus costly) decisions.

Diminishing Returns

Improvements to cost systems yield diminishing returns as the systems become more complex. Initial improvements to a simple cost system (e.g., implementing multiple cost centers rather than only one) significantly decrease the distortion of reported product costs and thus the cost of errors. As a result, the cost of implementing a marginally more complex system is more than offset by the benefits that result from having more accurate product costs.

Adding more improvements often requires making and handling increasingly expensive measurements that nonetheless improve reported product costs less and less. For example, tracing supervision costs more accurately might require that supervisors complete time sheets to show how they spend their time by products. But if having to complete these time sheets ends up consuming 20 percent of the supervisors' time, the benefits would probably not be justified by the additional costs.

Marginal Costs vs. Marginal Benefits

Increased accuracy is bought only at the cost of rapidly increasing measurement costs. Ultimately, the trade-off between measurement costs and the cost of errors means that the *optimal* cost system is *not* the most accurate cost system. Rather, the point (which is shown as optimum *a* on the graph in Exhibit B1.13) at which the marginal cost of an improvement just equals the marginal benefit of the improvement (in terms of more accurate product costs) defines the optimal cost system.

The position of the optimal cost system is affected by:

- Changes in measurement costs;
- The cost of making errors; and
- Product diversity.

Thus, if measurement costs can be reduced while the other two factors remain unchanged, the position of the optimal cost system will move to the right.

EXHIBIT B1.13

The Optimal Cost System

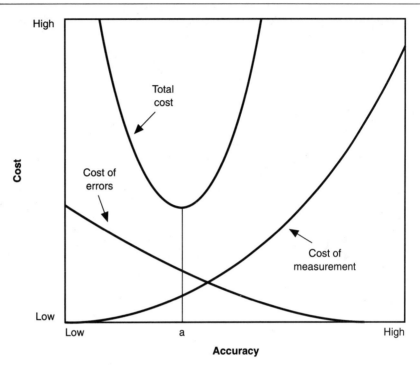

Note: Optimum a is the accuracy of product costs reported by the optimal cost system.

Exhibit B1.14 illustrates this movement. Similarly, if the cost of errors increases (because, perhaps, of increased competition) while the other two factors remain constant, the optimum system will again shift to the right. Exhibit B1.15 illustrates this movement.

Finally, an increase in product diversity reduces the accuracy of reported product costs and also moves the optimum to the right. The effect of the decreased accuracy is to increase the cost of errors and hence justify additional measurements.

Conditions Favoring the Use of Activity-Based Costing Systems

Measurement costs, the cost of errors, and product diversity all change continuously over time. Understanding how and why these changes occur provides insights into the conditions that favor the use of ABC systems.

EXHIBIT B1.14

Decreasing the Cost of Management

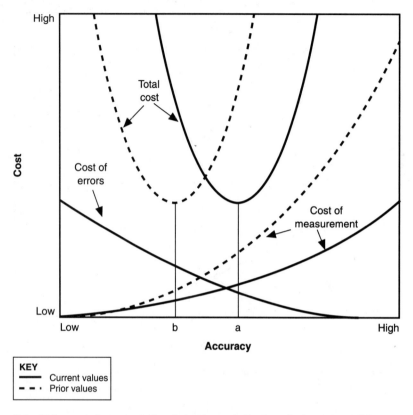

KEY
—— Current values
– – · Prior values

Note: Optimum a is the accuracy of product costs reported by the optimal cost system if the measu
costs decrease (but no other changes occur). Optimum b is the accuracy of product costs reported
existing cost system.

Decreasing Measurement Costs

High measurement costs often make it uneconomical to undertake measurements solely for product costing purposes. Fortunately, experience shows that
virtually all information that most ABC systems need is already available. Given
this availability, measurement costs typically consist of three elements:

1. The cost of routing information to the cost system;
2. The cost of making calculations needed to compute product costs; and
3. The costs of special studies required to determine relevant costs from
   reported product costs.

EXHIBIT B1.15

Increasing the Cost of Errors

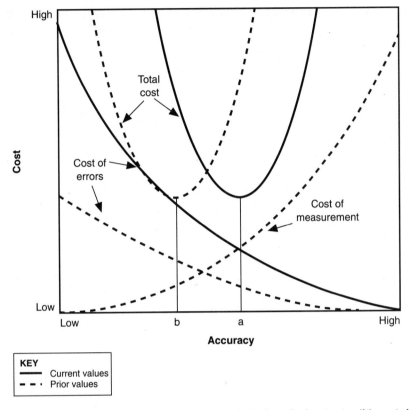

KEY
— Current values
- - · Prior values

Note: Optimum a is the accuracy of product costs reported by the optimal cost system if the cost of increase (but no other changes occur). Optimum b is the accuracy of product costs reported by the cost system.

Measurement costs are changed by the introduction of new information technology, such as computerized shop-floor planning systems, numerically controlled machinery, and more powerful, less expensive computers.

With a computerized production floor scheduling system, more information about products exists in electronic form. This information can then be supplied to the cost system at virtually no cost. For example, the control system for the shop floor captures information about the number of production runs. This information can be used, in turn, to estimate the number of movements of material that occur.

Cost systems perform many calculations to arrive at product costs. These calculations can comprise a major component of overall measurement costs. The cost per calculation has fallen dramatically in recent years with improvements in information processing technology. Indeed, this cost reduction has effectively removed any computational barrier to the development of ABC systems. For example, a powerful microcomputer can now run the ABC system of a sizable facility. Ten years ago, a mainframe computer would have been required; twenty years ago, such a system would have been impossible.

Increasing Cost of Errors

The cost of errors can take several forms. These include the following:

- Making poor decisions about products (e.g., aggressively selling unprofitable products, setting prices inappropriately, or introducing new products into unprofitable niches);
- Making poor product design decisions (e.g., increasing the number of unique parts in a product to reduce its direct labor content when the cost of maintaining those parts exceeds the labor savings);
- Making poor capital investment decisions based on overhead savings that do not materialize; and
- Making inaccurate budgeting decisions about the level of operating expenses required.

These costs arise for two reasons. First, the cost system fails to identify a problem. For example, if a product's reported profitability is high, management will have little reason to question whether that product should be discontinued. Second, failure to appropriately adjust reported product costs will potentially lead to erroneous decisions.

Cost systems report costs that can be modified to give relevant cost information. However, modifications typically require special studies, which usually are expensive. The degree of modification required for a given decision depends on the scope of the decision and the design of the firm's cost system.

The scope of the decision is important because it defines the magnitude of the risk associated with relying on incorrect cost information. The design of the cost system is important because it defines the accuracy of reported product costs and the ease with which they are modified. ABC systems reduce the need to perform special studies by increasing the accuracy of reported product costs and (unlike conventional systems) by reporting the costs of the four different categories of activities separately. For example, if relevant costs require knowledge of the cost of batch-level activities, a unit-based costs system provides little help compared with an ABC system.

First, ABC systems do not completely remove the need for modifications. Modifications are still required, because the assumption that the cost function of a firm is linear inevitably introduces errors. For example, when products contain common components, adding or dropping products will not necessarily change the number of batches of common components produced. Second, the cost system may not appropriately isolate the relevant costs for a particular decision. For example, a system might treat all costs associated with material movement as a single element, yet some decisions might affect only some of those costs. Third, some of the cost assignments might introduce distortions. This could occur, for example, if "number of setups" is used as an activity driver when setups vary according to products or manufacturing sequence.

Changes in Competition

The major cause of *changes* in the cost of errors is variation in the level of competition faced. Increased competition ordinarily increases the cost of errors, because there is a greater chance that a competitor will take advantage of any errors made. For example, an apparently low profit margin for an overcosted (but actually profitable) product—a product, moreover, that a competitor is aggressively chasing—might lead a company to abandon that product, which could prove to be a costly mistake.

By reducing the diversity of products offered, focused manufacturing makes the product costs that conventional cost systems report less distorted. The more accurate product costs that result potentially allow focused manufacturers to make better pricing or product mix decisions than full-range manufacturers. They can thus develop superior marketing strategies. Therefore, full-range manufacturers that suddenly face competition from more focused firms require more accurate product costs.

Creative competition can also change how a product is sold. This change alone can render a cost accounting system obsolete. To illustrate, consider the case of a company that bundled two products together: The first was a machine that customers rented, and the second was a fastener that customers purchased in large volumes and attached using the machine. Rental fees for the machines were purposely set low to attract customers.

Since the machines and fasteners were customized and had to be used together, customers became "captive." Thus, the company set the price of the fasteners high enough to cover not only the costs of the fasteners, but also the unrecovered costs of the machines, plus a profit. Reflecting this bundled-product marketing strategy, the firm's cost system *over*costed fasteners by tracing all overhead costs (including overhead related to the attaching machines) to fasteners and none to the machines.

A competitor, in an attempt to increase market share, found a way to unbundle the two products: It sold the fasteners at a 20 percent discount, which was approximately the amount that the fasteners were overcosted by the first company to subsidize the machines with which they were bundled. The competitor's unbundling of the fasteners and the machines forced the first firm to redesign its cost system so that it would report separate product costs for the machines and the fasteners.[8]

Deregulation can also force firms to compete in new ways. When a company's products and the prices that it charges are regulated, a firm survives by controlling its overall efficiency, not by managing its competitive position.

The cost systems of many regulated firms reflect this reality by measuring the cost of functional activities, not the cost of products. However, a more accurate knowledge of product costs becomes imperative when unregulated competitors appear, cut prices, and start "cherry picking" products. Thus, when deregulation looms on the horizon, managers of regulated firms often display a sudden and intense interest in knowing their product costs.[9]

Firms that were once captive suppliers but suddenly are allowed (or forced) to compete face a situation virtually identical to deregulation. The companies' transfer-pricing systems, which were formerly used to "price" products, often act much like a regulated pricing system.

One firm that recently went through this experience, for example, discovered that its cost system caused it to price products inappropriately. The prices attracted business that the firm did not want and caused the firm to refuse business that was actually profitable. Realizing that the cost system was the culprit, the company's management decided to develop a new cost system that more accurately reported product costs.[10]

Changing Overhead Structures

Over the last 150 years, overhead has relentlessly increased as a percent of value added.[11] This increase has caused many cost systems based on direct labor hours to report increasingly distorted product costs.

As overhead becomes more important, so does the effective management of overhead. Conventional cost systems, with their reliance on one (or a few) allocation bases that are based on production volume make it difficult (if not impossible) to understand the relationship (considering both mix and volume) between the products produced and the appropriate level of overhead. An ABC system, by contrast, provides insights into these relationships and thus can lead to better management of overhead.[12]

Increasingly Distorted Product Costs

As this chapter demonstrates, conventional cost systems can report highly distorted product costs when the products that a company manufactures consume a diverse mixture of resources. Actions such as the following increase product diversity and can thus reduce the overall accuracy of reported product costs:

- Introducing new products;
- Adopting new marketing strategies; and
- Changing production processes.

New Products

The introduction of a new product or product line whose cost structure differs significantly from the cost structure of existing products can increase the distortion of reported product costs. The distortions occur because cost systems report *average* product costs; the new averages are less representative of actual costs of both the old and new products produced than the old average was of the old products alone.

A classic example of this problem occurs when a cost center contains both manual and automated machines. As long as the products that pass through the center use different types of machines in about the same proportion, reported product costs are not significantly distorted. However, if a new product is introduced and it uses the automated machines more intensely, it will be undercosted if direct labor hours are used to allocate costs.

Costing distortions can increase gradually over time as the new products are produced in greater volumes relative to existing products. For example, one firm introduced a new line of plastic products. Since the firm did not have enough volume to justify doing its own molding, it purchased molded parts. However, the company fabricated its older, metal products by purchasing sheet metal, which was then cut and welded to create the desired shapes. The firm's cost system, which was based on direct labor, spread the support overhead for metal fabrication over both metal and plastic products, thus undercosting the metal products and overcosting the plastic ones.

New Marketing Strategies

Changing strategies for a product can also make a cost system obsolete. The decision to market in low-volume niches requires increased production of low-volume products. Conversely, the decision to produce standard parts in a specialty shop requires increased production of high-volume products. These changes result in distorted product costs if the cost system is not designed to appropriately attribute overhead to products when batch size diversity is high.

Conventional unit-based cost systems generally cannot differentiate adequately between overhead consumed by high-volume versus low-volume products (see the preceding discussion of batch size diversity). Fortunately, as long as the difference in volumes produced is low (e.g., a 5 : 1 ratio of items in the largest batches to items in the smallest batches), product costs are usually still reasonably accurate. But if the ratio exceeds 10 : 1, the risk of significantly distorted product costs increases.

For example, one company had a large variety of products. Some of the products were sold in high volumes, so some production lots contained thousands of items. Other products sold in low volumes and were produced in production lots containing as few as ten or twenty items. As a result, the firm's conventional unit-based cost system produced highly distorted product costs. The reported product costs led management to believe—erroneously—that the low-volume products were highly profitable.[13]

Changing Production Processes

Introducing a new production process can also cause a cost system to give distorted product costs. For example, the introduction of automated production processes (such as flexible machining) leads to the use of *less* direct labor but to an *increase* in the use of support functions such as programming and special engineering. As a result, the products manufactured on the new machinery are undercosted if direct labor is the only allocation base used. Conversely, products that are *not* manufactured on the new machines are overcosted.

One company, for example, completely revamped its production process. Machines that required continuous direct supervision were replaced with machines that required little supervision. This replacement allowed machine operators to watch over several machines at once, perform off-line setups, and also do inspections. But the company's cost system, which was based on direct labor, was *not* completely revamped at the same time. As a result, it failed to capture the changed economics of the company's production process and thus reported distorted product costs.[14]

COST SYSTEM OBSOLESCENCE

Even though a firm's measurement costs, cost of errors, and product diversity often change, firms seldom redesign their cost systems. As the years go by, therefore, the accumulated changes can render the company's cost system obsolete.

For example, at some point a firm may install a computerized system for controlling the shop floor. A few years later, the firm may face increased competition. Then, over the course of several years, the firm may add one or more new products to help improve its competitive position.

Individually, these changes might be insufficient, but in combination, they can render the firm's cost accounting system obsolete. Consequently, deciding if an ABC system is justified requires taking into account all the changes that have occurred since the existing cost system was installed.

The Cost of a New System

A cost system is obsolete and should be changed when the net present value of the benefits of having improved product costs exceeds the net present value of redesigning a new costing system.

Typically, cost accounting systems seem to last ten years or more. However, a cost system's longevity depends on the perceived costs of redesigning a new cost system. These costs create a significant barrier to the introduction of a new cost system. Total costs of a new cost accounting system include the following:

- Obtaining the support of management for a new system;
- Identifying a team (whether internal or external) to design the system;
- Designing and implementing the new system;
- Tying the new cost system into the company's other information systems;
- Training management in the use of the new system; and
- Creating a team to maintain the new system.

An ABC system is justified whenever the costs of installing and operating the new system are more than offset by the long-term benefits to be derived from the new ABC system. (These benefits are real, however difficult they may be to quantify.) This trade-off differs for every firm and depends on the factors already mentioned that affect the optimal cost system and the adequacy of the existing cost system.

It is therefore impossible to generate a set of simple decision rules to answer the question "Do I need an ABC system?" However, it is possible to define the conditions when an ABC is most likely to be justified. Specifically, implementing an ABC is advisable if the existing cost system was designed when measurement costs were high, competition was weak, and product diversity was low, assuming that measurement costs are now low, competition is fierce, and product diversity is high.

The Decision to Implement Activity-Based Costing

Any company that is about to redesign its cost system should consider implementing an ABC system even if all of these conditions do not exist. The best argument for doing this is that companies tend to keep their cost systems long after they have become obsolete. The long life expectancy of most cost systems and the time that it takes to install a new cost system make it dangerous to wait for all the appropriate conditions to occur.

Companies should monitor how well their cost systems perform and how much the three factors (i.e., measurement costs, the cost of errors, and the diversity of the firm's products) have changed over time. In other words, companies should anticipate the obsolescence of their cost systems before major problems occur. By doing so, a firm will have enough time to decide whether an ABC system is required. Ideally, an ABC system can be designed and implemented before an obsolete system can do much damage.

SYSTEM FOR IMPROVED PRODUCT COSTING

This chapter illustrates the need for ABC systems by demonstrating how conventional cost systems can report seriously distorted product costs.

Unit-based conventional cost systems report highly distorted product costs for two basic reasons. The first is a high cost of non-unit-level activities (e.g., batch-level activities or product-sustaining activities) relative to unit-level activities. At JDCW, for example, non-unit-level costs accounted for about 40 percent of all overhead. The second characteristic is a mix of products that consume unit-level and non-unit-level activities in different ratios. For example, JDCW produced some products in very low volumes, while similar products were produced in very high volumes.

ABC systems reduce the distortions inherent in conventional systems by representing the production process of a company as a hierarchy of four mutually exclusive and exhaustive categories of activities:

1. Unit-level activities, which are performed each time a unit is produced;
2. Batch-level activities, which are performed each time a batch of goods is produced;
3. Product-sustaining activities, which are performed as needed to support the production of each different type of product; and
4. Facility-sustaining activities, which simply sustain a facility's general manufacturing process.

ABC systems take advantage of this hierarchy by assigning the costs of the first three categories to products by using activity drivers that vary in proportion to the consumption of the activities. Thus, a full ABC system contains three different types of cost drivers:

1. Unit-level, which assume that resources are consumed in direct proportion to the number of units produced;
2. Batch-level, which assume that resources are consumed in direct proportion to the number of batches of each type of product produced; and
3. Product-sustaining, which assume that resources are consumed to develop or permit production of individual products.

Well-designed ABC systems match the level of the underlying activity and cost driver, thus avoiding the distortions inherent in conventional systems that rely entirely on unit-level bases.

This chapter also explains which firms are most likely to benefit from the additional accuracy provided by ABC systems. Specifically, the following factors suggest the need for an ABC system:

- Low measurement costs for the additional data required by the ABC system;
- High levels of competition; and
- A diverse product mix.

The chapter also explains how to determine the type and number of activity drivers to use to achieve a desired level of accuracy. Specifically, the following factors affect the *number* of drivers required:

- The desired level of accuracy of reported product costs;
- The degree of product diversity;
- The relative cost of different activities;
- The degree of batch-size diversity; and
- The use of imperfectly correlated activity drivers.

The following factors affect what *kind* of activity drivers to use:

- The cost of measuring the quantities associated with each activity driver;
- The correlation of the selected activity driver to the actual consumption of the activity by the products; and
- The behavior induced by the activity driver.

Finally, the chapter explains the design choices that have to be made in designing an ABC system.

Notes

1. For a description of the two-stage cost allocation procedure, see Robin Cooper, "The Two-Stage Procedure in Cost Accounting—Part One," *Journal of Cost Management* (Summer 1987): 43–51; and Robin Cooper, "The Two-Stage Procedure in Cost Accounting—Part Two," *Journal of Cost Management* (Fall 1987): 39–45.

2. The material in this section is adopted from Robin Cooper and Robert S. Kaplan, *The Design of Cost Management Systems* (Englewood Cliffs, NJ: Prentice Hall, 1991): ch. 5

3. For a discussion of the symptoms of a poorly designed cost system, see Robin Cooper, "Does Your Company Need a New Cost System?" *Journal of Cost Management* (Spring 1987): 45–49.

4. For a discussion of the significance of the correlation of direct labor hours and machine hours on reported product costs, see Robin Cooper, "When Should You Use Machine-Hour Costing?" *Journal of Cost Management* (Spring 1988): 33–39.

5. See Robert S. Kaplan, "John Deere Component Works," *Harvard Business School Case Series* 187-107/108.

6. For short case studies that illustrate five different ABC systems, see Robin Cooper, "The Rise of Activity-Based Costing—Part Four: What Do Activity-Based Cost Systems Look Like?" *Journal of Cost Management* (Spring 1989): 38–49.

7. Correlation of cost drivers is discussed in detail in Robin Cooper, "The Rise of Activity-Based Costing—Part Three: How Many Cost Drivers Do You Need, and How Do You Select Them?" *Journal of Cost Management* (Winter 1989): 34–46.

8 See Robin Cooper and D. Bottenbruch, "Mueller-Lehmkuhl GmbH," *Harvard Business School Case Series* 178-048.

9. For an example of the type of cost system that is common in regulated industries and the way that such a cost system changes after deregulation, see Robert S. Kaplan, "Union Pacific," *Harvard Business School Case Series* 186-176/177/178.

10. See Robert S. Kaplan, "John Deere Component Works."

11. See John G. Miller and T.E. Vollman, "The Hidden Factory," *Harvard Business Review* (September–October 1985): 142–150.

12. See Robert S. Kaplan, "John Deere Component Works."

13. See Robin Cooper, "Schrader Bellows," *Harvard Business School Case Series* 186-272.

14. See Robin Cooper, "Fisher Technologies," *Harvard Business School Case Series* 186-188.

Second-Generation Architecture

PETER B.B. TURNEY

Professor of Cost Management, Portland State University, and CEO,
Cost Technology, Portland, Oregon

This chapter is adapted, with permission, from Peter B.B. Turney, *Common Cents: The ABC Performance Breakthrough* (Portland, Ore.: Cost Technology, 1991).

INTRODUCTION

Activity-based costing (ABC) has come a long way in a short time. Although ABC was originally conceived as a methodology for improving the accuracy of product costs, by now it has become a comprehensive performance measurement system that supports a wide range of purposes. This "second-generation" perspective views ABC as a methodology for providing useful information about the performance of resources, activities, and cost objects. ABC is also the system that organizes and communicates this information.

A SECOND-GENERATION PERSPECTIVE

With a second-generation perspective of ABC, there is a shift of emphasis. The new emphasis focuses on the difference between ABC and activity-based management as well as on the use of ABC information.

Using Activity-Based Management

This second-generation perspective differentiates between ABC as a source of information and the discipline that can be called *activity-based management,* which uses ABC information to improve the management of activities. The goal of activity-based management is to increase the value of the products or services delivered to customers and, thus, the extra profit achieved by providing this added value.

Using Activity-Based Costing Information

Activity-based management uses ABC information to:

- Set and implement strategic priorities;
- Analyze and measure performance in the search for low-cost product designs, cost-reduction opportunities, and improvements in quality;
- Identify waste in supplier relationships; and
- Channel capital spending to the most profitable opportunities.

This chapter explains how second-generation ABC supports the goals of activity-based management and the areas that it analyzes. The chapter illustrates a two-dimensional ABC system that supplies both cost and operational information about performance. Then the chapter describes how to design a second-generation ABC using attributes and macroactivities. Finally, the chapter presents a case study (about TriQuint Semiconductor, Inc.) to illustrate these concepts and methods.

The second-generation perspective of ABC presented in this chapter and its link to activity-based management follow the framework established by *The CAM-I Glossary of Activity-Based Management.*[1] This glossary, which is reprinted at the end of this book, defines the standards for the industry in the area of ABC. The concepts, terminology, and the graphical depiction of the ABC model in this chapter all parallel the framework set by the glossary.

TWO-DIMENSIONAL ACTIVITY-BASED COSTING

Second-generation ABC has two main views. The first is the cost assignment view. Exhibit B3.1 illustrates the cost assignment view in the vertical part of the model depicted there. The *cost assignment view* reflects the organization's need to trace or allocate resources to activities or cost objects (including customers as well as products) to analyze critical decisions about such things as:

- Pricing;
- Product mix;
- Sourcing;
- Product design; and
- Setting priorities for improvement efforts.

The second part of the ABC model is the process view. Exhibit B3.1 illustrates the process view in the horizontal part of the model depicted there. The *process view* reflects the organization's need for information about events that influence the performance of activities and activity performance — that is, what causes work and how well it is done. Organizations use this information to help improve performance and thus increase the value received by customers.

The Cost Assignment View

The cost assignment view provides information about resources, activities, and cost objects. The underlying assumption is that cost objects create the need for activities and that activities create the need for resources.

EXHIBIT B3.1

The Two-Dimensional Activity-Based Costing Model

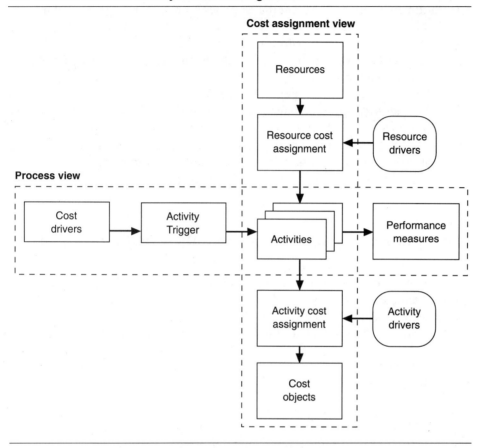

This cost information is quite different from that of early ABC systems. Today's cost information offers much more accurate product costs and also high-quality information about activities and cost objects.

Information About Activities

Unlike earlier systems, second-generation systems identify the significant activities and attach cost to them. Knowing the cost of activities makes it easier to understand why resources are incurred. Moreover, the information provided makes it much easier to address such questions as:

- Which activities require the most resources?
- What types of resources are required by these activities?
- Where do opportunities exist for cost reduction?

It was difficult to answer such questions with early ABC systems, which focused on accurate product costs rather than on improved information about activities.

Information About Customers

Second-generation ABC systems also have more points of focus. For example, they make customers a cost object. This addition makes good sense, because customer-support activities are costly in many companies, and different customers can require quite different levels of support.

Information About Nonmanufacturing Activities

Adding customers as a focus takes costing into new parts of the organization. Customer-support activities, for example, invariably take place outside the manufacturing plant—in marketing, order entry, and customer service. In contrast, early ABC systems resided exclusively within the walls of the plant, so their focus was exclusively on manufacturing activities.

It makes better business sense to focus on nonmanufacturing activities just as carefully as on manufacturing activities. To test this assertion, managers need only look at the income statement for their own company: If nonmanufacturing costs are calculated as a percentage of the sum of both manufacturing and nonmanufacturing costs, the percentage probably equals at least 50 percent of the total.

In summary, the cost assignment view allows management to obtain answers to the following kinds of questions:

- What are the high-cost activities?
- What opportunities exist for improving product and service design to reduce cost?
- What opportunities exist for shifting the focus toward more profitable products, services, or customers?

The Building Blocks

The cost assignment view is constructed from three main building blocks:

1. Resources;
2. Activities; and
3. Cost objects.

EXHIBIT B3.2

The Building Blocks of Cost Assignment in Activity-Based Costing

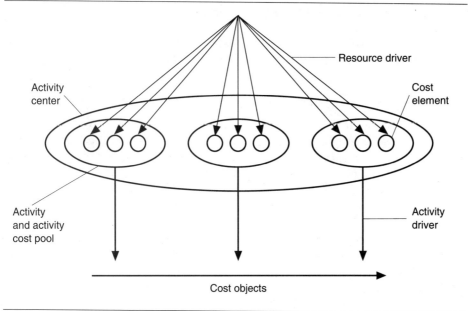

Cost objects

Resources are connected to activities by means of resource drivers; activities are connected to cost objects by means of activity drivers. Activity centers, cost elements, and cost pools also help describe the model, as shown in Exhibit B3.2.

Resources are economic elements that are applied or directed to the performance of activities; they are the sources of cost. Resources in a manufacturing company include:

- Direct labor and material;
- Production support (e.g., the cost for salaries of the material procurement staff);
- Indirect costs of production (e.g., the cost of power to heat the plant); and
- Costs outside of production (e.g., advertising).

Resources in a service company include the salaries of professionals, salaries of office support staff, and the costs of office space and information systems.

Resources flow to *activities,* which are processes or procedures that cause work to be performed in an organization. In a product support department, for example, activities can include processing engineering change orders (ECOs), answering phones, and testing products. Exhibit B3.3 illustrates these activities.

EXHIBIT B3.3

Activity-Based Costing Model for a Product-Support Department

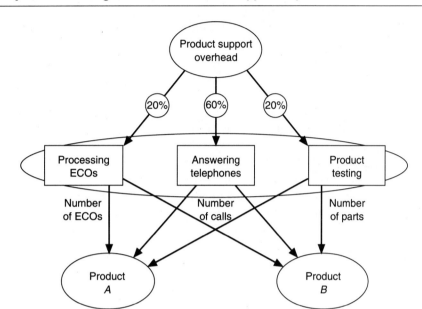

Typically, related activities are enclosed in an *activity center,* which reports pertinent information about activities in a function or process. Exhibit B3.3, for example, depicts an activity center that consists of all customer-support activities.

Various factors, which are referred to as *resource drivers,* are used to assign the cost of resources to activities. These factors are chosen to reflect the use of the resources by the activities. In Exhibit B3.3, for example, product support overhead is traced to the three activities. The percentages shown (20 percent, 60 percent, and 20 percent) are based on estimates of the effort expended on each activity. Specifically, the ten people in the product support department reported that they spent their time as follows:

- Four people in the department process engineering change orders half the time ($4/10 \times 50\% = 20\%$) but answer telephones the other half of the time ($4/10 \times 50\% = 20\%$);
- Four other people in the department do nothing except answer telephones ($4/10 = 40\%$); and
- The final two people in the department test products full time ($2/10 = 20\%$).

Each type of resource that is traced to an activity (e.g., the cost of salaries for people who answer telephones) becomes a *cost element* (i.e., an amount paid for a resource consumed by an activity) and is included in an *activity cost pool* (i.e., a grouping of cost elements associated with a particular activity). The activity cost pool is the total cost associated with an activity.

Each activity cost pool is traced to the cost objects by means of an activity driver. The *activity driver* is a measure of the use of the activity by the cost objects. It is used to assign resources from the activities to the cost objects.

To relate this analysis to Exhibit B3.3, each activity has a unique activity driver to trace its cost to the products. Answering telephones, for example, is traced to products based on the number of telephone calls. This tracing is reasonable because the product that creates the most problems for the customer is likely to generate the most phone calls.

The *cost object* is the final point to which cost is traced. A cost object is any activity, organizational unit, contract, or other work unit for which a separate measurement of cost is desired. It is, in short, the reason why work is performed in the company and may be either a product or a customer. Engineering, producing, marketing, selling, and distributing a product requires a number of activities. Supporting a customer also comprises a number of activities. The cost traced to each product or customer reflects the cost of the activities used by that cost object.

This vertical flow of information in ABC defines the economics of the company and the organization of work within it. It also provides the basic building blocks for creating accurate and useful cost information about the strategy and operations of the company.

The Process View

The horizontal part of the ABC model, as shown in Exhibit B3.1, contains the process view. It provides information about the work done in an activity and the relationship of this work to other activities.

To expand on this point, a process is a series of activities that are linked to perform a specific goal. Each activity is a "customer" (i.e., an internal customer) of another activity and, in turn, has its own customers. In short, activities are all part of a "customer chain,"[2] all working together to provide value to the outside customer.

At a valve manufacturer, for example, metal is melted in the foundry and then forwarded to molding. Molding pours the molten metal into the molds, allows them to cool, and passes them on to an activity that breaks and removes the mold to reveal the parts inside. All these activities—and many more—work together to provide finished valves to the company's customers.

On a more detailed level, the process view of ABC includes information about cost drivers and performance measures for each activity or process in the customer chain. These cost drivers and performance measures are primarily nonfinancial. They are useful in helping to interpret and improve the performance of an activity and of the process as a whole.

Cost Drivers

Cost drivers are any events that cause a change in the total cost of an activity. They are, in fact, the factors that determine the work load and effort required to perform an activity. They include factors relating to the performance of prior activities in the chain as well as factors internal to the activity.

Cost drivers tell *why* an activity (or chain of activities) is performed. Specifically, activities are performed in response to prior events. Scheduling a batch of parts, for example, is a response to a customer order or the scrapping of inventory—*the why,* in other words. In turn, scheduling the parts requires setting up equipment—*the effort.*

Cost drivers also tell how much effort must be expended to carry out the work. A defect in a part or data received from a prior activity, for example, can increase the effort required. Similarly, a requisition that contains the wrong part number requires correction before a purchase order can be completed. An engineering drawing that does not reflect the current process causes additional effort during machine setup.

Cost drivers are useful because they reveal opportunities for improvement. A reduction in the defect rate for incoming requisitions, for example, makes it possible to eliminate wasted effort and resources in the purchasing activity.

Performance Measures

Performance measures are indicators, either financial or nonfinancial, of the work performed and the results achieved in an activity, a process, or an organizational unit. They tell *how well* an activity is performed and communicate how well the activity is meeting the needs of its internal or external customers. Performance measures include measurements of:

- Efficiency of the activity;
- Time required to complete the activity; and
- Quality of the work done.

The efficiency of an activity is judged by first determining the activity's output volume. This value is then compared to the resources needed to sustain that activity and its output level. For a molding activity, for example, the number of molds processed in a month is computed. This measure of output is then divided into the resources required by that activity during the month. The result is a cost per mold—for example, $20—which may be compared with internal or external standards of efficiency.

Another dimension of performance is the time required to complete an activity. Measures of elapsed time are indirect measures of cost, quality, and customer service. The longer it takes to perform an activity, the greater the resources it requires. These additional resources include the salaries of staff required to do the work and the cost of equipment used to carry out the work. Also, the longer it takes, the more likely it is that work has to be redone to correct mistakes or defects. Conversely, the shorter the elapsed time, the quicker the activity's response to changes in customer demand.

A third aspect of performance is quality, which addresses questions such as: What percentage of the molded parts have to be reworked, and what percent are scrapped? The higher these percentages, the lower the quality of the activity, the higher its overall cost, and the greater the detrimental effect on the next activity in the process. The value received by the customer may also be diminished.

Performance measures focus attention on the important aspects of activity performance and stimulate efforts to improve. To recap, the ABC process view provides operational intelligence about the work going on in a company. This *operational intelligence* includes information about the external factors that determine the frequency with which an activity is performed, the effort required to carry it out, and information about the performance of an activity (e.g., the efficiency of the activity, the time required to complete it, and the quality of the work done).

This operational information allows management to obtain answers to questions such as the following:

- What events trigger the performance of the activity?
- What factors negatively affect the performance of the activity?
- How efficiently, how fast, and with what quality is the work carried out?

Moreover, the ABC process view brings the world of operations directly into the heart of the cost system. Cost and nonfinancial information join forces to provide a total view of the work done, thus facilitating the management of activities and improved performance.

An Illustration

Exhibit B3.4 illustrates a two-dimensional model of how ABC works. The total resource pool of $6 million is the total budget for the procurement department. Of this cost, $450,000 is traced directly to the purchasing activity. (The

EXHIBIT B3.4

An Example of Two-Dimensional Activity-Based Costing

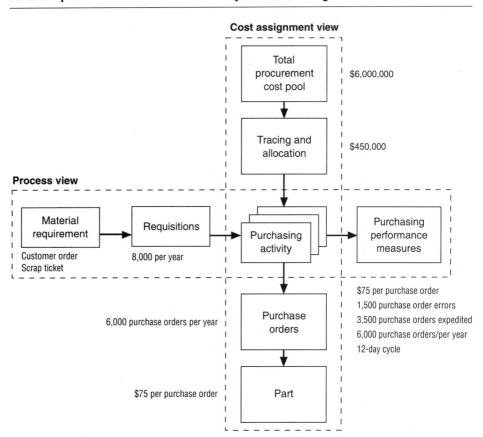

resource drivers include estimates of effort expended on the activity, and a specific measurement of the use of supplies.) The cost of the purchasing activity is traced to part numbers by means of the number of purchase orders per part number (the activity driver).

The number of purchase orders measures the output of the activity (the number of times the activity was performed). Other performance measures include the number of errors made, the number expedited, and the elapsed time required to complete a purchase order. A volume of 6,000 purchase orders and an activity cost of $450,000 yield a cost per purchase order of $75.

In this exhibit, the activity driver and the performance measure of output are one and the same. This matching of activity driver and performance measure is common in ABC, though there are exceptions. For example, if the number of purchase orders per part number is not captured by the company's information system, an alternative activity driver (e.g., the number of different parts) is required. Alternatively, if the effort required to complete a purchase order varies systematically from one type of part to another, a different activity driver (e.g., a direct measurement of the effort involved) may be necessary.

On the input side, the activity must cope with a volume of incoming requisitions of 8,000. A requisition is not a cost driver of the purchasing activity. Rather, it is the paperwork, or "trigger," that initiates the work. The volume of requisitions is determined by two cost drivers:

1. The number of customer orders; and
2. The number of scrap tickets.

Customer orders and scrap tickets are factors that trigger preparation of a purchase requisition (and the need to complete a purchase order).

Exhibit B3.4 shows the demand for the purchasing activity coming from purchases of parts. The level of work, however, is determined by the following cost drivers:

- End product demand (i.e., number of customer orders); and
- The quality of the parts and their processing (the number of scrap tickets).

An improvement in the quality of a machining activity, for example, reduces the number of scrap tickets. This, in turn, reduces the number of requisitions and the demand for purchasing replacement parts.

Performance is monitored by several measures:

- The cost per purchase order averages $75;
- The frequency of errors is 1 in 4 (1,500 out of 6,000 per year);
- Over one half of the purchase orders had to be expedited rather than completed in the normal processing cycle; and
- It took an average of twelve days to complete the processing of a purchase order.

A SECOND-GENERATION MODEL DESIGN

Designing a second-generation ABC model requires the capture of nonfinancial information as well as cost information. It also requires that the designer consider the use of ABC information for operational improvement as well as strategic improvement.

Including nonfinancial information in the ABC model is accomplished by using attributes. *Attributes* are labels that are attached to individual pieces of data to

EXHIBIT B3.5

Attributes for the Activity "Inspecting Incoming Materials"

Cost drivers	Performance measures
• Number of purchase orders	• Number of inspections
• Number of scheduled deliveries	• Number of material-related problems
• Percent of vendors uncertified	

Value status

• Non-value-added

---

convey the characteristics of that data. Operational and strategic needs are met through the use of macroactivities, which summarize detailed activity information.

Attributes

Attributes enhance the meaning of activity-based information by indicating whether an activity is value-added or non-value-added or whether the cost of an activity is fixed or variable in relation to the volume of work done.

Attributes also allow the identification of common threads in the data. For example, a manager may wish to review all activities related to preventing, detecting, and correcting defects in products. A label attached to each activity associated with these purposes allows the manager to prepare reports about the cost of poor quality.

Attributes include information about the performance of activities, the level of activities, the type of activities, and the cost behavior of activities. Each type of information is described below.

Performance Information

Attributes are used to describe the performance of activities. For example, Exhibit B3.5 shows attributes for the activity "inspecting incoming materials" about cost drivers, performance measures, and non-value-added activity.

Cost drivers, the factors that cause material receipts to occur, include the number of purchase orders issued, the number of regularly scheduled deliveries of incoming materials, and the percentage of vendors that are uncertified. This last cost driver reflects the progress of the company in certifying vendors for a level of quality that precludes the need for incoming inspection. It represents an opportunity for further improvement.

Performance measures for the activity include the number of inspections and the number of material-related problems discovered during manufacturing.

The second of these performance measures is also a cost driver for downstream activities that use the inspected materials.

The incoming inspection activity is a non-value-added activity—that is its attribute. It is non-value-added because the inspection activity can be eliminated without diminishing the value received by the customer. Customers do not value inspection; what they value is high quality. If high-quality incoming materials can be assured, then inspection is no longer required.

The value of attributes that describe performance is that they make it possible to use ABC for process improvement. They allow nonfinancial information to augment the cost information within the ABC system. This practice facilitates judgments about how work is carried out and how it can be improved.

Level of Activity

Identifying the purpose of an activity is one way to make sense of the work going on. Even small companies have many different activities, so grouping activities by common purpose is helpful.

There are two main categories of activities:

1. Those that work on cost objects; and
2. Those that sustain the organization.

Cost object activities benefit products or customers. Providing technical support to a customer is an example of a cost object activity (in which case the customer is the cost object). *Sustaining activities* benefit different parts of the organization, such as the plant or the division. Maintaining a plant's heating system is an example of an activity that sustains the plant as a whole.

Identifying activities by level proves valuable for both designers and users of ABC information. The level of an activity is a reminder to the designer to match activities with an appropriate activity driver. It helps the user group activities according to their relationship to cost objects and organizational units.

Type of Activity

Activities can also be marked by type. This designation facilitates process management by identifying related activities wherever they are performed in the company.

For example, Dayton Extruded Plastics is a manufacturer of vinyl extrusions for windows. The company was concerned about the time and cost required to get dies from engineering to production. The engineering department's job is to develop dies for new products, modify dies to reflect changes in product specifications, and overhaul dies at the end of their productive life. For each of these engineering initiatives, a new or modified die is prepared. Each die is tried (i.e., checked for its ability to produce good quality product) before production begins. This activity involves manufacturing engineering, product engineering, die engineering, the material laboratory, and quality control.

The first step in reducing cost and time was to understand the work involved in trying out dies. Accordingly, the attribute "trying out" was attached to all these activities (regardless of department). This attribute allowed Dayton Extruded Plastics to prepare a report listing cost and other information about "trying out" activities.

This use of attributes adds power to ABC's ability to report information about cross-functional processes. It allows managers to follow the chain of activities as it crosses organizational boundaries.

Cost Behavior

Attributes can reveal important characteristics of cost elements. They identify cost elements as fixed or variable, direct or indirect, or avoidable or unavoidable. Attributes about cost are used to support what-if decision analyses, which are simulations of cost impacts caused by changes in how activities are performed.

For example, the Business Products Division of Northern Telecom studied ways of reducing procurement costs. The Division looked at several alternative ways of procuring many thousands of low-cost, high-volume parts. It used information in its ABC system to model the cost impact of each procurement alternative.

Some alternatives changed the level of work done in some of the procurement activities. For these activities, it was necessary to identify the activity cost elements that would be variable with the changes in work load. One alternative eliminated several activities entirely. The requirement here was to identify those cost elements that would be avoided if the activity was eliminated. On average, the Division found that about 60 percent of the cost of these activities was avoidable.

The designation of cost attributes at Northern Telecom was done by the individuals doing the simulation. This procedure makes sense, because there is nothing black and white about cost behavior. The cost attribute is determined by the type of cost element and the circumstances of the change. Inevitably, it also depends on the user's judgment.

Macroactivities

Managing the level of detail in the ABC system is a key ingredient of successful use. When managers dig deep into an organization to identify the work that is done, it is not hard to turn up hundreds of different activities.

At one level, all this detail is very useful. The manager of a process engineering department, for example, needs detailed information about the cost and performance of activities in that department. Each detailed activity represents real work that must be managed and improved. But what about the cost of collecting all that detailed activity information? Surprisingly, the cost is quite low. In some cases, it is even "free," because the detail is typically received directly from the department managers.

Overwhelming Detail

At another level, however, the detail is overwhelming. A plant manager, for example, cannot pay attention to the smallest activity. For one thing, there is not enough time to do so. For another, the plant manager is not the person who actually brings about process improvement: Although the plant manager may provide coaching, help move constraints, and make resources available, the improvements are actually accomplished by those who do the work.

Similarly, the marketing department has no need for detailed activity information. Instead, they are interested in understanding the implications of product and customer strategies. For that purpose, information about broad groups of activities and their related activity drivers is sufficient.

This situation creates a dilemma in ABC. At the operating level, there is a need for detailed information about the work going on, including cost and process information about each activity. At the strategic level, however, the need is for summary information about activities; additional detail is unnecessary and even burdensome at this level.

For example, at Dayton Extruded Plastics, twenty-four activities were performed in the process engineering department. Exhibit B3.6 lists these activities. With minor modifications, these activities, which represented the components of the work done in the department, were all identified in interviews with the manager of the department.

At a strategic level, however, this much detail proved to be overwhelming. Across all the departments of the company, maintaining this level of detail meant including more than 400 activities in the ABC model.

Managers above the department level had no interest in this much detail. Nor was this much detail necessary to support product and customer costing. In reality, 400 activities did not require 400 activity drivers to report reasonably accurate cost; twenty drivers would have been sufficient.

How do managers resolve this detail dilemma? The answer is to use macroactivities. *Macroactivities* are summary activities. They are aggregations of several related detailed activities. Dayton Extruded Plastics used macroactivities to reduce the burden of detail within the system. In the process engineering department, for example, the twenty-four detailed activities were reduced to just five macroactivities.

EXHIBIT B3.6

Dayton Extruded Plastics: Detailed Activities in a Process Engineering Department

Administering	Monitoring the wear of production equipment
Assisting production	Recruiting
Cleaning areas	Researching rail coating
Cleaning dies	Setting up tools for production
Cleaning sizers	Supervising
Developing new processes	Training
Evaluating scrap	Troubleshooting
Evaluating shrinkage	Trying out dies with engineering changes
Fabricating production equipment	Trying out machines
Measuring die volume	Trying out materials
Measuring shrinkage	Trying out new dies
Meeting	Trying out reworked dies

Exhibit B3.7 depicts how Dayton Extruded Plastics accomplished this feat. The exhibit shows three activities associated with "trying out" dies. These are the detailed activities of interest to the department manager. The cost of each of the detailed activities was assigned to a single macroactivity. This macroactivity provided summary information for higher-level management and for strategic purposes.

What is unique about Dayton Extruded Plastics is the presence of two tiers of activity detail in the same system. This system allowed the company to avoid making a choice between a system that supported process improvement or one that supported strategy formulation, because its ABC system did both.

THE SEMICONDUCTOR INDUSTRY: A CASE STUDY

For a better look at an ABC system, a case study is now provided from the semiconductor industry. The company analyzed is TriQuint Semiconductor, Inc.

The case study illustrates the use of attributes and macroactivities. It also demonstrates how easy it is to use ABC for strategic purposes and also to improve processes.[3]

The Company

TriQuint Semiconductor is a manufacturer of gallium arsenide (GAS) integrated circuits (ICs). The company produces a limited mix of standard and custom ICs

EXHIBIT B3.7

Macroactivity at Dayton Extruded Plastics

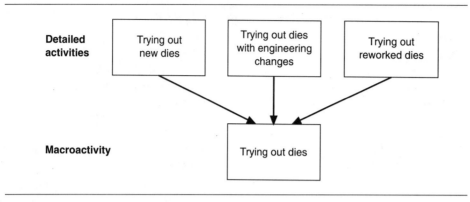

for the high-performance end of the market. Its customers are primarily in the telecommunications and computer industries. TriQuint Semiconductor is one of only a handful of companies that compete in the GAS IC market.

TriQuint Semiconductor is well known around the world for its ability to engineer high-quality ICs for custom applications. TriQuint Semiconductor is also well known for short engineering lead times: It can rapidly take a product from design, through the prototype stage, and then into production. The company has been less successful, however, in making the transition from custom prototypes to standard products. Its customers rave about the company's engineering capabilities, but are less likely to dedicate long-term production of their products to TriQuint Semiconductor.

To a degree, the company is a victim of the inability of gallium arsenide to score inroads against the dominant silicon variants of ICs. The gallium arsenide industry remains a collection of "boutiques" struggling to mature.

The bottom line for TriQuint Semiconductor is that its engineering prowess has given it a dominant share of the market. Unfortunately, it is also an unprofitable share of the market.

Terms of Reference

TriQuint Semiconductor set two objectives for its ABC system. The first objective was to provide information to support process improvement. The company believed that this would help eliminate waste, reduce process variability, and smooth the transition from prototype to production. An existing high level of cost provided a large opportunity for cost reduction and, thus, improved profits.

EXHIBIT B3.8

TriQuint Semiconductor, Inc.: The Design of an Activity-Based Cost System

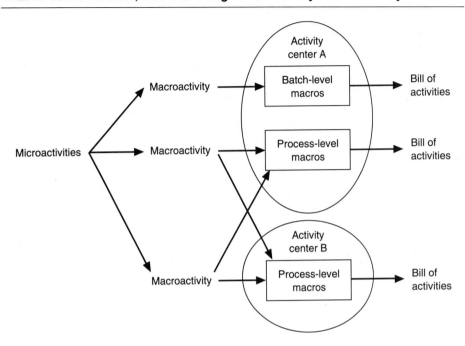

The second objective was to provide cost information for pricing purposes. Pricing was difficult for TriQuint Semiconductor for lack of published prices in the limited marketplace. Pricing was also important because cost was high, and the dominance of customer products meant that most products were unique.

The TriQuint Semiconductor ABC system focused initially on the "packaging" area of the plant. (Packaging here refers to the high-speed, high-density IC housings that enabled the ICs to be attached to printed circuit boards.)

The Design Approach

Exhibit B3.8 illustrates the cost flow in the TriQuint Semiconductor ABC system. The following discussion analyzes each part of the ABC system design.

Microactivities

The microactivities are the detailed activities at TriQuint Semiconductor. Exhibit B3.9, for example, shows information for the laser-cutting microactivity.

EXHIBIT B3.9

Microactivity at TriQuint Semiconductor, Inc.

Activity: Laser cutting

Activity level: Batch

Cost elements:

General ledger account	Account description	Cost
6720	Operating materials	$ 2,500
6654	Maintenance materials	3,500
6311	Salaries and benefits	15,075
	Total activity cost pool	$21,075

Performance measures:

Measure	Quantity	Cost per unit of measure
Number of parts cut	40,000	$ 0.53
Number of cuts per part	4	0.13
Cutting time	1,050 hours	20.07

This microactivity is the use of a laser to cut sheets of laminate into individual parts.

The information for laser cutting shows that it is a batch-level activity: Laminates are cut in batches, not individually. Key performance measures include the number of cuts per part. If this activity is done only once, it will cost less and take less time.

The microactivity in Exhibit B3.9 also shows the cost elements assigned to the activity. Salaries and benefits were traced to the activity by means of estimates of effort that were obtained in interviews with the manager of the laser-cutting process. Materials were traced based on records maintained by the process manager.

Macroactivities

The costs of microactivities were assigned to macroactivities. This decision was made to reduce the amount of information seen at higher management levels. Detailed activity information was also unnecessary for product costing purposes because several activities shared a common activity driver.

Exhibit B3.10 shows the macroactivity for cutting laminates. The exhibit includes the cost of three microactivities, including the laser-cutting activity in the previous discussion of Exhibit B3.9. Note that the total of each microactiv-

EXHIBIT B3.10

Macroactivity at TriQuint Semiconductor, Inc.

Activity: Cutting laminates

Activity level: Batch

Microactivities	Cost pools
Setting up laser	$ 5,400
Laser cutting	21,075
Testing cuts	7,300
Total activity cost pool	$33,775

Driver: Number of production runs

Driver quantity: 450

Cost per driver unit: $75

ity's cost pool is visible in Exhibit B3.10, but the detailed cost elements cannot be seen at this level.

A single activity driver is shown for this macroactivity: the number of production runs. The ABC system designers omitted the process information in the belief that process improvement would focus at the microactivity level rather than the macroactivity level.

Activity Centers

TriQuint Semiconductor also used the activity center as a flexible tool for reporting activities in different ways. The primary grouping of activities was by function. For example, all activities associated with electroless plating (which is a chemical method of applying a metallic substance) were placed in an electroless-plating activity center.

Within each activity center, the activities were also grouped by level of activity. In the electroless plating department, for example, there were groups of unit-, batch-, and process-sustaining activities. These groups were actually higher-level macroactivities that further reduced the detail.

The power of activity centers at TriQuint Semiconductor was the ability to change structure dynamically to meet management's reporting needs. There were several processes at TriQuint Semiconductor that cut across department boundaries, and activity centers were used to report information about them.

Exhibit B3.11 shows information about quality-related activities in three departments: one production department and two support departments. (Other non-quality-related activities in these departments are not shown.)

EXHIBIT B3.11

TriQuint Semiconductor, Inc.:: Activity Center

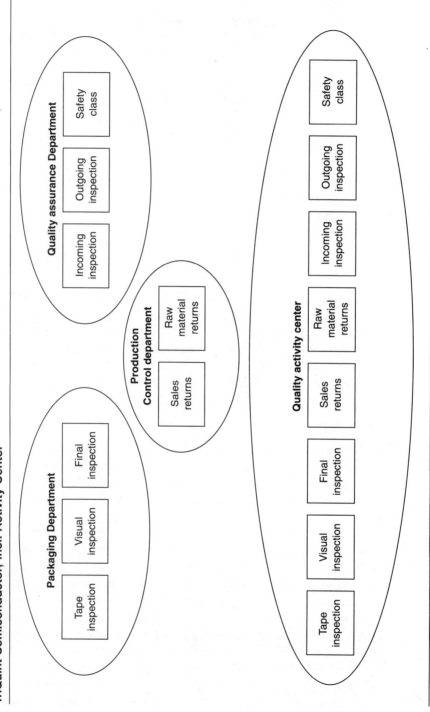

EXHIBIT B3.12

TriQuint Semiconductor, Inc.: Bill of Activities

Part number: XYZ123

Volume: 10,000 parts

	Driver	Cost per driver	Driver quantities	Total
Unit activities				
Electroless test	Number of units	$ 0.15	10,000	$ 1,500
Inspection	Number of units	0.20	10,000	2,000
Batch activities				
Laser cut	Number of runs	36.91	150	5,537
Laminate	Number of layers	0.25	105,000	26,250
Print setup	Direct labor hours	18.60	2,000	37,200
Product line activities				
MLC PL	Number of parts	0.77	10,000	7,700
Process-related activities				
Plating	Number of runs	92.80	375	34,800
Punching	Number of punches	0.02	200,000	4,000
Total cost				$118,987
Unit cost				$ 11.90

The bottom of Exhibit B3.11 shows a single activity center that contains all the quality-related activities. The value of the quality activity center was that it reported in one place all pertinent activity information about preventing, correcting, and detecting poor quality.

Bill of Activities

Exhibit B3.12 shows an example of a bill of activities for one of TriQuint Semiconductor's packages. A *bill of activities* is a listing of activities and associated costs required by a product or other cost object. In short, a bill of activities reports cost for each product. It contains information about the activities, activity drivers, and product cost.

A bill of activities can be structured in different ways and with varying degrees of detail, depending on management's preferences and needs. For example, activities can be "nested" according to their level (e.g., unit versus batch activities). Costs can also be separated according to whether the activity is value-added or non-value-added.

As shown in Exhibit B3.12, TriQuint Semiconductor's bill of activities is nested by activity level. It shows that the major cost of the product comes from two sources:

1. First, the cost of batch activities is heavy. Is this because the product was run in small batches? (Possibly the customer requires frequent just-in-time deliveries for this product.) Why is lamination so expensive?
2. Second, the product is a heavy consumer of an expensive plating process. Is this a reasonable charge for using this activity? Is the cost high because some of the capacity of the plating process is currently unused?

TriQuint Semiconductor's bill shows the cost of macroactivities, rather than the cost of underlying microactivities, to reduce the detail in the bill and to make it easier to read. Managers who want to look further can still go behind the macroactivities to analyze the detailed activities represented by each macroactivity. Finally, it is even possible to follow the trail from the microactivities and their cost elements back to the general ledger accounts.

PERFORMANCE INFORMATION FOR ACTIVITY-BASED MANAGEMENT

Modern ABC is a two-dimensional model that provides both nonfinancial and cost information. It is the main source of performance information for activity-based management.

The cost assignment view provides information about the use of resources by activities and about the use of activities by cost objects (e.g., products and customers). The process dimension provides information about why work is performed and how well the work is carried out.

Nonfinancial information is added to ABC by use of attributes, which are labels that supply information about the performance, level, type, and cost behavior of activities. The use of macroactivities in an ABC system provides:

1. A detailed level for operational improvement; and
2. A summary (macroactivity) level for strategic purposes.

Notes

1. Norm Raffish and Peter B.B. Turney, *The CAM-I Glossary of Activity-Based Management* (Arlington, Tex.: CAM-I, 1991).
2. Richard J. Schonberger, *Building a Chain of Customers: Linking Business Functions to Create the World Class Company* (New York: The Free Press, 1990).
3. This section of the chapter is based on a case study written by Anne Riley and Peter B.B. Turney.

Activity-Based Systems: Measuring the Costs of Resource Usage

ROBIN COOPER

Professor at the Claremont Graduate School

ROBERT S. KAPLAN

Professor at the Harvard Business School

Source: *Accounting Horizons*, September 1992, American Accounting Association, Sarasota, FL.

This paper describes the conceptual basis for the design and use of newly emerging activity-based cost (ABC) systems. Traditional cost systems use volume-driven allocation bases, such as direct labor dollars, machine hours, and sales dollars, to assign organizational expenses to individual products and customers. But many of the resource demands by individual products and customers are not proportional to the volume of units produced or sold.[1] Thus, conventional systems do not measure accurately the costs of resources used to design and produce products and to sell and deliver them to customers. Companies, including those with excellent traditional cost systems,[2] have developed activity-based cost systems so that they can directly link the costs of performing organizational activities to the products and customers for which these activities are performed.

ABC SYSTEMS AS RESOURCE USAGE MODELS

Activity-based cost systems estimate the cost of resources *used* in organizational processes to produce outputs.[3] Many people have attempted to interpret activity-based costs using their more familiar fixed versus variable cost framework, an interpretation inconsistent with an ABC system's measurements of resource usage costs. The conventional fixed versus variable cost classification arises from an attempt to classify the likely change in spending or *supply* of a resource. The measurement of unused capacity provides the critical link between the costs of resources *used*, as measured by an ABC model, and the costs of resources *supplied* or *available*, as reported by the organization's periodic financial statements.[4] The following equation, defined for each major activity performed by the organization's resources, formalizes this relationship:

Activity Availability = Activity Usage + Unused Capacity

A simple example illustrates the difference between the cost of resources supplied and the cost of resources used to perform activities. Consider a purchasing department in which the equivalent of 10 full-time people [the *resource supplied*] are committed to processing purchase orders [the *activity performed*]. If the monthly cost of a full-time employee is $2,500,[5] the monthly cost of the activity, "Process Purchase Orders," equals $25,000. Assume that each employee, working at practical capacity, can process 125 purchase orders per month, leading to an estimated cost of $20 for processing each purchase order.[6] Thus, the organization, each month, spends $25,000. This expenditure provides a capability to process up to 1,250 purchase orders [the *activity availability*] during the month. During any particular month, the department may be asked to process fewer purchase orders, say only 1,000. At an estimated cost of $20 / purchase order, the ABC system would assign $20,000 of expenses to the parts and materials ordered by the purchasing department that month. The remaining

$5,000 of monthly operating expenses represents the cost of unused capacity in the purchase order processing activity.

This example shows why companies need two different reporting systems. The periodic financial statements provide information on the cost of activities supplied each period (the $25,000 monthly expense in the purchasing department); and the activity-based cost system provides information on the quantity (1,000 purchase orders) and the estimated cost ($20,000) of activities actually used in a period. The difference ($5,000) between the cost of activities supplied ($25,000) and the cost of activities used ($20,000) equals the cost of unused capacity (or capacity shortage) during the period. And this difference is measured for each organizational activity, defined by the ABC system.[7]

The two systems provide different types of information for management. The cost of resources supplied is relevant for predicting near-term spending. Spending on many organizational resources will not vary with short-term fluctuations in activity volume and mix. That is why these costs have been classified as "fixed" in numerous accounting systems and textbooks.

But measuring and managing the operating expenses of most organizational resources as fixed in the short-run does not give much insight as to why the resources were acquired, what the resources are currently being used for, and the level of resources that will likely be required in the future. While the cost of supplying the resources may be fixed in the short-run,[8] the quantity of these resources used each period fluctuates based on activities performed for the outputs produced. Activity-based systems measure the cost of using these resources, even though the cost of supplying them will not vary, in the short run, with usage.

The ABC resource usage cost information can be used by managers to monitor and predict the changes in demands for activities as a function of changes in output volume and mix, process changes and improvements, introduction of new technology, and changes in product and process design. As such changes are contemplated, managers can predict where either shortages or excesses of capacity will occur. The managers can then either modify their decisions so that activity demand will be brought into balance with activity supply, or they can change the level of activities to be supplied in forthcoming periods.

For example, if newly designed custom products, with many unique parts and materials, are added to the mix, managers may forecast a much higher demand for the purchasing activity, perhaps now requiring that 2,000 purchase orders a month be processed. With no change in the process or efficiency of the processing purchasing order activity, this increase in demand will exceed available supply by 750 purchase orders per month, a shortage that can be relieved by hiring six more purchasing clerks. The ABC model, in addition, will trace purchasing costs directly to the newly designed custom products that are creating the demand for these additional purchasing resources, enabling managers to determine whether the revenues received fully compensate the organization for the cost of all the resources used to produce and deliver these products.

Of course, supplying additional purchasing clerks is only one possible action that the managers can take to the contemplated activity shortage. The engineering department can be asked to redesign the custom products so that they make more use of existing part numbers, an action that would reduce the amount of additional purchase orders required. Or the managers can search for process improvements or technology that would make the purchase order processing activity more efficient, perhaps raising the monthly output per person from 125 to 200 purchase orders.

Thus, measuring the *costs of resources supplied* indicates to managers the level of current spending (or, more generally, expenses) and the capacity to perform activities that this spending has provided. Measuring the *costs of resources used* by individual outputs provides information for managerial actions, as will be discussed more fully subsequently in the paper.

ISN'T THE UNUSED CAPACITY CALCULATION JUST A NEW NAME FOR THE VOLUME VARIANCE?

The calculation of unused capacity each period looks, at first glance, suspiciously like the traditional cost accounting volume variance. But the formulas:

Activity Availability = Activity Usage + Unused Capacity

or

Cost of Activity Supplied = Cost of Activity Used + Cost of Unused Activity

differ from the standard cost calculations of a volume variance in several significant ways.

First, and most obviously, volume variances are reported only in aggregate financial terms since traditional cost systems do not identify the *quantity* of overhead resources supplied or used. The activity-based approach reports both the quantity (number of purchase orders not written) and the cost of unused capacity. Second, traditional volume variances are often calculated with a denominator volume based on budgeted production, rather than practical capacity. In the activity-based approach, the "denominator volume" must always be the practical capacity of the activity being supplied, not the anticipated volume. And, third, the traditional cost accounting procedure of allocating overhead with a denominator volume is viewed as useful only for inventory valuation, not to provide information relevant for management; e.g.,

> The preselected production volume level of the application base used to set a budgeted *fixed-factory-overhead rate for applying costs to inventory* is called the denominator volume.

In summary, the production volume variance arises because the actual production volume level achieved usually does not coincide with the production level used as a denominator volume for computing a budgeted application rate for *inventory costing of fixed-factory overhead.*[9] (emphasis added)

Note how students are instructed that the calculation involves only the application of (so-called) *fixed*-factory overhead to units of production. Clearly, the volume variance is viewed, at least in textbooks (but not always in practice), as a cost accounting exercise for financial statements that is devoid of managerial significance.

These three differences between volume variances and measurements of unused capacity, while real, are not, however, the most important distinction. The cost accounting calculation that leads to a volume variance uses a measure of activity volume for the period (i.e., the denominator volume, also called the allocation base) that varies with the number of units produced. Direct labor hours, units of production, materials purchases, and machine hours are typical allocation bases used by traditional systems to assign factory expenses to products in production cost centers.[10] Implicitly, this procedure assumes that factory expenses are used by products in proportion to the overhead allocation base, i.e., proportional to volume of units produced. In practice, of course, this assumption is not valid.

Activity-based cost systems use separate activity cost drivers (the ABC generalization of an assignment or allocation base) for each activity. The activity cost drivers are not devices to allocate costs. They represent the demand that outputs make on each activity. For example, the activity cost driver for the setup activity could be the number of setups or the number of setup hours; the activity cost driver for processing purchase orders could be the number of purchase orders; the cost driver for administering and maintaining parts in the system could be the number of active part numbers. While some activity cost drivers are unit-related (such as machine and labor hours), as conventionally assumed, many activity cost drivers are batch-related, order-related, product-sustaining, and customer-sustaining.[11]

Because traditional cost systems use allocation bases that do not represent the demands for support resources by activities, the volume variance for a period can be zero even while substantial shortages or surpluses of capacity exist for many individual activities. For example, if actual production includes an unexpectedly high proportion of mature, standard products, produced in large batches, the demands for many batch and product-sustaining activities will be well below the quantity of resources supplied to perform these activities and much unused capacity will exist during the period. Conversely, if the actual production volume includes a substantial and unexpectedly high number of new, customized products, that are made in very small batches, the demand for batch and product-sustaining activities may exceed the quantity supplied. Shortages, delays, and overtime may occur in the batch and product-sustaining activities even though the total quantity of units produced during the period equaled the budgeted or anticipated amount.

The distinction between the measurement, by activity-based cost systems, of the cost of activities used (and unused) and the traditional cost accounting emphasis on fixed versus variable costs can be reconciled by examining closely the way managers contract for and supply resources to perform organizational activities.

RESOURCES THAT ARE SUPPLIED AS USED (AND NEEDED)

Some resources are acquired as needed. For these resources, the cost of resources supplied will generally equal the cost of resources used. For example, materials are usually ordered as needed so that materials expense equals the cost of materials used. And the cost of energy supplied to operate production machines also equals the cost of using that energy. Temporary employees hired on a daily basis from employment agencies and employees who are paid on a piece-work or overtime basis are additional examples. The company contracts with these workers to produce output and the workers are paid only when they are needed to produce output. Capital supplied by lenders is another example where the supply and the usage cost are identical (equalling the interest expense on the amount borrowed).[12]

In general, when the organization acquires a resource from outside suppliers, without long-term commitments, the cost of using the resource can equal the cost of acquiring (and supplying) the resource; for example, when the organization acquires the resource in spot markets. The costs of supplying such resources are apparently what many people have in mind when they refer to "variable costs." Such resources have no unused capacity. Whatever is supplied is used, or, alternatively, whatever is needed is acquired. This causes the costs of supplying the resource to be strongly correlated with the quantity (and hence the cost) of the resource used.

RESOURCES THAT ARE SUPPLIED IN ADVANCE OF USAGE

Organizations commit, however, to making many other resources available whether or not the resources will be fully used for current and future activities. This commitment can take several forms. The organization can make a cash expenditure to acquire a resource that provides service for several periods into the future. The most common example occurs when the company acquires or overhauls buildings and equipment. Such a transaction leads to an expense being recognized in each period during the useful life of the resource, with the organization gaining the capacity provided by the resource during each such period. The expense of supplying the resource will be incurred, each period, independent of how much of the resource is used.[13]

As a second example, the organization can enter into an explicit contract to obtain the use of a resource for several periods in the future. For example, a company leases buildings and equipment, or it guarantees access to energy or key materials through take-or-pay contracts. In this situation, a cash payment will occur and an expense will be recognized in each future period. Again, the amount of the cash payment and associated expense are independent of the actual quantity of usage of the resource in any period.

The third, and most important, example occurs when an organization enters into implicit contracts, particularly with its salaried and hourly employees, to maintain employment levels despite short-term downturns in activity levels. In this case, the spending (and expenses) associated with these employees will remain constant independent of the quantity of work performed by the employees.[14]

In each of the three contracting mechanisms, the organization acquires units of service capacity before the actual demands for the service units are realized. Consequently, the expenses of supplying the service capacity from these resources are incurred (or recognized) independent of usage. This independence in the short-run between the supply (or expense) of these resources and their usage has led this category of expense to be considered "fixed" with respect to current production volume and mix.

The separation between the acquisition of resource capacity and its actual usage arises from economies-of-scale in contracting for resources. For example, some service units come in lumpy amounts (e.g., physical capacity of machines, or the services provided by individual employees). Managers also find it less expensive to acquire some resources on a long-term commitment basis rather than to contract continually in spot markets to acquire resource capacity as needed.[15] These issues have been discussed at some length by scholars, such as Coase, Chandler, and Williamson.

Through any or all of these three contracting mechanisms, the organization acquires a capability or capacity to perform activities, and an associated expense of providing that capacity. The first step, therefore, in an activity-based analysis is to estimate both the expense of providing the capacity to perform an activity (the $25,000 monthly expense to process purchase orders), and the capacity or number of units of service activity that can be practically delivered (the 1,250 purchase orders per month) by the resources supplied. The expense of providing the activity capacity is divided by the number of available service units to obtain an estimate of the cost of supplying a unit of service of the activity (the $20 per purchase order cost).

MEASURING COSTS OF RESOURCES USED IN A PERIOD: THE ROLE FOR ACTIVITY-BASED COST SYSTEMS

The distinction between resources supplied as needed and resources supplied prior to (but in anticipation of) usage suggests that a relatively simple system

EXHIBIT 1

Example of ABC Income Statement

	Used	Unused	
SALES			20,000
Less: EXPENSES OF RESOURCES SUPPLIED AS USED			
Materials	7,600		
Energy	600		
Short-term labor	900		9,100
CONTRIBUTION MARGIN			10,900
Less: ACTIVITY EXPENSES: COMMITTED RESOURCES	Used	Unused	
Permanent direct labor	1,400	200	
Machine run-time	3,200		
Purchasing	700	100	
Receiving/Inventory	450	50	
Production runs	1,000	100	
Customer administration	700	200	
Engineering changes	800	(100)	
Parts administration	750	150	
TOTAL EXPENSES OF COMMITTED RESOURCES	9,000	700	9,700
OPERATING PROFIT			1,200

can be used for the periodic measurement of actual expenses (see Exhibit 1). In this system, short-term contribution margin is measured as price (or revenues) less the cost of resources acquired as needed: materials, energy, and short-term labor (and overtime). By assumption, the remaining operating expenses represent resources that have been acquired prior to actual usage. The costs of these resources should be unaffected by actual activity levels during the period. The periodic income statement can report, for each activity, the costs of resources used for outputs and the costs of resources unused during the period.

For management purposes, flexible budgets and variance analysis become unnecessary for these expense accounts. A simple comparison of actual of budgeted expenses, account by account, will suffice to provide feedback.[16] Basically, the authorized expenses have been determined either by prior commitments (acquiring plant, property, and equipment; signing take-or-pay contracts) or during the annual budgeting process. One manufacturing manager expressed this point quite forcefully:

> Cost variances are useless to me. I don't want to ever have to look at a cost variance, monthly or weekly. Once you've decided to run a product, you don't have many choices left. Resources are already committed regardless of how the cost system computes costs among alternative processes.

Monthly, I do look at the financial reports. . . . I look closely at my fixed expenses and compare these to the budgets, especially on discretionary items like travel and maintenance. I also watch headcount. But the financial systems still don't tell me where I am wasting money. I expect that if I make operating improvements, costs should go down, but I don't worry about the linkage too much. The organizational dynamics make it difficult to link cause and effect precisely.[17]

Managers may be encouraged to modify their use of resources in the short-run based on information on unused capacity. For example, when excess setup capacity exists, they can temporarily decrease batch sizes. Alternatively, managers may be expected to adjust downward the quantity of resources supplied when substantial amounts of unused capacity persist for several periods.

Several organizations, however, not understanding the important distinction between measuring the costs of resources supplied (and expensed) and the costs of resources used, have attempted to use their activity-based systems to budget monthly expenses. A good example of the problems arising from using an activity-based system for monthly performance measurement was documented in the Hewlett Packard: Queensferry Telecommunications Division case.

Hewlett Packard: QTD Case[18]

QTD had recently installed a new activity-based cost system. The system accumulated expenses at each process and assigned these expenses to products with a cost driver defined for each process (e.g., number of axial insertions). The system was developed primarily to provide process cost information to product engineers to help them design products that would be less expensive to manufacture. The system, however, was also used to monitor production performance. The two functions soon came into conflict when production volume dropped due to the postponement of a major contract. The lower production volume led to large monthly volume variances because operating expenses could not be reduced proportionately to the decline in volume. The controller commented:

> In a perfect world, spending would drop to offset lower production volumes. However, in environments like ours, where we retain our employees, it is almost impossible for spending to be cut back when volume drops in a period.

Higher cost driver rates were calculated, based on the lower production volumes, so that the accounts would "clear" each period without large volume variances. This change, however, negated the primary purpose of the newly designed system. With unused capacity expenses now loaded on to cost driver rates, the system no longer provided product designers with accurate information on the expenses of activities performed to manufacture their products.

Companies like QTD, that attempt to budget expenses each month from their activity-based resource usage model, will end up, each month, with a variance representing the unused capacity for every activity and resource for which usage and availability are not perfectly correlated. The unused capacity variance signals only that managers did not adjust the resource availability level to the amount actually required for the volume and mix of outputs produced that period. It is not helpful, however, to predict spending or expense changes.

Once decisions get made on resource availability levels in the organization, typically in the annual budgeting and authorization process, the expenses of supplying most resources will be determined for the year (unless managers deliberately act to eliminate or add to the resources). For example, the resources committed to the purchase-order processing activity will be determined annually as a function of the expected number and complexity of purchase orders to be processed. We would *not* expect, however, the size of the purchasing department to fluctuate weekly or monthly depending on how many purchase orders get processed during a week or a month. Therefore, even when usage of a resource drops, the expense associated with that resource continues at its previous level. The difference between the costs of resources supplied and the costs of resources used for producing products equals the cost of *unused capacity* for the period.[19] The difference should not be interpreted as a change in the cost of performing the activity.

RELEVANCE FOR MANAGERIAL DECISIONS: USING ABC TO INCREASE PROFITS

An improved costing system is a means to an end. The goal is to increase profits, not to obtain more accurate costs. How do activity-based cost systems help companies improve their profitability? We attempt to answer this question through the simple profit equation:

Profits = Revenues − Expenses

Pricing and Product Mix

Some companies use their ABC information to reprice their products, services, or customers so that the revenues (resources) received exceed the costs of resources used to produce products for individual customers. For example, prices are lowered to customers ordering standard products in high volumes, and prices are raised to customers ordering highly customized products in low volumes. Pricing strategies are part of a broader set of actions taken by managers to improve profits through changes in product and customer mix. For example, some companies, experiencing declining demand for their standard products, proliferated their product line to offer customized, low-volume varieties. This strategy was influenced by their belief that many costs were "fixed" and that the lost volume in standard products needed to be replaced with customized products that could "absorb overhead" and even sell at price premiums. With this traditional view, the labor hours, machine hours, and materials purchases could be approximately the same between the old product and the new product mix. But the new product mix included many customized, low volume products that made many more demands on resources performing batch and product-sustaining activities. Because sufficient unused capacity did not exist to perform these activities, the companies had to increase their spending so that more resources could be supplied to perform batch and product-sustaining activities. After the product proliferation had occurred, and the companies were incurring higher expenses for support resources, ABC models revealed that many of the newly-added products were unprofitable.[20]

Once this situation has been discovered, managers have typically first attempted to raise prices on the unprofitable products. If this action does not generate sufficient revenues to cover all their product-specific costs, managers contemplate eliminating unprofitable products. Or they consider outsourcing products to suppliers whose total cost of acquisition is below the cost of resources required to make the product internally. Of course, before outsourcing or dropping products, managers should verify that they can eliminate the resources no longer needed or can replace the lost volume with more profitable business. Thus before any decision is taken from activity-based product or customer costs, managers must assess the incremental revenue and spending consequences.

Critics of ABC have stated:

> Isn't this what we have been teaching (or practicing) as relevant costing or incremental analysis? Students in introductory cost and managerial accounting classes are already taught that costs unaffected by whether a particular product is retained or eliminated are irrelevant for that decision and should be excluded from the analysis. Why do companies need an ABC system? Why not just calculate the changes in spending that would occur for any contemplated decision, such as dropping or outsourcing a product, and make a decision based on that analysis? What purpose is served by building, maintaining, and attempting to interpret a generalized activity-based cost model?

Perhaps one can understand the demand for a generalized (activity-based) resource usage model from a similar situation that arises in physics. Introductory physics courses teach Newton's laws of motion, such as conservation of angular momentum or gravitational attraction. The principles are illustrated with problems that require calculating the interactions among two or three objects. Students who survive to more advanced physics courses encounter a subject called statistical thermodynamics, which provides predictions of the aggregate behaviors of large numbers of particles. A naive student might ask, "Why do we need to study thermodynamics as a separate subject? Don't Newton's laws of motion still apply to these particles?" The answer is, of course, they do, but to apply Newton's laws to the large numbers of particles being studied would exceed the lifetime and computational power of the universe. Therefore, physicists have devised laws to describe and predict the aggregate behavior of large numbers of interacting particles.

"Relevant costing" or "incremental analysis" situations are illustrated in introductory courses and books by simple examples with two or three products and simple overhead structures. An activity-based resource usage model can be viewed as the thermodynamic equivalent to the three product examples of introductory cost accounting courses. Consider, for example, the analysis that arises in the Bridgeton Industries case.[21] The plant initially produced five product lines. Because of competitive pressures, the plant's profitability had declined. Special studies were performed and eventually two product lines were outsourced. As the case proceeds, students learn that the total spending on resources declined by less than the loss in revenues so that the economies of the plant had deteriorated further. From a "relevant costing" perspective, how many special analyses would have been required to determine which product lines or combinations of product lines should have been dropped. Certainly each product line individually could have been analyzed. But because most resources come in lumpy amounts, perhaps substantial reductions in resource supply (and therefore spending) would occur only if at least two product lines were dropped, as was actually done. But why stop at two? Why not consider dropping all combinations of three, or four, or even all five product lines? In total, 2^5 or 32 combinations would have to be analyzed, with the relevant costs calculated for each of the 32 possible maintain/drop combinations.

The 32 possibilities may not seem insuperable, but for companies with hundreds and thousands of products, customers, processes, and facilities, the combinations, while still finite, would, as in thermodynamics, exceed the lifetime and computational power of the universe to enumerate much less evaluate. And retain versus drop is a relatively simple binary decision. What about shifts in product mix, improvements in production processes, and changes in product designs? Managers cannot possibly apply introductory cost accounting relevant cost calculations to all possible product and customer mix decisions. The activity-based cost model, like the thermodynamics model, provides an aggregate view of the economic laws of motion of a complex enterprise, with thousands of individual products, customers, and facilities.[22]

Borrowing another analogy, integral calculus teaches us that the sum total of doing lots of little things can amount to something substantial. An activity-based resource usage model forecasts the changes in aggregate demands for activities from making decisions on many products, services, and customers. In effect, the activity-based cost model performs the integral calculus function of adding up a lot of small effects into something quite substantial. It approximates the changes in resource demands that will occur from implementing new decisions on pricing, product mix, and customer mix. Before actually implementing the proposed decisions, of course, managers must assess the cash flow consequences by forecasting, as well, the increases and decreases in resource supply (including revenues) that they anticipate will occur. An activity-based cost model serves to direct managers' attention to where more detailed analysis will likely yield the highest payoffs. The ABC model reduces the dimensionality of decisions to where the cash flow consequences from only a few alternatives need to be examined closely.

Change Resource Usage

In addition to pricing, product and customer mix changes, which affect profits directly through changes in the margins earned between revenues received and resources expended, ABC models can help managers reduce resource usage, while holding revenues constant. When resource usage is reduced, some unused capacity will be created which can then be either managed away (enabling lower spending to occur) or used to process more throughput (enabling more revenues to be earned). Demands on support resources can be reduced by taking two types of actions:

- Reducing the number of times activities are performed, and
- Increasing the efficiency with which activities are performed.[23]

Reducing number of times activities are performed:

Changing from unprofitable to profitable product and customer mixes, as described above, enables companies to earn the same or even higher revenues while performing fewer activities. Managers can take additional actions to reduce the number of times activities are performed, especially activities performed by support resources. Marketing and sales executives in some companies have set *minimum order sizes* to reduce the large number of activities triggered by many small orders. As engineers *improve the design of products*, fewer engineering change notices are required. Other change activities are reduced when engineering managers discourage their employees from excessive tinkering with existing product designs, and marketing managers discourage or *charge premiums for customer-requested changes* in products and delivery schedules. In addition, design engineers, informed about the resource expenses associated with introducing and maintaining a large number of parts in the system, can develop product designs that use *fewer and more common parts*.[24] All these actions, individually and in combination, reduce the number of demands for activities performed by support resources, while maintaining existing (unit-driven) production volume.

Increasing efficiency (lowering the cost) of activities performed:[25]

A complementary set of actions can be taken to increase the efficiency of performing activities. The increased efficiency enables the same *quantity* of activities to be performed with fewer resources. Continuous improvement programs, such as *total quality management* and *cycle time reduction* (just-in-time), reduce the resources required to inspect products, changeover and setup machines, and move and store materials. Successful implementation of continuous improvement programs produces major reductions in the demands for resources to perform batch and product-sustaining activities.

Introduction of advanced *information technology* reduces by substantial amounts the expenses of many batch and product-sustaining activities. Computer-Aided-Design and Engineering (CAD/CAE) equipment reduces the expenses of designing products and making changes to existing products. They also standardize the maintenance of routings and bills-of-materials. Flexible Manufacturing Systems (FMS) and Computer Integrated Manufacturing (CIM) essentially eliminate many batch activities through automatic scheduling, materials movement, inspection, and tool positioning, gauging, and maintenance, plus instantaneous changeovers, between operations. In the theoretical limit, a CIM system requires the same resources to make 1 unit of 1,000 different products as it does to make 1,000 units of 1 product.[26] Electronic Data Interchange (EDI) and Electronic Funds Transfer (EFT) link companies with suppliers and customers, greatly reducing the expenses associated with purchasing, scheduling, receiving, shipping, invoicing, and paying for materials and products.

Improving Profits

Through a combination of reducing the quantity of activities performed and increasing the efficiency of performing the remaining activities, companies can maintain production throughput and, hence, revenues while reducing their demands for indirect and support resources. Ideally, managers can now obtain additional business, many of whose demands would be handled by resources currently in excess supply. This would enable the company to enjoy substantially higher profits because revenues would increase with only modest spending increases.[27] Alternatively, the unused capacity created can be reduced in the next budgeting cycle.

Budgeting: Changing the Supply of Resources to Match Resource Demands

As managers adjust their product and customer mixes, introduce new products, phase out mature products, improve operating processes, and introduce new technology, they change the demands for activities performed by indirect and support resources. The revised demands for resources to perform support activities can be estimated with an activity-based model. Differences between the demand for and the supply of resources can then be translated into expected changes in future spending on resources. Used in this way, the activity-based model becomes a central tool for management planning and budgeting. The budgets for each resource are determined based on the activities required for the forecasted product volume and mix, and existing production processes. For resources forecasted to be in short supply, the analysis provides a justification for additional spending to increase resource availability. For a resource forecasted to be in excess of predicted demands, managers can be requested to reduce the availability and hence the expenses of that resource. They can reduce the unused capacity by selling or scrapping machinery without replacement, by not replacing employees who retire or leave the organization voluntarily, by redeploying employees from activities where they are no longer needed to activities where capacity shortages exist, or, more drastically, by laying off now redundant employees. These actions enable the company to generate the same revenues with fewer resources, thereby allowing profits to increase.

Alternatively, companies may not exploit the profit opportunities from having created unused capacity. They may keep existing resources in place, even though the demands for the activities performed by the resources have diminished substantially. In this case, and only in this case, will the actions that reduced activity usage not yield any tangible benefits. Profits will remain the same, since revenues have remained constant and the expenses of resources supplied have also remained fixed. But the failure to increase profits is not due to costs being intrinsically "fixed." Rather, the failure is the consequence of managers being unable or unwilling to exploit the unused capacity they have created. The activity-based cost model focuses managers' attention on decisions that affect the resource demands by activities. If the decisions lead to lower demands for some resources, the company can then realize increased profits by either using these resources to generate higher revenues or by reducing spending on these resources. The costs of these resources are only "fixed" if managers cannot or do not exploit the opportunities from the unused capacity they helped to create.

SUMMARY AND CONCLUSIONS

Activity-based cost systems contain two important insights. First, the activities performed by many resources are not demanded in proportion to the total volume of units produced (or sold). The demands arise from the diversity and complexity of the product and customer mix.

Second, activity-based cost systems are not models of how expenses or spending vary in the short-run. ABC systems estimate the costs of resources used to perform activities for various outputs. During any given period, the production of products and services, and their marketing, sale, and delivery to customers, create a demand for organizational activities. The quantity of each activity supplied to outputs is estimated by activity cost drivers such as the number of setup hours, number of purchase orders processed, number of receipts, number of direct labor and machine hours, and number of parts maintained. By summing across the costs of all resources supplied to perform activities for individual outputs, the ABC model estimates the costs of resources used during the period by all the organization's output.

Activity-based systems model how activity usage varies with the demands made for these activities. If activity usage exceeds the quantity available from existing resource supply, then higher spending to increase the supply of resources will likely soon occur. If, however, activity usage is below available supply, spending or the expenses of resources will not decrease automatically. Management, to obtain higher profits, must take conscious actions either to use the available capacity to support a higher volume of business (i.e., by increasing revenues) or to reduce spending on resources by eliminating the unused capacity. Costs and profits are fixed only if management takes no action, and leaves the unused capacity undisturbed. Management behavior, not cost behavior, determines whether reductions in resource demands become translated into higher profits.

APPENDIX

Separate Systems for Measuring Resource Expenses and Resource Usage: A Case Study

The Union Pacific case study illustrates well how a service organization developed a system for measuring the costs of resource usage quite different from the system used for operational and expense control.[28] During the 1960s, the company had developed an extensive system for monitoring spending and expenses in its more than 5,000 cost centers around the country. Cost centers included freight and locomotive repair yards, switching yards, transportation crews, and maintenance of track and right of way. Expenses were recorded in up to 1,200 different account codes.[29] Each month, a cost center manager received a report on actual and budgeted expenses for each of these accounts, supplemented with data on Year-to-Date actual expenses compared with budget and with a similar period in the previous year. The 5,000 individual cost center expense control reports were aggregated into summary data for higher level managers all the way to senior vice-presidents in Omaha who received a one page summary of operations under their control. This extensive system of monthly reports was used to monitor and control cost center expenses and measure efficiency improvements.

In the deregulated environment of the 1980s, the company realized that despite extensive reporting of cost center expenses, it had no information to estimate the costs of resources used to move a carload of freight from one point to another. This gap occurred for two reasons. The railroad environment provides a vivid example of where almost complete separation exists between resource spending and resource usage. The monthly spending to maintain track and right of way and to repair locomotives and freight cars has no relation to the amount of traffic run that month. The monthly spending reflects the millions of gross ton miles hauled in many preceding months, and management's decision to replenish the supply of these resources so that they will be available for the future. The cost of using those resources occurred in the past; the spending to revitalize the depleted resources was occurring today.

Even apart from the temporal separation between resource usage and resource spending, the railroad like many other service organizations did not measure the use of resources by individual products within each cost center. For example, the railroad supplied switching yards and measured the expenses of operating switching yards. But it did not measure the quantity of use of switching yards by individual freight cars as they moved from shipper to customer.

The railroad had to develop entirely new analytic systems to measure the costs of activities performed to supply its customers with products and services. The costs of resources used to move a carload of freight from shipper to destination could not be estimated based on incremental spending since virtually no incremental spending occurred when the company picked up a freight car from a shipper, scheduled it, connected it to a train, switched it to several different trains, and finally delivered it to the customer. Yet the movement of the freight car required an extensive quantity of railroad resources to be supplied and available. And the actual running of the freight car placed incremental demands on several resources that would require additional spending sometime in the future. The company understood that it could not wait until the freight car, locomotive, or track was repaired to send out bills to all the shippers that made use of these resources in the past. It also understood that the amounts spent to supply train crews, scheduling and information systems, and switching yards were justified by the expected volume and mix of traffic to be carried. The company developed a system that estimated, move by move, the quantity and cost of all the resources used by individual carload moves, even though short-run spending was almost completely independent of these moves.

The railroad example provides a vivid example of the difference between resource usage and resource spending (or resource expenses). The power of the case, however, extends beyond railroads or even service companies since most manufacturing companies' resources are also now characterized by large distinctions between the use of the resources and the amount of current expenses to supply the resources.

Notes

1. Early versions of the transactional demand for resources appeared in J. Miller and T. Vollman, "The Hidden Factory," *Harvard Business Review* (September–October 1985): 142–150, and Robin Cooper and Robert S. Kaplan, "How Cost Accounting Systematically Distorts Product Costs," *Management Accounting* (April 1988): 20–27. A more comprehensive explanation of the impact of diversity and complexity on indirect costs was presented in the series of *Journal of Cost Management* articles by Robin Cooper, "The Rise of Activity-Based Cost Systems: Parts I–IV" (Summer 1988, Fall 1988, Winter 1989, and Spring 1989).

2. See, for example, Robert S. Kaplan, "John Deere Component Works (A) and (B), *Harvard Business School Cases #9-187-107* and *-108;* Robin Cooper and Karen H. Wruck, "Siemens: Electric Motor Works (A)," *Harvard Business School Case #9-189-089.*

3. We will use the term "outputs" to refer generically to products, services, customers, projects, facilities, or any object that creates a demand for or benefits from organizational activities. Activity-based cost systems assign the organization's operating expenses to outputs based on the activities performed for these outputs.

4. We have adopted the terminology of unused capacity, as suggested by Alan Vercio of Texas Instruments, rather than our initial term of "excess capacity." Not all "unused" capacity represents "excess" capacity.

5. This cost includes the costs of fringe benefits, secretarial and administrative support, equipment costs, and space charges associated with each purchasing department employee.

6. Note that this calculation does *not* use actual activity levels during the period; the denominator represents service capacity not actual usage of this capacity.

7. Later in the paper, we will show how to develop a new format for the periodic income or expense statement that highlights the costs of resources used and unused.

8. More accurately, the spending on (or expenses assigned to) these resources will be independent of the volume and mix of outputs produced during the period.

9. Charles T. Horngren and George Foster, *Cost Accounting: A Managerial Emphasis, Seventh Edition* (Prentice-Hall, 1991): 258, 265.

10. More complex traditional systems that use multiple allocation bases within the same cost center will have multiple volume variances, but each allocation base is still unit-level, driven by the volume of output.

11. The hierarchy of factory expenses was introduced in Robin Cooper, "Cost Classification in Unit-Based and Activity-Based Manufacturing Cost Systems" (Fall 1990): 4–13, and discussed further in Robin Cooper and Robert S. Kaplan, "Profit Priorities from Activity-Based Costing," *Harvard Business Review* (May–June 1991): 130–137.

12. Of course, the commitment fee associated with a line of credit is a counter-example, because the cost of supplying the resource (the right to borrow) is incurred whether the resource is used or not.

13. We are using the word "expense" in its traditional accounting sense; e.g., an outflow or other using up of assets or incurrence of liabilities (or a combination of both) during a period from delivering or producing goods, rendering services, or carrying out other activities that constitute an enterprise's ongoing major or central operations (W.W. Cooper and Yuji Ijiri, *Kohler's Dictionary for Accountants, Sixth Edition*, Englewood Cliffs, NJ; Prentice-Hall 1983: 203–204). To avoid confusion associated with financial accounting inventory valuation procedures that shift some period expenses forward in time to be matched against future revenues generated, we will assume, for purposes of this paper and without loss of generality, that units produced always equal units sold. This enables all period expenses to be recognized as expenses in the period they are incurred.

14. The actual expenses of providing this capability in a given period can even exceed the cash outlays in that period. This situation arises when cash payments made in much later periods, such as for vacations, pensions and other post-employment benefits, are attributed to the supply of the resource during the given period.

15. This prior commitment can also be made for strategic reasons; see Pankaj Ghemawat, *Commitment: The Dynamic of Strategy* (Free Press, 1991).

16. This distinction between the financial system required for periodic performance measurement (reporting on actual period expenses) and the activity-based system reporting on the costs of resource usage underlay the arguments in R.S. Kaplan, "One Cost System Isn't Enough," *Harvard Business Review* (January-February 1988). A good example of a company that separated its monthly reporting system from the system used to estimate the cost and profitability of its products is provided by the Union Pacific case study described in the Appendix.

17. Quote taken from Robert S. Kaplan, "Analog Devices: The Half-Life System," *Harvard Business School Case # 9-190-061.*

18. Robin Cooper and Kiran Verma, "Hewlett Packard: Queensferry Telecommunications Division," *Harvard Business School Case #9-191-067.*

19. During a period when usage exceeds normal capacity, the difference will represent a "favorable" over-utilization of capacity.

20. Unprofitable products are those for which the expenses assigned to maintain, produce, and deliver them exceed the net revenues received from their sale.

21. Robin Cooper, "Bridgeton Industries: Automotive Component and Fabrication Plant," *Harvard Business School Case #9-190-085.*

22. And even the thermodynamic extension is now known to be an approximation that ignores relativistic and quantum mechanical phenomena. Similarly, the activity-based resource usage model, as currently formulated, is likely just a first order, linear approximation to what may require stochastic, nonlinear formulations in certain situations.

23. These actions are iterative, not sequential, as managers continually adjust the volume and mix of their outputs, and manage the efficiency with which their activities are performed.

24. These design activities were the focus of the ABC systems described in the Tektronix and Hewlett-Packard cases: Robin Cooper and Peter Turney, "Tektronix (A)," *Harvard Business School Case #9-188-143*; and "Hewlett-Packard Roseville Networks Division," *Harvard Business School Case #9-189-117.*

25. Using activity-based information to focus improvement activities was discussed in H. Thomas Johnson, "Activity-Based Information: A Blueprint for World-Class Management Accounting," *Management Accounting* (June 1988): 23–30. Using an activity-based cost system for performance improvement was a central focus in the system described in Robert S. Kaplan, "Maxwell Appliance Controls," *Harvard Business School Case #9-192-058.*

26. In effect, CIM transforms batch and product-sustaining activities into unit-level activities so that product variety costs approach zero.

27. Spending will increase for resources for which availability and usage are tightly coupled (e.g., materials, energy), and for resources where unused capacity does not exist (perhaps direct labor or machine time). Also, it would be preferable for the added volume to generate revenues in excess of the expenses of resources used so that the new business can be sustained in the long run.

28. Robert S. Kaplan, "Union Pacific: Introduction, (A), and (B)," *Harvard Business School Cases 9-186-176, 177, 178.*

29. The larger number of account codes arose from regulatory reporting requirements specified by the Interstate Commerce Commission for Railform A.

CHAPTER THREE

Applications in Activity-Based Costing

This chapter is a continuation of chapter 2. The chapter provides examples and applications in four different areas:

1. Discrete part manufacturing
2. Continuous process manufacturing
3. Service companies
4. Customer-based cost objects

These four areas are only a sampling of the rich array of examples that are available in the literature. See the end of the book for additional references.

Reading 3.1 Discrete Part Manufacturing Applications

R. Cooper, "The Rise of Activity-Based Costing—Part Four: What Do Activity-Based Cost Systems Look Like?" *Journal of Cost Management* **(Spring 1989), pp. 38–49.**

In these early applications of activity-based product costing, Cooper provides illustrations from:

1. Tektronix Portable Instruments Division
2. Siemens Electric Motor Works
3. John Deere Component Works
4. Hewlett-Packard's Roseville Networks Division
5. Schrader Bellows

All of these companies are discrete part manufacturers. This means that they purchase or fabricate components that are assembled into completed units.

This article predates the ABC glossary now used by practitioners in this field. Thus, the term "cost driver" is used throughout the article instead of the agreed-upon term "activity driver." At this time, Cooper had yet to introduce the concept of activity levels; thus they are not explicitly identified in the article. For example, the number of part numbers used as an activity driver by Tektronix is an example of a driver for product-level activities, while the number of setups in

Siemens, John Deere, and Schrader Bellows are activity drivers for batch-level activities. In this article, Cooper uses an earlier term, "non-volume" activities, to refer to activities that occur at other than the unit level.

Reading 3.2 Continuous Process Manufacturing Examples

J. Reeve, "Cost Management in Continuous Process Environments," in *Handbook of Cost Management*, edited by Barry Brinker (New York: Warren Gorham and Lamont), C3, 1993.

I identify continuous processors as material-intensive, capital-intensive, and highly automated. The environment is characterized by a great deal of end product diversity on the customer side of the value chain, whereas the discrete part environment has component diversity on the vendor side of the value chain. The location of the relative complexity influences where overhead activities are located. The article also provides examples of Cooper's activity hierarchy concepts to customer and product hierarchies within the continuous process environment.

I provide two additional examples of ABC in a continuous process environment: one for a specialty chemical company and another for a distilled beverage company. The article also discusses the need to measure the cost of excess capacity, much as suggested by Cooper and Kaplan (Reading 2.3). The article also indicates that continuous processors are now experimenting with real-time financial information to help guide process decisions.

Reading 3.3 Service Company Applications

W. Rotch, "Activity-Based Costing in Service Industries," *Journal of Cost Management* (Summer 1990), pp. 4–14.

The Rotch article provides a number of examples of activity-based costing in service settings, such as hospitals, rail services, and data services. The article is brief, and provides only a high-level overview of activity-based costing issues with respect to service companies. The actual implementation of activity-based costing ideas in service companies is generally much more involved than indicated by the article.

Exhibit 1 provides some distinctions between cost management for manufacturing and service companies.

One striking difference between service and manufacturing companies is that service companies cannot inventory their product. Service companies often must commit resources to capacity (hotels, airplanes, communication networks, rental cars, hospital units) before the service is offered. These facilities-related costs are generally significant in service companies. Manufacturers can generally store

EXHIBIT 1

Manufacturing vs. Service Cost Management Issues

Issue	Manufacturing	Service
Direct materials	Important cost mgt. issue	Virtually irrelevant (except for transportation and power generation)
Cost structure	Variable costs are significant	Large percentage of costs are fixed
Cost behavior	Large percentage of costs vary with revenue volume	Very few of the variable costs vary directly with revenue volume; they are variable to other activities
Method for storing value	Inventory	Capacity to serve
Product costing	Extensive tradition (inventory valuation)	Little tradition in this area (no inventory valuation)
Product definition	Tangible	Intangible and hierarchical

value in inventory in expectation of an increase in demand. Service companies employ more of a *Field of Dreams* strategy—if we build it, they will come.

In addition, service companies generally have few costs that vary with revenue volume. Manufacturing companies have materials and labor that vary with units sold; thus the familiar two-axis break-even chart can be applied. This is not so with service companies. The variable costs of service companies are generally variable to non-volume activity bases. For example, an airline earns revenues from passenger miles. Very few costs are variable to passenger miles (fuel is to some degree). Crew salaries are variable to miles flown (regardless of flight occupancy rates), ground support costs are variable to the number of arrival and departures at a terminal (regardless of the length of flight), and reservation costs are variable to the number of passengers (regardless of the length of the flight). To take another example, an educational institution earns revenues from student credit hours. However, faculty salaries are variable to the number of sections (whether there are 5 or 50 students in a section); administrative costs are variable to the number of academic units; and student services are variable to the number of students. In both examples (as with most service companies), there are few costs variable with revenue volume.

An interesting exercise is to ask managers in a service enterprise, "what is your product?" Often you will get a variety of answers. A manufacturer can always answer this question clearly, but service companies seem to have some difficulty. Why is this? It's not that service companies have no product—they do. It's that the product can be defined at many different levels of aggregation, and often there is no agreement inside the organization at which level of aggregation the product should be defined. For example, the product of a bank could be loans, or commercial loans, or commercial loans less than $1,000,000, or John Jones' commercial loan. All are definitions of the product at increasing levels of resolution. When applying ABC, the cost object must be established within the appropriate level in the aggregation hierarchy. The downside, however, is that highly resolute product definitions require sophisticated data capturing mechanisms. For example, it's one thing to estimate the cost of an average rail move from New York to Chicago (one product definition) and quite another to measure the actual cost of specific moves day in and day out (a more resolute definition).

Service companies have no GAAP requirements for product costing. This is because there is no inventory; hence, there is no need to match cost of goods sold with revenue. In many service companies, product costing is an entirely voluntary effort for management needs only. Thus, service companies either have no product costing (no GAAP tradition), or in some cases, very sophisticated systems to support management decision making. It's either feast or famine with respect to this issue in the real world.

Reading 3.4   Customer Profit Applications

M. O'Guin and S. Rebischke, "Customer-Driven Costs Using Activity-Based Costing," in *Handbook of Cost Management*, edited by Barry Brinker (New York: Warren Gorham and Lamont), B5, 1993.

O'Guin and Rebishchke (OR) provide concepts and examples for using customers (or channels), rather than products, as cost objects. This is becoming a very popular application of the vertical dimension of the ABM model. Many companies wish to align the organization's resources with the relative degree of customer profit potential. ABC for customer costing can provide information to support such strategic efforts.

Managers may also find that activity information can be used to improve distribution channel decisions. *Distribution channels* are the means by which products and services are made available to customers. For example, an apparel manufacturer may provide customers access to clothing products through specialty retail stores, catalog sales, or manufacturer outlets.

Companies face decisions with respect to customers and distribution channels, such as the following:

- Does the retail channel meet our profitability criteria?
- Should the catalog channel be abandoned?
- Which customer is our most profitable and why?
- Which customer is our least profitable and why?
- Is our largest volume customer our most profitable?
- Which channel of distribution should the company emphasize?

EXHIBIT 2

The Relationship Between Product and Customer/Channel Costing

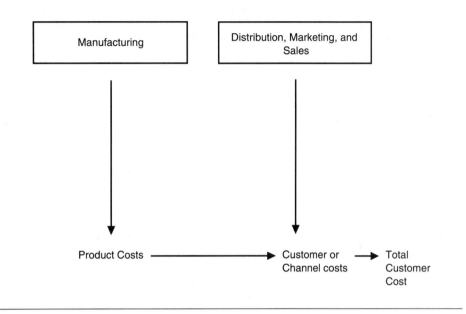

The relationship between product costing and customer/channel costing is shown in Exhibit 2. Product costs are generally determined from manufacturing costs. However, customer/channel costs are often determined from the distribution, marketing, and sales costs that are incurred after the product is manufactured. These post-manufacturing costs are considered period costs for GAAP. As a result, conventional management reporting practice will sometimes follow financial reporting requirements and avoid allocating these post-manufacturing costs. More contemporary managerial accounting practice, however, uses activity-based costing techniques to allocate these costs to customers or channels, and even products (such as advertising), for decision making.

Management uses activity-based approaches to assign post-manufacturing costs to customers to reflect the different ways in which customers consume resources. For example, one customer may frequently call on a vendor's technical support "hot line" because it has no in-house technical staff, while another customer may not require the "hot-line" support because it has an in-house staff. Differences such as these have an overall impact on the profitability of serving different customers or channels of distribution. Examples of other activities where customer/channels may have different resource demands are illustrated in Exhibit 3.

EXHIBIT 3

Examples of Customer/Channel Differences

Activity	High Cost Customer/Channel	Low Cost Customer/Channel
Shipping policies	Customer requires overnight shipping	Customer is satisfied with 3-day shipping
Inventory carrying requirements	Customer requires safety stocks close to its plant	Customer does not require safety stocks
Post-sale technical support	Customer requires specialized training to use product	Customer provides its own in-house training to use product
Field sales support	Customer requires shelf stocking from supplier's sales force	Customer performs shelf stocking with its own work force
Promotional support	Channel requires promotional displays	Channel requires no promotional displays
Order entry	Customer uses a salesperson to submit an order	Customer uses electronic data interchange (EDI) to submit an order
Credit and collection	Customer pays accounts in 90 days	Customer pays accounts in 15 days
Field service	Customer requires field service staff	Customer requires no post-sale service

Additional Readings

Antos, John. "Activity-Based Management for Service, Not-For-Profit, and Governmental Organizations," *Journal of Cost Management* (Summer 1992): 11–21.

Bellis-Jones, Robin. "Customer Profitability Analysis," *Management Accounting* (UK) (February 1989): 26–28.

Berlant, Debbie, Reese Browning, and George Foster. "How Hewlett-Packard Gets Numbers It Can Trust," *Harvard Business Review* (January–February 1990): 178–183.

Brignall, T.J., R. Fitzgerald, R. Johnston, and R. Silvestro. "Product Costing in Service Organizations," *Management Accounting Research* (December 1991): 227–248.

Campi, John P. "Total Cost Management at Parker Hannifin," *Management Accounting* (January 1989): 51–53.

Carlson, David A., and S. Mark Young. "Activity-Based Total Quality Management at American Express," *Journal of Cost Management* (Spring 1993): 48–58.

Carr, Lawrence P., and Christopher D. Ittner, "Measuring the Cost of Ownership," *Journal of Cost Management* (Fall 1992): 42–51.

Cooper, Robin A., and Robert S. Kaplan. *The Design of Cost Management Systems: Text, Cases, and Readings* (Englewood Cliffs, NJ: Prentice-Hall, 1991).

Cooper, Robin, Robert S. Kaplan, Lawrence S. Maisel, Eileen Morrissey, and Ronald M. Oehm. *Implementing Activity-Based Cost Management: Moving From Analysis to Action* (Montvale, NJ: Institute of Management Accountants, 1992).

Drumheller, Harold K., Jr. "Making Activity-Based Costing Practical," *Journal of Cost Management* (Summer 1993): 21–27.

Dugdale, David. "The Uses of Activity-Based Costing." *Management Accounting* (UK) (October 1990): 36–38.

Edersheim, Elizabeth Haas, and Joan Wilson. "Complexity at Consumer Goods Companies: Naming and Taming the Beast," *Journal of Cost Management* (Fall 1992): 26–36.

Eiler, Robert G., and John P. Campi. "Implementing Activity-Based Costing at a Process Company," *Journal of Cost Management* (Spring 1990): 43–50.

Howell, Robert A., and Stephen R. Soucy. "Customer Profitability—As Critical as Product Profitability," *Management Accounting* (October 1990): 43–47.

Johnson, H. Thomas, and Dennis A. Loewe. "How Weyerhaeuser Manages Corporate Overhead Costs," *Management Accounting* (August 1987): 20–26.

Jones, Lou F. "Product Costing at Caterpillar," *Management Accounting* (February 1991): 34–42.

Lee, John Y. "Activity-Based Costing at CAL Electronic Circuits," *Management Accounting* (October 1990): 36–38.

Lewis, Ronald J. "Activity-Based Costing for Marketing," *Management Accounting* (November 1991): 33–38.

Menzano, Ralph J. "Activity-Based Costing for Information Systems," *Journal of Cost Management* (Spring 1991): 35–39.

O'Guin, Michael. "Focus the Factory with Activity-Based Costing," *Managing Accounting* (February 1990): 36–41.

Ray, Manash R., and Theodore W. Schlie. "Activity-Based Management of Innovation and R&D Operations," *Journal of Cost Management* (Winter 1993): 16–22.

Roth, Harold, and Linda T. Sims. "Costing for Warehousing and Distribution," *Management Accounting* (August 1991): 42–45.

Schiff, Jonathan B., and Allen I. Schiff. "High-Tech Cost Accounting for the F-16," *Management Accounting* (September 1988): 43–48.

Shank, John K., and Vijay Govindarajan. "Transaction-Based Costing for the Complex Product Line: A Field Study," *Journal of Cost Management* (Summer 1988): 31–38.

Smith, Keith V., and Mark P. Leskan. "A Manufacturing Case Study on Activity-Based Costing," *Journal of Cost Management* (Summer 1991): 45–54.

Stuchfield, Nicolas, and Bruce W. Weber. "Modeling the profitability of customer relationships: Development and impact of Barclays de Zoete Wedd's BEATRICE," *Journal of Management Information Systems: JMIS* (Fall 1992): 53–76.

Turk, William T. "Management Accounting Revitalized: The Harley-Davidson Experience," *Journal of Cost Management* (Winter 1990): 28–39.

The Rise of Activity-Based Costing—Part 4: What Do Activity-Based Cost Systems Look Like?

ROBIN COOPER

Professor of Management, Claremont Graduate School
Peter F. Drucker Graduate Management Center, Claremont, California

Activity-based costing is an exciting approach to product costing. It provides cost system designers with new ways to cost products, focus managerial attention, and modify behavior. This article, part four in a series, explains how activity-based cost systems take advantage of the two-stage cost tracing procedure. It then describes five activity-based cost systems that demonstrate the range of design alternatives available. The first two systems are quite simple and use only a few cost drivers. The third system uses seven cost drivers, and the final two systems utilize many more.

This article is the fourth part of a series on activity-based costing and describes the activity-based cost systems implemented by five different companies. The first two systems are simple, the next somewhat more complex, and the final two quite complex. The aim of this article is to describe the range of design alternatives available for activity-based cost systems and to explore some practical design issues.

To help put this article in perspective, a look back at the first three parts of this series may be in order. Part one of the series[1] introduced the concept of activity-based costing. It demonstrated that if the product mix produced in a facility is diverse, an activity-based cost system will report more accurate product costs than a traditional volume-based cost system.

Part two of the series[2] continued the discussion of activity-based costing. It pointed out that firms that face intense competition and have both high product diversity and low measurement costs are best suited to take advantage of the increased accuracy offered by an activity-based costing system.

Part three[3] discussed the factors that should be considered when designing an activity-based cost system. In particular, it explored how many cost drivers should be used to trace the cost of resources consumed to the products produced in addition to what types of cost drivers to use.

TWO CLASSES OF COST DRIVERS

Activity-based cost systems achieve their improved accuracy over traditional volume-based cost systems by using two different classes of cost drivers. The underlying assumption for the first class of cost driver—those related to the volume of production—is that resources are consumed in direct proportion to the number of units produced. The underlying assumption for the second class of cost drivers—those unrelated to the volume of production—is that no direct relationship exists between resources consumed and the number of units produced.

Given the increased attention that activity-based cost systems have recently been attracting,[4] a natural question to ask is, "What do activity-based systems look like?" While it is still too soon to be certain (since only a few activity-based systems have been documented) they all appear to rely on a two-

FIGURE 1

Activity-Based Cost Systems as a Two Stage Allocation Procedure

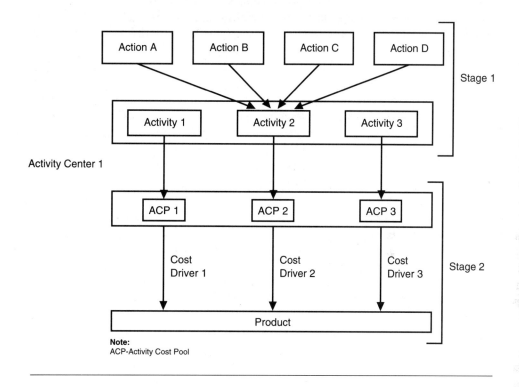

Note:
ACP-Activity Cost Pool

stage allocation procedure that indirectly traces the costs of resources consumed to products.[5] This procedure can be illustrated by a simple diagram (see Figure 1).

FIVE DESIGN CHOICES

In an activity-based cost system, five design choices have to be made:

1. Aggregating actions into activities,
2. Reporting the cost of activities,
3. Selecting the first-stage allocation bases,
4. Identifying the activity centers, and
5. Selecting second-stage cost drivers.

To reduce the cost of measurement, the level of aggregation of actions into activities has to be determined. For example, every time a machine is set up, new tools have to be drawn from the tool room, inserted, and qualified. The feeds and speeds of the machine must be altered, parts moved from inventory storage to the shop floor, the first part has to be inspected, the batch scheduled, and so on.

Aggregation. Aggregation, the first design choice, is necessary because tracing the consumption of resources by each action to the products would be prohibitively expensive. Treating collections of actions as activities removes the need to measure and track the performance of individual actions. For example, all of the actions associated with setups can be treated as the activity "setup."

Identifying activities is important because the costs of resources consumed by each activity are traced to products (in the second stage) using a single cost driver. As more actions are aggregated into an activity, the ability of this single cost driver to accurately trace the consumption of resources by actions—and therefore products—decreases.

For example, if the actions "material movement" and "setup" are treated as a single activity and traced to products using the cost driver "setup hours," the system assumes that the distance moved is directly proportional to the duration of the setup. On the other hand, if the driver "number of setups" is used, the system assumes that the distance moved is the same for each setup.

If, instead, two distinct activities—"setup" and "material movement"—are created and two separate drivers—for example, "setup hours" and "distance moved"—are used to trace the cost of these actions to the products, the activity-based system does not assume any relationship between setup duration and distance moved. This two-activity system can therefore report more accurate product costs than its one-activity counterpart. Its cost of measurement will be higher, however, because two sets of measurements must be made per product (setup hours consumed and distance moved) instead of only one (e.g., setup hours consumed).[6]

REPORTING THE COST OF ACTIVITIES

Once the activities have been selected, how to report the resources consumed by those activities can be determined. The second design choice, then, is the level of aggregation in reporting the resources consumed by each activity.

For example, the cost of the resources consumed by the activity "setup" can be reported separately or collectively. It is therefore possible to aggregate actions into activities but report the cost of those actions separately. Reported product costs are not affected by this design choice—only the level of reporting detail. For example, the system might report "setup" costs for product A of $6 or, alternatively, a "machine setup" cost of $4 and "material movement" cost of $2.

SELECTING THE FIRST-STAGE ALLOCATION BASES

The third design choice is the way the cost system traces the cost of resources consumed by an activity to the different kinds of activities. The costs of each kind of activity are traced to separate cost pools. Each activity cost pool contains the total costs of performing that kind of activity on all of the products.

For example, the activity "setup" might be performed on two different classes of machine. One class might require longer and more complex setups than the other. The cost system can ignore the differences between the two machine classes and identify only one kind of setup, or it can differentiate between the two types of machine and identify two kinds of setup. If two different kinds of setup are identified, the system designer has to choose how to trace the costs consumed by the activity "setup" to the two different machine classes.

The resources consumed in setting up the two machine classes can be measured directly or estimated indirectly. If they are measured directly, then the cost system (disregarding measurement error) will not introduce any distortion into reported product costs. If they are indirectly estimated, then distortion can be introduced by the estimation process.

For example, if setup costs are traced to the two types of machine classes using the allocation base "number of setup hours," then the cost system assumes that each machine class consumes the same quantity of resources per setup hour. For the machine class that consumes more resources per setup hour, reported setup costs will be too low. In contrast, the allocation base "number of setups" assumes that all setups consume the same quantity of resources irrespective of duration and machine class. In this system, the machine class that takes longer to set up will be undercosted. Thus, the level and nature of the distortion introduced depends on the allocation base used for indirect estimation in the first stage.

IDENTIFYING THE ACTIVITY CENTERS

The fourth design choice is to identify the activity centers. An activity center is a segment of the production process for which management wants to report the cost of the activities performed separately. For example, the receiving department might be treated as the activity center "receiving." The product costs reported by the system are not affected by this design choice—only the way in which they are reported. For example, the system might report a total cost of $50 or, alternatively, a cost of $30 for manufacturing and $20 for receiving. Reporting the cost of activities by activity center allows management to manage the activities better.

SELECTING SECOND-STAGE COST DRIVERS

Once the cost of the resources consumed by the activities performed in each activity center have been traced to the activity cost pools, the second-stage allocation bases or cost drivers can be selected. This is the final design choice.

For the activity "setup," the cost drivers "number of setup hours" or "number of setups" might be considered. The driver "number of setups" assumes that each setup consumes the same amount of resources, irrespective of the product being set up, while the driver "number of setup hours" assumes that the consumption of resources varies by product, depending on the time it takes to set up the machines. Again, the choice of cost driver of second-stage allocation bases determines the level of distortion introduced into reported product costs.

ADVANTAGE OF TWO-STAGE ALLOCATIONS

The advantage of the two-stage procedure over a single-stage procedure is that different measures of resource consumption can be used at each stage. For example, the driver "number of setup hours" can be used in the first stage and the driver "number of setups" in the second stage. Having two stages is frequently beneficial, because the information that is available about the consumption of resources by center is often different from that available by product.

For example, setup personnel might log their time spent in each center but not on each product. Using the allocation bases "number of setup hours" in the first stage allows the system to capture some of the differences in resource consumption by center even though this information is not available at the product level.

TWO SIMPLE ACTIVITY-BASED COST SYSTEMS

The Tektronix Portable Instruments Division (PID)[7] produces portable electronic oscilloscopes. The division recently implemented just-in-time production, total quality control, and people involvement in direct reaction to the entry of Japanese companies in the U.S. oscilloscope market.

These changes, coupled with a significant decrease in the direct labor content of the division's products over the last few years, has helped make PID's existing cost accounting system obsolete. In particular, the existing system required too many direct labor and work-in-process inventory measurements.

FIGURE 2

The Activity-Based Cost System at Tektronix: Portable Instruments Division

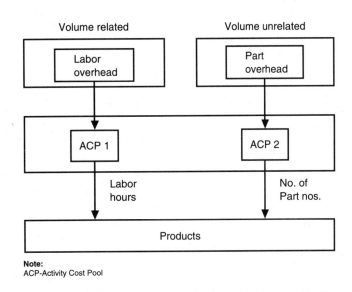

Note:
ACP-Activity Cost Pool

When redesigning their cost system, PID management increased the number of cost drivers from one—"direct labor hours"—to two—"direct labor hours" and "number of part numbers."[8] The new activity-based cost system is shown in Figure 2. It identifies only two activities: those related to direct labor operations and those related to the management of part numbers. The system aggregated many actions into these two activities.

Because the system identifies only two activities, it has only two cost pools per activity center, or one per activity. The costs of the resources consumed by the two activities are traced directly through the general ledger system into the cost pools. The company manufactures product lines primarily using cellular technology and treats each cell as an activity center.

Costs traced by cost driver. Approximately the same total costs are traced through each cost driver. The costs traced by the cost driver "number of part numbers" include:

1. Costs due to the value of parts,
2. Costs due to the absolute number of parts,
3. Costs due to the maintenance and handling of each different part number, and
4. Costs due to the use of each other part number.

211

EXHIBIT 1

Computing the Cost Per Part Number for the Cost Driver "Number of Part Numbers"

Total costs traced via cost driver	$60,000
Total number of different part numbers	÷ 100
Annual cost per part number	$ 600
Part A (high-usage)—volume used in year	1,000
Reported cost per unit	$ 0.60
Part B (low-usage)—volume used in year	10
Reported cost per unit	$ 60

The most significant of these costs are the costs associated with maintaining and handling each different part number. These costs include planning, scheduling, negotiating with vendors, purchasing, receiving, handling, delivering, and storing each part number. In general, as the number of different parts used in a facility increases, so does the number of these activities that have to be performed.

To trace the costs of activities related to part numbers to the products, management selected the cost driver "number of part numbers." This driver is used to trace a flat charge to each part number in a product, which depends on the volume of usage of that part. This flat charge is calculated in two steps. First, the total cost of all part-number-related activities is identified, and then the total cost is divided by the number of different part numbers to give a flat charge per part number. This charge, in turn, is divided by the volume of usage of each part to give a flat charge per part. Under this scheme, high-usage parts have a low cost per part, while low-usage parts have a high cost per part. (See Exhibit 1 for an example of how this cost driver is calculated).

Management selected this driver to reduce the number of low-volume parts used in the facility. Management believed its use would increase the product designers' awareness of the costs associated with part-number proliferation and in particular the high cost associated with designing products that relied heavily on low-usage parts. In addition, management believed that this awareness would provide incentives to the engineers to design products that contained more high-usage parts and fewer low-usage parts. Finally, management felt that although reducing the number of part numbers would not reduce overhead costs immediately or in direct proportion to the reduction of part numbers, it would eventually result in real cost savings.

The search for simplicity. The activity-based cost system at Tektronix was kept relatively simple because management considered reducing the number of part numbers to be vital.

Management believed that having only two cost drivers was beneficial because it allowed the cost system to send clear messages to the designers about what was strategically important—the reduction in the number of different part numbers used at the facility. Management was concerned that if multiple drivers were used, the pressure to achieve this strategic goal would be diluted or lost. Given this orientation, management was less concerned about the accuracy of the cost system than they were with the behavior it induced.

SIEMENS ELECTRIC MOTOR WORKS

Siemens Electric Motor Works (EMW)[9] produces low-wattage alternating current electric motors. It had recently implemented a new strategy of selling low volumes of customized motors. This strategy was designed to offset the lower labor rates of the Eastern Bloc countries with whom EMW competed. This new strategy requires EMW to manufacture products in lots that vary in size from one to over 100 units.

Previously, EMW had manufactured only standard motors in large lots. This change in strategy and hence manufacturing policy had made its existing cost accounting system obsolete. In particular, its existing cost system traced insufficient costs to the small lots and excessive costs to the large ones.

The firm's existing cost system used four cost drivers: (1) "material dollars," (2) "direct labor hours," (3) "machine hours," and (4) "reported cost to date." Due to its volume-based orientation, this system traced approximately 100 times as much overhead to lots containing 100 motors as it did to lots containing only one motor. This system treated each of the firm's 600 machine types as a separate production cost center.[10]

A special study by the company showed that about 7 percent of total costs were related to activities associated with shop floor orders and to the management of the production of the special components required by custom motors. At least part of each of the following departments' costs were considered driven by these activities:

- Costs Related to Order Processing
  - Billing
  - Order receiving
  - Product costing and bidding
  - Shipping
- Costs related to special components
  - Inventory handling
  - Product costing and bidding
  - Product development

FIGURE 3

The Activity-Based Cost System at Siemens Electric Motor Works

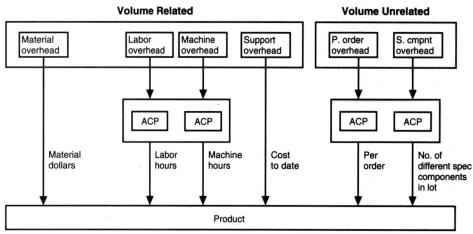

Notes: ACP-Activity Cost Pool
There are 600 manufacturing centers

—Purchasing
—Receiving
—Scheduling and production control
—Technical examination of incoming orders

Order-related costs were found to be approximately the same for each lot, regardless of its size. Special component costs, on the other hand, were found to be dependent on the number of different special components used by the motor in the lot.

Additional cost drivers for greater accuracy. To report more accurate product costs, management implemented a new cost system that, in addition to the original four cost drivers, used two new ones: "number of shop floor orders" and "number of different special components used per lot."

This new cost system adopted by EMW is shown in Figure 3. The driver "number of shop floor orders" charges a flat fee for each order, and the driver "number of special components" charges a flat fee per different special component. Thus a lot of one motor that contains N special components is charged the same order and special component overhead as a lot of 10 motors, where each motor contains N special components.

EXHIBIT 2

Computing the Cost Per Motor Using the Cost Drivers "Number of Shop Floor Orders" and "Number of Special Components" for a Production Lot Containing One Custom Motor

Cost of base motor*		$250	
Cost of special components*		50	
Total*			$300
Special components overhead	$ 40		
Order processing overhead	60		
Total lot related costs		100	
Number in lot		× 1	
Cost per unit			$100
Total cost			$400

* Includes direct material, direct labor, material overhead, production overhead, and support-related overhead costs.

The advantage of this new cost system is that it traces costs in ways that better approximate their consumption by products. Exhibit 2 shows the reported product cost for a lot of one motor, and Exhibit 3 the reported unit cost of the same motor if it were manufactured in a lot containing 100 units. EMW's activity-based cost system reports high costs for the low-volume motors and relatively low costs for the high-volume motors. In contrast, the traditional system would have reported unit costs of about $310, irrespective of the lot size.

The activity-based cost system at EMW was also kept simple, because management felt that the two additional drivers corrected enough of the distortion in the existing system for their current needs. Management had experimented with

EXHIBIT 3

Computing the Cost Per Motor Using the Cost Drivers "Number of Shop Floor Orders" and "Number of Special Components" for a Production Lot Containing 100 Custom Motors

Cost of base motor*		$250	
Cost of special components*		50	
Total*			$300
Special components overhead	$ 40		
Order processing overhead	60		
Total lot related costs		100	
Number in lot		÷100	
Cost per unit			1
Total cost			$301

* Includes direct material, direct labor, material overhead, production overhead, and support-related overhead costs.

additional cost drivers, but found that they had little effect on reported product costs. This suggests that the products manufactured in the facility are sufficiently similar enough that the simple activity-based cost system can capture most of the effects of product diversity.

A MEDIUM COMPLEX ACTIVITY-BASED COST SYSTEM

John Deere Components Works (JDCW)[11] produces screw machine parts. It had recently ceased to be a captive supplier to its parent, John Deere, and was now competing for business on the outside.

The manufacturing facility was designed to produce high-volume parts. Its existing cost system was quite sophisticated, and used three volume-related drivers to trace costs to products:

- Direct labor hours,
- Machine hours, and
- Material dollars.

Due to its volume-based orientation, this system systematically undercosted low-volume and overcosted high-volume production products. This distortion became apparent when the firm bid on several hundred parts and won only 20 percent of them, many of which were low-volume parts.

Reacting to the outcome of these failed bids, management designed a new cost system. The new system contained the original three volume-related drivers and four drivers that were not related to volume:

- "Setup hours,"
- "Number of production orders,"
- "Part numbers," and
- "Number of production loads."

General and administrative costs were allocated using the value added in production. This cost system is shown in Figure 4.

The cost driver "setup hours" was used to allocate setup-related costs to the products. The cost driver "number of production orders" is identical to the equivalent driver used at EMW. At JDCW, however, it is used to trace only production-order related costs to products.

The driver "part numbers" creates a constant charge for each part number. This charge includes the cost of establishing and maintaining records and system documentation plus a share of salaries in process engineering, industrial engineering, supervision, and materials control. The principle behind this driver is identical to the one behind the "number of part numbers" driver in PID's system.

FIGURE 4

The Activity-Based Cost System at John Deere Component Works

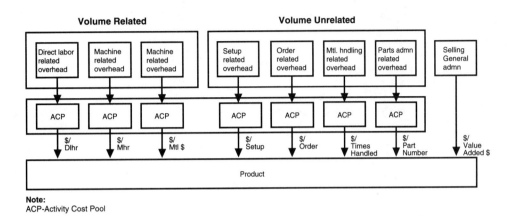

Note:
ACP-Activity Cost Pool

The driver "number of loads" is used to allocate the cost of material handling. These costs include moving barstock to the machines, moving the parts to the next operation, inspecting the parts, and a share of defective material costs. The computation of the driver "number of loads" shows an interesting twist on the relationship between volume-related and unrelated cost drivers. The firm moves products in loads of a maximum size. Consequently, as the lot size increases, the number of lots that have to be moved also increases, but in discrete steps. The cost driver "number of loads" is therefore only partially proportional to lot size. The computation of the cost driver "number of loads" was designed to handle this semi-proportionality (See Exhibit 4).

The change from the traditional cost accounting system to an activity-based cost system had a pronounced effect on reported product costs. The reported overhead costs of low-volume products approximately doubled, and the overhead cost of high volume products decreased by about 10 percent. The costs reported by the activity-based system better fit management's intuitions about product costs. This "better fit" increased management's confidence that the new system was reporting more accurate product costs.

TWO COMPLEX ACTIVITY-BASED COST SYSTEMS

Hewlett-Packard's Roseville Networks Division (RND)[12] produces electronic circuit boards that allow computers to communicate with other computers and peripheral devices.

EXHIBIT 4

Computation of "Numbers of Loads" for a Particular Product

1. Part weight $\times$ annual volume = weight/run
   runs/year for that part
2. Weight/run = loads/run;
   Pounds/load
3. Loads/run + 0.5 (then round to nearest integer)
   = Corrected loads per run
4. Corrected loads per run $\times$ runs per year $\times$ 2
   = Number loads/year moved for that part

Notes:
The correction factor of 0.5 in step 3 adjusts for partial loads. The correction factor of 2 in step 4 recognizes that loads are moved *to* and *from* machines.

The rapid change of technology in the last few years has reduced the life expectancy of RND's products dramatically while simultaneously increasing the number of products produced. In recent years, the company has introduced a new product every month. This rapid rate of product introduction requires an improved understanding of the economics of product design. The existing cost system was not designed to provide the required cost/design insights and consequently became obsolete.

The design engineers—reacting to the obsolescence of the existing system—designed their own private cost system and used the product costs it reported to make design decisions. When the accounting department learned about this private system, they used it as the basis for their new activity-based cost system. Over the next few years, management and engineering continuously added new cost drivers to the system as their understanding of the economics of design improved. By mid-1988, the system used approximately nine drivers:

- "Number of axial insertions,"
- "Number of radial insertions,"
- "Number of DIP insertions,"
- "Number of test hours,"
- "Number of boards,"
- "Number of solder joints,"
- "Number of parts,"
- "Number of manual insertions," and
- "Number of slots."

Additional drivers were added as management and the engineers became aware that the cost system was not adequate for their needs.

For example, one designer designed a product that required many axial but few DIP insertions. The cost system suggested that this product was expensive to manufacture. The engineer's intuition, however, was that the product was actually inexpensive to manufacture. A subsequent study showed that axial insertions were about one third the cost of DIP insertions. The cost system was therefore modified to differentiate between the two types of insertion. The complexity of the activity-based cost system thus reflects the complexity of the behavior it was designed to modify: the design of products.

Interestingly, until the latest round of changes, the system relied solely on volume-related drivers such as the number of axial insertions and the number of radial insertions. The choice of drivers was driven by economics of production. The costs unrelated to volume were relatively low, and were not as important in the other firms discussed in this article.

In mid-1988, however, the engineers proposed that a "slot charge" driver be established for DIP insertion.[13] The ability to automatically insert components is constrained by the slot capacity of the machines. In fact, given the current product mix, some automatically insertable components were being manually inserted. To reflect this capacity constraint, the engineers wanted to design a cost system that created an incentive to decrease the number of automatically insertable components used at the facility. This "slot charge" driver takes the total cost associated with slots and divides them by the number of slots to give a per slot "rent." This rent is then divided by the volume of each part used to give a per part cost. It is therefore very similar to the cost driver "number of part numbers" in Tektronix PID described earlier. At RND, however, the driver is used to trace only the costs related to insertion.

SCHRADER BELLOWS

Schrader Bellows (SB)[14] produces pneumatic products. The number of products manufactured at one of its facilities had proliferated over time. Although sales amounted to only $20 million, this facility produced over 2,700 different products from over 20,000 distinct components. These components were manufactured in lots of varying sizes, from under 100 to over 1,000.

The facility's existing cost system traced overhead to products using direct labor hours. It contained five manufacturing cost centers. Support-related overhead accounted for approximately 50 percent of all overhead and 25 percent of total cost. Management decided to retain the existing system for manufacturing overhead costs but to develop an activity-based cost system for support costs.

The support functions were treated as eight separate activity centers:

- Raw material inventory,
- Work-in-process inventory,

- Finished goods inventory,
- Production control,
- Purchasing,
- Setup,
- Quality control, and
- Manufacturing engineering.

The activity-based cost system designed for this facility contained the following cost drivers:

- Setup hours,
- Number of setups,
- Average dollar value of work-in-process,
- Number of direct labor reports,
- Sales dollars,
- Sales units,
- Direct labor hours,
- Cost of goods sold,
- Number of incoming shipments—purchased parts,
- Number of incoming shipments—raw material,
- Number of outgoing shipments,
- Number of parts purchased,
- Number of parts produced,
- Number of customer orders,
- Number of purchase orders cut,
- Number of supplies orders, and
- Number of purchase received.

The costs of the different activities performed in each center were traced to the cost pools using the work effort required to perform them. These costs were then traced to the products using the number of transactions or effort required to perform the activity on each product.

For example, the cost of the activities performed in the raw material inventory department were traced to cost pools using the percentage of work load performed by the people in that department. The costs were traced from the cost pools to the products by using the number of transactions generated by each activity. For example, the number of incoming purchased parts shipments was traced using the number of shipments. The complete structure of the activity-based cost system for this department is shown in Figure 5.

FIGURE 5

The Activity-Based Cost Systems for the Raw Material Department at Schrader Bellows

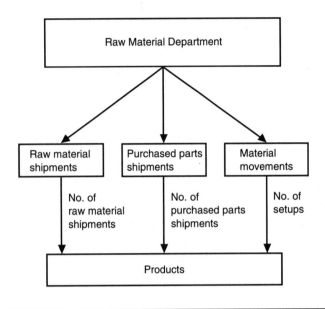

The activity-based cost system reported product costs that were significantly different from those reported by the traditional system. The overhead traced to products manufactured in low volumes was up to ten times the amount previously reported. The activity-based system at SB is complex, in part because the product mix is diverse. The facility produces several major product lines, each of which contains hundreds of very different products. This diversity requires a large number of drivers to capture accurately the economics of production.

CONCLUSION

The objective of this four-part series was to introduce and explore the concept of activity-based costing. Part one of the series illustrated the need for activity-based cost systems by demonstrating that traditional, volume-based cost systems can report seriously distorted product costs when the products manufactured are diverse. In particular, it demonstrated the effect of size and volume diversity on the accuracy of reported product costs. In addition, Part one demonstrated that, by contrast, activity-based cost systems can remove or reduce the distortion caused by product diversity.

Part two explained which firms were most likely to benefit from the additional accuracy provided by activity-based cost systems. It identified the factors that support implementing an activity-based cost system as the following:

- Low cost of measurement for the additional data required by the activity-based cost system;
- High levels of competition; and
- A very diverse product mix.

Part three explored the factors that affect the choice of the number of cost drivers to use and what kind of cost drivers to use to achieve a desired level of accuracy.

Part three identified several factors that affect the number of drivers required, including:

- The desired level of accuracy of reported product costs,
- The degree of product diversity,
- The relative cost of different activities,
- The degree of volume diversity, and
- The use of imperfectly correlated cost drivers.

The factors affecting what kind of cost drivers to use include:

- The cost of measuring the quantities associated with each driver,
- The correlation of the selected driver to the actual consumption of the activity by the products, and
- The behavior induced by the use of a cost driver.

One major finding in Part three was that, in most environments, volume diversity is likely to be the dominant source of distortion in reported product costs.

This article, the fourth part of the series, explains how activity-based cost systems take advantage of the two-stage cost tracing procedure. It then described five activity-based cost systems that were selected to demonstrate the range of design alternatives available. The first two systems discussed were very simple and had only a few cost drivers. The third system used seven cost drivers, and the last two utilized even more.

Competitive pressures. All of the activity-based cost systems described in this article were introduced by firms that faced intense competitive pressure. PID was reacting to the entry of the Japanese companies to their marketplace, EMW to the low labor rates of the Eastern Bloc, JDCW reacted to ceasing to be a captive supplier, SB to a loss in profitability, and RND to changing technology.

The complexity of the design of activity-based cost systems appears to be driven by a multitude of factors, including the objectives that management has in mind when designing the cost system. If a single objective dominates, as in the case of PID, then only a few cost drivers may be required to achieve the desired objective. As the design objectives, however, become more complex, as they did at RND, then multiple drivers may be required.

In addition, the complexity of a system appears to be driven by the diversity of the product mix. EMW, whose product mix has relatively low product diversity, requires only a few cost drivers to achieve the desired level of accuracy; RND and SB, on the other hand, which have high product diversity, require many drivers.

Cost drivers that adjust for volume diversity. Every activity-based cost system described in this article contained at least one cost driver designed to adjust for volume diversity. What is particularly interesting is the way the drivers were designed to handle different kinds of volume diversity. In PID, the driver adjusted for the volume diversity allocated with the volume of parts used in the facility. It was used to trace 50 percent of all overhead costs to products. In RND, a similar driver was used, but it traced only a small portion of overhead. In the other companies, several volume-diversity drivers were used. These adjusted for activities that are performed simultaneously on multiple product units (such as "cutting production orders" and "setting up machines"). The "number of loads" driver utilized at JDCW was interesting because it demonstrated how cost drivers can be designed to handle activities that are only partly proportional to the size of the batch.[15]

Activity-based costing is a relatively new concept: The oldest known system has been in use for only a few years. Despite the newness of these systems and their rarity, they have recently attracted a lot of attention. Activity-based costing is an exciting approach to product costing that provides cost system designers with new ways to cost products, focus managerial attention, and modify behavior.

Notes

1. See R. Cooper, "The Rise of Activity-Based Costing — Part One: What Is an Activity-Based Cost System?" *Journal of Cost Management* (Summer 1988): 45–54.

2. See R. Cooper, "The Rise of Activity-Based Costing — Part Two: When Do I Need an Activity-Based Cost System?" *Journal of Cost Management* (Fall 1988): 41–48.

3. See R. Cooper, "The Rise of Activity-Based Costing — Part Three: How Many Cost Drivers Do You Need, and How Do You Select Them?" *Journal of Cost Management* (Winter 1989): 34–46.

4. For example, see R. Cooper and R.S. Kaplan, "Measure Costs Right: Make the Right Decisions," *Harvard Business Review* (September–October 1988): 96–103.

5. For a description of the two-stage cost-tracing procedure, see R. Cooper, "The Two-Stage Procedure in Cost Accounting—Part One," *Journal of Cost Management* (Summer 1987): 43–51, and "The Two-Stage Procedure in Cost Accounting—Part Two," *Journal of Cost Management* (Fall 1987): 39–45.

6. The trade-off between the accuracy of the cost system and the cost of measurement is discussed in part two of this series.

7. Tektronix: Portable Instruments Division, *Harvard Business School Case Series 9-188-142, 143, 144.*

8. In addition, the firm discontinued measuring direct labor hours and now uses frozen standard direct labor hours to cost it's products.

9. Siemens: Electric Motor Works, *Harvard Business School Case Series 9-189-089, 190.*

10. This traditional cost system is as sophisticated as any system that this author has ever seen.

11. John Deere Component Works, *Harvard Business School Case Series 9-187-107, 108.*

12. Hewlett-Packard: Roseville Network Division, *Harvard Business School Case Series, N9-198-117.*

13. Each slot on an inserter allows a different component to be inserted. The number of slots, therefore, represents the capacity of the machine to insert different components without intervention.

14. Schrader Bellows, *Harvard Business School Case Series 9-186-272.*

15. This predominant use of cost drivers that adjust for volume diversity is in keeping with the theoretical finding of Part three of this series.

Cost Management in Continuous Process Environments

JAMES M. REEVE

Professor of Accounting, University of Tennessee—Knoxville, Knoxville, Tennessee

INTRODUCTION

The manufacturing environment of continuous and batch material processors (e.g., chemical, metal, food, and paper processors) differs significantly from the manufacturing environment of discrete part fabrication and assembly. Although many case studies and articles on cost management have described the problems and issues that discrete part and assembly manufacturers face,[1] a natural question is whether the cost management principles used in discrete part environments also apply to processing companies: That is, do continuous and batch material processors require different cost management principles?

To answer that question, this chapter outlines the cost management problems that continuous and batch material processors face and provides case studies to illustrate those problems. Specifically, the chapter discusses the following topics for continuous and batch material processors:

- Activity-based costing (ABC);
- Real-time cost management;
- Equipment (capital) costing;
- Constraint management; and
- Profit planning.

ACTIVITY-BASED COSTING

Most discrete part environments can be characterized as a *convergent* process. As the tree diagram in Exhibit C3.1 shows, part numbers are fabricated, finished, inspected, and assembled into subassemblies, which are themselves assembled into a completed unit.

In convergent processes, diversity at the component level requires that activities be tracked at this level. Therefore, convergent processes require extensive in-plant coordination, inspection, balancing, and change activities. Components must arrive at the right location, in the right quantities, at the right time, and with the right quality.

For this coordinated effort to occur, overhead activities such as procurement, material management, engineering support, quality control, and production control must be performed. In many convergent facilities, these overhead costs can become as large as direct material costs. It is not surprising, therefore, that some of the first applications of ABC occurred in discrete part environments. Activity-based cost drivers trace activities to component and subassemblies because of the significant resources necessary to support diversity and complexity in the manufacture of parts.

Continuous and batch material processing, by contrast, is a *divergent* process. Common raw material streams are routed through a common process. This stream of material is eventually split into many different end products, as shown

EXHIBIT C3.1

Comparison of Convergent and Divergent Processes

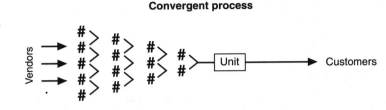

Convergent process

Characteristics:
- High in-plant coordination, inspection, balancing, and change activities
- Assembly-intensive
- Engineering-intensive
- Costs attach to part numbers through use of routings

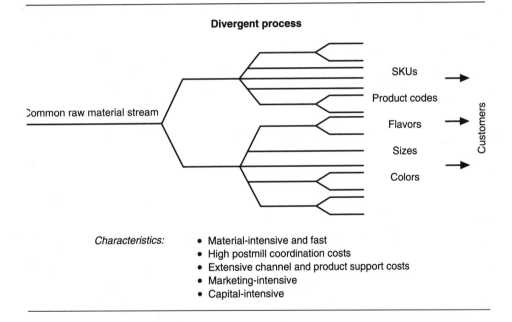

Divergent process

Characteristics:
- Material-intensive and fast
- High postmill coordination costs
- Extensive channel and product support costs
- Marketing-intensive
- Capital-intensive

at the bottom of Exhibit C3.1. The end products differ from the original raw material stream because of slight differences in how they are processed or because of the introduction of *minors* (i.e., additives), such as color. For example, end products for an textile mill may initially appear identical. In reality, however, thousands of different products can be produced because of such differences as thread count, color, and grade. Similarly, paper products can differ in terms of size, color, coatings, or packaging. The important point is that with continuous and batch material processors, the source of diversity and complexity

227

occurs toward the *customer end* of the value chain, while with discrete part manufacturers, diversity and diversity occur toward the *vendor side* of the value chain. (Note that some discrete part assembly manufacturers can have many part-number coordination activities and also a high end-product diversity if, for example, they make many custom-assembled products.)

Convergent vs. Divergent Processes

These fundamental differences between convergent and divergent processes cause problems among continuous processors about accepting ABC systems, because the examples used in explaining ABC systems do not apply to continuous processors. For example, many (though not all) product changeovers are done by continuous processors while the machine is running (i.e., "on the fly"). Therefore, product changeover activities tend to be less important in continuous process environments than they are in discrete part environments. Similarly, an ingredient card in a continuous process environment is much less complex than a discrete part manufacturer's bill of materials. Therefore, the overhead resources that must be devoted to the procurement and management of raw materials are comparatively small in a continuous process environment compared with the overhead resources devoted to procuring and managing raw materials in a discrete parts manufacturing environment. Consequently (unlike in a discrete part manufacturing environment, where there are often thousands of components), continuous processors have less need to capture activity and driver relationships for these activities.

The following section provides a framework for analyzing activities in a continuous process environment and discusses the use of ABC given this framework.

AN ACTIVITY DESIGN FRAMEWORK

Every activity has two important attributes: a cost object level and a frequency of occurrence at that level. Exhibit C3.2 depicts the activity design framework used for the examples in this chapter. The two major cost object hierarchies are:

1. The product hierarchy; and
2. The customer hierarchy.[2]

The usual two-stage allocation structure in ABC involves the assignment of resources to activities, then the assignment of activities to products. In the model used in this chapter, the second-stage tracing of activities should be to different product or customer levels within a hierarchy.

Within both hierarchies, the various cost attachment points are in increasing levels of aggregation from bottom to top. The lowest level of cost attachment can be added into higher levels due to logical construction. The third cost object is

EXHIBIT C3.2
Activity Design Framework

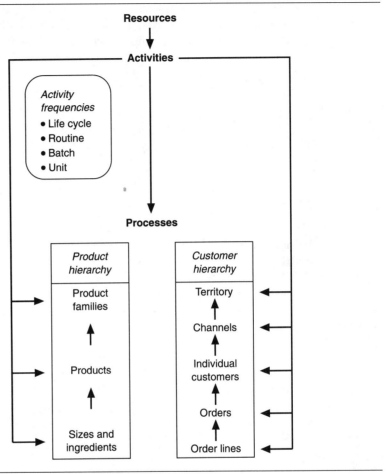

the process. Many activities in the continuous and batch material processor environment support processes (e.g., maintenance and process engineering) rather than products or customers.

Product Hierarchy

For the product hierarchy, the lowest level of cost attachment is the ingredient (or part number for convergent manufacturers). In discrete part manufacturing, the part number is an important cost attachment point, because many important activities relate to the management of part-number diversity. In a continuous and batch material processor environment, the ingredients listed on the formula card can be used as cost attachment points, but this occurs relatively infrequently. When ingredients are used as cost attachment points, it is usually for the activities of managing the vendor end of the value chain, such as raw material procurement, quality, movement, storage, and environmental assurance.

Overhead costs that are attached to ingredients through activities are rolled up into the final products themselves. The products form a second level of cost attachment. Activities attached at this level are related to managing the end products themselves. Examples include most activities at the customer end of the value chain.

Activity Frequencies

Activities can be associated with ingredients and products based on how frequently the activity occurs. (Frequency is an attribute of an activity. All activities have a frequency of occurrence—e.g., unit, batch, routine, life-cycle frequencies.) Activities can either be traced directly to the ingredient or product level, or they can be associated with the level on the basis of an activity driver that is related to the frequency of activity occurrence. Exhibit C3.3 provides a table that illustrates activities for the different product-level and activity-frequency combinations.

Frequency types are defined as unit, batch, routine, and product life cycle. *Batch activities* are those activities that are performed on a batch of products and activities that occur every time that a batch is processed; *unit activities* are those activities that are performed on a unit of the product and that occur for every unit of manufactured product.[3] Unit and batch activities generally occur during the processing and movement of a product. *Routine activities*, on the other hand, occur periodically to support, for example, ingredients, products, product families, and customers. They are generally related to nonmanufacturing events. Routine activities do not benefit the object hierarchy level in future periods, so they should be expensed as they are incurred. Examples include ongoing activities to support either ingredients or products (e.g., safety, environmental, formulation change, and product testing activities). *Life cycle activities* are infrequent; they benefit the product (or ingredient) for future time periods. The most typical are related to research and development (R&D) activities. Life-cycle frequency activities should be capitalized and amortized over a product's expected life to reflect their longer-term benefits.

Direct tracing is appropriate for both routine and life cycle activities. If the activity cannot be directly traced to a product or ingredient for lack of measurement, surrogate drivers (e.g., number of formulation changes or number of returned items) can be used.

EXHIBIT C3.3

Illustrations of Activity Frequency and Product Hierarchy Level Combinations

Activity frequency \ Product hierarchy level	Ingredient	Product
Unit	Processing activities of ingredients (e.g., preparing a color)	Processing or packing activities of final product
Batch	Activities related to inspection and quality testing of incoming raw material batches	Cleanout and changeover activities of pack lines for completed product
Routine	Environmental control activities related to hazardous chemicals used in various formulations	Customer-return activity on defective shipments
Life cycle	Ingredient research and testing	Research, development, and testing of a new product formulation

To avoid confusion, the notions of hierarchy and frequency should be separated. Some illustrations in this regard are:

- An example of a product-level batch frequency activity in a continuous process environment is a changeover to a different product specification. The changeover activity is related to the subsequent product batch, not the volume in the batch. As a result, the activity is proportional to changeover frequency, not production frequency.
- An example of an ingredient-level batch activity is quality testing of incoming raw materials. Since both small and large batches of raw ingredients require quality testing, quality testing is simply proportional to the number of incoming batches.
- An example of a unit activity frequency is the processing of a volume of a product or an ingredient. These activities are performed on all units of volume equally, so the costs are expected to change proportionally with the

volume. The activities that are traced to the ingredients, regardless of frequency, are accumulated up to the product level, where additional activities are added to the end product. Therefore, ingredients roll up into end product codes independent of frequency. It is not the frequencies that form the hierarchy; instead, it is the nature of the products that form the hierarchy.

Aggregation Levels

The highest level of aggregation in the product hierarchy is the product-family level. These represent activities to support the product family. These activities include:

- Brand management;
- Advertising; and
- Merchandising (to name only a few).

Frequently, brand managers are responsible for product families for which a number of different products vary on the basis of minor consumer-desired functionalities (e.g., size, flavor, or color). Promotional and merchandising efforts generally support a complete product family, but not any one product in the family.

Activities that are traced to lower levels can be rolled up to higher levels of aggregation. This feature does not hold in the opposite direction. Activities traced at higher levels can only be allocated down using arbitrary, frequently volume-based, allocation techniques. For this reason, the system designer wishes to attach activities to the lowest level possible in a hierarchy.

To see how this process works, consider the following example. A company incurred significant safety-related activities (routine frequency) related to chemical hazards (ingredient level). The resource categories (budget line items) related to safety included:

- Training;
- Special handling and storage needs;
- Direct injury claims; and
- Indirect labor.

A review of safety-related activities revealed that they were related to particular chemicals used in only some product lines. As a result of this insight, the company determined that the safety-related activities should be traced to the dangerous ingredients. Therefore, products that used these ingredients would be required to bear the cost of the safety activities. These activities did not change with the volume: They were incurred simply because the hazardous chemical existed.

The company could take several courses of action. For example, if products could be reformulated to eliminate the hazardous chemicals, the need for safety-related activities would also be eliminated. Or, if only 5 percent of the company's product line used the dangerous chemicals, the company could isolate the use of hazardous chemicals in one location to achieve economies of scale in the consumption of safety-related activities. In fact, this strategy is the one that the company chose to execute. In many of the company's plants, product lines with the hazardous chemicals were eliminated, which meant that expensive overhead incurred because of the dangerous chemicals was eliminated.

System Design Errors

Within this conceptual approach (see Exhibit C3.2), two cost system design errors can be made. The first design flow occurs when there is a mismatch between the activity driver frequency and the activity frequency. This error usually occurs when volume-based drivers (e.g., number of equivalent units, number of cases, number of hours, or number of tons) are used to allocate batch and directly traced activities to products or ingredients. Cost distortions result under such circumstances. Therefore, a first consideration is to assess whether activities that do not vary according to volume (e.g., batch-level activities, routine activities, and life cycle activities) are allocated using volume-based drivers.

The second design flaw occurs when an activity is traced to the wrong level. This error frequently occurs when an ingredient-level activity is traced to the product level. When this error occurs, the ingredient-level distinctiveness is averaged across the complete product line. One company, for example, incurred significant environmental control costs (e.g., because reports had to be made to regulatory authorities) for a particular chemical used in part of the product line. The costs were related to specific chemicals, yet the existing cost system allocated these costs across all products. Only products that used the environmentally controlled chemicals should have borne the cost burden, which could be accomplished by tracing the costs of environmental activities at the ingredient level.

Customer Hierarchy

The customer hierarchy includes many of the activities that occur after a product is produced. The customer hierarchy recognizes the activities that must be performed to manage sales relationships within various channels—activities that involve many sales, general, and administrative (SG&A) functions. The purpose of aggregating activities with the customer hierarchy is to achieve a different subgrouping (or slice) of the cost data to reveal customer and channel profitability. Without this information, diversity in the consumption of activities in terms of customers or channels is obscured.

Examples of activities that are related to each of the levels in the customer hierarchy (see Exhibit C3.2):

- *Sales order lines:* production planning activities.
- *Sales orders:* order-taking activities.
- *Individual customers:* sales effort and merchandising activities.
- *Channels:* special activities to support a channel in terms of promotion, sales effort, or special service.
- *Territories:* sales office management, warehousing, and transportation.

For each of the levels, a system designer attempts to assign activities to the lowest possible level and then aggregate upwards. Like the product hierarchy, costs aggregate upward, but can be allocated downwards only arbitrarily.

The notion of routine and life cycle activity frequency introduced for the product hierarchy can also be applied to the customer hierarchy. For example, routine sales visits are an activity that is necessary to support a given customer. Therefore, their costs should be considered a period cost that is traced directly to the customer level. New customer development efforts, on the other hand, are a life cycle activity for a customer. Therefore, their costs should be amortized over the future period of the customer's expected business. In this way, the cost of establishing new business is appropriately spread over the expected life of the business.

By following these practices, a company can assess the profitability of particular territories, customer relationships, and channel relationships. The mere cost of a product does not reveal these insights. If all activities are traced on the product hierarchy, then the cost to serve particular customers is disguised. Suppose, for example, that one customer buys a particular product in small quantities, while another customer buys the same product in large quantities. The product hierarchy will capture the batch frequency activities of these two orders and average their effects. Only by capturing the cost of a product by orders can a company distinguish the different costs of serving different customers to assess profitability by customer.

Process Activities

ABC systems in the discrete part environment are product-oriented. Thus, in discussions of ABC, one often hears the statement that "activities consume resources, and products consume activities." Activities are attached to components based on the performance of discrete and measurable events (e.g., moves, setups, and machine operations). The focus on products as the source of activities does not describe the continuous process environment as well as it does the discrete part environment. Many mill-related activities are not the result of discrete events related to the manufacture of products, but instead a result of *process* conditions. Such process-related activities cannot be related to product strategy in any meaningful way.

Divergent processes are material-intensive, capital-intensive, and fast. This description implies that cost systems for continuous processors must focus on process variables (such as the cost of material waste, equipment utilization, and equipment support) to a much greater extent than cost systems for most discrete part environments do. For example, running off-grade product in a continuous processing environment for an hour will cause the loss of expensive equipment capacity and tons of material. Minimizing these events is important, because equipment costs can be extremely expensive (e.g., $200 million for a new paper machine and up to $1 billion for a new pulp mill). The cost of equipment unreliability (in the form of unscheduled downtime, speed losses, and off-grade production) is a critical source of waste for continuous processors. Equipment unreliability, however, may relate not to products, but to operating policies, such as capital replacement policies, preventive maintenance programs, machine operating procedures, and existing of standard operating procedures.

As another example, significant engineering and continuous improvement activities relate to improving process operating characteristics. These engineering activities are not directly traceable to products but are caused, instead, by process needs. The engineering change and product design support processes typically found in discrete part manufacturing are not nearly as prevalent in the continuous processor. The significant engineering effort is not product-related, but process-related. For example, a study to improve variation in the cross direction of a sheet of aluminum improves all products produced in a particular rolling mill. The activity relates to improving the rolling mill's process rather than to any particular product (except arbitrarily).

Continuous processors also expend significant resources in maintenance activities. These activities are not product-driven, but are driven by process variables such as machine speed and shutdown or start-up frequency. Process-oriented cost drivers (e.g., start-up or shutdown frequency) explain the incurrence of maintenance activities with no cost tracing to products. Instead, the objective is to identify cause and effect with an eye toward process improvement. In the example, reducing shutdown or start-up frequency should lead to improved expenditure toward maintenance activities and also improved capital performance.

A continuous processor is concerned about the cost of these process activities. The cost of equipment unreliability, in terms of excess inventory, schedule changes, and lost equipment time, is a critical contributor to the cost of waste. Material losses due to process upsets, which are independent of the product produced, are critical control conditions in continuous mills. The material losses may have less to do with the product being run than with temperature, raw material variation, or standard operating procedures. The cost system for a continuous processor must therefore expand on ABC product costing to provide insight about the cost of important process activities. The identification of the causes of process activities must be developed in this context.

ACTIVITY-BASED COST APPLICATIONS

As noted, ABC costing techniques have not yet been widely employed in continuous and batch material processor environments. This situation should not be interpreted as a lack of need. Indeed, a strong case can be made that activity-based approaches are needed as much in continuous process environments as in the discrete part world. However, the design of a cost system and its focus must differ in a continuous process environment.

ABC systems of continuous processors must be oriented more toward the customer side of the value chain—for example, toward downstream product changeovers, postmill logistics, and marketing activities. The high product variety typical of a continuous mill can lead to complexity in the logistics system and in the marketing- or sales-related costs that are incurred to support so many products. These costs often represent 50 percent of total cost, though they are frequently aggregated because they are often treated simply as period costs.

Inside a continuous process plant, there is a need to account for batch frequency cost drivers that occur near the end of the process. For example, continuous processors experience their greatest batch diversity and switch-over costs near the end of a process; that is, commonality turns into diversity near the process finish. It is at the points of maximum diversity where cleanouts, package line changeovers, color changes, printing setups, and conversion changeovers occur most often. The basic principle in activity-based system architecture is to account for these batch-related costs for accurate product costing.

Two case studies below provide examples of the application of ABC principles in continuous process environments. Although the names of the companies (the Monarch Company and Anderson Beverage) are fictitious, the case studies are based on real companies; certain features of the companies, their products, and their activities, however, have been disguised. Nonetheless, the cases do not depart materially from the substance of the final ABC systems established in the actual companies.

Product Cross-Subsidies: A Case Study

The Monarch Co.—the subject of the first case study—is a batch processor of chemical products used in the commodity chemical industry. Its present cost system is a volume-based system that uses process plan hours as the basis for allocating overhead to products. Process plan hours is essentially the budgeted reaction or mix time for the products. (Reaction and mix are two different process steps that are allocated using process plan hours.) The activity-based system was developed by first interviewing department heads and translating general ledger items into activity pools. The interviews were conducted with department heads and selected subordinates to cross-verify the employees' understanding of basic departmental activities. Exhibit C3.4 shows the results of this part of the analysis.

The columns in Exhibit C3.4 represent activities, while the rows represent budgetary line items. The general ledger line items were spread to each of the activities based on the interviews. Care must be taken to capture the salient characteristics and drivers of the activities. Some of the activities (columns) in the exhibit are uniquely related to material processors. Examples include process change, environmental control, and product-traced utility activities. Product-traced utility is the category of utility costs that occurs due to unique product characteristics that incur special energy costs in the production process. In this case, some of the products required distillate to be burned in the process. As a result, energy cost is assigned to those products based on the amount of distillate burned in the process.

Exhibit C3.5 shows the activity drivers, product hierarchy levels, frequency types, driver quantities, and activity driver rates for each activity. Notice that costs attach to both the ingredient and product levels. Ingredient-related activities are common to all products formulated with those ingredients. Environmental control activities caused by the existence of toxic ingredients are an example; the toxic ingredients should bear the cost of the environmental activities. Therefore, products that include these toxic ingredients in their formulation bear the cost as the ingredient level costs are aggregated into the product level.

The "Frequency type" column in Exhibit C3.5 indicates types of activities — both unit-level and non-unit-level frequencies. Given this categorization, it can be concluded that the exclusive use of unit drivers in the cost system would likely cause significant distortions in the final product cost. In the case of Monarch, many activities (e.g., cost accounting, scheduling, customer service, and quality) are unrelated to the pounds produced (i.e., units of production). Instead, the activities are performed in proportion to the number of batches (orders) necessary to make a given number of pounds. This practice suggests that small batch runs are more expensive per pound than large batch runs because small batch runs consume accounting transactions, quality sampling, order planning, and order follow-up at the same level of intensity as larger batches.

Routine Activities

Routine frequencies shown under the "Frequency type" column of Exhibit C3.5 relate to activities that are caused not by processing pounds or batches, but by other events that affect ingredients and products.

EXHIBIT C3.4

The Monarch Co.: Activity Pools and Cost Drivers for a Chemical Batch Processor

					Activity				
Budget line item	Scheduling	Accounting	Customer service	Vendor partnering	Environmental control	Process change	Product-traced utility	Production	Quality
Indirect	$60,000	$ 95,000	$55,000	$115,000	$ 48,000	$165,000	0	$135,000	$ 60,000
Direct	0	0	15,000	24,000	0	0	0	330,000	45,000
Quality training	0	15,000	0	0	0	25,000	0	30,000	50,000
Depreciation	0	0	0	0	13,000	0	0	180,000	15,000
Electricity and fuel	2,000	2,000	0	2,000	6,000	2,000	$32,000	63,000	0
Repairs and maintenance	0	0	0	0	17,000	0	0	76,000	0
Safety	0	0	0	0	19,000	12,000	0	43,000	0
Craft services	0	0	0	0	11,000	22,000	0	33,000	8,000
Environmental waste disposal	0	0	0	0	23,000	0	0	0	0
Total activity dollars	$62,000	$112,000	$70,000	$141,000	$137,000	$226,000	$32,000	$890,000	$178,000

EXHIBIT C3.5

The Monarch Co.: Activity Descriptions

Activity	Driver	Product hierarchy level	Frequency type	Driver quantity	Activity driver rate ($)
Scheduling	Number of orders	Product	Batch	800	77
Accounting	Number of batches	Product	Batch	450	249
Customer service	Number of orders	Product	Batch	800	87
Vendor partnering	Number of ingredients	Ingredient	Routine	300	470
Environmental control	Number of toxic ingredients	Ingredient	Routine	20	6,850
Process change	Number of formulation changes	Product	Routine	95	2,379
Product-traced utility	Distillate pounds	Product	Unit	3,000	10.67
Production	Processing hours	Product	Unit	1,800	494
Quality	Number of batches	Product	Batch	450	396

Monarch has three activities that have a routine frequency:

1. Vendor partnering;
2. Environmental control activities; and
3. Process changes.

Vendor partnering activities at Monarch, for example, are caused more by the number of ingredients that are used than by the transactions required to purchase and receive raw materials (which are batch frequency activities). This explanation is offered because the activities in the procurement and raw material management groups relate more closely to vendor development, supplier selection, and vendor quality control than to order processing. As a result, these activities appear to be ingredient-driven. Ideally, these routine activities should be traced to each ingredient. However, this tracing is impractical, so it was assumed that all ingredients consumed an equal portion of these activities. Also included in this category of activities were depreciation charges for storage vessels and flow control valves. The reasoning behind this practice is that each ingredient requires storage vessels and flow valve support. As a result, products with ingredients that are not shared with other products bear the full burden of support costs incurred for those ingredients.

Process change activities are also routine to the end product. These activities reside predominantly in the process engineering department and are triggered by formulation changes. Each formulation change requires process engineering personnel to reconfigure the process requirements for the new formulation. Refor-

EXHIBIT C3.6

The Monarch Co.: Product Characteristics

Product	Number of orders	Volume (number of pounds)	Number of batches (batch size, pounds)	Number of formulation changes	Number of ingredients (toxic)	Distillate pounds	Processing hours
AF-11	40	500	5 (100)	5	20 (0)	100	60
MO-12	300	4,500	150 (30)	35	60 (8)	1,500	580
Glycerine	200	4,000	200 (20)	40	80 (12)	1,000	490
Anhydride	150	3,750	50 (75)	15	25 (0)	150	435
KD-44	30	625	25 (25)	0	60 (0)	150	80
Ammonia	70	1,100	10 (110)	0	15 (0)	0	130
Resin	10	150	10 (15)	0	40 (0)	100	25
Total	800	14,625	450 (375)	95	300 (20)	3,000	1,800

mulations frequently require process software changes, designed lab experiments, test run time on the equipment, and new capital. Monarch concluded that this activity was caused by the number of formulation changes. This treatment averaged the impact of these activities across all formulation changes, except for some expensive changes, which were directly charged to the responsible product. The overall result of this cost system design is to assign formulation change costs to those products that have a disproportionate number of formulation changes. The company is considering assigning these costs to the customer level on the grounds that many of the formulation changes result from changed specification by customers rather than errors in the original formulation.

Environmental control activities are the third type of routine activities identified at Monarch. These activities are related to toxic ingredients. The approach taken for the cost system at Monarch was to average the impact of these activities by dividing the cost of the activities by the number of toxic ingredients. Each ingredient required specialized storage, handling, testing, and reporting activities that were independent of the volume used in production.

Representative Products

Exhibit C3.6 shows seven representative Monarch products, along with the activity cost driver volumes associated with each product. A careful review of the cost driver data reveals some interesting product characteristics. For example, the products are diverse in terms of:

- Batch size;
- Batch frequency;

EXHIBIT C3.7

The Monarch Co.: A Comparison of Conventional and Activity-Based Product Costs

Product	Number of pounds	Total overhead cost using processing hours ($)	Conventional product cost per pound ($)	Activity-based product cost per pound ($)	Percent difference (%)
AF-11	500	61,600	123.20	123.57	0.30
MO-12	4,500	595,467	132.33	136.61	3.23
Glycerine	4,000	503,067	125.77	157.37	25.13
Anhydride	3,750	446,600	119.09	85.54	−28.17
KD-44	625	82,133	131.41	144.58	10.02
Ammonia	1,100	133,467	121.33	81.09	−33.17
Resin	150	25,667	171.11	268.71	57.04

- Sales order frequency; and
- Ingredient diversity.

Exhibit C3.7 shows that the largest-volume products (in terms of number of pounds) are:

- MO-12 (4,500 pounds);
- Glycerine (4,000 pounds); and
- Anhydride (3,750 pounds).

MO-12 and glycerine achieve volume by frequent sales orders multiplied by small batches; they are essentially made-to-order. Anhydride, by contrast, achieves volume through a make-to-inventory strategy that has fewer batch runs of larger size. Glycerine has the greatest ingredient complexity and also the most toxic ingredients.

In considering ingredient complexity, note that this example has been simplified by characterizing the products as having 300 unique ingredients, though the products actually share common ingredients. The costs are determined at the ingredient level and then rolled up into the products using the ingredient volume in the product. For example, if the cost of supporting a particular ingredient is $5,000 and 1,000 pounds of that ingredient are used in production, a product that uses 800 pounds is allocated $4,000 ($5,000 × 800/1,000), while a product that uses 200 pounds is allocated $1,000 ($5,000 × 200/1,000). Ingredient costs should also include the costs of catalysts and chemicals used to adjust acidity, viscosity, and other product attributes. Process control complexity is a product-level issue that is not illustrated here, but it can be approximated by the number of ingredients on the formula card for a particular specification. Intuitively, it can be seen that complex formulations are difficult to control and maintain for process equilibrium.

Note that glycerine has also experienced the greatest formulation changes. The formulation changes are the result of many small adjustments in the product characteristics required by various customers; glycerine is much like a custom product. Anhydride, by contrast, is made in larger batches and sold from tank storage inventory. Anhydride (which is essentially a commodity product) is subject to much less formulation change activity.

These sources of diversity are what caused Monarch's conventional cost system, which was based on processing hours, to distort the company's product costs. Exhibit C3.7 shows the product costs reported by Monarch's old cost system as compared with the product costs reported by the company's ABC system. As can be seen, the ABC system provides significantly different product costs. Cost per pound under the conventional cost system depends mainly on the processing hours required to make a product. Many activities that must be performed to produce these chemicals, however, occur at frequencies other than unit frequencies. The ABC system more accurately attaches cost to products (or to ingredients and, thus, to particular products) based on how frequently the activities occur.

Cross-Subsidies Under a Conventional Cost System

Two product pairs that illustrate cost cross-subsidies under the conventional system are the glycerine/anhydride and ammonia/resin pairs.

Glycerine and anhydride are both high-volume products. Glycerine absorbs batch-frequency activities much more often than anhydride, because glycerine is made in many small batches, while anhydride is made in fewer but larger batches. Glycerine has high order intensity, but a small volume per order. It also has a complex formulation that is subject to many formulation changes. Finally, glycerine has twelve toxic ingredients. All these product attributes suggest that glycerine should be expensive to support in terms of process control, environmental control, quality, and vendor partnering. These additional costs are captured by activity-based output measures (drivers). As a result, the ABC product cost per pound for glycerine is 25 percent higher than the cost reported by Monarch's conventional cost system. What is striking is the percentage difference, given the volume of glycerine sold. Usually, ABC systems show very large percentage differences on very small volume products. Here is a case where the activities necessary to support the product are so great that, even with large volume, the percentage difference in cost per pound is significant.

Anhydride has similar volume to glycerine but is a completely different product, because it is processed in large batches, stored in tanks, then sold as orders are received. As a result, anhydride requires fewer batch-frequency activities than glycerine. The ingredient complexity, toxicity, and product formulation change history for anhydride is much less than glycerine. As a result, anhydride requires much less technical support than glycerine. As a result (as shown in Exhibit C3.7), under Monarch's ABC system, the reported cost per pound of anhydride is 28 percent lower than the cost reported by the company's conventional cost system.

The ammonia/resin pair can be analyzed in much the same way. Ammonia is processed in large batches, has a simple formulation, and requires no energy to burn off distillate. Resin, by contrast, is processed in small batches, has a complex formulation, and requires some distillate burn-off. These differences suggest that the difference between the cost per pound of these two products is much higher than the difference implied by the conventional cost system.

Sales, General, and Administrative Activities: A Case Study

The SG&A budget for continuous and batch material processors is high. Each brand or specification must be managed with respect to movement, storage, promotion, and selling. Consequently, it is reasonable to apply ABC approaches to parts of the value chain that occur after production. As discussed previously, the greatest activity intensity is toward the customer side of the value chain for continuous and batch material processors.

The application of ABC principles to SG&A is illustrated here by a case study about Anderson Beverage, a company that has been in the business of distilling, fermenting, and bottling alcoholic beverages in the United States for over 100 years. The company's product lines are in the white distilled spirits markets (e.g., gin, vodka, and rum) and the white wine markets. Bottling operations are located around the globe, though the company was founded and still has its headquarters in California.

Anderson Beverage, which was concerned about the growth of its SG&A budget, decided to apply ABC to SG&A activities. The study was designed to determine SG&A costs that could be directly assigned to the various brands. The SG&A costs in question included sales costs, business-unit general costs, marketing costs, administration costs, and production administration costs. The actual ABC study considered over thirty different cost centers, though this case study considers only a small subset of the actual study.

Brands

Exhibit C3.8 provides descriptions of the brands and shows additional information about each brand. As can be seen, the brands exhibit a number of different characteristics. The brands are sold in different average batch sizes, as is reflected in the cases/order volume differences between the brands. Apparently, the wines (DuVal and Phillips) are sold in significantly higher batch sizes than

EXHIBIT C3.8

Anderson Beverage: Product Data

Brand	Type of beverage	Price range	Orders	Customer (retail)	Case volume	Cases/order	Orders/customer	SKUs	Ingredients
DuVal Wine	Wine	Premium	230	100 (90)	13,800	60	2.30	5	6
Brother's Gin	Spirit	Midrange	520	170 (140)	15,600	30	3.06	2	7
Anderson Vodka	Spirit	Midrange	450	150 (130)	15,750	35	3.00	2	6
Phillips Wine	Wine	Midrange	490	200 (165)	49,000	100	2.45	10	4
Coco Rum	Spirit	Premium	80	75 (70)	4,000	50	1.07	2	14
Guardsmen Vodka	Spirit	Premium	120	70 (65)	7,800	65	1.71	1	12

the spirits. As the column "Orders/customer" shows, the midrange brands (i.e., Brother's Gin, Anderson Vodka, and Phillips Wine) have higher order intensities than the premium brands. The midrange brands also have more customer accounts. The midrange brands appeal to a broader market segment, because they include grocery stores and brokers. The premium brands are not sold through these channels.

Diversity also exists in terms of the volume per order (orders/customer). Moreover, the wines appear to have greater stockkeeping unit (SKU, which is a product code) diversity. SKU diversity means that the wines are sold in a greater variety of sizes and "flavors" (e.g., Chardonnay, Chablis, and Sauvignon Blanc). Finally, diversity also exists in terms of ingredient complexity, because the premium brands—and also spirits in general—have more ingredients than the wines.

Naturally, all these sources of brand difference affect many activities. For example, quality-related activities relate to ingredient complexity, ordering activities to ordering frequency, merchandising activities to the type of customer (e.g., broker versus grocery store), and sales activities to the breadth of the customer base. The ABC system is constructed to capture and account for these differences between brands.

Departments

Four departments illustrate Anderson's ABC cost system:

1. Traffic;
2. Customer service;
3. Quality assurance; and
4. Field sales and administration.

In the Traffic Department, complexity comes from SKU, ingredient scope, and the manufacturing locale for shipments of finished goods.

The least complex brands are locally sourced. For example, the ingredients for Brother's Gin and Phillips Wine are produced in California. Traffic activity intensity increases for import or export shipments of brands because of the additional documentation required for governmental agencies. These sources of activity diversity were approximated by using an intensity factor approach. The factor was used to scale the impact of traffic-related factors that made a particular brand difficult to manage. Note that this approach provides an example of a "poor man's" approach to ABC. Instead of actually measuring the usage of the activities, the usage was estimated by the use of intensity factors. Exhibit C3.9 shows the brand allocations for the Traffic Department. As can be seen, DuVal Wine has the highest intensity factor because of its foreign sourcing and SKU diversity.

The Customer Service Department was handled in a similar way. Since customer service is generally a function of the availability of stock, customer

EXHIBIT C3.9

Anderson Beverage: Traffic Department Allocation

Traffic Department budget: $125,000

Brand	Case volume	Intensity factor	Weighted case volume	Allocation (%)	Allocation ($)
DuVal Wine	13,800	4.0	55,200	30.2	37,746
Brother's Gin	15,600	1.0	15,600	8.5	10,667
Anderson Vodka	15,750	2.0	31,500	17.2	21,540
Phillips Wine	49,000	1.0	49,000	26.8	33,507
Coco Rum	4,000	3.0	12,000	6.6	8,206
Guardsmen Vodka	7,800	2.5	19,500	10.7	13,334

service activities are generally caused by orders received. Out-of-stock items, however, require order changes and extra communication with distributors. Coco Rum and DuVal Wine caused the greatest out-of-stock problems due to their foreign sourcing. Coco Rum and DuVal Wine also cause more problems because of the need to manage foreign suppliers and to adjust orders to accommodate consolidated shipments in full container loads. Phillips Wine is a more complex brand because of the need to electronically transfer orders to the winery and handle subsequent order-shipment verifications. The intensity factors determined for the various brands were multiplied by the appropriate number of customer orders to adjust for these special circumstances.

The Quality Assurance Department has a large budget at Anderson Beverage. As a result, this department was segmented into the following activities (the percentages represent the estimated proportion of the department's total costs consumed by these activities):

- *Maintaining specifications:* developing and maintaining a product specification system for Anderson plants and co-packers for Anderson Beverage brands (40 percent);
- *Troubleshooting:* quality consulting and the troubleshooting of quality issues after a brand leaves the plant (20 percent); and
- *In-plant quality control audit:* executing policy making and audit functions related to plant sanitation, product sanitation, and quality control (30 percent).

A final activity had to do with developing new market share, which required identifying new venture initiatives such as wine coolers (10 percent). This activity was directly traced to the new venture products.

EXHIBIT C3.10

Anderson Beverage: Quality Assurance Activity Allocation to Brands

Quality Assurance Department budget: $565,000

	Activity		
	Maintain specs	**Troubleshooting**	**In-plant quality control audit**
Driver:	Number of ingredients ($)	Cases × complexity ($)	Cases × stock-keeping units ($)
Pool cost	226,000	113,000	169,500
Allocations:			
DuVal Wine	27,673	18,482	18,346
Brother's Gin	32,286	10,446	8,296
Anderson Vodka	27,673	10,547	8,375
Phillips Wine	18,449	65,624	130,282
Coco Rum	64,571	2,679	2,127
Guardsmen Vodka	55,348	5,222	2,074

These activities were used to prepare the costs per brand shown in Exhibit C3.10. From interviews, it was established that wines are approximately twice as complex to manage in the troubleshooting effort as the distilled products, because wines age longer and are subject to much more precise control conditions. Therefore, the case volume was multiplied by two to determine the allocation of troubleshooting costs to the brands. Developing and maintaining the product specification system are driven by ingredient complexity: The greater the number of ingredients in a product, the more complex the control environment. Brands having high SKU diversity are sold in a variety of sizes, flavors (e.g., dry or extra dry), and aging patterns. Finally, audit functions in the plant are driven by the number of SKUs, because each SKU requires quality support when scheduled into production.

The Field Sales and Administration Department was another high-budget department. Its efforts were broken down into three major activities (the percentages represent the estimated proportion of the department's total costs consumed by these activities):

1. *Order taking:* Salespersons are responsible for taking orders for brokers and major retailers. Anderson Beverage sells to grocery stores, state stores, brokers, large serving establishments (restaurant chains), and liquor stores (50 percent);

2. *Follow-up:* Salespersons are also responsible for follow-up with respect to ordering problems, product delivery problems, and quality problems (20 percent); and

EXHIBIT C3.11

Anderson Beverage: Field Sales and Administration Activity Allocation to Brands

Driver:	Order taking Number of orders ($)	Activity Follow-up Complexity × number of orders ($)	Merchandising Number of retail customers ($)
Pool cost	180,000	72,000	108,000
Allocations:			
DuVal Wine	21,905	12,690	14,727
Brother's Gin	49,524	14,345	22,909
Anderson Vodka	42,857	12,414	21,273
Phillips Wine	46,667	27,034	27,000
Coco Rum	7,619	2,207	11,455
Guardsmen Vodka	11,428	3,310	10,636

3. *Merchandising:* Salespersons must help manage retail shelf space and support merchandising strategies in retail stores—serving establishments, brokers, and state stores do not require merchandising support (30 percent).

Exhibit C3.11 shows the allocations of these three activities that were made to the brands. The midrange brands have much broader channel scope, since they include serving establishments and grocery stores. As a result, these brands have more orders and a larger customer base. The premium brands are sold to a few serving establishments and to premium liquor stores, but not to grocery stores.

The follow-up activity is similar to quality activities. Since wines occasion more follow-up problems than white spirits, they are weighted at twice their number of orders in allocating the follow-up activity. Merchandising is driven by retail customers only (i.e., only those customers that require support for shelf management and point-of-purchase displays). Therefore, merchandising activities are allocated to brands with a disproportionate customer base in liquor and grocery stores.

The traditional cost system allocated these costs on the basis of the sales volume of each brand. The ABC system demonstrated that such volume-related measures are inappropriate when the cost of a particular activity is not proportional to volume. As Exhibit C3.11 demonstrates, some activities relate more closely to the type of beverage (i.e., wines versus spirits) or to the price range of the beverage (i.e., premium versus midrange products). As a result, the activity-based allocations of the SG&A costs provided much more accurate product costs. Insights from this study were used to address pricing, sales territory, and product promotion strategies.

ACCOUNTING FOR CAPITAL INTENSITY

Gaining economies of scale has generally been considered critical to continuous processors. (Continuous processors are beginning to question the importance of scale economies in markets characterized by high varieties of end products. In such markets, new small-scale process technologies are being applied.) As a result, cost management systems should support capital use decisions that take into account variable product demand and product mix in future periods.

The approach used to identify the cost of equipment depends on whether a process is demand-constrained or process-constrained. A demand-constrained environment is one in which the firm has excess capacity. A facilities-constrained environment is one in which a firm is operating at full practical capacity and can sell essentially everything that it makes. In the long term, any given company usually experiences periods in both environments as industry scale and demand characteristics change over time.

A Demand-Constrained Environment

The critical cost management issue of a demand-constrained environment is reporting the cost of idle and misused capacity. The classical approach is full absorption costing, in which idle capacity costs are included in the unit cost of the product. This approach is consistent with reporting the cost at the point where it is incurred.

Alternatively, the cost of idle capacity can be separately reported at the divisional level as an expense line item. An example is an aluminum rolling mill. The cold rolling mill is able to process aluminum slabs into sheet aluminum at varying speeds without loss of quality. The rolling mill can run as fast as 6,000 feet per minute or as slow as 4,000 feet per minute.

The management of this mill is acutely aware of the benefit of producing sheet aluminum to order rather than to stock. As a result, the mill buffers variations in demand through adjustments in the processing speed at the rolling mill (rather than by carrying buffer stock of finished goods). The issue is how to report the appropriate unit costs. Exhibit C3.12 shows the two alternative approaches at the minimum and maximum speeds.

If the unit costs include the cost of idle capacity, the throughput of the plant directly affects the cost per ton. Thus, the conversion cost per ton is either $10 or $15, depending on processing speed. This is despite the fact that the processing speed is determined by demand, and despite the fact that the conversion cost per hour remains fixed (or nearly so). This varying cost per ton is not a useful performance measure for the mill because the additional unit cost during periods of slack demand is a reflection of market conditions rather than mill performance.

EXHIBIT C3.12

Capacity Costing at an Aluminum Rolling Mill

	Alternative 1 Capacity costs in unit costs		Alternative 2 Capacity costs separated	
	Fast	Slow	Fast	Slow
Conversion and capital cost per hour	$3,000	$3,000	$3,000	$3,000
Tons per hour	300	200	300	200
Capacity cost per hour				$1,000
Cost per ton (conversion)	$10	$15	$10	$10

When the idle capacity costs are separated from the unit cost, the cost per ton remains unchanged at $10 regardless of the processing speed. This cost per ton is based on the practical capacity of 6,000 feet per minute, regardless of whether that is the actual processing speed at any given time. If the actual speed is lower because of slack demand, then the idled capacity is reported as a separate expense line item (in this case, $3,000 − (200 × $10 per ton)). The capacity cost reflects the cost of running the mill at a speed that is lower than the practical capacity. The idle capacity cost should be reported as a divisional expense item above the mill level to properly reflect its importance to both manufacturing and marketing.

Separate reporting of capacity costs can be useful for both pricing and operational reasons. First, the pricing of products should not be influenced by falling demand. Such pricing strategies can exacerbate what is already a painful situation. In the worst case, a "death spiral" occurs: A company continues trying to recapture capacity costs (which lie buried in unit costs) by continually increasing prices in reaction to continually decreasing demand.

Second, many mills are attempting to embark on continuous improvement programs. In a capital-intensive environment, there are frequent opportunities to turn misused capacity into idle capacity. A problem is that if misused capacity (in the form of changeover time, time used to manufacture off-grade product, and unscheduled maintenance downtime) is treated the same as idle capacity, there is no incentive to turn wasted capacity into idle capacity.

Separating the pure idle capacity as a line item allows a company to improve unit cost by improving throughput *potential* through the removal of equipment waste. This can be very important even in periods of slack demand. When wasted capacity and idle capacity are merged and hidden in unit cost, strong incentives (e.g., entropy) exist for wasted capacity to grow into the space allowed for it (idle capacity). When demand returns, the company may wrongly conclude that the mill cannot accommodate the increased volume. The actual capacity potential is misused, which can lead to unnecessary purchases of additional equipment or facilities to increase capacity when demand returns.

A Facilities-Constrained Environment

A facilities-constrained environment differs significantly from a demand-constrained environment. In a facilities-constrained environment, the company must schedule the optimal product mix to achieve maximum profitability, given that the process is under capacity. The constraint management concepts of one pivotal treatise operate most forcefully in this environment.[4] Indeed, the economic principles of constraints are probably easier to apply in the continuous and batch material process environment than in discrete part manufacturing.

The concepts behind constraint theory are very powerful for maximizing short-term profit potential.[5] That is, if an organization has a constraint resource, profit will be maximized by using that resource to its best economic advantage—in other words, by maximizing the throughput of product with the greatest contribution margin per unit of constraining resource time. For this concept to work well in practice, three conditions must be present:

1. The firm must be at capacity;
2. The product routings must be fixed and invariant to product mix changes; and
3. The fixed cost must indeed be "fixed"—that is, the overhead must be mainly depreciation rather than expenses related to employees.

The first condition must hold true for the constraint theory to apply, because if no bottlenecks exist, the possibility of lost margin because of the wasteful use of a constraining resource does not exist. The second condition relates to the nature of the product and process combination, specifically if:

- The process routings stay fixed;
- The constraining resource is used by most of the product line; and
- The constraining resource does not "wander" (i.e., change location) due to product mix changes.

(In many convergent manufacturing environments, many different routings are possible, only some products are affected by a constraint, or the constraint changes or shifts if the product mix changes.)

The second condition focuses on "wandering" constraints. Wandering constraints require the economic analysis to be conditioned on the stability of the product mix, which is a strict assumption. For example, in a precision machining operation, some products may require milling, while others require lathing.

When the product mix is toward screw machine parts, then lathing operations can become the constraint, but when the mix is toward castings, then the milling centers become the constraint. Product mix changes therefore cause the constraint to wander, which makes the economic analysis more problematical.

The third condition relates to the nature of the cost of the operating system. (A constraint hour, it has been suggested, is a system hour.) The underlying assumption, therefore, is that almost all conversion costs are fixed, which suggests that these costs cannot be actively managed. ABC would imply otherwise. Therefore, an overhead structure that consists mostly of people-related expenses can be redeployed to best advantage under activity-based approaches, whereas an overhead structure composed mainly of depreciation for equipment is truly a committed, fixed cost of doing business. This equipment is added or deleted in large chunks; it is difficult to sell, install, or use elsewhere for a different purpose. These conditions make the application of constraint theory attractive.

For continuous processors, the constraining resource does not shift as readily with product mix changes as it does in discrete part manufacturing. Therefore, a particular resource can be identified as a constraint across most products over a lengthy time horizon. Similarly, in continuous and batch material processor environments, the overhead is composed largely of equipment depreciation (which is often over 50 percent of all overhead costs). This is an environment that therefore supports maximization of throughput.

One case study has been reported about the application of constraint theory to cost paperboard products.[6] In this study, the paper machine was the fixed constraint; it also accounted for a significant portion of the operation's total overhead. The product costs were recast to include the opportunity costs of paper machine time. These opportunity costs were estimated by attributing the lost margin from changeover time, off-grade production time, and unscheduled downtime to the related product specification. The final accounting reports demonstrated that the cost of scrap was much higher than the company had thought, because the cost included not only the material cost but also the value of lost time on the constraint resource. This lost time represented lost opportunity in the form of margin from sales that were never made because the product was not made. Products that had short runs but long grade changeovers became very expensive under this costing approach. Likewise, products that did not run well on the machine and were characterized by low yields became very expensive as the margin opportunity of lost throughput was included in the cost of these products.

PROFIT AND COST PLANNING WITH STRUCTURED MATRIXES[7]

The structured matrix is an emerging planning and costing tool that was developed by Hoesch AG and later adapted and improved by a number of Japanese users, including Kobe Steel, Nippon Kokan, and IBM-Japan. There is, as yet, no application of this approach in the United States. The structured matrix provides a methodology for modeling the relationship between input (influence) and output (target) values within the form of a matrix. The matrix can either be linked with other matrixes to model sequential processes or layered into a hierarchy. The hierarchical structure can be used to manage varying levels of data aggregation. In this way, shop data can be rolled up into mill data, which can then be rolled up into macroprofit models that incorporate financial data. The structured matrixes provide a methodology for decomposing a complex set of relationships into ones that can be understood by management at any level of detail desired.

Advantages

The advantages of the structured matrix are many. Foremost among these is that a decision support system built around the structured matrix is flexible, friendly, and adaptable. This environment exists because the matrix structure is formed independent of its values. Therefore, the underlying programs that process the matrix are developed independent of the matrix content (which is unlike simulation approaches). In other words, the matrix is not a rigid construction but one that can be adapted easily to new realities by adding or deleting columns or rows, or by changing cell contents to describe new relationships. The matrix provides detailed information about the nature of engineering relationships (which can be matrixes in and of themselves) or can be used at the macro level for material, cost, or profit planning. In this way, different user needs can be accommodated on the same platform.

A matrix can be distributed across many different users and departments. As a result, the organization can be linked to the same economic description of the firm, which strongly supports cross-functional and fast decision making. Users can use the matrix model at any link in the chain or any layer in the hierarchy and then conduct "what if" analyses to plan the impact of process or product changes. Therefore, all types of planning and cost estimating can be cross-verified, because the matrix is the universal method for planning change.

Common Applications

The structured matrix is now being used in a variety of organizations—from steel producers to banks. Common applications include:

- Consolidation of balance sheet and trial balances;
- Profit planning and budgeting;

- Allocation of selling quotas;
- Cost control, cost calculations, and cost allocations;
- Utility consumption and energy-balancing calculations;
- Production and materials planning;
- Purchase planning;
- Capacity planning; and
- Exchange rate planning.

Details about the use of a structured matrix are beyond the scope of this short introduction, but they include issues such as:

- Defining hierarchical tables;
- Building the structure map;
- Responding to logic, value, and linkage changes; and
- Adapting to nonlinear cell relationships.

The original matrix applications were started in continuous and batch material processor environments. This is not surprising, since material planning and cost estimating tools (e.g., material requirements planning) are much less well-developed for continuous and batch material processors. A similar pattern of adoption can be predicted for the United States.

In summary, the matrix approach appears to hold powerful promise in linking the increasingly disparate parts of an organization by providing a user-friendly decision-support system that incorporates transparent engineering detail for the support of cost and profit management.

AN EMPHASIS ON CONSUMERS AND PROCESS ACTIVITIES

The cost management needs of continuous and batch material processors are different from the needs of discrete part manufacturers. These different needs call for a different perspective about applications of ABC. Specifically, ABC for continuous processors should be oriented toward the customer side of the value chain and should emphasize process activities.

The direct and support-related equipment activities in processors require a cost management focus on:

- The cost of idle and misused capacity;
- Maintenance activities; and
- Process engineering activities.

In process-constrained environments, the opportunity cost of misused constraint resources should be explicitly considered in the determination of product cost. Finally, structured matrixes represent an emerging cost and profit management tool that is likely to become more widely recognized and used in the United States. Structured matrixes should prove to be particularly useful for continuous and batch material processors.

Notes

1. See, e.g., most of the illustrations in the series of columns about activity-based costing by Robin Cooper in *Journal of Cost Management:*

   - Cooper, "Cost Management Concepts and Principles: The Rise of Activity-Based Costing — Part One: What Is an Activity-Based Cost System?" *Journal of Cost Management* (Summer 1988): 45–53.
   - Cooper, "Cost Management Concepts and Principles: The Rise of Activity-Based Costing — Part Two: When Do I Need an Activity-Based Cost System?" *Journal of Cost Management* (Fall 1988): 41–48.
   - Cooper, "Cost Management Concepts and Principles: The Rise of Activity-Based Costing — Part Three: How Many Cost Drivers Do You Need and How Do You Select Them?" *Journal of Cost Management* (Winter 1989): 34–35.
   - Cooper, "Cost Management Concepts and Principles: The Rise of Activity-Based Costing — Part Four: What Do Activity-Based Cost Systems Look Like?" *Journal of Cost Management* (Spring 1989): 38–49.

   See also articles on the interplay between just-in-time (JIT) manufacturing and cost management systems. For example, the Harvard Business School cases cited in Cooper, "The Rise of Activity-Based Costing — Part Four: What Do Activity-Based Cost Systems Look Like?" include:

   - "Tektronix Portable Instruments Division," *Harvard Business School Case Series 188-142/143/144;*
   - "Siemens Electric Motor Works," *Harvard Business School Case Series 189-089/090;*
   - "John Deere Component Works," *Harvard Business School Case Series 187-107;*
   - "Hewlett Packard's Rosewell Networks Division," *Harvard Business School Case Series 189-117;* and
   - "Schrader Bellows," *Harvard Business School Case Series 186-272.*

   All these examples are discrete part examples. Additionally, much of the JIT literature espouses simplicity in cost system design through the use of material backflushing techniques, wider transaction gates, and the elimination of direct labor as a cost function. These JIT ideas merely emulate typical process costing technology, so it is unclear if any of these suggestions for achieving "simplicity" have great bearing in the continuous process environment.

2. This discussion has been motivated by Cooper, "Cost Classification in Unit-Based and Activity-Based Manufacturing Cost Systems," *Journal of Cost Management* (Fall 1990): 4–14; Turney and Reeve, "The Impact of Continuous Improvement on the Design of Activity-Based Cost Systems," *Journal of Cost Management* (Summer 1990): 43–50; and Peter B.B. Turney, *Common Cents: The ABC Performance Breakthrough* (Cost Technology: Hillsboro, OR.), 1993.

   Note that the concepts of activity levels and activity hierarchies are not new in the cost management area. Authors that have discussed these concepts include Dunne and Wolk, "Marketing Cost Analysis: A Modularized Contribution Approach," *Journal of Marketing* (July 1977): 83–94;

Crissy and Mossman, "Matrix Models for Marketing Planning: An Update and Expansion," *MSU Business Topics* (Autumn 1977): 17–26; and "Report on the Committee on Cost and Profitability Analyses for Marketing," *The Accounting Review Supplement* (1972): 575–615.

3. This discussion is based on Cooper, "The Rise of Activity-Based Costing—Part Four: What Do Activity-Based Cost Systems Look Like?"; Kaplan, "Contribution Margin Analysis: No Longer Relevant/Strategic Cost Management: The New Paradigm," *Journal of Management Accounting Research* (Fall 1990): 2–15; and Greenwood and Reeve, "Activity-Based Cost Management for Continuous Improvement: A Process Design Framework," *Journal of Cost Management* (Winter 1992), pp. 22–40.

4. J. Cox and E. Goldratt, *The Goal* (Croton-on-Hudson, NY: North River Press, 1986).

5. For a related discussion, see Kaplan, "Contribution Margin Analysis: No Longer Relevant/Strategic Cost Management: The New Paradigm."

6. T. Albright and James M. Reeve, "A Case Study on the Impact of Material Yield Related Cost Drivers on Economic Improvement," *Journal of Management Accounting Research* (Fall, 1992), pp. 20–39.

7. This section is based on personal discussion with Takayuki Toyama of IBM-Japan, who has been involved in developing and implementing MATPLAN, which is a decision-support tool based on the structured matrix.

Activity-Based Costing in Service Industries

WILLIAM ROTCH

Johnson and Higgins Professor of Business Administration at Darden Graduate School of Business Administration at the University of Virginia in Charlottesville.

ABC has mainly been applied to manufacturing companies, but it can also prove useful to service enterprises. This article identifies how ABC is applied in manufacturing settings, then discusses any special challenges that service companies encounter in trying to use ABC systems.

A number of articles and cases recently have described and analyzed activity-based costing (ABC). Since ABC has mainly been applied to manufacturing companies, however, the question arises whether ABC can also be used in service businesses. To answer this question, this article first considers how ABC works in manufacturing settings to identify key characteristics of both the manufacturing setting and of the cost systems. This background provides a point of departure for considering the suitability of ABC to service business and also any special challenges that arise in using ABC in those businesses.

ABC SYSTEMS IN MANUFACTURING

As a number of recent articles and cases explain,[1] ABC deals with indirect costs, which are costs that are not easily traceable to outputs (output being defined as all tangible and intangible benefits provided for customers). In the short run, many indirect costs are fixed. ABC, however, implicitly takes a longer-term view by recognizing that, over time, these indirect costs can be changed and hence are relevant to management choices.

The following two sections explain the two primary benefits derived from using ABC.

More accurate costs for output. More accurate costs are possible when support costs (e.g., setup and inspection) that are not driven by volume are allocated to products by using a volume-related base (traditionally, direct labor hours or dollars). By shifting the allocation base to an activity that is related to output or output characteristics, the link between the use of resources and product output becomes more accurate. An activity such as "product runs," for example, could be used to capture all the setup, inspection, and material-handling costs caused by production runs. Then, if a company has product diversity in terms of run length, short-run products will not be undercosted and long-run products will not be overcosted. How much the accuracy of costs improves depends on how different the products are in their use of the activities.

Behavioral influence. Besides more accurate output costs, ABC can provide benefits by influencing the behavior of design engineers, production managers, or marketing strategies. Identifying and costing activities provide potentially powerful information such as the following:

EXHIBIT 1

Link Between Strategy and Activities

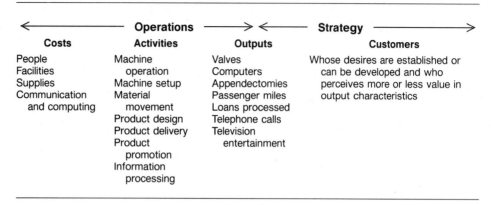

← Operations →		← Strategy →	
Costs	**Activities**	**Outputs**	**Customers**
People	Machine	Valves	Whose desires are established or
Facilities	operation	Computers	can be developed and who
Supplies	Machine setup	Appendectomies	perceives more or less value in
Communication	Material	Passenger miles	output characteristics
and computing	movement	Loans processed	
	Product design	Telephone calls	
	Product delivery	Television	
	Product	entertainment	
	promotion		
	Information		
	processing		

- Knowing the high cost of parts handling (a defined activity) can encourage design engineers to simplify production design;
- Recognizing that volume-based overhead allocations can give false signals (e.g., knowing that automation-related support costs will not go down by reducing direct labor) helps production managers determine the optimum level of production technology); and
- Knowing even the approximate cost of various customer services can guide marketing strategists toward a profitable mix of service and volume.

RELATIONSHIP BETWEEN ACTIVITIES AND STRATEGY

Activities and strategies are closely linked in ABC because strategic choices drive activities. ABC deals with activities and costs that can be changed only gradually, which reflects the long-term perspective taken by ABC and its concern with strategic issues. Support costs ordinarily cannot be changed much in one week. Over time, however, changes that occur in a company's production methods, product design, and marketing strategy ultimately affect the company's indirect support costs. This important linkage is illustrated by Exhibit 1, which shows the relationship between strategy and activities (which, together, comprise the firm's operations).

Strategy. A company's strategy can be seen as a plan to provide certain outputs to attract and serve customers. Those outputs, whether manufactured products or units of service, have characteristics that cause certain activities to take place, and those activities cost money. When a company's strategy changes—say, toward greater customer service and shorter production runs—certain activities (e.g., setups and product design) occur more often or are used more. The costs of these activities, therefore, increase. Unless they can measure the link between output characteristics (e.g., better customer service) and activities (e.g., improved product design because of an expanded product design department), managers cannot compute the cost of strategic choices. If they use traditional systems based on direct labor hours or machine hours, these managers may well have misleading information.

Several examples of how strategic choices can influence or drive activities are given in the following cases.

The Schrader Bellows case. In the Schrader Bellows case,[2] the company's strategy was to offer a broad line of valves and to respond favorably to customer requests for rush orders and specially designed products. The result was many short runs and interruptions of longer runs. All support activities that were driven by the frequency of production runs were heavily used (the application of ABC to Schrader Bellows is discussed next).

Siemens Electric Motor Works. The Siemens Electric Motor Works case[3] found that 40 percent of its support-related manufacturing costs (or 10 percent of total costs) were driven by two kinds of activities: order processing and the handling of special components. The company's strategy had led it toward producing custom motors and away from long-run, commodity-type motors. As a result, 90 percent of all orders were for custom motors. The average order was for less than ten units although almost half the motors sold were on orders for 100 or more units. The company's strategy clearly made both order processing and component handling into large and costly activities, especially for small production runs.

A hospital. A Pennsylvania hospital decided in 1986 to become certified as a trauma center. That strategic decision set in motion a number of activities and affected some existing ones. The hospital recruited four doctors to staff the trauma center so that it could be covered twenty-four hours a day. Each of these doctors received compensation guarantees. Other incremental one-time and continuing expenses were incurred for facilities, equipment, training, and support staff. Although a few activities and staff members were unique to the trauma center, many were used by other hospital services. A continuing review of the strategy of maintaining a trauma center benefited from knowing the link between the new trauma center's work and related support activities.

ABC PROCESS

There are three essential steps in establishing an ABC system:

1. Defining the activities that support output (which often requires defining output—or characteristics of output—in a way that describes how the output drives activities). In the Schrader Bellows case, for example, the traditional output definition would be "a valve" with certain specifications. With ABC, the output is defined as "a valve with a particular average number of units per run." This output definition highlights the activity "making runs," which is different from making units. Note also that the activity "making runs" is chosen to capture output diversity because runs in Schrader Bellows varied greatly in length.

2. Defining the links between activities and outputs. Again using the Schrader Bellows example, the link between the activity "runs" and the output would be "cost per run" and the "average units per run" (or runs per unit) for each valve produced.

3. Developing the cost of activities (often costs are customarily gathered by function or organizational unit, so special allocation methods have to be used to relate costs to activities). In the Schrader Bellows case, the activity "making runs" was supported by a number of functions (such as setup, inspection, material handling, and labor reporting). The costs of those functions combined to become the cost of the activity "making runs."

Schrader Bellows. While each of these steps is essential, the difficulties that they present vary from company to company. Exhibit 2, for example, portrays these steps for the Schrader Bellows case. The exhibit shows how both the traditional and the new cost systems looked, using the same framework.

Under the "old way," the activities are the work done in manufacturing departments, and the link is overhead cost per direct labor hour. The "new way," by contrast, uses a number of activities (e.g., purchasing and shipping), each with its own appropriate link to output. (Exhibit 2 focuses on only one activity: setting up and making a run.)

The Schrader Bellows ABC system was not easy to set up. All three steps required some ingenuity. Activities had to be defined so that they reflected what people in the support groups actually did and also in a way that could be linked to product output. Relating costs to activities required data gathering on how people spent their time, which was not information that was readily available.

Structure of ABC systems. At this point, one might ask whether ABC is just a traditional two-stage overhead allocation system that uses more overhead cost pools and a variety of appropriate allocation bases. Technically, ABC is just that,

EXHIBIT 2

The Schrader Bellows Case: An ABC Case Study

		The Old Way		
Support Costs	**Links**	**Activities**	**Links**	**Products**
Inventory management	Mostly based on direct labor; setup on estimates of time	Manufacturing departments (machining, assembly, etc.)	Overhead rate per labor hour	Valves with specified amount of direct labor
Production control				
Purchasing				
Setup				
Quality control				
Engineering				

		The New Way (ABC Costing)		
Costs	**Links**	**Activities**	**Links**	**Products**
Same as above	Percentage of time spent in support of specified activities	*A run* Setting up and making a run of a component or finished product	Cost per run	Run cost of products with specified number of units and runs
		(Other activities Purchasing Shipping Handling customer orders Direct labor etc.)	Other appropriate links	Cost of purchasing Cost of shipping Cost of handling order Overhead related to labor
				Total cost per item

but companies using it seem to have obtained some important benefits that are not obvious when viewing cost systems from an overhead cost pool perspective.

One benefit is that learning about the links between output characteristics and activities helps managers make product decisions directly, even without dollar figures. A circuit board manufacturer discovered, for example, that certain board designs required more hand work. The manufacturer also recognized that the hand work was expensive and prone to quality problems. Therefore, the manufacturer concluded that changes in board design could eliminate the manual operation. Alternatively, if changes were not feasible for particular applications, the price of the boards might be raised. Defining the linkages between board designs and product costs, therefore, helped the manufacturer identify where improvements could be made.

Another benefit seems to arise from defining activities according to how they relate to output characteristics rather than in relation to organizational units, which are more oriented toward input characteristics. It is obvious, for example, that the cost of a setup is the time that setup people spend in setting up for a new run. But if the activity is defined more broadly as a production run, many other costs are also caused by setups, including the following:

- Material movement;
- Inspection; and
- Labor reporting.

Although the activity "setups" is indeed an overhead pool, notice that the pool is defined by an *output-related activity* (runs) rather than by an organizational unit (the setup department).

ABC may also make it easier to include activities outside the factory walls (e.g., marketing and distribution) in product costs. Reorienting and broadening the definition of activities in this way makes the allocation of overhead cost pools more useful in making strategic choices that depend on product costs.

Another benefit of ABC comes from its untraditional way of looking at the relationship between outputs and activities. ABC rejects any clear split between fixed and variable costs and accepts the notion that many costs that are usually considered fixed in fact change over time largely because of changes in strategy. Therefore, not only are these "fixed" costs relevant for strategic decisions, but also the most effective way to control them may be through changes in output strategies.

When management simplifies a product, as IBM did with its ProPrinter, the need for many activities is reduced, so costs can be cut. IBM achieved significantly lower product cost by designing the ProPrinter with fewer parts, thus reducing the costs of parts manufacturing, storage, and handling. By highlighting non-value-adding activities (such as labor reporting) and high-cost activities (such as managing part numbers), ABC systems direct management attention to likely areas for improvement.

The structure of an ABC system (with its use of activity cost pools), therefore, resembles the structure of a traditional overhead cost pool system. The benefits of an ABC system lie in choosing activities that are oriented toward output characteristics and that capture output diversity. The analytical process of defining activities and of establishing their linkages to output helps managers to evaluate the cost of strategic choices and to discover ways to reduce costs.

ABC SYSTEMS IN SERVICE ENTERPRISES

Given that ABC systems work in a manufacturing setting, can they also work in service enterprises? If so, what would an ABC system for a service company look like, and would the service setting present any special challenges?

Although differences between manufacturing and service enterprises tend to get blurred because of an emphasis on service in the strategies of many manufacturing enterprises, service enterprises do have several distinctive characteristics:

- Output is often harder to define;
- Activity in response to service requests may be less predictable; and
- Joint capacity cost represents a high proportion of total cost and is difficult to link to output-related activities.

Output in a service enterprise. Output in a service enterprise is sometimes described as a "package of service benefits,"[4] many of which are intangible: for example, speed of service, quality of information, or satisfaction provided. But —just as in a manufacturing environment—these benefits drive activities that cost money. Viewed in this way, service enterprises have characteristics similar to manufacturing although the intangible nature of service output makes costing more difficult.

Despite these difficulties, service businesses are beginning to develop systems that look very much like ABC even though that term is usually not used. Here are some examples, including discussions of any particular difficulties that these service enterprises encountered in implementing an ABC system.

ALEXANDRIA HOSPITAL

Consider another hospital, Alexandria Hospital, for example. A hospital's "product" can be defined as a patient's stay and treatment. The total charge for each stay includes charges for many different services (e.g., tests, medications, treatments, supplies, and a daily rate). The daily rate usually covers three kinds of costs:

- "Hotel" cost for the room;
- Meal costs; and
- Costs of nursing services.

In most hospitals, a different daily rate is charged for different types of care. The private room charge for stays in the intensive care unit, for example, is higher than the private room charge for stays in the obstetrics unit. Within each unit, however, all patients are charged the same daily rate for the same type of room.

The Alexandria hospital recognized that patients in the same unit require and receive different amounts of nursing care and that overall nursing care

EXHIBIT 3

Alexandria Hospital: Example of an ABC in a Hospital

		The Old Way		
Costs	**Links**	**Activities**	**Links**	**Service Output**

Nurses
Nursing
  supervision and
  support
  supplies
Facilities
Dietary
Overhead
	Costs related to
	patient nursing,
	occupancy, and
	feeding
		Patient care,
		including
		nursing,
		occupancy, and
		feeding
			Cost per day
			(about $500)
				A patient day's
				stay in the
				hospital

		The New Way		
Costs	**Links**	**Activities**	**Links**	**Service Output**

Nurses
Nursing
  supervision and
  support
	Costs related to
	nursing and
	acuity level
		Nursing care that
		varies with
		acuity
			Cost per day for
			each acuity
			level ($50 to
			$600)
				Nursing service
				for specified
				acuity level

Supplies Facilities Dietary Overhead	Costs related to hotel and dietary functions	Occupancy and feeding	Cost per day ($335)	Occupancy per day Total cost per day

accounted for about half the total daily rate. There was diversity in service provided, and the amount of money involved was significant.

In a recently installed system[5] designed to measure more accurately how much nursing care each patient requires, each unit's head nurse rates each patient and arrives at a level of "acuity" on a 5-point scale. Level 5 patients in the cardiac care unit, for example, need more than ten times as much nursing care as level 1 patients (twenty-four hours versus two hours). The hospital's financial office uses projected costs and patient mix to compute a nursing service charge per day for each level of acuity, and the patient's bill shows nursing service as a separate line from the daily rate. The result is that each patient's charges more accurately reflect the actual service received. In addition, the acuity ratings are used to prepare a flexible budget for nursing in each unit.

The hospital's new system is actually an ABC system (although the hospital does not call it that). Under the previous system, the activity was "patient care and feeding" (see "Old Way" under Exhibit 3), and the hotel, feeding, and nursing costs were bundled into one cost per day.

The new system redefines the hospital's "product" by specifying characteristics that related to separable activities: "nursing care" and "occupancy and feeding" (see "New Way" under Exhibit 3). The nursing activity is driven by acuity

EXHIBIT 4

Union Pacific: Example of ABC for a Railroad

Support Costs[a]	Link	Activity	Link	Service Output or Output Characteristic
Maintenance of ways and structures	Groups of support costs allocated to activities in appropriate ways	Moving freight trains	Cost per gross ton mile	Gross ton miles per shipment
Equipment maintenance and depreciation		Switching freight trains	Cost per yard/ train switching minute	Yard/train switching minutes per shipment
Transportation, including switching costs and fuel station platform labor		Handling and depreciation of freight cars	Cost per freight car mile	Freight car miles per shipment
		Handling freight in and out of freight cars	Cost per ton of freight	Tons of freight per shipment
				Total cost of a specific shipment

[a] Each of these groups of costs corresponds to a function of railroad operation as well as the organization structure, and each group of costs supported three or four of the activities.

Source: Adapted from teaching notes prepared by Professor Robert S. Kaplan for three cases he wrote about Union Pacific in the *Harvard Business School Case Series* (cases 186–176, 186–177, and 186–178).

levels. "Occupancy and feeding" was considered a daily cost that was the same for all acuity levels.

UNION PACIFIC[6]

In any given hour, the Union Pacific Railroad operates up to 200 trains, covers over 21,500 route miles (using 2,400 locomotives), and moves some 80,000 freight cars. Thousands of shipments are processed every day, each different from the others. To cost this traffic, Union Pacific uses a form of ABC that is sufficiently real time to recognize that the cost of a particular shipment is influenced by the other shipments that ride with it. Exhibit 4 depicts this system.

If Union Pacific were to use a costing system with one all-encompassing activity, that activity would be "moving freight," and the link to output would be cost per ton mile. But since ton miles of freight are not all alike, Union Pacific devised a system that relates characteristics of freight shipments to activities and the costs of those activities.

Essentially none of the railroad's operating costs relates directly to a shipment; all are support costs. The costs are collected by function and organizational unit. In that form, however, they cannot easily be linked to the distinctive characteristics of shipments. To accomplish this goal, Union Pacific has defined a series of activities that can be linked to shipments and developed a mechanism for collecting the costs of those activities. For example, each shipment will be on a freight car that will be handled one or more times in one or more switching yards (an activity). The route and train specifications determine how many switching minutes will be needed. The cost of that switching activity is an accumulation of several functional support costs, such as maintenance of track in the yards, depreciation and maintenance of switching equipment, and labor costs in the yards.

Union Pacific's system enables it to develop the actual cost of each shipment, gathering data each day from many locations on movements of trains and shipments. Furthermore, by using the same activity cost information, Union Pacific can estimate the cost of future shipments, which helps the marketing department identify profitable business.

AMTRAK[7]

Although many of Amtrak's costs are similar to Union Pacific's, the unit of service output is different. For Union Pacific, the output is a shipment. For Amtrak, the output is service on a specific route with a defined frequency of trips and a specified makeup of cars and engine (the "consist"). Whereas Union Pacific's diversity of output precluded use of ton miles as the definition of output, Amtrak's diversity meant that the single definition "route miles" would not produce accurate costs. Exhibit 5 depicts Amtrak's costing system.

Cost categories are the same as activities in this instance. Of all the costs listed, only train and engine crews and on-board service are directly related to a train on a route. All the other costs are indirect. Most of them, however, represent activities that are closely related to departments and functions for which costs can be computed without extensive allocation.

For Amtrak, the problem is in defining the links between activities and output. The links between some are easy—fuel, for example. Even though fuel is not metered by train, engineered consumption standards can be reliably used to estimate fuel consumption by route. Maintenance is more difficult, partly because locomotives and cars are shifted around from route to route. Output

EXHIBIT 5

Additional Amtrak: Example of ABC for a Railroad

Costs and Activities	Percent	Link	Service Output
Train and engine crews[a]	18%	Direct charge	Trip-specified consist
Fuel	11	Estimate based on route specs	Trip-specified consist
Yard and mainline operations; other transp.	6	Cost per train trip	Trip
Locomotive maintenance	6	Locomotive miles	Trip-specified locomotive(s)
Car maintenance	18	Cost per car miles (80%) and trips (20%)	Trip-specified consist
Maintenance of way	3	Rate per train unit per track mile	Trip
Onboard service	10	Direct charge	Trip-specified consist
Station services	3	Cost per route and per train	Trip-specified route
			Total trip cost
Depreciation, administration, etc.	18	Percentage of total cost	Route-specified frequency
Sales, marketing, reservations	7	Percentage of projected sales	Sales
	100%		Cost of route with a given frequency and consist

[a] Approximate percentage of total cost.

diversity is also problematical. For example, does a 400-mile trip cause 4 times as much locomotive maintenance as a 100-mile trip? Probably not although Amtrak has used a straight mileage measure (that particular type of diversity was evidently not considered material).

Defining the links between activity usage and product definition may also involve deciding which activity costs should be considered variable. If a strategic, longer-range perspective is taken, all (or almost all) costs are variable. Amtrak has called variable costs "short-term avoidable," a concept that was developed in the political context of decisions about dropping specific routes. Specific costs (or percentages of costs) are defined as short-term avoidable.

For other decisions (about frequency or consist, for example) different definitions of relevant costs are used. A particularly thorny issue has been how to handle costs that follow a step function. A certain station and its staff might be able to handle ten trains a day. Additions in frequency from six to ten trains would, therefore, cause no increase in cost, but adding an eleventh train would increase costs significantly. Should the linkage between activity and "product" assume average activity cost or somehow recognize the actual costs? In the expectation that a series of decisions are likely to come along, average costs probably make more sense.

With Amtrak, defining service output and support activities has been fairly clear: Establishing the links between the two, however, has proven difficult.

DATA SERVICES, INC.[8]

Data Services, Inc., a subsidiary of Armistead Insurance Company, was set up to market Armistead's unused third shift of computer time. By the end of two years, Data Services had established a service that provided data analysis for about forty fast-food franchisors, each with varying numbers of units. The data analysis was performed on each unit. The number of units per franchise ranged from under five to several hundred. Data Services charged an installation fee and a monthly service fee per unit. Unfortunately, the operation taken as a whole was not profitable. Armistead Insurance Company wanted to know what the trouble was.

This case requires defining the service output in a way that will suggest useful links to the support activities. Data Services was not just selling computer time. The company was providing an information system that required four types of support activities:

- Selling the system;
- Installing the system;
- Maintaining relations with each franchisor; and
- Processing data from each unit.

There were costs associated with each of these activities although Data Services charged only for installation and data processing.

Exhibit 6 depicts Data Services' old and new ways of costing its service output. Under the new system, the costs that were previously collected by function were allocated to the three distinct activities shown in the center column of Exhibit 6. This allocation made it possible for Data Services to compute the cost of acquiring a customer (including the installation costs) and the cost of servicing a customer (including the cost of monthly visits to each franchisor's headquarters plus the cost of servicing each of the franchisor's units).

The issues involved in determining pricing and market strategy for Data Services focused on the different sizes of franchisors. Specifically, what was the relative profitability of franchisors of different sizes, and how should that information influence Data Services' marketing and pricing? Only by separating out customer acquisition costs and linking service costs to different sizes of customers could Data Services see the strategic reorientation needed to become profitable. The result was that Data Services charged higher per-unit fees for small franchisors and paid special attention to streamlining the customer-acquisition process.

EXHIBIT 6.

Data Services, Inc.: Activity-Based Product Costing in a Service Industry

The Old Way				
Costs	**Links**	**Activities**	**Links**	**Services**
Data entry Service agents SG&A Computer Travel, etc.		Running Data services (the total enterprise)	Cost per month or year	Data analysis service for customers

The New Way				
Costs	**Links**	**Activities**	**Links**	**Services**
Data entry Service agents SG&A Computer Travel, etc.	Cost of specific visits Travel, analysis Setup	Customer acquisition and installation	Cost per successful customer acquisition	Customer under contract Total customer acquisition cost
	Cost of specific visits Travel	Servicing customers	Cost per month per customer company	Customer satisfaction
	Cost of data analysis	Servicing units	Cost per unit or shift served	Data reports to the units Total customer service cost

ABC FOR SERVICE INDUSTRIES

The two questions stated at the beginning of this article were whether ABC could be used in service enterprises and, if so, whether doing so presented any special challenges. To answer the first question, it appears that ABC can indeed be useful to service enterprises, at least in some instances. Robin Cooper and Robert S. Kaplan have pointed out the conditions that make manufacturing enterprises good candidates for ABC (e.g., diversity of resource consumption; products and resource consumption not correlated with traditional, volume-based allocation measures).[9] The implication is that while ABC is useful in some manufacturing enterprises, it may not be useful in others.

The Cooper-Kaplan conditions also apply to service enterprises. All the examples described in this article show diversity of resource consumption. Traditional allocation bases fail to capture that diversity:

- In the Alexandria hospital example, patients require different levels of nursing care. Although this diversity is significant, it was missed altogether by the all-in-one rate that the hospital had formerly used in charging patients.

- In the Union Pacific example, the cost differences between shipments was not captured by a gross-ton-mile measure.
- In the Amtrak example, the cost of a route could not be computed accurately using a single measure such as route miles.
- In the Data Services example, the varying size of customers in terms of units served per franchisor created output diversity. The all-inclusive monthly expense for servicing franchisors did not reflect that diversity.

Identifying and costing activities. Identifying and costing activities may reveal opportunities for more efficient operations. The Data Services case provides an example because Data Services chose to isolate and cost out customer acquisition activities. This decision made it possible to focus on opportunities to streamline the selling process. These opportunities might not have been discovered if the company had not learned how high the selling costs really were.

Special challenges. The differences between service enterprises are at least as great as the differences between service and manufacturing enterprises as a whole. However, service companies and manufacturing companies can present similar problems. Schrader Bellows and Data Services, for example, have much in common: both have product setup costs and other costs that vary with volume. Both must also grapple with strategic issues about selling and pricing products with varying unit volumes.

However, service enterprises can present special difficulties in allocating costs to activities. Consider, for example, the hospital trauma center. Certain personnel and facilities costs are directly attributable to the center. But the center also draws on other resources, such as helicopter transportation, laboratory work, and regular nurses, physicians, and staff. Specifying resource use by the trauma center is difficult, so it is not easy to define the links between the trauma center as an element in the hospital's strategy and the activities that support it. The need to be responsive to unpredictable external demands adds another element of uncertainty. Service cannot be inventoried, so unused capacity is often an unavoidable cost.

Output diversity. Service enterprises also present difficulties in defining output diversity. In manufacturing, parts are specified, and it is clear when one product uses many parts and another uses only a few. But in service settings, diversity that draws on support activities in different ways may be hard to pin down. For example, a bank's checking account customers do not all use the same services or provide the same revenue. To try to control this tendency, some banks have begun to segment customers and offer varying service packages. Each package drives a known mix of activities that the bank hopes will please the customer and that will have a predictable cost. Such a strategy does not eliminate diversity, but it does make the diversity somewhat more measurable.

Some service enterprises have quite clearly definable measures of output diversity and clear links between relevant output characteristics and support activities. The four cases described in this article are examples. Other service enterprises are far more difficult to analyze. For such companies, implementing an ABC system would be expensive and the benefits of doing so would be questionable: The information produced is likely to have a wide range of uncertainty.[10] In such situations that basic framework used in Exhibits 2–6 can still be followed but without the efforts to quantify the links. Certain kinds of service may be known as "hard to execute." As a result, they may draw excessively on support activities. In a printing plant, for example, certain jobs with tight schedules may required more attention than jobs with more relaxed timetables. The jobs with tight schedules interrupt the smooth flow of work and place extra burdens on setup activity.

Other support activities may be identified as not being essential to the service strategy. Although this framework fails to quantify costs and relationships, the conclusion that can be drawn from it can still prove helpful.

ABC can be successfully applied in some service enterprises. It provides an analytical framework that can be useful even in settings where it would be impractical actually to quantify costs and relationships.

Notes

1. A number of articles have described and analyzed ABC systems in the past few years. At the center of these is Robin Cooper's four-part series called "The Rise of Activity-Based Costing" in the *Journal of Cost Management:* "Part One: What Is an Activity Based Cost System?" (Summer 1988): 45–53; "Part Two: When Do I Need an Activity-Based Cost System?" (Fall 1988): 41–48; "Part Three: How Many Cost Drivers Do You Need, and How Do You Select Them?" (Winter 1989): 34–54; "Part Four: What Do Activity-Based Cost Systems Look Like?" (Spring 1989): 38–49.

   Note also these other important articles on ABC systems: H. Thomas Johnson, "Activity-Based Information: Blueprint for World-Class Management," *Management Accounting* (June 1988): 23–30; Robin Cooper and Robert S. Kaplan, "Measure Costs Right: Make the Right Decisions," *Harvard Business Review* (September–October 1988): 986.

   An application of ABC is described in the following articles: Gary B. Frank, Steven A. Fisher, and Allen R. Wilkie, "Linking Cost to Price and Profit," *Management Accounting* (June 1989): 22.

   Among the case that deal with ABC systems are the following: Robin Cooper, "Schrader Bellows," *Harvard Business School Case Series 186–272*; Robert S. Kaplan, "John Deere Component Works (A) and (B)," *Harvard Business School Case Series 187–107/108*; Robin Cooper and Peter B.B. Turney, "Tektronix: Portable Instruments Division (A), (B), and (C)," *Harvard Business School Case Series 188–142/143/144*; Robin Cooper and K.H. Wruck, "Siemens Electric Motor Works (A) and (B)," *Harvard Business School Case Series 189–089/90.*

2. See Cooper, "Schrader Bellows."

3. See Cooper and Wruck, "Siemens Electric Motor Works."

4. See, e.g., W.E. Sasser, R.P. Olsen, and D.D. Wyckoff, *Management of Service Operations* (Boston: Allyn and Bacon, 1978).

5. This system is described in William Rotch and W. Schell, "Alexandria Hospital," *University of Virginia Darden Graduate Business School Case No. UVA-C-2007* (1987).

6. This system is described in Robert S. Kaplan, "Union Pacific Introduction, (A) and (B)," *Harvard Business School Case Series 186–176/177/178.*

7. This system is described in William Rotch and S. Allen, "Amtrak Auto-Ferry Service," *University of Virginia Darden Graduate Business School Case No. UVA-C-988.*

8. The names of these entities have been disguised. This cost system is described in J.L. Colley, Jr., R.A. Gary IV, J.C. Reid, and R.C. Simpson III, "Data Services, Inc. (B)," *University of Virginia Darden Graduate Business School Case No. UVA-OM-582.*

9. See Cooper and Kaplan, "Measure Costs Right: Make the Right Decisions."

10. See "The Rise of Activity-Based Costing—Part Two: When Do I Need an Activity-Based Cost System?" Cooper discusses the cost/benefit balance. If applied to many service enterprises, the cost curve will rise steeply with increasing accuracy requirements, and the benefit curve, shown as the cost of errors, will be uncertain. See also Robin Cooper, "You Need a New Cost System When . . . ," *Harvard Business Review*, (January–February 1989): 77–82, in which he uses the same cost/benefit curves.

Customer-Driven Costs Using Activity-Based Costing

MICHAEL C. O'GUIN

Manager, National Cost Management Practice, Price Waterhouse,
Newport Beach, California

STEVEN A. REBISCHKE

Senior Consultant, National Cost Management Practice, Price Waterhouse,
Newport Beach, California

INTRODUCTION

In the 1980s, the competitive "call to arms" was quality. Companies focused their improvement efforts on increasing the quality of their products through a myriad of technologies and techniques. They found that improving the customer-perceived quality of their products provided a competitive advantage in the marketplace.

Changes in technology and in organizational structure (which accompanied the push to improve product quality) have profoundly changed how most managers look at and manage their businesses. A few companies today—while continuing to focus on providing superior product quality—are applying these same basic precepts about quality to virtually every other aspect of operations. These companies have embarked on what will undoubtedly be the focal point for developing and sustaining distinct competitive advantages in the 1990s: strategies based on customer service.

Despite what some quality experts argue, however, quality is not free, and neither is providing superior customer service. The key is to provide superior customer service to the right audience at the lowest possible cost. Strategic planning is as simple—and as difficult—as that objective. Success lies in an organization's ability to integrate and balance these sometimes-conflicting requirements without sacrificing either service or profitability.

To achieve this balance and develop the most profitable customer service strategies possible, companies must have information systems that provide insights into the probable impact that alternative service strategies will have on profits. Knowing which customers, markets, and distribution channels are profitable and also why they are profitable is critical to achieving (and then sustaining) long-term competitive advantage.

This chapter explains the concept of customer-driven costs, then develops an activity-based framework for analyzing these costs. The chapter suggests how managers can use this activity-based information to design long-term customer, market, and distribution channel strategies to improve profitability.

THE EFFECTS OF CUSTOMER DIVERSITY

As most managers are well aware, much diversity exists in the service and support requirements of different customers, markets, and distribution channels. These differing requirements manifest themselves as a network of activities that a company must perform to meet those different requirements.

Customer Costs vs. Product Costs

The difference between product costs and customer-driven costs is the resource-consuming activities that trigger them. Product costs are a function of product design, operations design, business systems, and product mix, whereas customer-driven costs derive from specific customers (or groups of customers) and their buying characteristics. The diversity involved in serving different market segments is illustrated by the following case study.

The Wheelchair Manufacturing Industry: A Case Study

Legacy is a $50 million wheelchair manufacturer that sells its wheelchairs to dealers, who then sell the wheelchairs to end users. End users are divided into two distinctly different market segments: the home care segment and the rehabilitation segment. Here is how diversity affects the costs of serving these two different market segments:

- *The home care market* serves temporary wheelchair users. Typically, these users are elderly persons who use the chairs for an average of six months. These wheelchairs are high-volume, low-cost, simple products.
- *The rehabilitation market,* on the other hand, serves victims of injuries, strokes, or spinal disease. These end users typically use their wheelchair for the rest of their lives. Their wheelchairs are customized or "prescribed" for each user's particular needs. For example, each chair is fitted to the customer's body dimensions and has unique features (e.g., removable left arms for persons with left-side paralysis or detachable arm rests for personal computer users). These end users are knowledgeable buyers, given the importance of wheelchairs to their life-style. In addition, this market segment also includes sophisticated sports and power chairs.

Establishing Service and Support Requirements

Clearly, diversity exists in the product requirements needed to serve Legacy's two different market segments. There is also, however, much diversity in Legacy's service and support requirements.

For example, since the home care wheelchairs are simple products used for an average of only six months, each wheelchair requires little order entry or maintenance effort, technical service, or engineering support. But the rehabilitation wheelchairs, on the other hand, are custom-fitted to each user's size and disability. The rehabilitation users are relatively sophisticated about their wheelchairs; they use them for an average of ten years or more. Because of all the options available for the rehabilitation wheelchairs, it takes at least twenty minutes longer to order a rehabilitation product than it takes to order a home care wheelchair. It also takes at least two days for Legacy to train a dealer on how to "prescribe" a rehabilitation chair. After taking an order, the factory must assemble the product to order with its appropriate options. If a dealer or customer service representative makes a mistake in ordering a rehabilitation wheelchair, it must be returned to the factory for rework.

Diversity manifests itself as a cost factor in other ways as well. Consider, for example, the engineering resources required to serve these two quite different markets. While no rehabilitation product line is more than four years old, the current line of home care products was introduced and developed between 1970 and 1977. Continuous innovation and a steady stream of new products are required to be competitive and profitable in the rehabilitation market. As a result, approximately 80 percent of the company's total spending for research and development (R&D) and for engineering goes toward product innovations for the rehabilitation market. Since the home care market supports a relatively "low tech" wheelchair that is essentially a commodity item, the remaining 20 percent of the total spending for R&D and engineering goes toward improving the quality and decreasing the costs of Legacy's manufacturing.

Consider also the diversity in product liability that Legacy faces in serving these two distinctly different markets. While the home care products are sold largely to inactive, elderly patients, the rehabilitation products target injury patients who live and work in their customized wheelchairs for ten or twenty years. The rehabilitation market includes power wheelchairs. Not only are users of power wheelchairs much more seriously disabled than users of home care wheelchairs, but they also frequently use their wheelchairs to travel to and from work. The motor and batteries make the power wheelchairs heavy, which makes them liable to tip over. Consequently, the rehabilitation products create much more liability exposure than the home care chairs. Like most companies that provide medical service products, Legacy's product liability insurance is expensive. But since Legacy's traditional cost system excluded the costs associated with product liability insurance sales, order entry, R&D, engineering, distribution, and marketing from the company's product costs, the traditional cost system painted a misleading picture about the relative profitability of the two different market segments.

Choosing Customers and Customer Service Attributes

Two critical elements in any competitive strategy are selecting which customers to target and determining which service attributes are most critical to provide. Without an understanding of which customers are most profitable and why, a company may focus its resources on the wrong markets, the wrong mix of customers, or the wrong service attributes.

Unfortunately, Legacy had never considered customer service in determining its competitive strategy. Since it did not know the costs of providing its services, it was never able to tie services into its pricing strategy except on an ad hoc basis. Not surprisingly, Legacy had little idea which service attributes were important to customers. Moreover, it had only an intuitive "feel" about the relative profitability of the two market segments it served. It had never included customer costs (which comprised approximately 25 percent of total costs) in its strategic cost analyses. Instead, customer costs were simply considered "part of the cost of doing business." Consequently, Legacy's pricing policies did not reflect the different costs associated with serving each market segment.

Before conducting a strategic cost analysis, Legacy had for some time been shifting its resources away from the home care market in an attempt to increase its share of the more glamorous rehabilitation market. When customer costs were included in the cost analysis, however, the home care market was found to be far more profitable than the rehabilitation market. This information, along with the implementation of a disciplined approach to improving customer service, helped Legacy refocus its competitive strategies and thus improve its overall profitability significantly.

THE EFFECTS OF DIVERSITY

Serving different customers and markets and employing different distribution channels (each with its own set of customer service requirements) create a large degree of complexity in a company's operations. Complexity is one of the major drivers of overhead cost in any organization.

Complexity is a function of an organization's product mix, customer mix, business process design, business systems, and product design. Each of these factors influences the set of activities required of the organization to develop, manufacture, and sell products. The many types of customer service diversity include:

- Intensity of customer service requirements;
- Technical service requirements;
- Engineering support requirements;
- Order frequency;
- Delivery frequency;
- Geographic distance;
- Supporting documentation requirements;
- Sales and promotional support; and
- Advertising.

Clearly, this list is not exhaustive. Each organization and the customers, markets, and distribution channels that it employs form a unique set of diversities that must be managed.

Two different companies that produce exactly the same product can have quite different cost structures, depending (for example) on their target customers, distribution strategies, and promotion programs. The product-driven costs for each of these companies would be the same, but the customer-driven costs would differ. (Indeed, the same would be true for one company that sold the same product to two different sets of customers.)

The Light Consumer Goods Industry: A Case Study

Consider, for example, another case study—that of Kanoe, Inc., a manufacturer of recreational boats. Kanoe sells to two different types of customers: buying groups and distributors. Each type of customer is examined in detail below.

Buying Groups

A buying group is a collection of independent stores that organizes to negotiate buying agreements with manufacturers. This arrangement allows a large group of small stores to leverage their buying power. Besides affording the manufacturer lower margins because of the collective buying agreement, group buying arrangements also place large demands on the service support the manufacturer must provide.

Two characteristics of the buying groups that cause high service costs are:

1. The stores are physically dispersed; and
2. Each purchases its own products.

Since the stores make their own buying decisions, each must be visited by a salesman. The sheer geographic diversity of the buying group, therefore, demands a great deal of sales force time.

Due to their size and customer base, these small stores typically order in small quantities. Each order triggers a series of activities and transactions, including:

- Entering orders;
- Verifying the customer's credit;
- Creating a pick list;
- Preparing a bill of lading;
- Calculating the freight charges;
- Packing and shipping the order; and
- Generating the invoice.

The volume of activity that these small orders create clearly drives up the service costs per unit of the product being sold.

Distribution Channels

A different situation exists in serving Kanoe's distributors channel. Distributors typically have only one buying decision maker and shipping location (although sometimes there are several). Their distributors, therefore, require little sales force time compared with the time that must be devoted to the buying groups. Distributors typically order products once a month in large quantities and take delivery at only one shipping destination. A distributor, therefore, requires only one bill of lading and one invoice each month. Moreover, a distributor usually receives large shipments, such as full truckloads.

Clearly, buying groups cause a much greater percentage of the total transactions and activities that Kanoe must perform than the distributors for the same sales volume. It follows, therefore, that a greater share of the costs incurred to perform these activities costs should be attributed to the buying groups.

ACTIVITY-BASED CUSTOMER COST INFORMATION

Just as activity-based costing (ABC) can help companies account for manufacturing diversity, ABC can also be used to account for the diversity of customer-driven costs. By focusing on activities and the different activity requirements placed on the organization by different customers, ABC provides visibility into the activity cost structure of customer-driven costs.

Customer costs typically make up 20–25 percent of the total cost of delivering products and services. By their very nature, customer service, sales promotion, and distribution-related costs are both labor-intensive and transaction-intensive. Tracing these labor and transaction costs to their sources helps a company identify the relative profitability of customers, markets, or distribution channels.

Strategic Importance

Knowing and understanding the sources of profitability are critical for managers who set strategies that ultimately determine the long-term viability of an organization. Costing out the activities required to provide different services to different customers, markets, or channels (and thus identifying the relative profitability of each) serves as the basis for appropriate allocations of resources and for initiatives designed to increase profitability.

Customer-Driven Activities

Perhaps just as important as the strategic importance of knowing and understanding an organization's customer costs are the identification, analysis, and evaluation of customer-driven activities. Customer-driven costs are driven by activities that constitute the extended product. These activities can be a significant source of competitive advantage or disadvantage, depending on how resources are deployed to meet customer needs.

Defining those attributes of the extended product that customers value most and analyzing the activities of the company that constitute those attributes make it possible to analyze the relative cost impact of alternative customer-service strategies. This analysis provides a means for improving the efficiency and effectiveness of those attributes that companies choose to provide as a part of their competitive offering.

EXHIBIT B5.1

Traditional Costing vs. Activity-Based Costing Systems

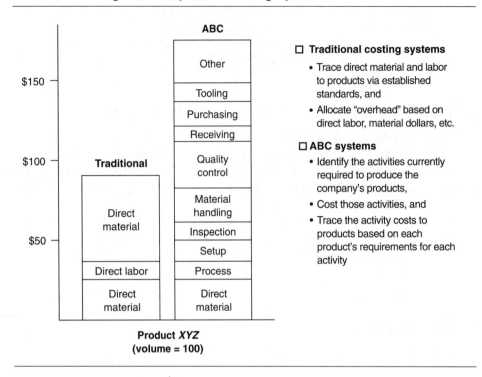

Product *XYZ*
(volume = 100)

☐ **Traditional costing systems**

- Trace direct material and labor to products via established standards, and
- Allocate "overhead" based on direct labor, material dollars, etc.

☐ **ABC systems**

- Identify the activities currently required to produce the company's products,
- Cost those activities, and
- Trace the activity costs to products based on each product's requirements for each activity

THE TREATMENT OF CUSTOMER-DRIVEN COSTS

The treatment of product costs has undergone few changes in the past fifty years, and the same can also be said about customer-driven costs. Although manufacturers are beginning to switch to ABC systems for product costing purposes, few companies have looked at their customer costs. Most companies still use percentage of sales dollars (or some other relatively arbitrary method) to allocate "below the line" expenses to products—if they are allocated at all. But ABC can also be used help deal with customer-driven costs. Exhibit B5.1 depicts the differences between traditional and ABC costing systems and some of the differences that encourage manufacturers to switch to ABC.

The Traditional Treatment

Companies have traditionally given little thought to including customer-driven costs in their strategic cost analyses; "back of the envelope" methods have predominated. Clearly, these methods do not accurately reflect the diversity of serving one customer rather than another. As noted earlier, this situation is partially the result of the relatively small role in strategy formulation that customer service has historically played.

Economies of scale and low-cost-producer strategies have dominated managerial thinking for many years. People typically measure the attributes of performance they perceive to be important. Since performance measures are a derivative of strategy, if customer service is not an element of strategy, customer cost information will not be measured.

The Role of External Financial Reporting

A related factor is the role that financial accounting systems (which were designed in the past to meet external reporting requirements) have played in supplying cost information for internal management needs. Customer-driven costs are not part of "product cost" as that term is defined under generally accepted accounting principles (GAAP). To value inventory under GAAP, customer-driven costs (and engineering costs) must be separated from manufacturing costs. Only the costs of supporting the production of a product can be included in inventoriable product costs.

Inventoriable costs become expenses only when inventory is sold. Noninventoriable costs, by contrast, are expensed immediately and considered "below the line" costs. These costs are usually unrelated to the volume of production and are, therefore, considered fixed. Since these costs are generally dwarfed by manufacturing costs and assumed to be fixed, there has been little interest in developing any rigorous methodology for assigning these costs.

The Pet Food Industry: A Case Study

Much has been written about the problems with traditional cost accounting systems and the information that they produce. Distorted cost information used for decision making can lead to suboptimal strategies and to misallocations of resources, as shown in the following case study.

Consider the impact that misleading cost information had on a pet food company that was considering building a new 400,000-square-foot warehouse because its existing warehouses were full. A project team was assigned the task of investigating the cause of the capacity shortage. As the team visited each warehouse, it found that each warehouse was, indeed, filled to capacity—primarily with dog food.

The team did not understand why this overstocking occurred until it learned the method that was used to allocate warehousing costs: The company's storage and distribution costs were allocated based on product value. The use of this method meant that a 4-cubic-foot bag of dog food was allocated $3.89 in warehousing costs, while a single case of gourmet cat food was allocated $12. This seemingly inexpensive storage cost for the bulky bags of dog food led the dog-food product managers to keep excessive inventories of dog food on hand all the time.

After all, if the cost information that the dog-food product managers received told them that it cost little to carry huge quantities of finished goods inventory, what product manager *wouldn't* want to keep vast quantities of finished goods inventory on hand? This large inventory translated into immediate service to customers. It also meant increased machine and labor utilization in the plant due to large lot sizes, driving down reported product cost. In short, it was a situation that was almost too good to be true. (In fact, the warehouse order sizes caused the large manufacturing batch sizes. The factory was also carrying large inventories due to this cost allocation scheme.)

By simply changing the allocation of distribution costs to cubic feet and number of units handled, both behavior and operating policies changed. The dog food product managers learned to manage inventory and no longer ordered in large batches, so the inventory of dog food shrank and the need for a new warehouse evaporated.

As this case study shows, arbitrarily spreading distribution costs over products distorts the underlying economics of storage and distribution and can lead to poor decision making and to dysfunctional behavior.

Activity-Based Costing Treatment

Most of the attention about ABC systems that have been developed and implemented so far has focused exclusively on the activities and costs inside the factory walls—in other words, on the same activities and costs that are reflected on the income statement as "cost of sales." An activity-based approach to the treatment of sales, general, and administrative (SG&A) expenses (the so-called below-the-line costs) has, for the most part, been omitted, both in cost management literature and in the actual development of ABC systems.

Customer-Driven Activity-Based Costs

Conceptually, there is nothing different about the development of customer-driven costs using an ABC system. The treatment of customer driven costs is based on the same premise as product-driven costs using an ABC system: That is, activities consume the resources of the organization, and cost objects (e.g., components, products, customers, or markets) consume those activities by creating the need for their performance.

In other words, an ABC system traces costs to the activities that consume resources and then traces those activity costs to the cost objects that consume the activities. Exhibit B5.2 shows how costs are traced under ABC. The difference lies in the particular cost object to which the activity cost is attached. Product-driven ABC costs are attached to such cost objects as components, subassemblies, and

EXHIBIT B5.2

Tracing Costs Under Activity-Based Costing

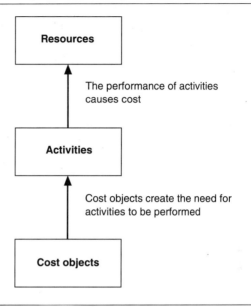

Resources

↑

The performance of activities causes cost

Activities

↑

Cost objects create the need for activities to be performed

Cost objects

assembled products. Customer-driven ABC costs, on the other hand, are attached to such cost objects as customers, markets, and distribution channels.

Levels of Attachment

In applying ABC to customer-driven costs, it is important to understand the concept of *attachment*. Costs are attached to different types of cost objects at different levels. For example, a market is a higher-level cost object than an individual customer.

Some costs—promotional programs, for example—are targeted not at individual customers but at the entire market. Therefore, it is inappropriate to assign these promotional costs to a cost object lower than the entire target market. The number of levels of cost attachment varies from one company to the next. Exhibit B5.3 shows the levels that, however, generally describe most manufacturing organizations:

- For product-driven activity costs, there are four levels at which costs are attached through the use of cost drivers: unit-level, batch-level, product-level, and plant-level.
- For customer-driven activity costs, there are usually four or five levels: order-level, customer-level, channel-level, market-level, and enterprise-level.

EXHIBIT B5.3

Assigning Costs to Different Levels: The Hierarchy of Costs

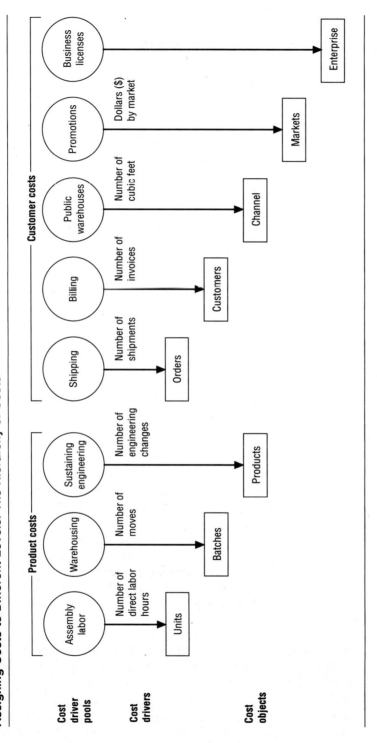

EXHIBIT B5.4

Example of a Company With Multiple Channels of Distribution

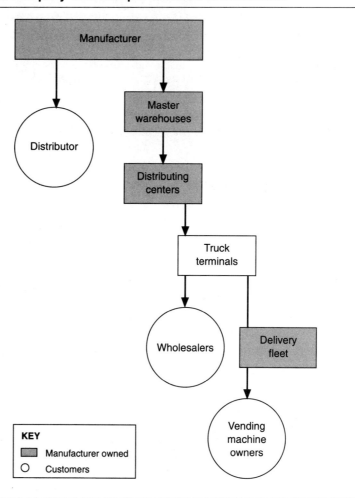

The number of levels of customer activities may vary. Some companies (e.g., Philip Morris) distribute their products through a large number of distribution channels, including distributors, wholesalers, retailers, dealers, cooperatives, and vending machines. Each distribution channel has different steps. Exhibit B5.4 depicts a company with multiple distribution channels. In the case of distributors, for example, products are delivered directly from the factory to the distributors. Products going to wholesalers, on the other hand, may go from master warehouses, to distribution centers, on to truck terminals, and finally to the wholesalers. Products that are sold through vending machines often go through even more steps—from truck terminals, to delivery trucks, to local agents, and finally to the individual vending machines.

From this case study, it can be seen that the number of activities (and thus the costs) required to sell products through vending machines varies substantially from the number of activities (and thus the costs) required to sell to distributors. To support vending machine sales, a manufacturer must maintain master warehouses, local distribution centers, and a fleet of delivery trucks. While wholesalers and vending machines should share the costs of maintaining the master warehouses and local distribution centers, only the vending machine sales should bear the cost of supporting the local delivery fleet.

CUSTOMER-DRIVEN ACTIVITIES

This section explains how customer-driven costs should be broken down into the following different levels of attachment:

- *Order-level costs:* Order-level costs are the costs of activities attributable directly to the selling and delivery of orders to individual customers (e.g., order entry, shipping, billing, and freight).
- *Customer-level costs:* Customer-level costs are the costs of non-order-related activities that are attributable to individual customers (e.g., sales force, credit and collections, returns, and catalogs).
- *Channel-level costs:* Channel-level costs are the costs of activities that are particular to a distribution channel and are not driven by customer orders or particular customers. (These activities can include maintaining master warehouses, a delivery fleet, and certain promotional campaigns.) Distribution channels are the method by which customers have products delivered. Not only can markets be served by more than one channel of distribution, but one customer may buy the same product through different channels. Channel conflict and overlaps between markets are common, which makes the segregation of channel and market activities challenging.
- *Market-level costs:* Market-level costs are the costs of activities relating to a particular class of customers. These activities are performed to define and analyze customer needs, develop new technologies to satisfy customer needs, and create name recognition. They include advertising, R&D, and market research.
- *Enterprise-level costs:* Enterprise-level costs are the costs of activities required to remain in business that are unassignable to any lower level (e.g., pension liability, licenses, taxes, and board of director fees).

Each type of cost is discussed on the following pages.

Order-Level Costs

Order-level costs are those costs directly traceable to processing and delivering individual customer orders. These costs include discounts and the costs triggered every time an order is placed (e.g., order entry, order picking, shipping, freight, and invoicing).

Customer-Level Costs

Customer-level costs include all costs associating with maintaining a customer, including:

- Making sales calls;
- Evaluating a customer's credit;
- Sending samples, catalogs, and other mailings;
- Handling information requests; and
- Managing collections.

Since many customer-level costs are triggered by the acquisition of a new customer, it is often useful to segregate the costs of maintaining a customer from the cost of acquiring new customers. This distinction substantially improves cost planning.

Channel-Level Costs

Some companies have channel-level costs, which are the costs of maintaining a separate channel of distribution (e.g., a series of warehouses or a fleet of delivery trucks). These channel-level costs include the costs of:

- Managing the channel;
- Maintaining the channel; and
- Advertising, promoting, and marketing the channel.

Channel-level costs do not include the costs of taking orders or delivering through a particular channel. Those costs are order-level costs, even though they may be associated solely with a particular channel. A channel's order-level costs are simply treated as another activity center at the order level.

Market-Level Costs

Many costs are not traceable to individual customers or even to particular distribution channels. Costs for marketing and advertising, for example, apply broadly to entire classes of customers or markets. Market-level costs, therefore, include costs incurred to develop and maintain a presence in a marketplace or to attract new customers. These costs are independent of the number of orders received, the number of customers served, or the channel of distribution used. They typically include costs for:

- Advertising;
- Promotion;
- Product liability;
- Trade shows;
- Marketing staff; and
- General R&D, but not engineering R&D. (Engineering costs are driven by and directly traceable to products, while general R&D is associated with satisfying the needs of a particular group of customers—i.e., a market.)

Enterprise-Level Costs

Enterprise-level costs are costs that a company incurs simply to exist. These costs include costs for:

- Executive salaries;
- Licenses;
- Director's fees;
- Taxes; or
- Outstanding liabilities (e.g., pension obligations, accrued taxes, liens, or debt payments).

Costs should be segregated so that only relevant costs are considered in an analysis. For example, when evaluating the costs of ordering products, customer-level costs should be segregated because they are not directly affected by changes in ordering policies. Similarly, customer-level costs are not affected by new promotional programs or by other market-level costs. On the other hand, decisions such as whether to abandon a market involve most costs, including order-level, channel-level, and customer-level costs.

THE TWO-STAGE COST MODEL

ABC can be seen as a two-stage model. ABC establishes a relationship between resources and activities and products/customers. In the first stage, resources (e.g., salaries, utilities, fringe benefits, depreciation, rent, and supplies) are directly traced to activity centers based on some measure of usage. Each activity center represents a business process, the resources for which are, in turn, directly consumed by products or customers. Usage is tracked by use of a cost driver. By dividing the total cost of an activity by the number of outputs, a cost per unit of activity is calculated. The cost per unit of activity is applied to the consumption of activities by specific cost objects (usually products or customers) to calculate costs per cost object. Customer-driven activities (e.g., sales calls, order entry, and product delivery) are distinct from product-driven activities, because customer-driven activities are directly consumed by the customers.

Although it might be argued that customers consume products and, therefore, that all activities exist to be consumed by customers, the objective of an ABC system is to reflect the consumption of costs as close to the events that trigger them as possible. The cost assignment should represent the clearest possible cause-and-effect relationship. Product-driven costs are consumed by customers only after the customers consume the products. Therefore, the linkage between product activities and customers becomes long and sometimes obscure. Instead of trying to model how customers—through their choice of products—trigger product activities, products are used as surrogate cost objects. In this way, costs are assigned to products, then product and customer costs are assigned to customers.

An ABC system assigns all costs to products or customers based on the activities that they consume. But since products or customers consume many costs in a company only indirectly, an ABC system assigns costs in two stages. Exhibit B5.5 depicts the ABC structure for customer-driven costs. The following sections provide more detail about each of the two stages.

The First Stage

In the first stage, customer-driven resources (e.g., salaries, operating supplies, depreciation, data processing, and maintenance) are traced to activity cost pools by means of first-stage cost drivers.

A first-stage cost driver is defined as a measure of resource consumption by activity. Examples of first-stage cost drivers include:

- Square footage;
- Direct trace (e.g., electricity via meters);
- Head count assignment;
- CPU time;
- Number of work orders; and
- Percent of time spent per activity.

The difference in the first stage between traditional cost systems and ABC systems is critical. While traditional cost systems often have a similar first stage that involves the allocation of resources to cost pools, the nature of these cost pools is significantly different from the cost pools used in an ABC system. Specifically, traditional cost pools are predominantly oriented around product lines or

EXHIBIT B5.5

Activity-Based Costing Structure for Customer-Driven Costs

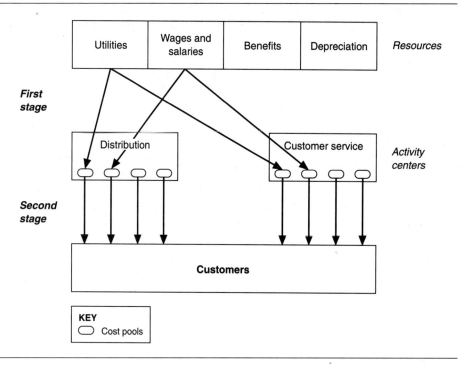

market segments, while ABC cost pools are oriented around activities. Once customer-driven overhead resources are traced to activity cost pools, the first stage of the model is complete, because the total cost of each activity has been identified.

The Second Stage

In the second stage of the activity-based model, second-stage cost drivers are used to compute the cost per unit of activity for each cost object and level of attachment. A second-stage cost driver can be defined as a measure of activity consumption by cost object (e.g., a customer or a distribution channel). Examples of second-stage cost drivers include:

- Number of sales calls;
- Number of customer orders;
- Number of credits;

- Number of bills of ladings;
- Number of invoices;
- Freight charges;
- Number of returns;
- Number of customer inquiries; and
- Number of customer inquiries expedited.

The unit cost of the activity is then attached at the appropriate level to a cost object based on how much of that activity the cost object requires.

The selection of second-stage cost drivers is critical. It is important to identify measures of output that are proportional to the cost objects' consumption of an activity's resources. In this way, the more cost driver units a customer triggers, the more cost the customer will be assigned.

Selecting second-stage cost drivers depends on the availability of relevant data as well as on a cost driver's correlation with resource consumption. Data about customer cost drivers are usually not as readily available as data about product cost drivers, because distribution information systems are usually given a low priority.

In many cases, customer activities are driven by a customer transaction of one kind or another. The right-hand column of Exhibit B5.6, for example, shows second-stage cost drivers for a pump manufacturer. As can be seen, costs are assigned to orders, customers, and markets.

Customer Service

A customer service center takes customer orders and answers customer inquiries. The principal costs of a customer service center are for salaries and telephone lines. Both resources are consumed according to how much time customers spend on the telephone with the service representatives. To assign customer service costs, the company may therefore record either the length of telephone calls or the number of calls by customers. The company can use bills from the telephone company to identify both the number and length of outbound calls. Then, by cross-referencing the origination numbers of telephone calls to customers, the company can automatically generate cost drivers. Alternatively, the company could keep manual records. Either way, the company would assign customer service costs to customers based on each customer's use of the customer service department (i.e., whether usage is measured by the number of telephone calls or by time spent).

Finished Goods Inventory

Some customers, by negotiating quick delivery terms or by demanding private-label products, create the need to carry finished goods inventory. The

EXHIBIT B5.6

Second-Stage Cost Drivers for Pump Manufacturer

Activity center	Cost pool	Cost driver
Distribution	Shipping dock	Number of line items ordered
	Shipping office	Number of bills of lading
	Distribution center	Number of line items filled by distribution center
	Distribution center	Number of bills of lading through distribution center
	Freight	Way of bill sampling
Customer service	Industrial customer service	Number of customer orders
	OEM customer service	Number of units ordered
Sales	Sales force	Number of sales calls
	National accounts	Estimate by account representative to national accounting
	Commissions	Commission formula by customer
	Discounts	Sales records by customer
	Net pricing	Complicated calculation by customer
Marketing	Industrial marketing	N/A (direct to industrial market)
	OEM marketing	N/A (OEM market)
R&D	Industrial R&D	N/A (industrial market)
	OEM R&D	N/A (OEM market)
Administrative	Billing	Number of invoices
	Credits	Number of credit requests and adjustments
	Accounts receivable	Average dollars outstanding by customer

costs of carrying this inventory should be assigned to the companies that create the need. The warehousing space required depends on the physical size of the inventory required.

Sales Force Costs

In most companies, sales force costs are high and vary considerably by customer. Some customers, for example, buy only simple products that are easy to provide, while other customers buy complex products that require prolonged and costly negotiations. Since salespeople usually earn sales commissions based on the account involved, sales commission records tend to be accurate. However, sales should not be used as the basis for assigning other sales force costs. Sales representatives spend much of their time on accounts that end up buying from a competitor (or that never buy anything at all), which means that no commission is paid. In highly competitive markets, such customers tend to absorb a high proportion of sales representatives' time.

Typically, the job of the sales force is to make sales calls, develop personal relationships with customers, distribute literature, and negotiate sales. All these tasks are directly related to the number of sales calls made to a particular customers. Therefore, sales force costs are often assigned based on the number of sales calls per customer. Since few systems record this information, manual records usually have to be used. Fortunately, most sales managers manually record this information anyway.

APPLYING COSTS TO CUSTOMERS

Cost driver information generated from the two-stage cost model discussed in the preceding section can be used to assign costs accurately to customers. The four steps for doing so are analyzed next.

Establishing Customer Classifications

Before costs can be assigned to customers, a preliminary step of establishing customer classifications must be completed. Specifically, customers must be categorized into channels and markets so that costs can be applied accurately. Since many customer-driven costs are not assignable to individual customers, customers must be aggregated into groups.

This aggregation allows costs to be assigned to the appropriate group of customers. For example, if Apple Computer attends a trade show for computer dealers, its costs for attending the show should be assigned only to the appropriate group of computer dealers. Customer groups (such as computer dealers in this example) are classes of customers that use the company's products in the same manner and that have similar business characteristics. If these conditions are met, the result should be groups of customers with similar buying habits (e.g., similar buying frequency, order size, or product and service mix).

For example, a manufacturer of saw chains would segregate original equipment manufacturers (OEMs) from distributors and retailers. Each of these groups has very different buying characteristics:

- *OEMs* regularly buy large quantities of saw chains. They demand substantial price discounts and also design engineering assistance when developing new chain saws.

- *Distributors* buy "the whole catalog" over the course of a year because they buy the saw chains and, in turn, resell the chains to a huge number of small users. Therefore, distributors order small shipments of a large variety of products, with large volume fluctuations over the course of a year.
- *Retailers,* on the other hand, order only a limited number of items but require just-in-time (JIT) shipments to each of their stores. This practice creates many order picking, shipping, and freight transactions. Retailers also demand plastic see-through packing for consumers. Since consumer use of chains is seasonal, retailers order most of their chains during the spring months, which causes scheduling problems for manufacturers.

As can be seen, each of these different customer groups creates a different set of challenges and costs for the manufacturer. The virtue of establishing customer classifications in these cases is that, as a group, the customers' problems will be similar. By grouping customers into classes and identifying the profitability of each group, management obtains an understanding about the costs and benefits of each type of customer.

Validating the Classifications

The second step in applying costs to customers is to validate the customer classifications. Often, a company's marketing department fails to maintain classification records or does a poor job of establishing them in the first place. In addition, it is not uncommon for a customer to change its classification over time. For example, a wholesaler can grow into a distributor, or a buying group can transform itself into a cooperative. Therefore, company customer classifications tend to be error-prone and must be reconsidered periodically.

When conducting an ABC study, customer classifications are validated by analyzing whether all the members of a given group actually do buy alike. For example, do they:

- Order at roughly the same frequency?
- Buy in small or large quantities?
- Require much sales support (e.g., sales calls or customer service calls)?

If a member of a given customer group behaves differently from the group, its classification should be reviewed, validated, or changed.

Creating Bills of Activities

The next step in applying costs to customers is to create a bill of activity for each customer. A bill of activity is a routing of each activity that a customer consumes. This routing should reflect how the customer acquires products and how much activity each customer consumes.

For each customer, the bill of activity defines how many cost driver units the customer caused. The ABC system then applies a cost per cost driver unit to that customer. For example, if a customer placed 200 customer orders and the cost driver rate for each order was $50, the customer would be assigned $10,000.

Resolving Channel Conflict

When creating a bill of activity for each customer, channel conflict must be kept in mind. Frequently, customers end up using competing channels of distribution over a given year.

For example, although a retailer usually buys its steel-belted radial tires directly from the manufacturer, it sometimes receives an order that is so large that it buys tires from a local distributor. While the retailer does not earn as high a margin on units bought through the distributor, it keeps the sale by occasionally buying through the distributor. A customer may have more than one bill of activity for a given product. One cannot assume that a customer always buys its products in the same way.

Evaluating the Costs

The last step in applying costs to customers is to evaluate the costs of serving individual customers or groups of customers, along with their channel-specific costs.

In analyzing costs, the costs must be segregated by level of attachment. To analyze customer profitability, only order-level and customer-level costs should be included. Market-level costs would include all costs except enterprise-level costs. This allows management to assess the profitability of its different channels. Combining channel-level and market-level costs makes it possible for management to judge the true profitability of different market segments.

DEVELOPING COMPREHENSIVE BUSINESS STRATEGIES

To develop comprehensive business strategies that encompass customer service strategies, managers need accurate and relevant customer cost information in a timely manner. Management needs to know which services provide a competitive advantage. This, in turn, requires knowing how much the various customer services actually cost and how important they are to customers. Management also needs to know which customers result in the most profit. Finally, management needs to know which customers, markets, and distribution channels to target (including the resources required for the various channels).

EXHIBIT B5.7

Customer Costs for Packaged Food Manufacturer

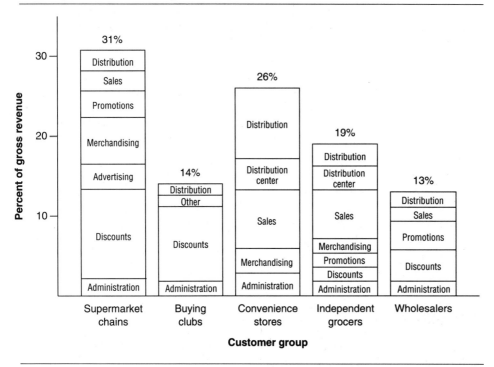

While the answers to these questions depend on many factors (e.g., the prospects for growth of each different market, the company's distinctive competence, competitors' strengths and weaknesses, the company's access to distribution channels, and the level of investment needed), the most important issue usually is which customers are most profitable. While managers often know intuitively that it costs more to serve some customers than it does to serve others, ABC can provide this information. ABC tells managers how much more one market or channel costs than another. An ABC cost study also pinpoints exactly what activities cause the difference.

The Packaged Foods Industry: A Case Study

Consider another case study—that of a packaged food company. Exhibit B5.7 portrays the customer costs for that company. This company sells its product to five major customer groups. Customer costs vary from a high of 31 percent of gross revenues for supermarket chains to a low of 13 percent for wholesalers.

Supermarket chains, with their significant buying clout, can negotiate large discounts and also expensive marketing program support. Since supermarket chains own their own distribution centers, the packaged food company has to make shipments to only a few locations, which keeps administrative and distribution costs low.

By contrast, convenience stores (which operate with low inventories at many locations) generate vast numbers of transactions for ordering, picking, billing, and shipping. While the supermarket chains buy in quantities of full truck loads, convenience stores order in quantities that require pallets to be broken. Thus, for example, the packaged food company's shipping department can use a forklift to load an entire truck bound for a supermarket chain in the time it takes to load only eighteen cases in a truck bound for a convenience store.

The Pursuit of the Wrong Customers

A marketing strategy is like a supertanker: Although the helm can be turned, it takes a long time before the ship can change direction. Therefore, if a company finds itself chasing its less-profitable customers, it can take years to effectively reorient that company's marketing strategy. The company must reeducate its end customers, reconfigure its manufacturing and distribution processes, and possibly introduce different types of products.

By pursuing the wrong customers, a company misses opportunities and squanders resources. Information about customer profitability is critical when management must make resource allocations between market segments.

Uncovering unprofitable customers is important strategic information. Armed with this information, managers generally have three alternatives:

1. Improve the efficiency of providing customer service to the unprofitable customer to achieve a profitable relationship;
2. Renegotiate pricing agreements; or
3. Drop the customer and its business.

Different Prices for Different Customers

Knowing customer-driven costs suggests one should charge different prices to different customers. The functioning of the marketplace would improve if all customer-driven costs could be charged directly back to each customer through pricing. However, federal laws and regulations such as the Robinson-Patman Act specifically prohibit the practice of pricing discrimination.

The Robinson-Patman Act allows price differentials if cost differences occur in providing a product or service. Should a customer pricing differentiation strategy be chosen, customer-driven activity-based costs can provide the data to substantiate cost differentials charged. Ironically, small business are typically the customers with relatively high transactions costs and are the ones most likely to be hurt by activity-based pricing.

Treatment of Undesirable Customers

Undesirable customers, once they are identified, should be transformed into profitable customers, if possible. The first step in this conversion is to uncover why the customers are unprofitable to serve. For example:

- Do they buy low-margin products?
- Do they require an abnormal amount of sales, customer service, or engineering support?
- Are they given discounts that are simply too high?

Fortunately, ABC identifies the factors that cause high customer service costs. If sales expenses are too high, the sales force could be refocused. If more drastic action is required, a company can sell through telemarketing or through manufacturer's representatives. (For example, it may cost a company roughly $100–$150 for a personal call by a sales representative as opposed to roughly $25–$35 for a call by a telemarketer.) Naturally, a telephone call is less effective than a face-to-face meeting, but telemarketing can efficiently supplement a sales force. Sales management can also change the commission structure to encourage sales representatives to sell high-margin products to the desirable customers.

Customer Partnerships

Developing customer partnerships is a large factor in customer margin contributions. If a customer frequently orders large volumes of products, management may consider installing electronic data interchange (EDI) at the customer's facility. With EDI, the customer can electronically inquire on the supplier's inventory availability and can place new orders without manual intervention, thus saving both parties time and money. This practice also allows both companies to handle smaller order quantities economically. Since the ABC system calculates the cost per order entry, the system provides all the information needed for the financial justification of the EDI system.

Should a customer's contributions to profits be negative, that customer's discounts should be scrutinized. Sales contracts typically are based solely on sales volume. Service costs are generally ignored because suppliers lack service cost information.

With ABC, however, a company will have access to service cost information on which to negotiate more profitable as well as less costly sales contracts. For example, a company that implements ABC soon will know the following information:

- How much shipping a full truck (as opposed to ten smaller shipments) saves;
- How much a faxed order (as opposed to a telephone order) costs; and
- What the cost of stocking a private-label product is.

Renegotiated Contracts

In many cases, a company can increase a customer's margin contributions by forcing that customer to renegotiate its sales contract even before the contract expires. Sales contracts typically require minimum sales volumes to qualify for certain discounts, though this is a provision that is rarely enforced. With the information that ABC provides, management can make a case for enforcing or renegotiating contract terms, thereby increasing sales volume or reducing discounts.

Distribution policies can also be changed to reduce costs. By raising the minimum order quantity, money is saved on shipping, billing, and freight. Assume, for example, that a company had a minimum order quantity of three units. Using ABC rates, a calculation can be made about the reduction in billing, order entry, shipping, and freight transactions that would result by raising the minimum order quantity from three to five units. Changes in the number of transactions multiplied by the variable cost of each shipping and billing transaction plus freight savings provides an estimate of the savings to be realized from the higher minimum order quantity. Against these savings, management can weigh the market impact.

Alternatively—again using information from the ABC system—management can charge handling fees and require customers to pay freight on small orders. Using ABC data, a company can even determine how much it would cost to offer three-day (as opposed to ten-day) delivery times.

Self-Induced Unprofitability

Sometimes high customer service costs occur not because of the customer but because of the company itself. At one company, for example, high customer service costs made many customers appear unprofitable. The problem actually stemmed, however, from the company's use of confusing and obsolete product literature. It took a customer an average of 20 minutes to determine which product to order. The company was imposing this cost and frustration on its own customers!

When talking to customer service representatives, the customers in this case always asked many questions, which consumed both parties' time. After the company replaced its catalog, customer service overtime disappeared and the customer service telephone bill dropped by 20 percent.

Another option when dealing directly with small, high-cost customers is to require them to make their purchases indirectly through distributors. Distributors consolidate many small orders into large ones and usually have a limited number of shipment locations to keep order and freight costs down. Since distributors create few customer orders, bills of lading and invoices, they are relatively inexpensive to serve. The distributors make their money by selling products from many manufacturers to the small accounts to which manufacturers cannot afford to sell directly.

ABC provides an early warning system. If the business environment changes, customer buying habits will probably change as well. ABC can alert management immediately to such changes. By forecasting and tracking the number of units per order, days outstanding, returns, product mix, and sales volumes, a company can spot changes in a customer's buying characteristics. If the number of units per order drops as a customer begins buying more build-to-stock units, for example, the customer may be implementing JIT. If so, it would probably be wise to discuss long-term contracts and EDI with the customer.

A STRATEGY FOR IMPROVED CUSTOMER SERVICE

Using ABC to analyze customer-driven costs provides a company with significant competitive insight, especially as companies move toward improved customer service strategies. ABC systems identify the activities that are performed, cost those activities, and then trace them to the customer/market/channel that requires those activities to be performed. In doing so, a company can identify the true sources (i.e., customers, channels, and so forth) of profitability. However, there is an added benefit to developing an ABC system. By identifying and costing the customer-driven activities that are currently performed, a company can match those activities (services) against those that the customers value. Activities that are not of value to customers are targets for elimination. High-cost activities that customers value are targets for improvement.

As the ABC system is maintained over time, customer activity requirements, costs, and profitability can be rationalized against the revenue generated by a customer/market. In doing so, a company is provided with feedback on the efficacy of customer service strategies and of initiatives designed to improve customer service levels.

OPERATIONAL COST MANAGEMENT

CHAPTER FOUR

Improving Performance

Managers not only need cost management information for strategic decisions, but also for operational control and improvement. A new responsibility of management is to own and continuously improve processes. *Process management* focuses on the definition, direction, and improvement of processes toward the delivery of customer value. Processes are activities that transform inputs to outputs. Examples of processes are the sales order process, the scheduling process, the order filling process, the vendor selection process, and the customer service process. Frequently, transforming inputs to outputs will connect the boundaries between functions. For example, the vendor payment process involves the accounting, procurement , and receiving functions. Management of the process assures that the functions work together to provide timely and accurate payments to vendors, who are the customers of this process.

Managing boundaries between functions is critical to assuring smooth process flows and coordinated objectives for the overall benefit of the process customers. Accounting professionals will need to develop performance and cost information to support the processes of the organization, as opposed to merely the functional departments. All four articles in this section are related to using cost management information to improve processes.

Reading 4.1   The Horizontal View of ABM

M.R. Ostrenga and F.R. Probst, "Process Value Analysis: The Missing Link in Cost Management," *Journal of Cost Management* (Fall 1992), pp. 4–14.

Ostrenga and Probst (OP) provide a brief overview of Ernst and Young's methodology, termed Process Value Analysis (PVA).[1] PVA is an example of a methodology that incorporates both the vertical and horizontal dimensions of the ABM cross model. In this article, OP provide examples of how the horizontal dimension of the ABM model is brought into the analysis. In their example, activities can be arranged into processes, the cost drivers for processes can be identified, the activities within the process can be labeled as value added or non-value added, and finally, performance measures (cycle time, time/shift) can be used to support process improvement. In addition, OP combine their process analysis into a more traditional ABC product cost determination (the vertical dimension of ABM). OP's Exhibit 9 shows how a complete ABM model should be able to provide both product and *process* information. The key characteristics of the process view of ABM are:

1. Characterizing resources as activities.
2. Labeling activities into meaningful categories, such as value added or non-value added.
3. Linking activities into processes.
4. Identifying cost drivers of processes.
5. Measuring the performance of the process.

Reading 4.2   Performance Measurement—The Balanced Scorecard

R.L. Lynch and K.F. Cross, "Performance Measurement Systems," in *Handbook of Cost Management*, edited by Barry Brinker (New York: Warren Gorham and Lamont), E3, 1993.

Lynch and Cross (LC) explain the role of performance measures in guiding strategy and improving operations. LC indicate that some of the best companies in the U.S. are relying less on financial performance measures, such as return on investment (ROI) and residual income, and relying more on a broader set of non-financial measures that take into account customer perspectives and innovativeness. Such an expanded set of *key performance indicators* are unique to each organization, but all stress customer value. Examples include measures of product quality, customer complaints, warranty experience, customer retention rates, product availability, on-time performance, customer satisfaction, new product time to market, and market share.

Organizations are concerned that traditionally defined performance measures expressed in terms of financial numbers may be too internally focused. Under traditional financial measures, some claim the pulse of profit focuses the company too greatly on short-term objectives and cost cutting. When profit projections are not being met, managers begin to micro-manage the company. The results are harmful behaviors that remove attention from the customer. These newer non-financial measures combined with conventional financial measures can provide the organization with a balanced perspective that takes into account both internal and external performance. The performance pyramid in Exhibit E3.2 captures this notion well.

LC's observations are supported by survey evidence. For example, one survey indicated the following:[2]

	Strategic	Tactical	Operational
Percentage of financial measures in top half of ranked importance	34%	29%	25%
Financial measures as a percentage of primary measures	37%	24%	22%

As you can see, financial measures are more valued at the strategic level and less valued at the operational level.

Reading 4.3   Quality Costs

J.P. Simpson and D.L. Muthler, "Quality Costs: Facilitating the Quality Initiative," *Journal of Cost Management* **(Spring 1987), pp. 25–34.**

Simpson and Muthler (SM) provide an overview of the quality cost concept. The costs of quality are determined from an activity analysis. An *activity analysis* is a study of activity costs for the purpose of either identifying overhead cost reduction opportunities or enhancing the effective use of overhead resources in an organization. The primary approach to conducting an activity analysis is to allocate resources, such as employee salaries, to activities by way of an activity by resource worksheet. An *activity by resource worksheet* spreads the general ledger costs (the resources) to activities based upon resource drivers. For example, employee salaries can be traced to activities based upon employee effort among the activities. This is, of course, merely the first stage of the ABM cost assignment view (vertical dimension). The activities are then categorized in order to discover cost reduction or effectiveness opportunities.

There are a number of ways in which consultants and internal accountants categorize activities. One common approach is to identify the value-added and non-value-added activities, as shown in Reading 4.1. Another approach for categorizing activities is to label the activities according to the costs of quality. Under this approach, management is using the activity information to discover if overhead resources are being used effectively in enhancing quality.

As indicated by SM, the costs of quality are typically categorized as:

Cost of controlling quality:
  Prevention
  Appraisal

Costs of failing to control quality
  External failure costs
  Internal failure costs

One survey estimated the cost of quality to be approximately 20–30% of sales.[3] The percentage of quality cost allocated to each category has historically been about:[4]

External failure	25–30%
Internal failure	30–35%
Appraisal	20–25%
Prevention	5–10%

As you can see, companies have been spending their quality dollars in the wrong way. The failure costs have been much larger than the costs associated with discovering and preventing failures. Management has been allowing defective products to be made before discovering a quality problem. This practice results in higher quality costs due to the effort of correcting failures. Instead, companies should be investing in prevention, so that defective product can be eliminated.

Reading 4.4 The Theory of Constraints

G.B. Frank, S.A. Fisher, and A.R. Wilkie, "Linking Cost to Price and Profit," *Management Accounting* **(June 1989), pp. 22–26.**

Fisher and Wilkie (FW) provide an example of how a constraining resource impacts product costing and performance improvement priorities. The authors do not use the term "theory of constraints" in their article, so a brief discussion follows.

The theory of constraints (TOC) has been advocated as a new method of managing service and manufacturing operations. Although the concept is really not all that new, it has received considerable attention as of late because of a very influential book, titled *The Goal*.[5] To understand the concepts behind TOC, consider the following scenario.

Have five students line up in a row. Provide each student with two dice, except for the student in the third position, who gets one die. Place four poker chips between each student (work in process). The object is to move poker chips from the beginning of the line (upstream) to the end of the line (downstream). Poker chips are moved from upstream to downstream based on the roll of the dice. Have a stack of poker chips (raw material) in front of the first position. Have the students roll the dice ten consecutive times on an instructor's count. When the simulation is finished, answer the following questions.

1. How many chips do you think were processed over the ten turns? (Have the output counted at this time.)
   Ans: On average the complete line can only move as fast as the slowest operation. Thus, even though all positions have two dice, except position three, they do not add to throughput capacity. The average output is based on position three, which is 3.5 per turn. Over ten turns the expected output of the line is 35 chips.

2. What happened between position 2 and 3, and why?
   Ans: Poker chips stacked up in front of position 3. There is no place for these chips to go. Positions 1 and 2 are paced at an average roll of 7 (the average of two dice), but position 3 only has a single die. Thus, position 3 cannot keep up. As a result, chips pile up in front of position 3.

3. Was the additional production from positions 1 and 2 "productive?"
Ans: Not really. These positions produced chips that cannot get through the line. If position three does not receive any more capacity, then these chips will *never* get through the line. One of the concepts of TOC is that throughput only "counts" if the production results in sales. Throughput to inventory is not value added. Thus, the buildup of chips in front of position 3 by keeping positions 1 and 2 busy is getting us nowhere. The extra dice of capacity in positions 1 and 2 is waste.

4. What is happening in positions 4 and 5?
Ans: They are operating way below capacity. They are rolling averages of 7, but can only move averages of 3.5. In other words they are starved for work because position 3 operates at a much slower pace than do 4 and 5. The extra dice of capacity in positions 4 and 5 is waste. Clearly the chain is only as strong as the weakest link.

5. How can I avoid some of these problems?
Ans: Naturally, the firm would want to remove the constraint at position 3 by purchasing another die. However, if this was not done, the theory of constraints suggests that the constraint should be the drumbeat for the rest of the line. Thus, whatever position 3 rolls becomes the automatic roll for everybody else. In this way the line becomes balanced to the constraining resource. This does not solve the problem of the excess capacity at positions 1, 2, 4, and 5.

Now that you have some idea of TOC, what are the financial implications? In the words of TOC advocate, Eli Goldratt, a constraint hour becomes a system hour. The constraint resource is the economic leverage point for the whole system. The relative profitability of products and improvement priorities are driven by the constraint resource.

An example of this is provided by FW in GenCorp. GenCorp's PPV ratio is a measure of the relative contribution margin of each product per constraint hour. The equation in FW's Table 1 provides the overall basis for managing the operations. The objective is to maximize aggregate PPV. This can be accomplished by:

1. Raising price
2. Improving constraint throughput by improving yields, reducing constraint downtime, and reducing product changeover time on the constraint
3. Incurring lower cost for materials
4. Improving the processing time of the constraint resource

Although TOC concepts are very powerful in limited situations, TOC has not gained widespread acceptance. This is because not all firms have had success in implementing TOC. Moreover, there is some criticism that financial decisions driven by TOC can be very short-term oriented.[6]

Notes

1. A more extensive discussion of Ernst and Young's methodology is provided in M.R. Ostrenga, T.R. Ozan, R.D. Mcilhatten, and M.D. Harwood, *The Ernst and Young Guide To Total Cost Management* (New York: John Wiley, 1992).

2. A.J. Nanni, J.R. Dixon, and T.E. Vollmann, "Strategic Control and Performance Measurement," *Journal of Cost Management* (Summer 1990): 37.

3. "The Quality Review," Spring 1987, Gallup Poll.

4. James B. Simpson and David L. Muthler, "Quality Costs: Facilitating the Quality Initiative," *Journal of Cost Management* (Spring 1987): 25–34.

5. E. Goldratt and J. Cox, *The Goal* (Croton on the Hudson, NY: North River Press, 1986).

6. For some additional points on this criticism, see R.S. Kaplan, "Contribution Margin Analysis: No Longer Relevant/Strategic Cost Management: The New Paradigm," *Journal of Management Accounting Research* (Fall 1990): 3–5.

Additional Readings

Ayers, James B. "Understanding Your Cost Drivers — The Key to Disciplined Planning," *Journal of Cost Management* (Fall 1988): 6–15.

Bailes, Jack C., and Ilene K. Kleinsorge. "Cutting Waste with JIT," *Management Accounting* (May 1992): 28–32.

Beaujon, George J., and Vinod R. Singhal. "Understanding the Activity Costs in Activity-Based Costing Systems," *Journal of Cost Management* (Spring 1990): 51–72.

Beheiry, Mohamed F. "New Thoughts on an Old Concept: The Cost of Quality," *CMA Magazine* (June 1991): 24–25.

Beischel, Mark E., "Improving Production with Process Value Analysis," *Journal of Accountancy* (Sept. 1990): 53–57.

Borthick, A. Faye, and Harold P. Roth. "Accounting for Time: Reengineering Business Processes to Improve Responsiveness," *Journal of Cost Management* (Fall 1993): 4–14.

Campbell, Robert J. "Pricing Strategy in the Automotive Glass Industry," *Management Accounting* (July 1989): 26–34.

Carr, David K. "Managing for Effective Business Process Redesign," *Journal of Cost Management* (Fall 1993): 16–21.

Carr, Lawrence P., and Lawrence A. Ponemon. "Quality Costs: Managers' Perceptions About Quality Costs," *Journal of Cost Management* (Spring 1992): 65–71.

Cross, Kelvin, and Richard Lynch. "Accounting for Competitive Performance," *Journal of Cost Management* (Spring 1989): 20–28.

Darlington, John, John Innes, Falconer Mitchell, and John Woodward. "Throughout Accounting: The Garrett Automotive Experience," *Management Accounting* (UK) (April 1992): 32–35, 38.

Dhavale, Dileep G. "Activity-Based Costing in Cellular Manufacturing Systems," *Journal of Cost Management* (Spring 1993): 13–27.

Edersheim, Elizabeth Haas, and Betty Vandenbosch. "How to Make Accounting Count: Causal-Based Accounting," *Journal of Cost Management* (Winter 1991): 5–17.

Fisher, Joseph. "Use of Nonfinancial Performance Measures," *Journal of Cost Management* (Spring 1992): 31–38.

Foster, George, and Charles T. Horngren. "Cost Accounting and Cost Management in a JIT Environment," *Journal of Cost Management* (Winter 1988): 4–14.

Gilmore, James H. "Reengineering for Mass Customization," *Journal of Cost Managment* (Fall 1993): 22–29.

Goldratt, Eli M., and J. Cox. *The Goal* (Croton-on-Hudson, N.Y.: North River Press, 1984).

Greene, Alice H., and Peter Flentov. "Managing Performance: Maximizing the Benefit of Activity-Based Costing," *Journal of Cost Management* (Summer 1990): 51–59.

Greenwood, Thomas G., and James M. Reeve. "Activity-Based Cost Management for Continuous Improvement: A Process Design Framework," *Journal of Cost Management* (Winter 1992): 22–40.

Greenwood, T.G., and J.M. Reeve, "Process Cost Management," *Journal of Cost Management* (Winter 1994): 4–19.

Howell, Robert A. and Stephen R. Soucy. "Operating Controls in the New Manufacturing Environment," *Management Accounting* (October 1987): 25–31.

Kammlade, John G., Pravesh Mehra, and Terrence R. Ozan. "A Process Approach to Overhead Management," *Journal of Cost Management* (Fall 1989): 4–11.

Kaplan, Robert S. "Measures For Manufacturing Excellence: A Summary," *Journal of Cost Management* (Fall 1990): 22–29.

Kaplan, Robert S., and David P. Norto. "The Balanced Scorecard: Measures that Drive Performance," *Harvard Business Review* (January–February 1992): 71–79.

Lessner, John. "Performance Measurement in a Just-in-Time Environment: Can Traditional Performance Measurements Still Be Used?" *Journal of Cost Management* (Fall 1989): 22–28.

Low, James T. "Do We Really Need Product Costs? The Theory of Constraints Alternative," *Corporate Controller* (September–October 1992): 26–36.

MacArthur, John B. "Theory of Constraints and Activity-Based Costing: Friends or Foes?" *Journal of Cost Management* (Summer 1993): 50–55.

Maisel, Lawrence S. "Performance Measurement: The Balanced Scorecard Approach," *Journal of Cost Management* (Summer 1992): 44–49.

McGroarty, J. Stanton, and Charles T. Horngren. "Functional Costing for Better Teamwork and Decision Support," *Journal of Cost Management* (Winter 1993): 24–36.

McNair, C.J. "Interdependence and Control: Traditional vs. Activity-Based Responsibility Accounting," *Journal of Cost Management* (Summer 1990): 15–23.

_____. "Do Financial and Nonfinancial Performance Measures Have to Agree?" *Management Accounting* (November 1990): 28–36.

Moravec, Robert D., and Michael S. Yoemans. "Using ABC to Support Business Re-Engineering in the Department of Defense." *Journal of Cost Management*, (Summer 1992) 32–41.

Morrow, Michael, and Martin Hazell. "Activity Mapping for Business Process Redesign," *Management Accounting* (UK) (February 1992): 36–38.

Morse, Wayne J., and Kay M. Poston. "Accounting for Quality Costs in CIM," *Journal of Cost Management* (Fall 1987): 5–11.

Nanni, Alfred J., Jr., J. Robb Dixon, and Thomas E. Vollman. "Strategic Control and Performance Measurement," *Journal of Cost Management* (Summer 1990): 33–42.

Ostrenga, Michael R. "Activities: The Focal Point of Total Cost Management," *Management Accounting* (February 1990): 42–49.

_____. "Return on Investment Through the Cost of Quality," *Journal of Cost Management* (Summer 1991): 37–44.

_____. "How Activity-Based Costing Helps Reduce Cost," *Journal of Cost Management* (Winter 1991): 29–35.

Turney, Peter B.B., and Bruce Anderson. "Accounting for Continuous Improvement," *Sloan Management Review* (Winter 1989): 37–47.

Process Value Analysis: The Missing Link in Cost Management

MICHAEL R. OSTRENGA

Principal with Ernst & Young in Milwaukee and director of Cost Management
Consulting Services for Wisconsin

FRANK R. PROBST

Professor of accounting at Marquette University in Milwaukee, Wisconsin

Much of the existing literature on activity-based costing (ABC) shortcuts the necessary link between costing rates and operational cost drivers. The focus on activities in ABC is often restricted to improvements in product costs to the exclusion of process improvements and cost reductions. Process value analysis (PVA) is a methodology for reducing costs and improving processes by identifying resource consumption within a process and the underlying root causes of cost (i.e., cost drivers). The linkage between PVA and ABC is critical. Activities are the focal point of total cost management; they must be managed to gain and sustain a competitive advantage.

In today's rapidly changing manufacturing environment, it has become increasingly difficult to answer the following three basic operating questions:

1. What do our products actually cost?
2. Why do they cost that much?
3. What can be done to reduce the cost?

Existing financial information systems continue to reflect a financial statement orientation. The emphasis continues to be on cost allocation and overhead absorption, when what we really need are:

- Relevant measures of product cost; and
- Techniques to better understand the sources of cost to facilitate cost reduction.

This article discusses an improved costing methodology called *process value analysis* (PVA) that addresses the three questions listed above. PVA gives a better understanding of cost behavior and about the root causes of costs (i.e., cost drivers) than traditional costing techniques. PVA facilitates the improvement of processes and also the reduction of costs; it also serves as a foundation for more accurate product costs.

Activity-based costing has been widely advanced as a method for improved product costing. Experience shows, however, that ABC by itself may actually distort product costs. This distortion (which is described in the sections below) can be eliminated by integrating PVA with ABC.

WHAT IS ABC?

The objective of ABC is more accurate product costs. This objective is achieved by identifying the types and amounts of activities consumed by each product. Product costs are thus based on the cost of all activities consumed.

An activity cost is actually an overhead rate that is developed by assigning costs to activity pools, then dividing these cost pools by a quantifiable assignment base. Accurate product costs are developed by applying overhead to each product based on the consumption rate of each activity.

SHORTCOMINGS OF CURRENT ABC METHODOLOGIES

The primary limitation to the development of more accurate product costs is the determination of cost behavior. The important thing to remember is that cost is incurred at the process level, not at the product level. Understanding cost behavior requires identifying the causal relationship between the resources (i.e., the costs) consumed in a process and the underlying reason why the costs are incurred.

Identifying activity cost pools. The *first* area where conventional ABC falls short lies in the identification of activity cost pools. Many ABC methodologies force-fit the definitions of activities from an existing dictionary of activities without ever analyzing the process. What may appear to be logical relationships between activities and costs often prove to be inadequate in practice.

Major activities need to be tied to the process in which they represent the significant resources in terms of cost and time. This ensures that proper recognition is given to those activities that increase value as well as to those that impede the workflow (i.e, non-value-added activities, or waste).

Definition of "driver." The *second* limitation of ABC is the definition of the term "driver." Often no clear distinction is made between the root cause (i.e., the cost driver) of an activity and the activity driver that is used to assign cost to products (or to other possible cost objects, such as customers or regions).

The distinction is critical. To initiate process improvements, identifying the true root cause of a cost is essential. Otherwise, only symptoms are treated. In other words, the activity itself—rather than the cause of the activity—is attacked, so the cost tends to resurface elsewhere in the process.

A driver can be thought of as the root cause of an activity. This can be the fact, event, circumstance, or condition prevalent in the process that causes the activity. This activity driver can be operational, policy-related, or environmental as it relates to the activity; it need not be a quantifiable basis of cost assignment.

The terms "stage-one driver" and "stage-two driver," which have been used in some literature about ABC, actually do not refer to drivers at all. Instead, they are methods of assigning cost from the general ledger to process pools and a measure of activity output consumed by products. A stage-one driver, in other words, is simply a resource driver, and a stage-two driver is simply an activity driver. Thus, for example, a stage-one driver is used to assign costs from a general ledger to a cost pool. For costing purposes, it is preferable to call a stage-one driver a "resource driver" and a stage-two driver an "activity driver." The term "cost driver" should be reserved for references to the root cause or actual driver of a cost.

This distinction can be illustrated by discussing a common activity driver—number of moves. While number of moves is a possible quantifiable base for applying cost to products, it is not necessarily a cost driver. Rather, the physical layout of a plant, a process imbalance, or a lack of standardization of parts may be the actual *driver* that *causes* the number of moves.

Definition of value-added vs. non-value-added. The *third* area where ABC falls short is in the definition of value-added and non-value-added activities. Some methodologies do not address the distinction at all. Others address it mainly from an operational improvement perspective without making the important distinction between the development of activity-based costs for process improvement and the proportion of non-value-added costs at the product level.

Selection of activity drivers. The *fourth* and final area where ABC falls short is in the selection of activity drivers. As pointed out above, activity drivers may not be the true drivers of cost. Activity drivers should be tied (i.e., correlated) to the actual cost driver to properly reflect the behavior of costs.

For example, using material handling as a major activity might generate an activity-based cost related to the number of moves. While using the number of moves as an activity driver may be appropriate for part of a process, it may not necessarily be appropriate everywhere material handling occurs.

Only by understanding cost behavior through PVA is it possible to make this determination. If material handling occurs mainly because of the number of parts, the number of parts issued to assembly might well be a more appropriate activity driver for material handling in subassembly and final assembly than number of moves.

In this case, the consumption factor at the product level would be the number of part numbers on the respective bills of materials. Conversely, the number of moves may be the appropriate activity driver for fabrication where pallets and batches are moved to the subsequent operations.

PROCESS VALUE ANALYSIS

As the experience of a Midwestern manufacturer of heavy equipment has recently demonstrated, the limitations of ABC can be overcome by integrating it with PVA. A useful linkage can be developed to reduce process costs and to provide more reliable product costs. After the PVA methodology is described below, this linkage is illustrated by means of an extended example.

PVA is a methodology for reducing costs and improving processes. This is accomplished by identifying:

- Resource consumption within a process; and
- The underlying root causes of cost (i.e., cost drivers).

PVA starts with the premise that costs are incurred at the process level, which is where resources are consumed. The level of costs is determined by the configuration, complexity, flow design, flow flexibility, and similar attributes of a process. Process costs can reduced by means of any of the following methods for reducing waste:

- Simplification;
- Reducing variation;
- Improvements in process layout;
- More compact design flows; and
- Synchronous processing.

With the exception of a pure product-focused work cell (i.e., one in which the production process and product flow are virtually identical), product routings follow diverse process paths. Each process has a series of inputs, transformation activities, and outputs through which a variety of products flow. Useful product costs and valid performance measures must reflect the diversity of activities consumed to support each part or product.

Accordingly, PVA provides:

- A framework for understanding cost behavior patterns;
- Support for the selection of activities within a process to which costs should be applied;
- Cycle time analysis;
- Identification of value-added vs. non-value-added activities;
- Identification of operational cost drivers;
- Identification of opportunities for process improvements;
- Measurement base for continuous improvement efforts; and
- Foundation for improved product costing.

The use of PVA as a foundation for product costing generates cost information that reflects the physical environment, as the list above indicates. The dual focus on process and product costing offers the advantages listed below.

Process costing facilitates:

- Flexible budgeting to reflect changes in activities;
- Costing the effect of changes in the physical process or in activities;
- Investment justification; and
- Performance measurement.

The *product costing* perspective (which ABC offers in conjunction with PVA) supports:

- More accurate product costs;
- "Total costing" (including imputed interest and economic resources included in sales, general, and administrative expenses) rather than just manufacturing costing;
- Life cycle costing; and
- Target costing.

ABC: AN EXTENDED EXAMPLE

The linkage between PVA and ABC can be demonstrated by using a series of examples from a study performed for the heavy equipment manufacturer mentioned above.

The initial focus is on product costs, as Exhibit 1 shows. Product costs are developed from a bill of materials, a labor routing (i.e., a bill of labor), and an overhead rate based on direct labor. As Exhibit 1 shows, Product B is charged with twice the overhead of Product A because Product B consumes twice as much labor in terms of dollars.

This traditional approach does not differentiate between the various costs of activities actually consumed by each product. For example, the amount of scheduling, setup, material handling, and inspection actually consumed by Products A and B have no demonstrated relationship to the amount of direct labor used by each product. Therefore, applying overhead on the basis of direct labor leads to distortions in the product costs.

Exhibit 2 illustrates the use of ABC to develop product costs. First, costing rates based on activity drivers are calculated for three processes; steel cutting,

EXHIBIT 1

Traditional Product Costing

	Product A	Product B
Material	$300	$300
Direct labor	48	96
Overhead	144	288
Total	$492	$684

Source:
  Material   – Costed bill of material
  Direct Labor – Process routing, standard labor
  Overhead   – 300% of direct labor

EXHIBIT 2

Activity-Based Cost Rates

Process	Activity	Cost	Activity Driver	Quantity	Activity Driver Rate
• Steel cutting	• Setup/scheduling	$200,000	No. of work orders	1,000	$ 200
	• Conversion[a]	100,000	No. of machine hours	5,000	20
	• Inspection	100,000	No. of setups	100	1,000
	• Maintenance	150,000	No. of machine hours	5,000	30
		$550,000			
• Assembly	• Changeover	$100,000	No. of scheduled batches	1,000	100
	• Conversion[a]	50,000	No. of parts	50,000	1
	• Inspection	125,000	No. of scheduled batches	1,000	125
	• Retrofit	75,000	No. of ECMs	500	150
		$350,000			
• Material handling	• Move material	500,000	No. of moves	12,000	42
		$1,400,000			

[a]Conversion cost = energy and machine depreciation.

assembly, and material handling. Exhibit 2 identifies these activity-based rates and shows supporting activities, costs, and activity drivers.

In Exhibit 3, these cost rates are applied to products A and B based on the activities consumed by each product. Specifically (as Exhibit 2 shows), the cost per work order is $200. This rate is used in Exhibit 3 to charge product A with $2 of scheduling cost in the steel cutting operation based on 100 units of product A per batch. The costs of conversion, inspection, and maintenance are likewise assigned to the products based on their activity drivers and volumes.

This use of activity drivers reduces the distortion in product cost shown in Exhibit 1 and goes a long way toward establishing useful product costs. As Exhibit 3 shows, Product B's ABC cost is $16 more ($595–$579), or about 3 percent higher, than Product A's ABC cost. This compares to the 42 percent difference calculated under the traditional costing approach illustrated in Exhibit 1.

IMPROVING THE ABC METHODOLOGY

Despite this improvement over traditional costing, the ABC methodology can itself be improved. First, note that the methodology illustrated treats all material handling alike. As Exhibit 2 shows, a single cost pool is used to arrive at a cost of $42 per move. This $42 is then applied to material handling wherever it occurs, as shown in Exhibit 3.

A PVA study, however, showed that material handling was extensive in all processes. This finding necessitated identifying material handling costs within

EXHIBIT 3

Activity-Based Product Costs

| A | B | C | D | Product A | | | Product B | | |
| | | | | E | F | G | H | I | J |
Manufacturing Overhead	Batch-Related	Output Measure	Cost Rate	Output Measure Volume	Per Piece[a] Consumption of Batch[a]	(DxExF) Total	Output Measure Volume	Per Piece Consumption of Batch	(DxHxI) Total
• Steel cutting									
— Setup/scheduling	×	No. of work orders	$ 200	1.0	1/100	$ 2.00	1.0	1/100	$ 2.00
— Conversion	×	No. of machine hours	20	0.5		10.00	1.0		20.00
— Inspection	×	No. of setups	1,000	1.0	1/100	10.00	1.0	1/100	10.00
— Maintenance	×	No. of machine hours	30	0.5		15.00	1.0		30.00
• Assembly									
— Changeover	×	No. of setups	100	1.0	1/500	0.20	1.0	1/500	0.20
— Conversion	×	No. of parts	1	25.0		25.00	10.00		10.00
— Inspection	×	No. of scheduled batches	125	1.0	1/250	0.50	1.0	1/250	0.50
— Retrofit	×	No. of ECNs	150	1.0	1/500	0.30	1.0	1/500	0.30
• Material handling									
— Move material									
Steel sheets		No. of moves	42	3.0		126.00	2.0		84.00
Assembly		No. of moves	42	1.0		42.00	1.0		42.00
Subtotal						$231.00			$199.00
Direct material						300.00			300.00
Direct labor						48.00			96.00
Total						$579.00			$595.00

[a] That is, 100-piece work order with one piece consumption = 1/100; similarly, one engineering change notification (ECN) for a 500-piece work order with one piece consumption = 1/500.

each process to give a more accurate picture of total process costs and the source of these costs.

After the PVA study, the cost charged to the material handling activity within each process was based on resource drivers of how many forklift trucks, automated guided vehicles, cranes, and employees supported each process area. These resource drivers provided a logical assignment basis for developing the material handling cost pools. (Some ABC methodologies would call this a "stage-one driver" allocation. However, these factors are clearly not root cause "drivers" of the activities. Rather the true cost drivers were related to process imbalance, machine downtime, stocking levels, and the like, all of which became the focus of PVA process improvement initiatives.)

Value-added vs. non-value-added. The typical ABC approach does not distinguish between value-added and non-value-added activities. While some methodologies do incorporate this distinction, without a PVA study to establish the process orientation and internal customer requirements, the selection may be more intuitive than real.

Selecting activity drivers. In this generic ABC example, the selection of activity drivers to be used in developing the rate for tracing costs to products is generalized as the number of moves. In the PVA study, the activity driver selected for steel cutting was the number of moves. For assembly, it was the number of parts.

EXHIBIT 4

Summary of PVA Results

Process	Major Activities	VA/NVA	Operational Activity Driver	Hours Cycle Time/ Part	Time/ Shift	Process Activity Cost Pools
Steel cutting	● Product flow-related					
	— Material handling	NVA	Process layout	0.3		— Material handling
	— Queue	NVA	Process imbalance	3.4		— Conversion
	— Conversion	VA	Lineal inches	0.2		— Inspection
	— Inspection	NVA	No. of parts	0.1		— Maintenance
						— Setup/scheduling
	● Process-related					
	— Setup/scheduling	NVA	No. of work orders		0.5	
			No. of unscheduled changeovers		1.0	
	— Downtime	NVA	Machine reliability		0.5	
				4.0	2.0	

Cycle efficiency = 0.2/4 = 5%
Lost capacity per shift = 1.5/8 = 19%

Process	Major Activities	VA/NVA	Operational Activity Driver	Cycle Time/ Part	Time/ Shift	Process Activity Cost Pools
Assembly	● Product flow-related					
	— Material handling	NVA	No. of options, features	0.3		— Material handling
	— Conversion	VA	No. of parts assembled	0.3		— Conversion
	— Inspection	NVA	No. of units	0.5		— Inspection
	Retrofit	NVA	Process specification	0.4		— Retrofit
						— Changeover
	● Process-related					
	— Changeover	NVA	No. of schedule changes		0.5	
				1.5	0.5	

Cycle efficiency = 0.3/1.5 = 20%
Lost capacity per shift = 0.5/8 = 6%

Exhibit 4 shows the results of PVA and identifies several important aspects of the process.

- The time spent adding value to the product was limited to 5 percent in steel cutting and 20 percent in assembly. Thus, non-value-added costs were incurred 95 percent of the time in steel cutting and 80 percent of the time in assembly (e.g., for queue or storage time), which inhibited the throughput velocity at which resources were converted to cash.

- Lost capacity on a per-shift basis amounted to almost 19 percent in cutting (1.0 hour setup + .5 hour downtime / 8 hours per shift) and 6 percent in assembly (.5 hour / 8 hours per shift changeover). Note that for product cycle time analysis, the product is in a state of queue while the process is tied up for setup or repair.

- The operational cost drivers identified represent root causes for use in planning operational improvements. These "true" cost drivers should not be confused with the term "cost drivers" as used in the past to describe a

EXHIBIT 5

PVA/ABC Linkage

Process	Process/Activity	VA/NVA	Cost	Output Measure	Quantity	Cost per Output Measure
• Steel cutting	• Material handling	NVA	$300,000	No. of moves	10,000	$ 30
	• Setup/scheduling	NVA	200,000	No. of work orders	1,000	200
	• Conversion[a]	VA	100,000	No. of machine hours	5,000	20
	• Inspection	NVA	100,000	No. of setups	100	1,000
	• Maintenance	VA	150,000	No. of machine hours	5,000	30
			$850,000			
• Assembly	• Material handling	NVA	200,000	No. of parts	50,000	4
	• Changeover	NVA	100,000	No. of scheduled batches	1,000	100
	• Conversion[a]	VA	50,000	No. of parts	50,000	1
	• Inspection	NVA	125,000	No. of scheduled batches	1,000	125
	• Retrofit	NVA	75,000	No. of ECWNs	500	150
			$550,000			
			$1,400,000			

[a] Conversion Cost = energy and machine depreciation.

cost assignment base. These true operational cost drivers can, however, be used to support the selection of activity drivers for ABC.

- The process or activity pools were selected based on the significant activities defined in the activity analysis and cycle time analysis portion of the PVA. The selections were supported by interviews with functional area representatives. The analysis revealed that a manageable number of activities could be defined for each process to provide a significantly improved cost perspective while keeping the level of complexity reasonable.

This example shows only two of the many processes analyzed. It should be noted that several activities were common among the processes analyzed. However, they were structured as specific activities within each process rather than as generic process pools. This treatment is due to the different operational cost drivers identified for certain activities depending on which process they supported.

Exhibit 4 shows the material handling example introduced earlier. Steel cutting is "driven" by the existing process layout. This layout caused more move frequencies to occur in order to overcome the lack of synchronization. Conversely, the driver of material handling in assembly was the complexity caused by numerous product options and features. This allowed for further differentiation in cost behavior and the selection of appropriate activity drivers.

LINKING ABC WITH PVA

To link PVA with ABC, look at Exhibit 5, where the general process of material handling is *now* presented as a significant activity within each process. Here the

EXHIBIT 6

Integrated PVA/ABC Product Costs

A Manufacturing Overhead	B Batch-Related	C Output Measure	D Cost Rate	Product A — E Output Measure Volume	Product A — F Per Piece Consumption of Batch	Product A — G Extended VA	Cost NVA	Total	Product B — E Output Measure Volume	Product B — F Per Piece Consumption of Batch	Product B — G Extended VA	Cost NVA	Total
● Steel cutting													
— Setup/scheduling	X	No. of work orders	$ 200	1.0	1/100		$ 2.00	$ 2.00	1.0	1/100		$ 2.00	$ 2.00
— Material handling	X	No. of moves	30	3.0			90.00	90.00	2.0			60.00	60.00
— Conversion		No. of machine hours	20	0.5		$ 10.00		10.00	1.0		$ 20.00		20.00
— Inspection	X	No. of setups	1000	1.0	1/100		10.00	10.00	1.0	1/100		10.00	10.00
— Maintenance		No. of machine hours	30	0.5		15.00		15.00	1.0		30.00		30.00
● Assembly													
— Changeover	X	No. of setup batches	100	1.0	1/500		0.20	0.20	1.0	1/500		0.20	0.20
— Material handling	X	No. of parts	4	25.0			100.00	100.00	10.0			40.00	40.00
— Conversion		No. of parts	1	25.0		25.00		25.00	10.0		10.00		10.00
— Inspection	X	No. of scheduled batches	125	1.0	1/250		0.50	0.50	1.0	1/250		0.50	0.50
— Retrofit	X	No. of ECNs	150	1.0	1/500		0.30	0.30	1.0	1/500		0.30	0.30
Subtotal						$ 50.00	$203.00	$253.00			$ 60.00	$113.00	$173.00
Direct material						270.00	30.00	300.00			270.00	30.00	300.00
Direct labor						38.00	10.00	48.00			76.00	20.00	96.00
Total						$358.00	$243.00	$601.00			$406.00	$163.00	$569.00

activity driver used for material handling in the steel cutting process was the number of moves, but the activity driver used for the assembly process was the number of parts. This is the critical linkage of PVA information with ABC. The activity drivers selected are based on the insights gained from the operational cost drivers (and from the quantifiability and availability of data).

Exhibit 6 shows the calculation of costs for Products A and B using the PVA/ABC linkage. The extended cost in column G clearly identifies value-added and non-value-added cost components. The validity of the resulting product costs is based on the clear distinction between the cost driver and the activity driver. The specific drivers for each process in Exhibit 6 are listed below:

Steel Cutting	Cost Driver	Activity Driver
Setup scheduling	Product variety	No. of work orders
Material handling	Process layout	No. of moves
Conversion	Process time	No. of machine hours
Inspection	Poor tooling condition	No. of setups
Maintenance	Lack of preventative maintenance	No. of machine hours

Assembly		
Changeovers	End item configuration	No. of setup batches
Material handling	Product features options	No. of parts
Conversion	Parts to assembly	No. of parts
Inspection	Product specifications	No. of scheduled batches
Retrofit	Lack of collaborative design	No. of emergency changes

Does this distinction make a difference? Exhibit 7 summarizes the calculation of product costs for Products A and B using the three approaches described. The different product costs under the three approaches is due primarily to the

EXHIBIT 7

Cost Comparison

Product		Traditional Costing	Conventional ABC	PVA/ABC VA	PVA/ABC NVA	PVA/ABC Total
A	Material	$300	$300	$270	$30	$300
	Labor	48	48	38	10	48
	Overhead	144	231	50	203	253
	Total	$492	$579	$358	$243	$601
B	Material	$300	$300	$270	$30	$300
	Labor	96	96	76	20	96
	Overhead	288	199	60	113	173
	Total	$684	$595	$406	$163	$569

EXHIBIT 8

Cost Comparison Graphs

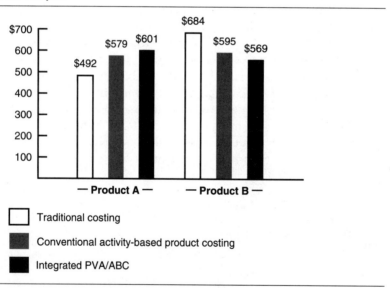

- ☐ Traditional costing
- ▨ Conventional activity-based product costing
- ■ Integrated PVA/ABC

number of parts on the bill of material for Product A vs. Product B (25 vs.10). The marked differences in product cost are presented graphically in Exhibit 8. Since product costs are used extensively (e.g., for pricing support, promotions, sales mix decisions, and product profitability evaluations) an improved perspective on product costs will have important ramifications.

OTHER BENEFITS OF LINKING PVA/ABC

The benefits of the proposed linkage extend beyond more useful measures of product cost to process improvement and cost reduction opportunities.

Operational changes planned as a result of the improved awareness of cost behavior obtained from the integrated PVA/ABC initiatives for the company on which this case study was based include the following:

- Delivering material to point of use to reduce queue and storage;
- Instituting compact process layouts to reduce material handling requirements;
- Synchronizing process flow to reduce queue, material handling, lost material, and damage;
- Processing of mating parts sequentially to reduce handling, work-in-process levels, and matching;
- Improving preventive maintenance programs; and
- Focusing on setup reduction efforts.

Beyond the operational improvements prompted by PVA, the company now has the methodology and techniques in place to do the following:

- Better understand cost behavior;
- Provide a focused plan of cost reduction through operational improvement;
- Provide more accurate product costs;
- Make investment decisions by focusing on changes in processes and the impact on activity costs;
- Grow the business in a more profitable way; and
- Understand the cost of providing internal services to the company.

Much of the existing literature on ABC shortcuts the linkage between costing rates and operational cost drivers. Additionally, the focus on activities is restricted to improvement in product costs to the exclusion of process improvement and cost reduction. Accordingly, the emphasis should be on linking ABC with PVA.

As these examples suggest, the linking of ABC with PVA offers both operational and strategic advantages by providing a foundation for cost management. This linkage is illustrated in Exhibit 9.

RELEVANCE FOUND?

Observers of the manufacturing scene agree that cost accounting has not kept pace with technological innovation. The cost equation has changed, but the methodology for providing cost information has not changed correspondingly.

EXHIBIT 9

"The Linkage"

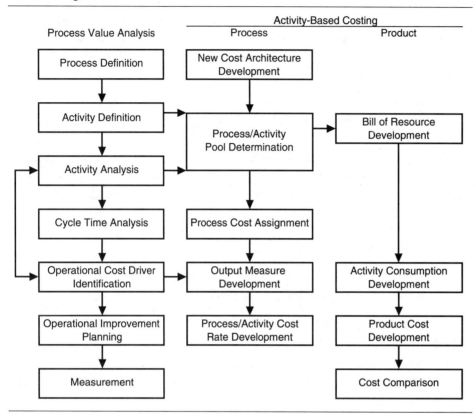

Efforts to reduce cost have been frustrated by attempts to manage cost at the product level. The measurement of product costs does increase the awareness of cost, but ABC is generally promoted in too narrow a scope. Activity-based product costs fail to identify *how* costs are incurred, *where* resources are consumed, and *what* the underlying cost behavior patterns are.

PVA establishes the foundation for understanding cost; it also sets the direction for cost reduction and process improvement. ABC should establish the relationship of cost to the activities performed within the process. This one-two punch provides the necessary linkage to employ the remaining tools of total cost management—investment justification, performance measurement, responsibility accounting.

The linkage between PVA and ABC is critical. Activities are the focal point of total cost management; they must be managed to gain and sustain a competitive advantage.

Performance Measurement Systems

RICHARD L. LYNCH

Quality Manager, The Faxon Company, Westwood, Massachusetts

KELVIN F. CROSS

Senior Vice President, Gray Judson Howard, Cambridge, Massachusetts

INTRODUCTION

Consider the effect that a properly designed performance measurement system can have on a business. Well-designed performance measures can:

- Track performance against customer expectations, thus bringing the company closer to its customers and making everyone in the company involved in the satisfaction of customers.
- Serve as the links in the chain of internal customers and suppliers. They turn department rivalries into cross-functional teams that work on common goals.
- Identify waste in its various guises—delays, defects, mistakes, and surpluses—and lead to reduction of waste.
- Make fuzzy strategic objectives concrete, thus accelerating the rate at which organizations learn.
- Build consensus for change by rewarding the right behavior.

Of course, there is also a negative side to performance measures: The wrong measures can subvert strategic intent, pit one department against another, and protect internal bureaucracies. Even worse, the wrong measures encourage people to devote time and effort to activities that are irrelevant to customers and stockholders alike. It is critical, therefore, for companies to "measure the right stuff."

The purpose of this chapter is not to state what to measure, because that depends on customer expectations, strategic intent, work flows, and so on. Instead, this chapter proposes a model or framework for identifying the critical measures in an operation and linking those measures together to help bring about continuous improvement.

THE IMPORTANCE OF PERFORMANCE MEASURES

Effective performance measurement systems can help the U.S. manufacturing industry prosper. Sound performance measurement systems provide (1) a link between activity accounting and performance measures, and (2) a focus on cost drivers.

The Link Between Activity Accounting and Performance Measures

Management accountants have taken their share of the heat for the troubles that U.S. manufacturing companies have encountered in recent years. Operating managers charge that the product costs and performance measurements accountants provide contribute to poor make-buy decisions, high inventories, and poor quality. Now, however—under the banner of activity accounting—management accountants are helping to solve some of these problems by:

- Providing better information about product costs; and
- Identifying the cost drivers of the business.

A Focus on Cost Drivers

Activity accounting is defined as a collection of financial and operational performance information about significant activities that a business performs. A part of activity accounting deals with identifying the causal factors or cost drivers behind the activities. Consider the following situations, for example:

- Reducing the number of vendors reduces purchasing *activities* related to qualifying vendors, negotiating contracts, and the like;
- Reducing the number of parts in a product reduces assembly activity;
- Reducing the number of engineering change orders reduces the amount of rework activity; and
- Reducing setup time reduces machine setup activity.

A major benefit of activity accounting is that managers are forced to view operations as the management of activities, not cost—whether, in other words, they are doing things well. But an even more fundamental question is whether they are doing the right things in the first place.

Performance measures—indicators of the results of a process or of an organizational unit—must be viewed from the customer's perspective: In other words, is the organization doing the right things, and if so, is it doing them well?

REDESIGNING MEASURES FOR BUSINESS PERFORMANCE

For the first time since World War II, managers in the United States are now starting to look inward for the eroding market shares of U.S. companies in almost every industry—from textiles, steel, and automobiles to semiconductors, photocopiers, and computers.[1] Faced with global competition and rapid changes in the external marketplace, U.S. companies are scrambling to restructure their companies for survival in the 1990s.

Here are some examples:

- Caterpillar is investing nearly $2 billion on training and to modernize factories so that Caterpillar can compete on a global basis with the Japanese company Komatsu.
- General Motors (GM) has begun to recognize that automation alone is not the answer. GM has overhauled its management system at its New United Motor Manufacturing, Inc. (NUMMI) operation, a joint venture with Toyota in California, and also at its new Saturn Corp. GM is placing more emphasis on simplifying the work and on giving the workers more accountability for their work.
- Faced with dwindling market share, Harley-Davidson has dramatically reconfigured its plants and scrapped miles of automated material handling equipment.

Desperate times call for new measures to support these new initiatives. In fact, a recent article in the *Harvard Business Review* made the claim that "within the next five years, every company will have to redesign how it measures its business performance."[2]

Weak Performance Measurement Systems

These changes will not be easy. Management expert Peter Drucker has stated that performance measurement is one of the weakest areas in management today. Several studies have documented how frustrated managers feel about existing performance measurement systems. Most notable was the 1987 survey, jointly sponsored by the National Association of Accountants and Computer Aided Manufacturing-International (CAM-I), in which 60 percent of the 260 financial officers and 64 operating executives surveyed stated that they were dissatisfied with their performance measurement system.[3]

These findings can probably be corroborated in many organizations, because resentment about existing performance measures seems to be widespread. At dozens of companies (including Armco Steel, Hewlett-Packard, Wang Laboratories, Becton Dickinson, and Weightwatchers International), the same complaints can be heard over and over again:

- "The measures are too financial."
- "The measures are not customer-driven."
- "It's not clear how my department's measures are linked to the company strategic objectives."
- "The measures are irrelevant."

All too often, management's response is that "people don't understand the measures." Debate turns to stalemate as the focus on corrective action gets sidetracked.

Common Problems

Even if management is receptive to change, the comments listed above are often too imprecise or abstract for corrective action to be taken. To get at the root problems, companies must listen carefully to the message, then dig deeper. For example, the "too financial" comment may point to the following situations:

- Purchase price variances (PPV) motivate buyers to increase order quantities to get the best price, which too often means sacrificing quality and timely deliveries. The net result is mythical cost savings in procurement, but excess inventory, inspection, and rework costs in production.
- Machine utilization variances motivate workers in a particular work cell to produce more subassemblies than are needed (and often the wrong subassemblies for future consumption). As a result, misallocations of resources occur, because parts that could have been used for salable subassemblies are wasted on subassemblies that cannot be sold.
- The scrap component built into standard cost models assumes waste; managers have no incentive to eliminate waste unless it exceeds the standard.
- Absorption variances motivate managers to produce excess inventory to absorb more expenses.

These "discoveries" are not random occurrences: They are a structural part of a company's formal management and reward structure. The challenge that today's operating and financial managers face is to redefine those systems and rewards to match the realities of today's operational strategies.

RECALIBRATING MEASUREMENT TOOLS

Companies begin tinkering with performance measurement systems for several reasons. They learn about what other companies are doing by attending seminars or reading books. Sometimes, internal specialists create interest through pilot programs that introduce new measures. Pressures from a major customer, parent company, or strategic partnership may also force a company to start reporting quality and delivery measures. A crisis (such as lost market share or red ink on the P&L) can also trigger top management's attention.

When times get rough, it is only natural for managers to reexamine their company yardsticks. Usually, however, the response is all too familiar. Here are examples of what often happens:

- Each department is asked to measure its own activities;
- A temporary task force is formed to study critical success factors;
- Managers are asked for a new laundry list of measures; or
- Cost-cutting goals are set.

These solutions attack symptoms of the problem or the wrong problem entirely. The impact of the changes they cause is usually negligible or short-lived. To design a new performance measurement system, the changes that have rendered the old yardsticks ineffective must be recognized.

The Change From a Seller's to a Buyer's Market

One of the main reasons that the old yardsticks do not measure up is that they were designed in a time of a "seller's market." In the early years of mass production, virtually anything that was made could be sold, since the products were so much cheaper than handmade goods. Over the years, manufacturers got accustomed to demand exceeding supply. The attitude of most manufacturers was: "This is what we make—if you want it, buy it." This "product out" mentality translated into an internal focus on performance measures: units shipped and product margins.

In a seller's market, customers take what they can get: In the extreme, they even accept having to pay a high price for a standard product of marginal quality with a long or unpredictable lead time for delivery. In other words, the company can sell whatever it builds. In this environment, the strategy for the business—and the imperative for manufacturing—is simple: Increase output. Nothing else matters. Manufacturers, therefore, learned to produce to their own specifications, not the customer's.

In recent years, however, the seller's markets have dried up. In the automotive industry, for example, the 1980s brought global competition and a crushing blow to the domestic oligarchy. Even in rapid-growth, high-technology industries now, a seller's market does not last long.

In a buyer's market, it is not enough simply to get the product out. Today, customers demand products that:

- Meet or exceed explicit customer expectations;
- Are delivered on time (not early or late);
- Are defect-free;
- Have short lead times; and
- Have low prices and low cost of ownership.

Companies must develop performance measures that track these customer demands.

Pressure From the Competition

Customers (and stockholders) determine what is important to measure, but the competition determines how good performance according to those measures must be. Successful manufacturing and service companies alike now compete on three fronts:

1. Customer satisfaction;
2. Flexibility; and
3. Productivity.

Customer satisfaction occurs when performance equals or exceeds expectations concerning quality, delivery, and responsiveness. Flexibility is certainly another major competitive factor. For example, turnaround time for Toyota's suppliers has been cut from fifteen days to same-day delivery. Motorola produces intercom pagers in just two hours, a job that took three weeks just a few years ago. Many companies have adopted computer integrated manufacturing to allow for rapid changeovers for increased responsiveness.

While customer satisfaction and flexibility are new fronts in the battle for tomorrow's customers, fighting on the third front—productivity—has increased in intensity but in a new context. Productivity is defined in terms of meeting the objectives of customer satisfaction and flexibility *at a low cost.* Global competition and eroding margins in mature industries have forced companies to restructure and to do more with less.

This backdrop sets the stage for building a new performance measurement system.

Different Starting Points for Performance Measures

Total quality management (TQM), just-in-time (JIT) manufacturing, and activity accounting are "hot" topics in manufacturing today. Although each initiative has its own approach and starting point for measurement, all have a common theme that bears on performance measures: continuous improvement (*kaizen* in Japanese). Exhibit E3.1 shows the common measurement criteria for today's continuous improvement initiatives.

TQM can be defined as a new way to manage by involving everyone in meeting or exceeding customer expectations. TQM concepts and practices focus on three major areas of activity:

1. Customers;
2. Continuous improvement of processes; and
3. Total company involvement in quality.

EXHIBIT E3.1

Common Measurement Criteria for Today's Continuous Improvement Initiatives

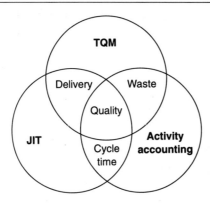

Regular, on-time delivery and high-quality products or services are the key measures of customer satisfaction, as Exhibit E3.1 shows. Note that waste is really a measure of the cost of quality—that is, the costs associated with internal failures (e.g., rework or yield loss), appraisals (e.g., inspections), and returns from customers. TQM shares common success criteria with JIT and activity accounting, which are discussed next.

The objectives of JIT are continuous improvement in terms of improved responsiveness, reduced defects, and faster cycle times, all of which contribute to the reduction of waste. Activity accounting collects financial and operational performance information about the significant activities of the business. A major application of activity accounting is called activity-based costing (ABC), which traces costs to products according to the activities performed on them. ABC involves analyzing the key cost drivers of the activities that consume major costs. In a sense, therefore, ABC cost drivers, such as setup time and number of engineering change orders, are actually cycle time and waste measures.

Companies such as Analog Devices, Xerox, and Motorola have launched performance measurement programs as part of their quality improvement efforts. Northern Telecom and Harley-Davidson began tinkering with performance measures following their experiences with JIT. Others companies (such as Hewlett-Packard, Caterpillar, and John Deere) took a new look at performance measurement through activity accounting.

Whatever the starting point, quality, delivery, cycle time, and waste are emerging as the core performance criteria for success in the 1990s.

Out With the Old, In With the New

Understanding and promoting the "new" operating initiatives of TQM, JIT, and ABC do not ensure success. Nor is it enough simply to add a few new quality or cycle time measures to the existing system to keep the pressure on. The existing system may be part of the problem; therefore, care should be taken to eliminate all unnecessary and counterproductive measures.

A good starting point for this analysis is to profile existing measures by type, use, frequency, and purpose. This leads to appropriate action:

- If too many measures exist, which ones can be eliminated?
- Some measures may have been required long ago but may no longer be important. Can they be dropped?
- Are compensation and reward plans in line with strategic objectives? For example, if a company is pursuing a JIT strategy, is the company rewarding buyers on purchase price variance, which may add to lead times?

Next, the system should be critiqued:

- Are hidden measures the real driving force? (For example, do not get caught without a spare.)
- Are some measures simply wrong? (Some people will need convincing.)
- What measures are missing?
- Why does the company have masses of data and no information?[4]

THE POWER OF THE PYRAMID

Performance measures are an integral part of the management system. Performance measures are effective when they:

- Support the priorities of top management consistently throughout the organization;
- Can be aggregated in a way that gives decision makers the right information at the right time;
- Balance and integrate the financial and nonfinancial measures of the business;
- Are communicated horizontally in the internal customer-supplier networks.

Exhibit E3.2 shows a performance pyramid that represents a model for achieving these objectives.

EXHIBIT E3.2

The Performance Pyramid

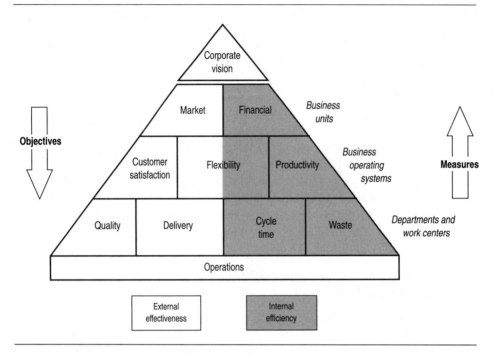

At the top level of the performance pyramid, senior management must articulate a vision for the business. For example, Seiko had a vision that watches were a fashion business rather than a timekeeping business. This vision sparked a whole new era in which new products were introduced on a daily basis.

At the second level, objectives for each business unit must be defined in terms of the market and also in financial terms. Strategies must be formulated to describe how these objectives will be achieved.

At the third level, more tangible operating objectives and priorities can be defined (in terms of customer satisfaction, flexibility, and productivity) for each business operating system (e.g., new product introduction, order fulfillment, or after-sales service).

At the base of the pyramid, objectives are converted into specific operational criteria (quality, delivery, cycle time, and waste) for each department or component of the business system.[5]

The performance pyramid is split in half to show the pressures and influence of the marketplace (on the left-hand side of the pyramid) and also the pressures and influence from stockholders and creditors (on the right-hand side). At the business unit or corporate level, market measures, such as market share and relative market share, are achieved through customer satisfaction and flexibility. Traditional financial measures of profitability, cash flow, and return on assets are achieved by meeting flexibility and productivity objectives. This strategy is not to suggest that the business unit measures are wrong; the problem has been how they are driven down into the organization.

Connecting With Success

The three objectives of business operating systems must be further translated to provide a clear foundation or framework for specific operational measures. But how does one measure customer satisfaction or flexibility? Even measuring productivity is not straightforward in a JIT environment or in an environment where direct labor makes up less than 10 percent of product cost.

Certainly, some measures reflect on the performance of the business system. For example, measures such as renewal rates, number of complaints, and independent surveys are all measures of customer satisfaction. Likewise, quoted lead times and inventory turns are measures of flexibility. Similarly, productivity can be measured in terms of cost of sales, asset turnover, breakeven time, or added value per employee.

The problem with these measures is one of focus and accountability. These measures are all global in the sense that they combine two or more of the four basic performance criteria shown at the base of the performance pyramid. For example, inventory turns has components of both delivery and cycle time. Similarly, total factor productivity (outputs/inputs) has both delivery and cost components. Global measures also tend to spill across business systems and therefore to summarize the performance of the company as a whole. For example, product ratings have to do with design, manufacture, and also after-sales service.

Concrete and Specific Measures

Measures need to be concrete and specific—measures, in other words, that managers and workers can identify with on a day-to-day basis. These measures must also be explicitly linked to the value added to the end customer. Exhibit E3.3 shows a business system scorecard outlining these links. If each department in a business operating system (e.g., departments A, B, and C in Exhibit E3.3) reports on quality, delivery, cycle time, and waste, it is easy to roll up the data to assess the business operating system as a whole.

Since quality and delivery measures for the business operating system are determined by the end customer, they are reflected in the last department's external measures. In other words, a business operating system as a whole performs only as well as the department nearest to the customer. The managers of

EXHIBIT E3.3

Business System Scorecard

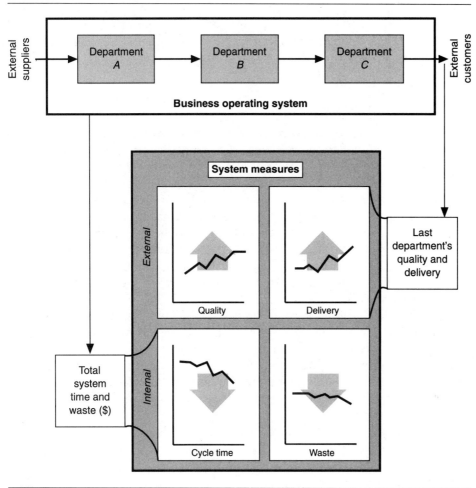

each department in Exhibit E3.3 must, therefore, focus on the next department's needs (i.e., the "internal customer") within the context of the overall values set by paying customers at the end of the process. The cycle time measurement for the business operating system as a whole is simply the sum of the critical path cycle times in each department. Waste in the business operating system can be shown as the dollarized sum of each department's waste. However, it is important to tie cost (the operational variable) into the financial reports to avoid mixed signals.[6]

The Pursuit of Continuous Improvement

The foundation of an effective performance measurement system is a tightly defined linkage between measurements at the local operational level and the objectives and priorities of the business operating system. The elements of this linkage are found in four principal local operating performance criteria:

1. Quality;
2. Delivery;
3. Cycle time; and
4. Waste.

The objective of any function or department in the business operating system is to increase quality and delivery performance and to decrease cycle time and waste.

Quality

Quality means meeting or exceeding customer expectations (i.e., for both internal and external customers) 100 percent of the time through the delivery of defect-free products or services. It is no longer acceptable to think of quality as conformance to specifications. Instead, quality has a far broader meaning in today's marketplace.

Aspects of quality include the following:

- Features;
- Performance;
- Durability;
- Reliability;
- Ease of servicing;
- Aesthetics; and
- Perceived quality.[7]

For internal customers, examples of quality measures include:

- Parts (per volume) accepted by the materials department;
- Cycle count accuracy;
- Planning accuracy;
- Number of vendors or parts requiring no inspection; and
- Completeness of new product documentation when introduced to manufacturing.

For final customers, examples of quality measures include:

- Percentage of problem-free installations at customer sites at the first attempt; and
- Percentage of lots accepted.

Delivery

Delivery refers to the quantity of product or service delivered on time to the customer or user (including internal customers). As JIT takes hold in more and more companies, on-time means just that: Shipping early is as unacceptable as shipping late. Appropriate measures include:

- Percentage delivered to schedule;
- Percentage delivered to rush order; and
- Percentage of time products are released on schedule.

Cycle Time

Cycle time is the sum of process time, move time, inspect time, queue time, and storage time. Only process time is considered value-added time. (Throughput time means the same thing.) Examples of cycle time include:

- Development time to bring a new product or service to market;
- Manufacturing lead time;
- Departmental throughput time; and
- Work station setup time.

Waste

Waste refers to the non-value-added activities and resources incurred to meet customer requirements. Waste includes all effort and costs associated with failures, appraisals, and surpluses. This definition has some major implications, because it means that efforts spent to repair defects or to produce 110 units to get 100 good ones is not only poor-quality performance, it is costly performance as well.

Problems with waste are internal in that money and effort are expended to get a product right before it is passed on to the next customer (which often means a downstream department.) At the business operating system level, the main objective is to improve productivity by reducing overall costs. At the departmental level, the objective becomes more specific: to measure and eliminate waste. Cost of rejected materials, rework, in-process scrap, incoming inspection, warranty costs, surpluses, accidents, and returns are typical examples.

THE WHO, WHAT, WHERE, WHEN, AND HOW OF PERFORMANCE MEASUREMENT

Changes to a performance measurement system occur in several steps. A company must plan the change, implement the change, monitor the new system, and then continually improve it.

Who Is Responsible for Changing the Yardsticks

Line managers are responsible for changing the yardsticks. In the past, often it was a finance or accounting manager who accepted this responsibility. In an environment in which only meeting the numbers was important, it was natural to use the same information that the accountants collected in the standard cost system to evaluate the business. Today, however, financial managers are part of the cross-functional team of managers responsible for meeting the goals of customer satisfaction, flexibility, and productivity, which often differ for different business systems. Focus shifts from the same measures for everyone to measures that count to the end customers and the bottom line of the business system.

What Gets Measured Gets Done

With the right measurement criteria in place (i.e., for measuring quality, delivery, cycle time, and waste), employees, teams, and departments can work together to meet the needs of customers and the goals of the organization. If an important aspect of performance goes unmeasured, it will probably get worse. Consider, for example, the case of a semiconductor company that improved its on-time delivery from 70 percent to 97 percent over a period of three years. After sustaining that performance for one year, the measure was dropped from the quarterly general manager's review. Sure enough, after just three quarters, performance slipped to 89 percent.

There are really two aspects of performance:

1. Maintaining the current level of performance (control and the standard-do-check-act cycle); and
2. Continuously improving it (improvement and the plan-do-check-act cycle).

Control and the Standard-Do-Check-Act Cycle

The word control suggests "keeping things in line," "not rocking the boat," "no surprises," and "keeping things the way they are." Certainly, control has its place in the world of external financial reporting and auditing, where there are given standards. Managers work, controllers check, and exceptions are acted upon to prevent further surprises. Control also has a place in performance measurement. People work to hold the gains that they achieved in prior periods.

This standard-do-check-act (SDCA) cycle, however, is only one part of anyone's job. The word "standard" in this context refers to a work standard: For example, a work standard instructs an operator to produce a part at a specified thickness. The operator does the work, frequently checking the output. If the part produced fails to meet the standard, corrective action must be taken to ensure the proper thickness.

Improvement and the Plan-Do-Check-Act Cycle

Everyone in the organization has the responsibility to improve. When a known problem exists (e.g., late deliveries, long cycle times, rework, or yield loss), the objective is not to keep things the way that they are (by, for example, building rework into the standard in the product cost model). Instead, the objective (and challenge) is to correct the problem, hold onto any gains that are achieved, and then to continuously improve. This is the plan-do-check-act (PDCA) cycle for improvement. Both cycles occur simultaneously in the workplace.

For example, when a problem has been identified and a team is assigned to solve the problem, the PDCA cycle begins. Data are collected, root causes are analyzed, and solutions are planned. The team then implements the plan and conducts necessary training. The plan is then evaluated against a specific measure. If results are satisfactory, then an improvement has been made and a new standard has been created. This standard is passed on to the SDCA cycle to control and hold the new gains. When the next problem is tackled, the standard is improved again and revised in the SDCA cycle.

Motivating Continuous Improvement Where It Counts

Performance measurement systems can no longer focus solely on past performance: Rather than looking in the rear mirror, managers must learn how to read the road ahead. One author[8] likens control systems of tomorrow to heat-seeking missiles that can make in-flight corrections to stay on the track of an elusive target ahead:

> Strategic control takes the tracking and checking up characteristics of the control function, and rather than locating them in what has already happened, it places them in the future. It continually tracks how the future "X" is changing as you get closer to it, so that, although you are still managing to stated future objectives, the objectives are updated daily to correspond to the shifting reality.[9]

EXHIBIT E3.4

Linking Day-to-Day Measures to the Customer

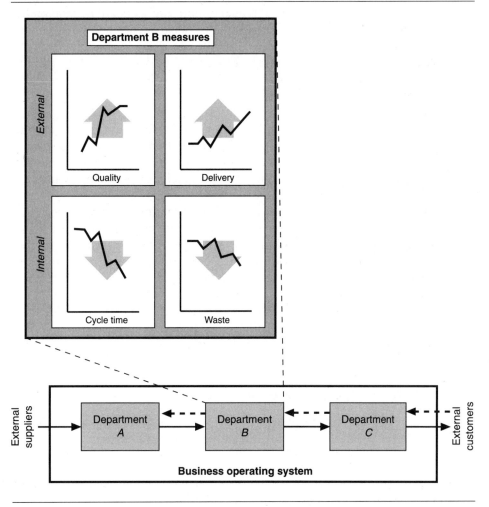

Exhibit E3.4 shows a simple "map" of key internal suppliers and customers, which forms the basis for determining where performance measures need to be put in place. Department *C* must have measures important to the customer, Department *B* must have measures important to Department *C,* and so on.

This approach is a powerful mechanism for managers to make sure their day-to-day performance measures are tracking close to their customer-driven targets.

343

Information When It Is Needed

"Measuring the right stuff" is only half the battle. Access to that information at the right time is just as critical. The frequency and level of detail depend on how managers use the information. For example, departments need to meet frequently (at least weekly) to review local performance in terms of quality, delivery, cycle time, and waste. This information should be detailed and stated in the language of operations (i.e., in nonfinancial terms). It is at this level that priorities are interpreted and early-warning signals identified. Action needs to be taken regarding scheduling, problem solving, and so on.

At the business system level, information can be summarized and reported on a monthly basis. The purpose of this information is to evaluate how the business operating system as a whole performs, to share information horizontally in the business operating system, and to target quality or productivity improvement efforts in the business operating system.

At the corporate or business-unit level, information can be further aggregated (in terms of both marketing and financial measures) and reported quarterly. These data can be used to evaluate the effectiveness of strategies, support longer-term resource decisions, and identify cross-functional or cross-divisional issues. These measures represent the results of overall performance from both a long-term and short-term perspective. Market and financial measures have a symbiotic relationship. Market share success affects future financial performance, yet financial performance today is required to compete in the future. This delicate balance is a key to successful performance.

How to Develop Custom-Tailored Measures

Once management is committed to revitalizing its performance measurement system, attention turns to implementation. Exhibit E3.5 shows a detailed plan that provides a useful road map.

The key point in Exhibit E3.5 is that performance measures are part of a dynamic system that must be responsive to changes in customer expectations, shifts in strategic focus, or changes in the work flow.

AN EFFECTIVE MANAGEMENT ACCOUNTING TOOL

Performance measurement has long been one of the most effective tools in the management accountant's toolbox. However, as is the case in many professions, tools sometimes need to be updated. The purpose of performance measurement today is to bring about improvement, not to punish shortfalls in performance. Performance measures can be used to continuously encourage day-to-day actions

EXHIBIT E3.5

Implementation Plan

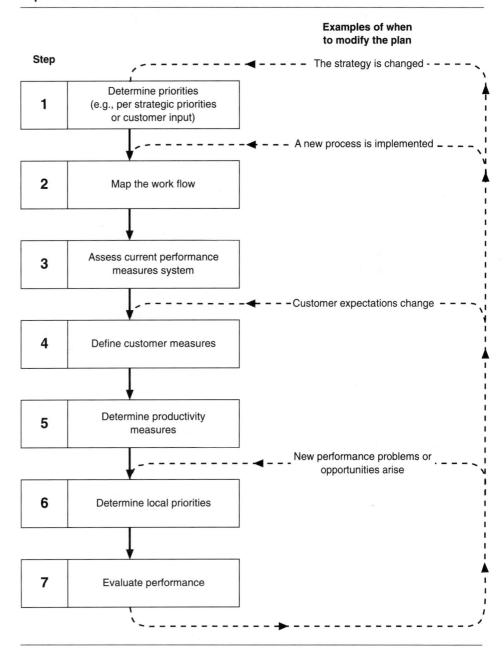

that improve quality and delivery while reducing cycle time and waste. The right performance measures can sustain goals of new strategies, processes, restructurings, and programs like JIT or TQM. In short, "measuring the right stuff" in day-to-day operations and encouraging the right actions are catalysts to effective profit management.

Notes

1. MIT Commission on Industrial Productivity, *Made in America: Regaining the Productive Edge* (Cambridge, MA: MIT Press, 1989).

2. Robert Eccles, "The Performance Measurement Manifesto," *Harvard Business Review* (January–February 1991): 131–137.

3. Robert A. Howell, James D. Brown, Stephen R. Soucy, and Allen H. Seed, *Management Accounting in the New Manufacturing Environment* (Montvale, NJ: National Association of Accountants, 1987).

4. Richard L. Lynch and Kelvin F. Cross, *Measure Up: Yardsticks for Continuous Improvement* (Cambridge, MA: Blackwell Publishers, 1991): 125–129, 148–149.

5. This section was adapted with permission from *ibid.*

6. C.J. McNair, Richard L. Lynch, and Kelvin F. Cross, "Do Financial and Non-Financial Performance Measures Have to Agree?" *Management Accounting* (November 1990): 28–36.

7. David A. Garvin, *Managing Quality* (New York: The Free Press, 1988).

8. Stanley M. Davis, *Future Perfect* (Reading, MA: Addison Wesley Publishing Co., 1987).

9. *Ibid.*

Quality Costs: Facilitating the Quality Initiative

JAMES B. SIMPSON

Supervisor-Cost Analysis in the Controller's Office at the Ford Motor Company.

DAVID L. MUTHLER

Manager in the Manufacturing Excellence Practice at Ernst & Whinney.

Many companies are now realizing the enormous financial losses that result from poor quality control. Consumers also believe that purchasing a quality product will save them money in the long run. As a result, companies in many different industries are implementing quality cost programs. Although senior management is heavily involved, these programs affect virtually every department in a company and every quality cost must be accounted for. This article discusses the external, internal, appraisal, and prevention costs involved in a quality cost program and suggests methods for creating and implementing an effective program.

During the last few years, international competition has put tremendous pressure on US industry, and market share for US corporations has been eroding in almost every commodity. In addition, consumers are now willing to pay premium prices for quality products. They believe that if they pay more initially for a quality product, the total cost over the life of the product will be less than if they buy a product of lower quality. This is especially evident in the automotive industry. The rise in consumer quality expectations has started a ground swell in US industry. This push for quality is being termed the "second industrial revolution." Larger corporations are beginning to realize that quality is a systematic approach to the search for excellence.

The Ford Motor Company's statement of guiding principles begins as follows:

> *"Quality comes first*—To achieve customer satisfaction, the quality of our products and services must be our number one priority.

> *Customers are the focus of everything we do*—Our work must be done with our customers in mind, providing better products and services than our competition.

> *Continuous improvement is essential to our success*—We must strive for excellence in everything we do: in our products and in their safety and value, in our services, in our human relations, in our competitiveness, and in our profitability."[1]

This approach affects all aspects of the corporation and can begin only with the commitment of senior management. Every department must work together to achieve quality control. However, quality is a concept that people sometimes have difficulty describing—like excellence or goodness. One way to further a company's push for quality is by converting the language of quality into dollars. This conversion not only gives everyone a common language, it also quantifies the characteristic. Once a characteristic is quantified, it can be measured, tracked, and analyzed. Managers can now understand how quality affects the corporation and can analyze where to make the best investments in the quality effort. For example, in a division of a large corporation, before quality costs were completely understood, quality improvement projects were regularly rejected by a senior manager. The manager believed that "quality is free, and we cannot afford to spend any more on it." After working with a cost-of-quality program, however, this manager began to understand quality costs and their interrelationships. Quality improvement projects are now evaluated on their return on investment, just as all other projects. As a result, the major product of this division is now the best of its class.

Quality costs are as important as labor costs, engineering costs, and marketing costs. They can also be substantial, as David Garvin points out: "Research suggests that poor quality costs a typical company 10 to 20% of its sales revenue. These dollars go for a broad range of activities: inspection and testing to ferret out mistakes, rework and scrap, warranty claims, and product liability suits."[2] Because these costs are so high, quality improvement projects can substantially affect company profits. In fact, when a corporation understands its total quality cost picture, it usually finds that the quality system can provide one of the most attractive return-on-investment opportunities available. For example, a medium-sized company that had problems with quality started a cost-of-quality program. In two years, the company improved its quality cost picture by more than $2.76 million.[3]

QUALITY COSTS DEFINED

Quality costs can be found in virtually every department. Most managers don't realize that they incur quality costs and are responsible for them. Unfortunately, most accounting systems are not equipped to report quality costs because these costs are typically associated only with the quality control department. Virtually all departments, however, have quality costs. This is often overlooked because quality has not been recognized as a functional profit center. The quality control department and the controller's office must pull these costs together. A more formalized system can then be established by the controller's office. Quality costs are basically divided into four major categories: external failure, internal failure, appraisal, and prevention (see Exhibit 1). Because these costs are not listed in the chart of accounts, management must take the time to study and understand them.

External failure costs. When a customer receives a defective product, external failure costs result. Repairs caused by defects, the shipping and handling of the product, the warranty adjustments needed to replace or discount the product, and the salaries of the personnel needed to administer these activities are included in external costs. In addition, the costs of investigations of defects in the field are also counted. These costs are incurred when a company's field service engineer visits a customer location to investigate an external failure. The findings are then reported to the appropriate department for corrective action.

EXHIBIT 1.

Examples of the Four Cost-of-Quality Areas

External Failure Costs	Internal Failure Costs	Appraisal Costs	Prevention Costs
• Warranty adjustments	• Scrap	• Receiving inspection	• Quality engineering
• Repairs	• Rework	• In-process inspection	• Quality planning done by any activity
• Customer service	• Reinspection of rework	• Laboratory inspection	• Design and development of quality equipment
• Returned goods	• Downgrading because of defects	• Outside laboratory endorsements	• Design verification and review to evaluate the quality of new products
• Returned repaired goods	• Losses caused by vendor scrap	• Setup for testing	
• Investigation of defects	• Downtime caused by defects	• Maintenance of test equipment	• Quality training
• Product recalls	• Failure analysis	• Quality audits	• Quality improvement projects
• Product liability suits		• Calibration of quality equipment	• Quality data gathering analysis and reporting
		• Maintenance of production equipment used for quality	• Statistical process control activities
			• Other process control activities used to prevent defects

When products are recalled, costs for owner notification, replacement, shipping and handling, and administration are incurred. Product liability involves the cost of liability insurance and any legal fees or other costs that are the result of a lawsuit. Another cost that should be included in this category but is difficult to determine is loss of goodwill. Consumers tend to spread the word faster when they are unhappy with a product than when they are happy. In addition, product recalls are often published in newspapers and magazines or announced on the radio or television. Although it is difficult to predict the consumer's reaction to negative publicity and its affect on future sales, an estimate of these costs should be made and included in the external failure costs.

Internal failure costs. These costs are generated by defects that are found before a product reaches the customer. Internal failure costs are easy to identify because many accounting systems already track them. Scrap is the result of defects that cannot be repaired or discounted. The cost of scrap includes the labor and overhead required to make the part, but it does not include waste generated in the usual course of processing (i.e., chips, trimmings, or offal that results from machining or stamping operations). Most accounting systems allow for this type of waste. When costs are incurred as a result of defect repairs, the expense of the extra operations performed and the cost of reinspecting or retesting the product should be included. In addition, many industries (e.g., textiles) downgrade or discount flawed products. The amount of this discount should be added to the internal costs.

The cost of any downtime or work stoppage caused by such defects as mismachined parts from a previous operation is also an internal cost. Losses and downtime caused by vendor scrap and rework are harder to capture but are nevertheless included. The salaries of the individuals required to troubleshoot or investigate the problems caused by defects can be costly. For example, when a machining line is stopped for tool breakage because the castings from the foundry have hard spots, a metallurgist, tool engineer, manufacturing engineer, and quality engineer are called in to investigate and solve the problem. These individuals participate in the review of defects to determine whether the articles are scrap, rework, or discounted and are members of a material review board.

Appraisal costs. The costs associated with inspecting a product to ensure that it meets with customers' requirements are considered appraisal costs. Here, the term "customer" refers to both internal and external customers. The internal customer is the next person in the company that uses the output of an operation. For example, assembly departments are usually the customers of machining or fabricating departments. The external customer is the consumer who purchases the product.

The cost of checking incoming materials (receiving inspection) to ensure conformance to requirements (e.g., checking the hardness of castings or measuring dimensional characteristics before releasing materials to production) is also an appraisal cost, as is any in-process checking or testing performed by quality control inspectors, production workers, or engineering personnel. Quality audits are associated with this area and can be performed on the shipping dock before release to the customer, in the field at the customer's location, or in storage areas for evaluation of shelf life. Laboratory costs are included in this category, as well as endorsements from such outside testing facilities as Underwriters Laboratories or the Consumer Product Safety Commission.

Appraisal costs also encompass the cost of noncapitalized equipment (e.g., gauges, micrometers, scales, or other quality control equipment or supplies used for testing or inspecting products). The depreciation expense for capitalized quality control equipment is also figured in, as are the costs for maintenance and calibration of quality control equipment. The cost of maintenance and calibration of some production equipment used for inspection is an appraisal cost. This includes such items as a built-in automatic gauging station or a probe on a machining line.

Administrative costs that come mostly from the quality control department are considered appraisal costs. Several companies, however, have removed inspectors from this process and have made production personnel responsible for checking their own products. If this is the case, a portion of the production management and labor costs should be added.

Prevention costs. These costs are associated with actions taken to plan the product or process to ensure that defects do not occur. Quality engineering costs fall under this category. These costs involve the activities that establish the inspection and testing plans or procedures. This advanced quality planning includes not only quality engineering but manufacturing engineering, design or product engineering, purchasing, and production personnel. These activities also include working with suppliers to improve the quality of incoming products. This involves visits to suppliers' and customers' locations to conduct reviews and jointly establish the quality plan. Supplier certification programs are also prevention costs (e.g., Ford's Q-1 and General Motors' SPEAR).

Because prevention is a cross-functional activity, it presents difficulty in establishing quality-related costs for departments other than quality control. As a result, estimates must be made and refined as experience is gained with the cost-of-quality program.

The design and development of quality control equipment (e.g., gauges, test fixtures, and quality data-gathering equipment, including computer hardware and software) are prevention costs. Design reviews or testing done to evaluate the quality of a new product in order to prevent defects or to create a more robust design (one that is more easily manufactured or is less likely to be defective) is also included in this category.

Training personnel in techniques or concepts that are designed to improve quality (e.g., statistical process control, design of experiments, employee involvement, quality circles, and reliability methods) are prevention costs that are easily captured. Another prevention cost is the evaluation of the ability of machine tools or processing equipment for consistency manufacturing products to specifications before and after they are installed in the plant. Quality improvement projects and quality data gathering, analysis, and reporting, including the cost to maintain these systems, are also involved.

QUALITY COST RELATIONSHIPS

Management must understand the relationship between the four cost-of-quality areas to identify and make informed decisions on quality improvement projects. For example, if appraisal costs are increased, more products are checked and more defects are caught before they reach the customer. This lowers the external failure costs because fewer defective products are shipped. Higher internal failure costs can result, however, because the amount of scrap, rework, and retest increase accordingly. Overall, the total quality costs should be lower because it is usually cheaper to repair the goods at the plant than in the field. A major computer manufacturer reported:

> "The earlier you detect and prevent a defect, the more you can save. If you throw away a defective two-cent resistor before you use it, you lose two cents. If you don't find it until it has been soldered into a computer component, it may cost $10 to repair the part. If you don't catch the defect until it is in the computer user's hands, the repair will cost hundreds of dollars. Indeed, if a $5,000 computer must be repaired in the field, the expense may exceed the manufacturing cost."[4]

Exhibit 2, adapted from Juran and Gryna, graphically displays the relationship between the costs of control (prevention and appraisal) and the costs of failure (internal and external).[5] As more is invested in control activities, the failure costs decrease. Even though prevention actions are usually long term, they tend to eliminate the source of the defects; appraisal actions catch the defect only after it has been made. Therefore, effective prevention actions reduce failure costs as well as appraisal costs. The vice-president of a major automotive supplier commented that his organization finds it difficult to identify and initiate more preventive actions, although he realizes that this category yields the highest return on investment. Appraisal actions are relatively easy — it's simply a matter of adding more inspectors or automated inspection equipment. The development of robust designs and processes, however, is a much tougher assignment.

Exhibit 2 also demonstrates that quality costs cannot be reduced to zero. Ideally, failure costs could go to zero but prevention and appraisal would still be required. For example, in 1983, the XYZ Corporation was being pressured by its customers for quality improvements. The board of directors decided that XYZ should embark on a quality improvement program. First, management compiled the cost of quality, which was running at a level of 18% of sales. Exhibit 3 illustrates these cost relationships. External failure costs made up the bulk of the quality costs for 1983. Management then took immediate action to stem the flow of defects by adding more inspection and increasing the amount of sorting. They also embarked on a quality training program and began training all employees in employee involvement and statistical process control. As a result, external failures dropped drastically in 1984 and customer relations were improved, but the internal failure costs increased significantly. Instead of shipping defects to customers, the company was now catching the defects and containing them in-house. The final result was an overall reduction in quality costs for 1984. In 1985 training was completed, the statistical process controls were added, and employee involvement groups were growing. Although appraisal costs continued to increase, failure costs were reduced and the total quality cost picture improved.

Preventive actions were continued that year with experiments-design training for engineering personnel and the institution of a supplier quality assurance

EXHIBIT 2.

Graphic Display of Quality Cost Relationships

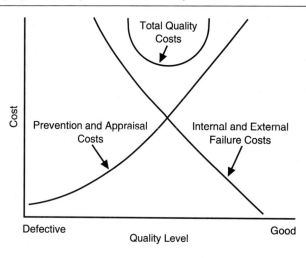

EXHIBIT 3.

Example of Quality Cost Reduction (XYZ Corporation)

Quality Cost Category	1983	1984	1985	1986
		($ in thousands)		
External failure	$4,000	$ 800	$ 400	$ 200
Internal failure	200	2,400	1,400	600
Appraisal	400	800	1,200	800
Prevention	200	400	400	400
Total	$4,800	$4,400	$3,400	$2,000

program. In 1986, preventive actions continued to pay off with a further reduction in external, internal, and appraisal costs. As a result, quality costs have now been reduced to 7.5% of sales, customer relations have improved dramatically, the company's quality position in the industry is strengthened, and the profit picture has improved. This example shows that increases in preventive costs should reduce other quality costs. More robust designs and processes, as well as improved process controls, help to reduce external failures, internal failures, and appraisal costs. Ultimately, total quality costs are lowered. An ounce of prevention is indeed worth a pound of cure.

THE QUALITY COST SYSTEM

Quality costs must be captured and reported to management in a meaningful way. A joint effort by the quality control department and the controller's office is necessary in establishing a usable reporting system. Because most cost accounting systems don't reflect these specific quality cost categories, quality control and the controller's office must determine which accounts contain valid quality costs. Management must determine how to reorganize and restructure the existing accounting system to provide accurate quality cost data.

Because the objective is to establish a long-term reporting system, it may be necessary to revise the chart of accounts to reflect each quality cost category. Once established, the usual cost accounting process can provide the cost data associated with each account. Typically, it is the quality control manager's responsibility to identify and define what quality cost elements are needed to ensure that the resulting data adequately meets the needs of management. This involves establishing and defining a company-specific cost-of-quality program. The accounting department must then devise a system for identifying the cost elements. Both departments should keep in mind that the raw data is usually provided by other departments and, as such, should be obtained with a minimum of inconvenience to regular operations.

Any changes must be organized in such a way as to benefit all levels of the company (i.e., plant, division, and corporate). A uniform accounting system is needed to collect and consolidate data at any level. Once the objective and purpose of the program has been defined, quality control personnel and the controller's office can establish the cost-of-quality accounts. They may still have to examine the existing chart of accounts to determine valid quality costs and interview department managers to determine what kind of quality control activities are being performed. Some costs must be simply estimated; for example, the process engineering department may not be able to find an account that totals the portion of the engineer's time spent investigating quality problems.

Developing and implementing source documents for all of these quality costs elements is necessary if the system is to function properly. Time sheets and labor accounts must be structured for easy identification of the hours associated with a specific quality cost category. For example, the hours spent reworking defective components should be charged to a special account that automatically ends up in the internal failure group of accounts. The same holds true for scrap material. Special coding may be necessary to segregate internally generated scrap and scrap from external sources (e.g., returned goods). Proper identification and reporting of quality costs keeps management apprised of potential areas of concern (e.g., excessive scrap or rework) and allows for the formulation of action plans that reduce costs. Many large companies further subdivide these quality cost accounts to provide cost data by product line or commodity.

REPORTING QUALITY COSTS

Any reporting system is only as good as the data provided. It is essential that the reports are user-oriented. Senior management requires a summary of comparable data, whereas a warranty analyst requires specific details. Therefore, individual reports must be tailored to the end user.

An established accounting system and the provision of raw data are worthless if the data is not collected and reported in a meaningful way. Reporting formats must be established and analytical techniques implemented for proper interpretation of the quality costs. The quality control and accounting departments must design report formats and bases for comparison. Basic data collection makes use of the company's experts, in general avoids jurisdictional disputes, and lends credibility to the numbers. Senior management usually depends on the accounting department for unbiased financial information.

Exhibit 4 represents a typical reporting format. The quality cost categories (accounts) are listed and totaled. Comparison bases and ratios of the various bases to cost categories are also illustrated. Usually these reports provide monthly costs, year-to-date costs, and variances to established budgets. Some reports may include a comparison with the previous year's cost data. Establishment of comparison bases is an important element for measuring the cost of quality. Some of the more meaningful bases of measurement include:

- Percentage of sales dollars—Usually appeals to most members of management.
- Direct labor hours produced—Useful for short-term activity.
- Per unit of product—Useful for comparison of similar product lines (e.g., transmissions and engines).

In time, managers learn to interpret the significance of the ratios and bases. Through the reporting format, useful indexes are agreed on; they then become the accepted bases for comparison. Exhibit 5 illustrates the method a major automotive supplier used to graphically present its cost of quality. These graphs show the relationship of all quality cost categories. Using graphs to present cost data can have a greater impact on management than a tabular report.

What is done with the data after it has been summarized and provided to management? At this point, various analytical techniques are applied. For example, if a company wishes to attack internal failure costs, and scrap is the most significant portion of the budget, it may be necessary to break it down by product or commodity. One of the most powerful management tools is Pareto Analysis. This technique is widely used to work on the bulk of the problem area with the least amount of analytical study. Exhibits 6 and 7 demonstrate an example of Pareto Analysis. Exhibit 6 shows that three product lines out of eighteen can account for 80% of the total scrap. Further analysis (see Exhibit 8) explains that

EXHIBIT 4.

Quality Cost Report

Prevention Costs	Month	Year to Date ($ in thousands)	Variance B/W* to Budget (Year to Date)
• Quality control administration	$15	$60	($2)
• Quality planning	8	20	8
• Training	4	15	4
• Quality improvement programs	7	30	(10)
Total prevention	$34	$125	—
Appraisal Costs			
• Inspection/testing	$45	$235	($18)
• Maintenance/calibration	14	62	(4)
• Outside testing fees	9	25	(3)
• Quality audits	14	37	7
Total appraisal	$82	$359	($18)
Internal Failure Costs			
• Scrap	$57	$327	($45)
• Rework	18	84	(19)
• Discontinued material	13	60	(25)
• Retesting	23	95	(22)
Total internal	$111	$566	($111)
External Failure Costs			
• Warranty defects	$22	$82	($6)
• Product recalls	—	15	(15)
• Product liability	15	60	10
• Repairs and adjustments	35	122	(32)
Total external	$72	$279	($43)
Total quality costs	$299	$1329	($172)
Bases			
• Sales	$4,950	$22,412	($1,372)
• Direct labor hours	650	2740	(226)
Ratios			
• Internal to direct labor	$.17/hr	$.21/hr	
• Total to sales	6%	5.9%	
* Better than/worse than budget			

the part was scrapped because of its oversize condition. With this information, management can investigate the reasons for the oversize condition and formulate a plan to correct the situation.

When quality costs are being reported, managers must remember the interrelationships between the four cost areas. With this in mind, they can then compare improvement program proposals. They can quantify improvements, calculate return on investment, and track the progress of each program. Caution is required, however, as W.E. Deming notes:

EXHIBIT 5.

Supplier Cost Summary

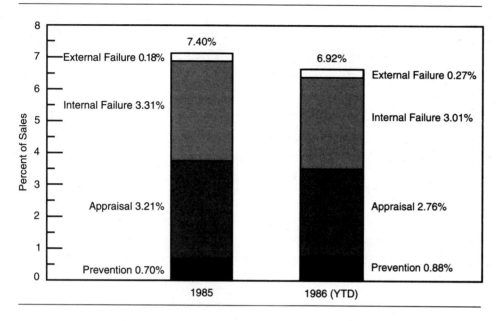

1985   1986 (YTD)

EXHIBIT 6.

Scrap by Product Line

Product Line	Total Scrap	Cumulative Scrap	% of Total	Cumulative %
527M	$80	$80	32%	32%
119J	65	145	26	58
212F	55	200	22	80
520M	20	220	8	88
306M	10	230	4	92
Other (13)	20	250	8	100
Total	$250		100%	

"1. Costs are sometimes elusive; difficult to estimate. For example, no one knows the cost of a defective item (e.g., TV-tube) that reaches a customer. A customer dissatisfied with an item of small cost (e.g., a toaster) may be influential in the decision on a huge contract, and see to it that some other manufacturer gets it. 2. Same for benefits. Benefits are even more difficult to evaluate in dollars. However, by use of the idea of a trade-off, one benefit against another, a scale of ranks for benefits can sometimes be achieved."[6]

EXHIBIT 7.

Pareto Diagram of Scrap from Exhibit 6

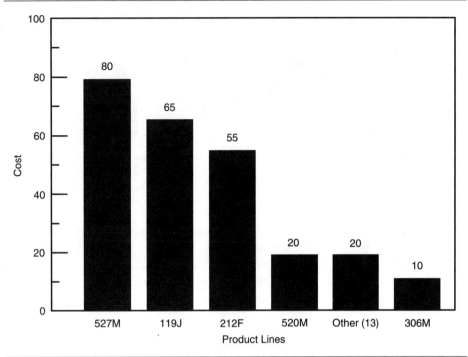

EXHIBIT 8.

Scrap by Causal Fator

Product Line	Oversize	Undersize	Porosity	Cracked	Total
527M	$50	$5	$10	$15	$80
119J	40	10	10	5	65
2121F	20	10	20	5	55
Total	$110	$25	$40	$25	$200

Target for Cost Reduction Action

After a company compiles its quality costs, it often asks, How do these costs compare with other companies? This is difficult to answer because no detailed studies have been published. It is also a misleading comparison because each company is different. Comparing plants within the same corporation is difficult

EXHIBIT 9.

Comparison of Quality Cost Categories

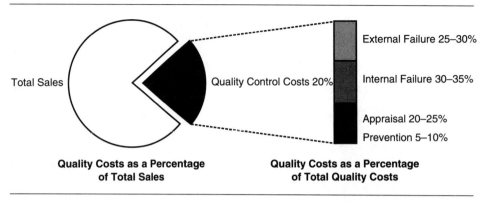

Total Sales

Quality Control Costs 20%

External Failure 25–30%

Internal Failure 30–35%

Appraisal 20–25%

Prevention 5–10%

**Quality Costs as a Percentage
of Total Sales**

**Quality Costs as a Percentage
of Total Quality Costs**

because of the numerous product mixes, processes, age of facilities, equipment, and work force—the differences are almost endless. Even though it is futile to make comparisons, each department or plant should be tracked so improvements can be monitored. Management must also realize the proper ratio between the quality costs. A.V. Feigenbaum suggests that the ratios in Exhibit 9 are probably typical,[7] and further states:

> "[T]his cost analysis suggests that we have been spending our quality dollars the wrong way; a fortune down the drain because of product failures; another large sum to support a sort-the-bad-from-the-good appraisal screen to try to keep too many bad products from going to customers; and comparatively nothing for the true defect prevention technology that can do something about reversing the vicious upward cycle of higher quality costs and less reliable product quality."

Management also needs to know what the percentage of quality costs are compared with sales. A previous section noted that quality costs were as high as 20% of sales. Phil Crosby suggests, however, that 2% to 3% is required to be competitive worldwide.[8] It is not an easy task to lower quality costs to this level, but it can be very profitable. Management must also remember that quality is a long-term commitment; it doesn't happen overnight. Improvement projects may not affect the total quality costs in the same reporting period in which they are installed, and several reporting periods may be required before results are shown.

For example, in 1982, Ford rewrote its quality manual for suppliers. To continue doing business with Ford, suppliers had to increase their preventive costs in the following areas: quality planning, work force training in statistical methods, and implementation of statistical process controls. Implementation had to begin by October 1983. The companies that put in an all-out effort to comply are now reaping the rewards. In these companies, appraisal costs have been reduced, internal failure costs have been cut by more than half, and external failure costs are almost nonexistent (see Exhibit 5 for actual data).

CONCLUSION

Financial organizations have much to offer in the pursuit of quality by way of tracking quality costs. A company can create a successful quality cost program by keeping the following points in mind:

- Use quality costs as benchmarks—Remember, initially they will be estimates.
- Get started as soon as possible—Waiting for total or complete costs could delay the quality cost program by years.
- Make sure the costs chosen are valid quality costs—This avoids departmental differences.
- Use the costs to determine the progress of each plant or department—Avoid comparisons.
- Use the quality cost data to take action and change the process—Just encouraging people to do better doesn't help. They are probably doing the best they can with what they have to work with.
- Be patient—Commitment to quality requires long-term thinking.

Deming, who helped teach the Japanese about quality improvement, notes that 85% of a company's problems are the responsibility of management. Therefore, the quality cost program should be used as a management tool to help identify the problems, reveal where improvements can be made, and monitor the ongoing improvement.

Notes

1. *Continuing Process Control and Process Capability Improvement* (Ford Motor Co, September 1985).

2. D.A. Garvin, "Product Quality: Profitable at Any Cost," *The New York Times* (March 3, 1985).

3. A.V. Feigenbaum, *Total Quality Control,* 3rd ed, (New York: McGraw-Hill, 1983).

4. Garvin.

5. J.M. Juran and F.M. Gryna, *Quality Planning and Analysis* (New York: McGraw-Hill, 1980).

6. W.E. Deming, *Quality, Productivity, and Competitive Position* (Cambridge MA: Institute of Technology Center for Advanced Engineering Study, 1982).

7. Feigenbaum.

8. P.B. Crosby, *Quality Is Free* (New York: McGraw-Hill, 1979).

Recommended Reading

Groocock, J.M., *The Cost of Quality* (New York: Pitman Publishing Corp, 1974).

Guide for Reducing Quality Costs (Milwaukee: American Society for Quality Control, 1977).

Juran, J.M. and D.M. Lundvall, *Quality Control Handbook* (New York: McGraw-Hill, 1983).

Karabastos, N.A., "Mae-Goodwin Tarver: Quality Pays for Itself," *Quality* 24, (1985).

Quality Cost Analysis (Dearborn Heights: Multiface Publishing, 1979).

Quality Costs — What & How (Milwaukee: American Society for Quality Control, 1971).

Rotherberg, J., "Cost/Benefit Analysis," *Handbook on Evaluations* 2 (1975).

Linking Cost to Price and Profit

GARY G. FRANK, PH.D., CMA, CPA
Assistant Professor, School of Accountancy, University of Akron.

STEVEN A. FISHER, DBA, CMA
Assistant Professor in the School of Accountancy at the University of Akron.

ALLEN R. WILKIE, MBA
Operations Controller of GenCorp Polymer Products.

Source: Published by *Management Accounting,* June 1989, Institute of Management Accountants, Montvale, NJ.

The current revolution in U.S. manufacturing continually challenges cost accountants and cost accounting systems in manufacturing firms. The evolving role for cost accountants increasingly will be to direct attention toward opportunities for performance improvement and to assist functional area managers to exploit these opportunities. Cost accounting systems will need to evolve into cost management systems.

The emphasis of cost management extends beyond cost control to encompass complex relationships between cost and pricing. Under the cost management philosophy, accounting systems serve as catalysts for organizational change.

Firms seeking to implement cost management must tailor the approach according to their own needs, but they can find direction from the experience of firms that have adopted this philosophy, such as GenCorp Polymer Products (GPP). GPP successfully made the transition to cost management in response to changing production technologies.

THE GPP MANUFACTURING ENVIRONMENT

The Mogadore plant of GPP's Latex Division is situated on 43 acres in Mogadore, Ohio, just outside Akron. The oldest building dates from the early 1900s and was originally used to manufacture bicycle tires. Since 1952 the facility has been used exclusively for latex production. The plant's annual capacity of 200 million dry pounds makes it the world's largest producer of styrene butadiene (SBR) latex.

Latex is the generic description of any synthetic rubber or plastic produced by pulverization. GPP manufactures 60 different SBR latex products from the same feedstocks, applying the same technology. The industry has multiple producers, and product markets are highly competitive on price. Deep price discounting in the early 1970s by competitors seeking greater market share convinced GPP that its success in the synthetic rubber latex industry depended on becoming the leader in product quality and innovation.

FOCUS ON PRODUCT QUALITY

Product quality as viewed by GPP is multidimensional. It includes producing latex consistently to precise tolerance, but it goes beyond that to encompass both yield and output of the production process.

GPP has applied a broad program to achieve industry leadership in product quality. Its Latex Division works in partnership with suppliers to ensure standard quality of material inputs. Extending quality control upstream enhances consistency and reduces testing costs at the plant substantially.

This overall quality effort has included focusing on human resources. The firm's emphasis on training and personnel development and its policy of internal advancement have resulted in low turnover, high employee loyalty, and high productivity.

GPP's quality strategy has been furthered through Computer-Aided Manufacturing (CAM). The initial change from localized manual control to computer process control occurred in 1974. Recently, the plant brought on line its second-generation computer, a Foxboro Fox 1A manufacturing process computer (commonly found in fully integrated oil refineries). The application of CAM has enhanced productivity and product consistency dramatically. This is despite the age of the plant and the fact that the 18 reactor vessels in the plant have been added during multiple expansions and vary in size from 3,500 to 7,500 gallons.

Manufacturing scheduling and the conversion process are regulated automatically by the Fox 1A process computer, which receives continuous input on the 18 reactor vessels from more than 6,000 sensors and controls. The database developed from continual monitoring of reactor processing allowed GPP to tailor recipes for each product to the characteristics of individual reactors. CAM has significantly reduced cycle times, increased reactor loadings, and improved product consistency.

PRODUCT INNOVATION—KEY TO COMPETITION

Product innovation is the second component of GPP's strategic plan for the Latex Division. SBR latex can be processed in almost infinite variations for different industrial and commercial applications. The primary markets in which GPP's Latex Division competes are: paper coatings, textile backings, tire cord adhesives, and latex saturates. The Division has modified and reformulated products continuously within each of these markets to meet customer needs.

Two factors have played crucial roles in allowing GPP to compete as a high-tech supplier in the SBR latex industry. First, GPP pioneered computerized control of the reaction process. Through CAM, GPP can manufacture products to tailor-made recipes easily, according to customer formulation. Consequently, the plant currently can manufacture 60 different products even though it was designed originally to accommodate only eight or nine product formulations.

Second, GPP has a strong commitment to research and development. The company has established a latex research and development laboratory immediately adjacent to the production facility. This proximity facilitates the type of coordination between production and research that is required for achieving both process and product innovation. Close ties between production, marketing, and R&D have made the Latex Division extremely responsive to market needs.

From a production viewpoint, the Mogadore plant is a resounding success. GPP's strategy to survive the industry shakeout predicted for the late 1970s was both sophisticated and successful. Emphasis on both process and product innovation has allowed GPP to succeed while smaller, less innovative producers were forced out.

A FLY IN THE OINTMENT

The production-oriented culture of GPP's Latex Division promoted a highly efficient and profitable operation. The Division's bottom line was very good, sales were on target, and production consistently set new records. Given these circumstances, there seemed to be no pressing need to examine critical relationships between product pricing and true costs of production. In fact, the cost accounting system established when the plant switched to latex production was virtually unchanged, despite major changes in the production process.

In the fall of 1985, however, the plant approached its capacity limits. Until then no internal factors had ever threatened sales. But at production capacity management faced the problem either of rationing or dropping selected products. A group of production, accounting, and marketing managers met to evaluate alternatives. Eventually, discussion centered on adjusting the product mix to maximize profits. To do this, one or more products would have to be discontinued temporarily.

Working with the plant controller, the newly hired division controller analyzed the cost of products to determine their relative profitability. One product was identified as the prime candidate to be dropped. However, production and marketing managers were unwilling to accept this verdict because the product ran through the plant smoothly, had high production yields, and sold in large volume. When presented with the cost analysis, the president of the latex subsidiary said that the problem was not with the product but rather with the costing system.

THE EXISTING COST SYSTEM

GPP's cost accounting system had been structured primarily for financial reporting and had little relevance for either pricing or product decisions. Because GPP's focus was on plant performance, the system met the normal information requirements of plant management. As long as the plant remained highly profitable, nobody questioned the decisional purpose and assumptions that structured the cost system.

Without a crisis, there was actually little reason to modify the cost system. Inventory level was low compared with total production, so even a distorted inventory valuation would not materially affect financial statements. Performance evaluation was based primarily on yield of process, which functioned well

TABLE 1

Application Rates

$$\frac{\text{Budgeted Overhead}}{365 \,/\, 18 \text{ reactors}} = \text{rate per reactor per day}$$

Revenue Per Reactor Run	−	Materials and Freight-out	=	Contribution Margin	÷	Product Standard Processing Time	=	Product Profit Velocity (PPV)

within the plant's production culture. Accounting data did not normally affect product pricing because competitors' prices determined GPP's price for many products. Cost determination was significant only for unique products, but management assumed products had similar conversion costs, even the unique ones. As a result, all products were costed at standard.

GPP's standard cost system attached materials, labor, and overhead to the product based upon its recipe. The system recognized direct material as a major cost component and regularly adjusted standard cost of materials for changes in yield and price. The treatment of direct labor cost and overhead under the cost system was more problematic.

Products were costed at standard direct labor, but technological change had undermined the relation between products and labor. With the change to computer-aided manufacturing, direct labor ceased to exist as a measurable production component.

Nowhere in the production process do employees handle or transform product, except in limited premixing operations. Production is centrally controlled by CAM. Of the 130 production employees, only one worker's efforts can be associated readily with specific products. Nevertheless, products were costed based on direct labor, even in some cases on the basis of labor classifications that had ceased to exist.

No distinction was made between variable and fixed overhead. Management had determined that more than 93% of plant operating costs are fixed over a reasonable range of activity and so felt little need to identify elements of variable overhead. The system based overhead application on a single plant-wide rate, using a two-stage application procedure that assigned overhead initially to reactors and then to product processed through the reactor vessel. The application rate was calculated as shown in the upper part of Table 1.

Overhead attached to product based upon the pounds of latex produced within a given reactor. If $1,250 of overhead were charged per reactor per day, and reactor 13 produced 40,000 pounds of latex in the day, each pound produced through this reactor would absorb $1,250/40,000, or $0.03125.

Originally, all reactors in the plant were the same size. GPP deployed larger reactors as the plant expanded but did not modify the cost system to reflect this change so calculation of the overhead application rate ignored differences in reactor size. A 3,500-gallon reactor bore the same overhead as a 7,500-gallon reactor. Consequently, the overhead absorbed by a pound of product was influenced by the reactor that processed the product. The overhead application system distorted product cost, as any product could be processed in any reactor. The one actually used was simply a function of scheduling.

As the management accounting team reviewed the cost accounting system, it became convinced that the system could not provide a measure of product cost useful for product mix and pricing decisions. The accounting system had been designed for macro control of the plant and to obtain an inventory value for financial reporting. Thus, the cost system provided the data necessary to assess production efficiencies and overall plant performance, and the inventory cost fully accounted for overhead and met the objectives of valuation under GAAP. But the cost system was not sufficiently refined to determine the relative profitability of products so it failed to provide management with the necessary information to allocate production capacity across products.

The cause of the problem was simple, in retrospect. The components of manufacturing cost had changed with the production process, but management had not modified the cost accounting system to recognize these changes. It was necessary to develop a cost system that could be responsive to GPP's evolving technology.

TOWARD AN EFFECTIVE COST SYSTEM

The plant controller and division controller formed an ad-hoc task force to assess management needs. GPP's management information system was relatively sophisticated and its database extensive. The basic problems appeared to be identifying the decisional needs of management and ordering the data in a form amenable to those requirements.

The focus of their investigation was to determine what factors drive the cost of production and how this cost should be assigned to specific products. The ultimate goal was to develop a cost system useful for product mix and pricing decisions. To identify the parameters of the system, its goals, and the data to be generated, the investigators conducted interviews with technical personnel, including the technical director, the vice president of manufacturing, the purchasing manager, and the sales manager. These interviews were structured to determine each functional area's requirement for and uses of accounting information.

Interviews, in combination with analysis of historic cost data, identified the following as primary factors driving the cost of production: material recipe, material prices, reactor loading (pounds of material input), reactor cycle time, reactor cleaning time, and frequency of cleaning. Once the team identified the factors driving production cost, natural pools for cost aggregation became apparent. Specifically, the task force decided to group direct labor with overhead as conversion cost. Furthermore, the team determined that conversion cost was fixed; neither labor nor plant operating costs vary over the anticipated range of plant operations.

The task force reconstituted cost pools to conform to the behavior of costs within the revised production process. At this stage, the team had not yet determined how costs should attach to product. The cost driver activities were identified within weeks, but the primary activity determining income-generating capacity remained unclear. The leap of logic that served to restructure the cost system occurred when the cost team broke out of a production mind-set to a view that encompassed both production and sales.

The team had experimented with alternative cost allocations using pounds of product as a denominator. Such an approach was consistent with the production emphasis of the plant, but it failed to relate the analysis to product markets. The breakthrough occurred when the cost team shifted its focus to the limiting production factor—reactor capacity. When the team integrated production limitations with its knowledge of cost drivers, it finally identified the higher order correlation. The activity of interest was pounds of product per reactor hour; costs and profits were driven by this activity.

The cost team had to resolve two problems before it could develop performance measures tied to the activity. First, any product could be produced by any reactor, despite variation in reactor size. A common production denominator was necessary for meaningful comparisons. Accordingly, the cost team assumed a standard 6,000-gallon reactor.

Second, a global performance measure was sought, one useful to marketing, production, and purchasing. Such a measure would foster goal congruence across these functional areas, thereby improving strategic decisions that typically span functional boundaries, such as product decisions.

Contribution margin per reactor hour would have been the criterion to maximize if reactor vessels were a common size. The need to assume a standard-sized reactor determined that a comparative rather than an absolute measure was appropriate. This disqualified unadjusted contribution margin per reactor hour. Consequently, the calculation of contribution margin by product per reactor hour of a standard 6,000-gallon reactor determined the Product Profit Velocity (PPV) ratio.

The PPV ratio is calculated as shown in the lower part of Table 1. PPV is contribution margin per standardized reactor hour by individual product.

The ratio emphasizes factors that are controllable by marketing, purchasing, technical engineering, and production. Revenue Per Reactor Run is determined by product price and yield. Materials cost is influenced jointly by purchasing, production, and product formulation. Product processing time depends on production and research and development. While the actual contribution margin

TABLE 2

PPV Ranking of Products

Ranking	Product	Revenue per reactor run	−	Materials and Freight-out	=	Contribution Margin	÷	Product Standard Proc. Time	=	PPV
1	A	$40,000		$27,500		$12,500		15 hours		833.3
2	F	58,560		22,000		36,560		44 hours		830.9
3	D	50,400		24,371		26,069		32 hours		813.4
4	E	54,050		21,806		32,244		40 hours		806.1
5	C	45,580		21,655		23,925		30 hours		797.5
6	B	41,160		26,250		14,910		20 hours		745.5

per hour per product varies depending upon the reactor used, Product Profit Velocity allows comparison of products and provides functional managers with a goal to optimize.

Conversion costs—labor and overhead—are fixed in this technology and therefore irrelevant to the analysis. While conversion cost must be allocated to products for inventory valuation, within the plant's process technology the allocation can be only arbitrary. The failure to recognize that conversion costs were not controllable had distorted operational decisions affecting product mix and pricing.

IMPLEMENTATION

The data requirements for PPV calculation are met by the existing information system. The new analysis requires data accumulation only along different dimensions to meet cost objectives. The revised system is run parallel with the original system to provide support for product mix and pricing decisions. The existing cost system was maintained for financial reporting.

The president of the subsidiary had given approval to these modifications, but the team felt the need to sell the costing innovations to functional managers to gain their acceptance. The team held meetings with key personnel: production, purchasing, technical, and sales managers. The cost team presented the rationale for measuring PPV and its use for comparative analysis of products.

The team developed a ranking of products based on the Product Profit Velocity ratio. Products with higher PPV make a greater contribution to firm profitability. Table 2 shows an abbreviated version of the product ranking presented to management. From the table it is clear that management needs to focus attention on the product with the lowest PPV, Product B, to seek means to increase its ratio. Similarly, in times of capacity limits, product B appropriately would be discontinued to allow greater capacity to be dedicated to products with higher PPV.

By presenting this list to functional managers, the team shifted discussion to actions each manager could take to improve the ratings of products in the bottom 10% of the ranking. What had been perceived as an accounting problem was now viewed as a cross-functional or boundary-spanning management issue. The plant manager's contribution to enhance PPV was to improve cleaning times and scheduling to reduce cycle times. The purchasing manager and technical manager were to search for alternative materials that would result in higher yields and lower input prices. The sales manager was to review pricing to determine if product prices should be raised.

ASSESSMENT

PPV gave functional managers a common performance goal. GPP's use of it as the criterion measure of performance at the Mogadore plant had an immediate effect on product mix and pricing decisions. The ranking of products by this ratio identified poor performance. As the plant was operating at capacity, the appropriate action was to change the product mix in favor of products with higher loadings on the PPV ratio. External factors constrained the rate at which these changes could occur. GPP was very concerned about maintaining customer goodwill. The price of lower-ranked products was substantially increased when alternative sources or substitute products existed; this satisfied customers' needs for choice and at the same time achieved GPP's goal.

When the company found the product underpriced but lacking a substitute, it told its customers to expect significant price increases over time. GPP used pricing to shift product demand and product mix toward products with higher Product Profit Velocity ratios.

The initial adjustments had to focus on pricing. Short-term changes in material mix or production were not possible. However, the PPV ratio is designed to encourage adjustments in materials, production, or prices that will move the plant incrementally toward maximum profitability. Product performance is reviewed monthly. Products falling in the lowest stratum of the ranking are automatically evaluated. Management believes that these products hold the highest potential for improvement and should be the focus of its attention. This philosophy goes beyond management by exception because it encourages management intervention not only when out-of-control situations have developed but also when potential opportunities exist.

SYSTEM OF THE FUTURE

The only certainty for today's managements is that their firms will feel the impact of technological and economic change. Firms that survive and grow will be those that adapt, and flexible accounting systems are central to a firm's adaptation. Such systems provide relevant and reliable information to facilitate management's efforts to control cost, to measure and improve productivity, and to devise improved production processes.[1]

For accountants, setting up an innovative accounting system means casting away their limited focus on cost control and broadening their horizon to total cost management. Accountants must demonstrate creativity in cost identification, measurement, and presentation. They must be aggressive in seeking innovative avenues, both to reduce cost and to maximize profit.

The new class of accountant can be likened to a product engineer who adapts products to the firm's R&D capabilities, existing production technology, and consumer tastes. The accountant must be able to design cost systems that capture and communicate relevant information to ensure that optimal cost and product tradeoffs are identified by management.

As H. Thomas Johnson has noted, "Activity-based cost information provides a clear view of how the mix of a company's diverse products, services, and activities contribute in the long run to the bottom line."[2] The focus on activities that drive costs provides great opportunity for an expanded partnership between functional managers and accountants. The philosophy of cost management is based on the belief that the only way to change costs is to change activity. Consequently, accountants must view the firm's activities critically and construct systems of analysis that will allow comparison of the efforts of functional areas.

Notes

1. H. Thomas Johnson and Robert S. Kaplan, "The Rise and Fall of Management Accounting," *Management Accounting,* January 1987, pp. 23–24.

2. H. Thomas Johnson, "Activity-Based Information: A Blueprint for World-Class Management Accounting," *Management Accounting,* June 1988, pp. 23–30.

CHAPTER FIVE

Japanese Cost Management Approaches

There has been recent interest in Japanese cost management practices. Published cases and readings on the subject indicate that the Japanese use a number of different approaches than those found in North American companies. Although we do not have a complete taxonomy of Japanese cost management practices, a number of approaches emerge as potentially useful to North American companies. The two areas that I believe may hold the greatest promise for being adopted by U.S. companies are explained in the two readings selected for this chapter; namely, target costing and Kaizen costing.

Reading 5.1   Target Costing

R.J. Aalbregtse, "Target Costing," in *Handbook of Cost Management*, edited by Barry Brinker (New York: Warren Gorham and Lamont), D2, 1993.

Aalbregtse describes a practice used by many Japanese manufacturing companies, termed the *target cost concept*.[1] Under this concept, management estimates the product unit cost that allows the company to compete effectively in the market and earn a normal profit. The product is then designed to achieve this target cost. The following equation illustrates the target cost concept:

Sales price (as determined from the market)
Less: Target profit
Target cost

The sales price is given by the market. Thus, the target profit can only be achieved by designing and manufacturing a product to achieve a specified target cost. This is different than the cost-plus approaches that achieve a target profit by adding a markup to cost. The cost-plus approaches assume that the resulting price will be accepted by the market. In contrast, target costing begins with a price acceptable to the market and "backs in" the cost required to achieve a profit. As a result, target costing places downward pressure on cost.

Most cost information focuses on when cost is incurred, such as during production. However, target costing attempts to bring attention to the design stage, where decisions can be made to improve the eventual cost of the product. Exhibit 1 illustrates the importance of the design stage in the product introduc-

EXHIBIT 1[2]

Product Introduction Stages—Committed and Incurred Costs

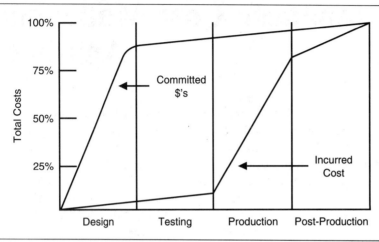

tion process. During the design phase, up to 80% of a product's cost is *committed*, or "designed in," even though very little cost has actually been incurred. This means that a poor design will "lock in" a high cost structure, while a good design can produce tangible cost savings during production. To illustrate, consider two hand drills. One drill is designed with 20 different fasteners, while a second drill is designed with only 4 different fasteners. The second drill will cost less than the first drill because fewer parts will result in fewer quality problems, easier assembly, easier production control, less purchasing, less vendor support, and less inventory. Thus, the superior design of the second drill has *committed* the company to a lower cost structure, even before the first drill is actually made.

Reading 5.2   Kaizen Costing

Y. Monden and J. Lee, "How a Japanese Auto Maker Reduces Costs," *Management Accounting* **(August 1993), p. 22–26.**

A potentially promising approach to U.S. cost management practices is the Japanese concept of Kaizen costing. There are few case studies on this approach; however, this article by Monden and Lee (ML) provides some insight into the approach. Kaizen is a Japanese term that means "continuous improvement." Thus, Kaizen costing is based on continuously improving cost competitiveness. The method is based upon setting aggressive cost reduction targets throughout the operations of the firm. The cost reduction targets motivate process improvement activities. One of the attractive characteristics of this approach is that it formally links process improvement with cost reduction, i.e., back into personnel

374

plans, material costs, manufacturing variable costs, and facilities costs. Some argue that this is what is missing from U.S.-style continuous improvement efforts —they are disconnected from translating the process improvement into cost reductions. In their Table 4, ML provide an interesting comparison between Kaizen costing and western style standard costing. The distinction appears dramatic.

Notes

1. Over half of the respondents to a survey of Japanese manufacturers indicated that they use target costing. See P. Scarbrough, A.J. Nanni, and M. Sakurai, "Japanese Management Accounting Practices and the Effects of Assembly and Process Automation," *Management Accounting Research* (March 1991): 27–46.

2. Source: *Cost Management for Today's Advanced Manufacturing: The CAM-I Conceptual Design*, edited by Callier Berliner and James A. Brimson (Boston: Harvard Business School Press, 1988): 157.

Additional Readings

Dolinsky, Larry R., and Thomas E. Vollmann. "Transaction-Based Overhead Considerations for Product Design," *Journal of Cost Management* (Summer 1991): 7–19.

Hiromoto, Toshiro, "Another Hidden Edge — Japanese Management Accounting," *Harvard Business Review* (July–August 1988): 22–26.

Huthwaite, Bart. "The Link Between Design and Activity-Based Accounting," *Manufacturing Systems* (October 1989): 44–47.

Kato, Y., "Target Costing Support Systems: Lessons From Leading Japanese Companies," *Management Accounting Research* (March 1993): 33–48.

Martin, James R., Wendi K. Schelb, Richard C. Snyder, and Jeffrey S. Sparling. "Comparing the Practices of U.S. and Japanese Companies: The Implications for Management Accounting," *Journal of Cost Management* (Spring 1992): 6–14.

Monden, Y., and M. Sakurai, ed. *Japanese Management Accounting: A World Class Approach to Profit Management.* (Cambridge, MA: Productivity Press, 1989).

Sakurai, Michiharu. "Target Costing and How to Use It," *Journal of Cost Management* (Summer 1989): 39–50.

Scarbrough, P., A.J. Nanni and M. Sakurai, "Japanese Management Accounting Practices and the Effects of Assembly and Process Automation," *Management Accounting Research* (March 1991): 27–46.

Takeuchi, Hirotaka. "Productivity: Learning From the Japanese," *California Management Review* (Summer 1981): 5–19.

Tanaka, Tako, "Target Costing at Toyota," *Journal of Cost Management* (Spring 1993): 4–11.

Yoshikawa, Takeo, John Innes, and Falconer Mitchell. "Cost Management Through Functional Analysis," *Journal of Cost Management* (Spring 1989): 14–19.

_____. "Cost Tables: A Foundation of Japanese Cost Management," *Journal of Cost Management* (Fall 1990): 30–36.

Target Costing

R. John Aalbregtse

Associate Partner, Andersen Consulting, Detroit, Michigan

INTRODUCTION

Target costing is a cost management tool for reducing cost over the entire life cycle of a product. Target costing can also be used to reduce investments required in design, production, and distribution.

This chapter analyzes target costing by introducing the basics of target costing and showing how target costing can help translate customer requirements into actual product features. Finally, the chapter shows how target costing can be applied to bring about continuous improvement (*kaizen* in Japanese) throughout a product's life cycle.

A BENEFIT TO COST PLANNING

Target costing is a method used in product design that involves estimating a target cost for a new product, then designing the product to meet that cost. Target costing can yield three benefits to the cost planning process:

1. Reduced product cost;
2. A faster product development process; and
3. Less risky new product introductions.

The means to realizing these benefits are:

- Using information and target cost factors during product conceptualization and design;
- Linking customer requirements to design cost and product performance specifications; and
- Emphasizing continuous product and process improvements.

The Concept

Target cost is the maximum manufactured cost for a given product—a cost that will allow an expected return to be earned within a given market niche and also allow the product to gain market share. A target cost can be computed by taking the expected market price within the appropriate niche and subtracting from it the expected margin on sales.

Target costing is not a tool for day-to-day cost control. Rather, it is a cost planning tool that focuses on controlling design specifications and production techniques, thus contributing to the goal of delivering a competitive product to the marketplace.

Target costing has been applied primarily in discrete manufacturing industries that have short product life cycles. In the electronics and automotive manufacturing industries, for example, a significant amount of design work goes toward meeting continuously changing market conditions. By setting a target cost during product design, it is possible for new computers or new cars to be cost-competitive in the first year they are manufactured. The use of target costing means that a manufacturer does not have to rely on a traditional experience curve to reduce product cost to a competitive level over the first two or three years of a product's life cycle.

The Basic Approach

Target costing starts with the identification of four items:

1. *Customer requirements:* understanding market requirements and the performance levels of competitors' products;
2. *Future cost structures:* making target cost development an aspect of the ongoing design process;
3. *Product design:* considering the impact of various cost drivers during product design; and
4. *Continuous improvement:* fostering continuous improvement of cost drivers during all stages of the product's life cycle, production, and distribution.

Each of these elements is discussed below.

CUSTOMER REQUIREMENTS

The first element of target costing is understanding customer requirements, including the performance and cost characteristics of competitors' products. This understanding is a key condition for the success of target costing. A manufacturer must carefully define and select a market niche where there is opportunity to penetrate the market and gain market share. Target costing can then be applied during the product design phase to create a product that meets the customer's requirements and beats the competition.

Gathering Market Information

Gathering market information is an important step in the targeting costing and product development process. The characteristics of the selected market niche

EXHIBIT D2.1

Bicycle Market Characteristics

Characteristic	Casual tourers	Campers	Road racers
Price			
Sensitivity	High	Medium	Low
Range	$225–400	$250–500	$500+
Delivery	Off-the-shelf	Off-the-shelf	Special order
Service	In-store is important factor	Do-it-yourself	Do-it-yourself
Maintainability	Routine maintenance important	Important	Performance more important
Durability	Key feature	Key feature	Less important due to frequent repurchase
Technology	Not very important	Not important	Key: Demand latest
Quality	Appearance	Rugged and sturdy	Name-brand componentry Quality image
Performance	Ride comfort Wide gear range Smooth shifting	Ride quality Very wide gear range Frame stiffness Low internal friction	Narrow gear range High frame stiffness Low wheel inertia Low internal friction

reflect customer values and expectations about:

- Price;
- Quality;
- Delivery;
- Service;
- Technology; and
- Product performance.

The data can come from market research studies, customer surveys, sales force feedback, comparisons with the competition (including reverse engineering of products), and improvements identified for existing products.

For example, Exhibit D2.1 outlines the market requirements for three segments of the two-wheel bicycle market. Casual tourers tend to purchase bicycles for occasional use and expect to keep their bicycles for a long time (from ten to fifteen years). The second segment—campers—puts its bicycles to hard use, so the campers expect a smooth ride with good reliability and durability. Finally, racers are consummate bicyclists who look for the latest technology and the highest performance. They tend to trade up frequently, and price is only a minor factor in their purchase decisions.

The bicycle manufacturer that is used as an example throughout this chapter decides to develop a new product for the casual tourer market segment and determines that the target price should be $350. Many of the examples illustrated in this chapter are based on the steps required to determine the target cost for the new "Tourist" model bicycle (a fictitious product used as an example here).

Documenting Customer Requirements

A structured method for documenting customer requirements and competitor comparisons helps ensure that all relevant market factors and product characteristics are considered during product development. *Quality function deployment* (QFD) is a structured approach to documenting customer requirements and translating those requirements into technical design characteristics for each stage of product development and production. QFD provides a framework for the thorough documentation of:

- Product characteristics;
- Competitor performance comparisons;
- Target performance values; and
- Customer rating comparisons.

Charts are used to document product quality and to deploy the quality function. These charts include the following:

1. Customer requirement planning matrix;
2. Product characteristics deployment matrix;
3. Process planning and control chart; and
4. Quality control planning chart.

Exhibit D2.2 shows an example of a QFD planning matrix for a touring bicycle. The left-hand column contains documented customer requirements, which are obtained from:

- Customer surveys;
- Experience with previous products; and
- Market research studies.

The columns across the top of the exhibit contain specific product characteristics that are needed to meet the outlined customer requirements. These characteris-

EXHIBIT D2.2

Casual Tourer Bicycle Planning Matrix

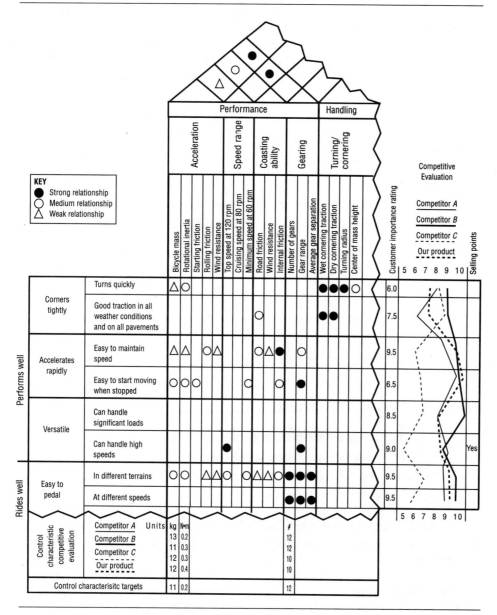

tics are determined from:

- Experience with previous products;
- Engineering studies;
- Calculations and modeling; and
- Experimentation.

Correlations between product characteristics and specific customer requirements are identified by means of symbols. Specifically, filled-in circles indicate a strong relationship, an empty circle indicates a medium relationship, and a triangle indicates a weak relationship.

The customer requirement planning matrix shown in Exhibit D2.2 is used to document whether identified product characteristics adequately address customer requirements. An absence of symbols indicates:

- Areas where customer requirements have not been addressed; or
- Weak relationships between customer requirements and product characteristics.

In either case, the design has little probability of fully meeting customer expectations.

When this is the case, additional design characteristics must be identified if the customer requirements in question are determined to have high importance ratings. If the importance ratings are low and the manufacturer has a superior rating compared with competitors, it may indicate that a weak relationship with the identified product characteristics is sufficient to meet customer expectations. (However, it may also indicate that other product characteristics exist to satisfy the customer requirement, but they have not yet been identified.)

Customer input is solicited for two reasons:

1. To rank the importance of each customer requirement; and
2. To understand market perceptions about competitors' products—for example, how the products meet customer requirements in comparison to existing or prototype products. (This comparison is documented on the right-hand side of the matrix shown in Exhibit D2.2.)

Performance tests are conducted to determine specific performance data for each relevant product of a competitor. This information is shown at the bottom of the matrix in Exhibit D2.2. From this information, best-in-class (BIC) performance targets can be established as inputs to the design process.

The QFD process generally uses charts such as those listed previously to document the translation of customer requirements into process plans and quality control plans. This process yields the competitor comparisons, performance targets, and process plan data for use in target costing.

EXHIBIT D2.3

Product Characteristics: Casual Tourer Segment

Characteristic	Competitor A	Competitor B	Competitor C	Ours	Target
Price ($)	400	375	270	345	350
Mass (kg.)	13	11	12	12	11
Rotational inertia (nm.)	64	62	71	60	55
Wind resistance (Cd)	0.41	0.35	0.49	0.38	0.33
Gear range	1 : 25	1 : 28	1 : 22	1 : 26	1 : 28
Tire pressure (psl)	95	120	100	95	110

Comparing Competitors' Products

When developing a competitive comparison, a manufacturer should select two sets of competitors:

1. Competitors that represent a cross-section of global competition within the market niche; and
2. Any up-and-coming competitors that may not yet have significant market share.

The representative products of each competitor chosen should have price and performance parameters similar to those planned for the new product. For example, Exhibit D2.3 shows a sample of several competitors' bicycles that have characteristics and performance levels similar to those required for the casual tourer target market. As can be seen, the product selection criteria are based on customer requirements and product characteristics documented in the QFD product planning matrix shown in Exhibit D2.2.

Generally, the selection of competitors and representative products for comparison is made by a cross-functional team composed of members from product planning, sales and marketing, and engineering. The data used to make the decision are based on:

- Published performance data and specifications;
- Customer input;
- Competitive test data; and
- Information from annual reports, trade shows, and other external sources of information that may provide insight into plans for new products.

Once the selection process is completed, the manufacturer should obtain several samples of each chosen product for performance testing and reverse engineering (i.e., tearing down the product to analyze its design). The testing should be conducted in a manner that allows direct comparison between the product that is being planned and various competitors' products. The comparative test results are documented at the bottom of the product planning QFD matrix, as noted above.

Applying Reverse Engineering

Reverse engineering determines BIC design characteristics and provides information about competitors' materials and processes. The purpose of this information is to help the manufacturer established a competitively based target cost.

Reverse engineering should involve a cross-functional team of people from product and process engineering, manufacturing, industrial engineering, procurement, and estimating. During the process, it is a good practice to keep one example of each competitor's product in working condition while the other one is disassembled for analysis. It is also helpful to take photographs during the disassembly process and to tag and catalog all parts as they are removed. Detailed data (such as torques, fits or clearances, fluid levels, electrical readings, and pressures) should be measured and documented.

Bills of material and estimated routings can be developed once the tear-down process is complete. The bills of material outline the description, quantity, weight, and material type for each component. Notes should be kept about each component to describe whether the component is similar to one used on the manufacturer's product and whether it should be considered a purchased part or a manufactured part. Procurement and estimating personnel use this information to develop estimated purchased costs for each purchased component or raw material.

Process engineers then review the components designated as manufactured parts and develop estimated routings for all parts similar to those manufactured in house. If the information suggests that certain competitors do—or do not—produce the components in-house, adjustments can be made when the manufacturer's own cost is compared with the estimated competitor's cost.

The estimated routings reflect judgment about the following:

- The type of manufacturing processes used for each component;
- The time required to manufacture the component; and
- The manufacturing philosophy of each competitor.

These conclusions are based on:

- The physical characteristics of the component;
- Published process information on the competitor;
- General industry practices;

- Information from equipment and component suppliers; and
- Tours of competitors' facilities.

Manufacturing philosophy also plays a role. Thus, consideration should be given to differences between the manufacturer and its competitors in terms of volume, use of automation, application of just-in-time (JIT) or lean manufacturing concepts, and use of participative or team-based manufacturing operations.

Value-Adding vs. Non-Value-Adding Data

Reverse engineering can provide solid data about the materials and "value adding" processes that are used in manufacturing components, though it provides no information about "non-value-adding" processes that increase the cost of components. Non-value-adding costs, such as inspection, material handling, setup, maintenance, supervision, and administrative costs, all must be estimated or inferred from plant tours, company publications, or other external data sources (e.g., consultants, suppliers, customers, government surveys, newspapers and magazines, or subscriber databases).

One of the target costs used in the conceptual design process should be based on incorporating world-class or "best" practices (i.e., the best competitor design characteristics identified through reverse engineering) into an optimal design. Even though it may not be possible to produce the optimal design today, the target cost provides a perspective on where competitors' product costs may go in the future. This optimal-design target cost should figure heavily in the conceptual design process. It helps to ensure the competitiveness of the new product design when it finally gets to market.

FUTURE COST STRUCTURES

The second element of target costing is making target cost development an aspect of the design process. Competitors' activities have an impact here as well in the form of their present and future cost structures. A manufacturer should therefore develop estimates of competitors' cost structures by analyzing the internal costs of existing products, categorizing them by cost driver, and developing comparative ratios by cost driver to translate internal costs into estimated competitor costs.

A *cost driver* is any event that causes a change in the total cost of an activity. It can be thought of as an activity, a requirement, or a specification that creates cost during the conversion of resources into a finished product. The broad categories of cost drivers used for comparison are related to four areas:

1. *The organization:* Organization costs include all labor and benefits for hourly and salaried workers.

EXHIBIT D2.4

Tourist Bicycle Cost Structure

Material	$150.00
Direct labor	30.00
Burden	90.00
SG&A	30.00
Total product cost	$300.00

2. *Sourcing or logistics:* Sourcing and logistics costs include all raw materials, supplier development costs, and transportation costs.
3. *Manufacturing processes:* Manufacturing process costs include all nonlabor burden costs (e.g., maintenance supplies, depreciation, process scrap, and utilities).
4. *Design:* Product design costs include design scrap, offal, and material design premiums related to differences in specifications, the number of components, or the type of materials selected.

Cost Structure Analysis

The first step in analyzing cost structures is to gather cost information about one of the manufacturer's current products—one that has design and performance characteristics similar to those of the new product under development and also similar to those of competitors.

Relationship to Cost Driver Categories

Traditional cost structures are expressed in the form of material, labor, burden, and sales, general, and administrative (SG&A) costs. The cost structure for target costing should reflect the four key driver categories (i.e., organization, sourcing or logistics, manufacturing processes, and design) listed previously to provide greater insight into the causes of current cost levels. The categorization of costs in this manner makes it easier to compare the company's cost structure with competitors' cost structures; it also exposes hidden cost opportunities that are not readily visible in standard cost accounting systems. Experience shows that 15–45 percent of a product's cost structure is due to non-value-adding activities or ineffective product design. Cost structure analysis provides a vehicle to identify waste to be eliminated during the design of future products and processes and through continuous improvement.

To illustrate, consider the bicycle manufacturer again. The manufacturer plans to produce a new line of casual touring bicycles. The current production bicycle selected for comparison has a total cost of $300. Exhibit D2.4 depicts the

EXHIBIT D2.5

Tourist Bicycle Material Cost

Basic material	$132.00
Design potential	15.00
Scrap-reduction potential	2.00
Specification-related potential	1.00
Total material cost	$150.00

EXHIBIT D2.6

Tourist Bicycle Direct Labor Cost

Value-added labor	$22.50
Inspection	4.50
Material handling	2.50
Setup	2.00
Rework	3.50
Downtime	10.00
Total direct labor cost	$45.00

cost structure according to the manufacturer's cost accounting system. To better understand the internal or current product cost structure, each of the standard cost elements should be reviewed and outlined in more detail.

In this hypothetical example, a comparison with the competitors' products indicates that the use of different materials for the frame could reduce total material cost by 10 percent and that changes to the tube-forming process could reduce design scrap by 4 percent. In addition, a 10 percent improvement in yield could be achieved in the gear-forming operations if minor changes were made to material specifications. Exhibit D2.5 shows the resulting material cost structure. Note that the total material cost of the product has not changed, but the detailed analysis of material costs in Exhibit D2.5 identifies opportunities for improvement.

Direct labor can be restated in the same way. The first step is to include the fringe and benefit costs and split the resulting cost between value-added and non-value-added operations. Value-added activities actually alter the product in a way that provides value to the consumer. Non-value-added operations include inspection, material handling, setup, rework, and downtime. Exhibit D2.6 shows how the direct labor costs could be restated. In this case, the total direct labor cost has increased due to the inclusion of fringe and benefit costs, but it is evident that only one half of the direct labor costs add value to the product from the customers' perspective.

Burden costs should be split between labor-related costs and other costs. Labor costs should be categorized by salaried and indirect hourly workers and should include the associated fringe and benefit costs. The costs for each group should fall into the following categories:

- Production supervision (e.g., salaried only);
- Manufacturing engineering;
- Material control;
- Quality control;
- Tool rooms;
- Maintenance; and
- All other.

Nonlabor burden costs should fall into the following categories:

- Process scrap;
- Utilities;
- Data processing;
- Supplies;
- Freight;
- Depreciation and taxes; and
- Tooling.

Exhibit D2.7 shows an example of a burden cost breakdown for the Tourist bicycle.

SG&A costs also should be split between labor-related and non-labor-related costs for product development, sales and marketing, and administration. Exhibit D2.8 shows an example breakdown for the Tourist bicycle's SG&A costs.

For the sake of simplicity in this example, assume that one half of the burden and SG&A costs were found to be non-value-adding from the end consumer's standpoint. Adding the $18 of non-value-added material costs and $22.50 of non-value-added direct labor costs brings the total non-value-added cost for the Tourist bicycle to $93, or 31 percent of the total cost.

The target cost set for the new bicycle under development should take into account a desired reduction in the level of non-value-added costs as well as the need to beat the competitors' estimated cost levels.

Competitor Cost Modeling

The manufacturer should develop cost models to help estimate the production cost of competitors' products. Generally, the process involves developing factors

EXHIBIT D2.7

Tourist Bicycle Burden Cost

Indirect hourly labor

Quality control	$ 4.50
Tool room	3.50
Maintenance	9.00
Material control	5.50
Manufacturing engineering	2.50
All other	3.00

Salaried labor

Production supervision	5.50
Quality control	4.50
Tool room	1.50
Maintenance	3.00
Manufacturing engineering	3.50
All other	1.00

Other burden (nonlabor)

Scrap	4.00
Utilities	3.50
Data processing	2.50
Supplies	3.00
Freight	7.50
Depreciation and taxes	3.50
Tooling	4.00
Total burden cost	$75.00

that adjust current product costs for competitive differences in labor rates, labor hours, purchasing and production scale, economic differences, and complexity. Exhibit D2.9 shows a high-level example of a competitor cost model.

Comparative Factors

After reviewing the cost structure of an existing product, as outlined in the prior discussion, comparative factors are developed for each element of the cost structure to convert current costs into estimated competitors' costs. The factors shown in the middle column of Exhibit D2.9 are composites of a number of individual comparative factors.

For example, the material factor of 1.07 is composed of individual factors for purchasing scale, economic differences such as exchange rates and commodity

EXHIBIT D2.8

Tourist Bicycle Sales, General, and Administrative Cost

Labor-related

Product development	$ 8.00
Sales and marketing	7.00
Administration	5.00

Other costs

Product development	3.00
Sales and marketing	6.00
Administration	1.00
Total SG&A cost	$30.00

EXHIBIT D2.9

Competitor Cost Model

	Current cost	Comparative factor	Estimated competitor cost
Material	$150.00	1.07	$160.50
Direct labor	45.00	0.85	38.25
Indirect labor	50.00	0.70	35.00
Depreciation	3.50	0.90	3.15
Scrap	2.50	0.50	1.25
Tooling	4.00	0.75	3.00
Utilities	2.00	1.50	3.00
Other burden	43.00	0.85	36.55
Total	$300.00		$280.70

prices, and content differences relating to types of material and level of vertical integration.

Similarly, the direct labor factor of 0.85 is composed of individual factors related to differences in labor rates and labor hours, which are influenced by differing levels of automation, vertical integration, efficiency, and manufacturing philosophy. The indirect labor factor of 0.7 is composed of individual factors relating to labor rate, headcounts, production volumes, vertical integration, and level of production complexity.

Other comparative factors are developed along similar lines for input into the cost models. (Using a spreadsheet software program allows easy modification and flexible "what if" analyses.) Developing several different models allows comparisons of product design, manufacturing processing, and best practices.

Best Practices Model

The models of best practices consider the best design characteristics, the best manufacturing processes, and the best economics as factors. These are identified by means of the reverse engineering studies, industry benchmarks, industry trade associations, surveys, plant tours, and information gathered from consultants. The resulting models help set ultimate targets within a given industry; the company can use them to drive continuous improvement and help assure that it designs and produces products that will achieve the targeted market share.

The product costs determined through the modeling of best levels of performance are an indication of the magnitude of improvement that may occur in a given market segment or niche. No competitor may have achieved these levels of performance yet, but some competitor could conceivably achieve these higher performance levels within the time frame of the new product's life cycle. Therefore, the information obtained through the best practices cost models is an important input to the conceptual design process for new products.

Competitor Information

Depending on the level of accuracy required for the target cost, competitor information is available from a variety of sources. For discrete products, the best data sources (in terms of cost and ease of access) are product tear-downs and external data sources. These external data sources include:

- Annual reports;
- Marketing brochures;
- Commercially available information databases (e.g., LEXIS/NEXIS, Trade and Industry ASAP, IEEE, Dun and Bradstreet);
- Government reports (e.g., the Commerce Department's *Annual Survey of Manufacturers* and also its *Census of Manufacturers*); and
- Local news sources (e.g., newspapers, news magazines, and industry publications).

Generally, product tear-downs and external data sources yield enough information to develop target costs that are sufficiently accurate relative to the competition. In some cases, however, specific information about yield, throughput, manpower levels, and capacity utilization may be needed to develop meaningful target costs. When this situation occurs, it may be necessary to tour competitors' plants or to participate in an industry benchmarking study. Reciprocal visits with competitors can often be arranged. Trade associations usually know about benchmarks or may even publish them, depending on how open—or closed—the industry is.

When developing competitor cost comparisons, the manufacturer should pay particular attention to identifying and analyzing differences in capacity costs. In particular, the company should factor out cost disadvantages that may be incurred due to excess capacity, which can distort competitor cost estimates. The company should analyze any costs related to excess capacity to determine their cause and how they should be handled.

Excess capacity costs should be excluded from product costs and treated as a general cost of doing business at the divisional or business-unit level (i.e., at some level at which the unit's management can make decisions regarding better use of excess resources).

Internal Cost Models

Cost models for internal costs relate cost drivers to specific elements in the cost structure of a product. Similar in nature to competitor costs models, internal cost models generally are developed using spreadsheet software to provide what-if comparisons that identify the sensitivity of final product costs to certain costs drivers. Cost drivers that have important effects on unit cost obviously provide the greatest opportunity for value analysis and cost reductions.

The basis of the internal cost model is also the cost structure analysis conducted for the manufacturer's current product. From 10 to 20 key cost drivers are identified, and relationships are established between the drivers and each element of the current cost structure. Examples of cost drivers include:

- Downtime;
- Scrap;
- Absenteeism;
- Overtime;
- Rework;
- Level of inspection;
- Level of non-value-added activities;
- Level of maintenance;
- Preventative maintenance ratio;
- Production volume per day;
- Vendor scrap; and
- First-time quality and tooling expenditures.

By comparing differences between current cost driver levels and projected levels, the cost models develop ratios to apply to current costs for purposes of estimating future costs. The projected cost driver levels can be based on specific action plans, annual goals, projections, or best practices.

The models are useful in value engineering new and existing products, developing annual budgets and investment justifications, setting performance measures, and fostering continuous improvement. Each of these uses for internal cost models is explored in detail later. (See, e.g., the discussions of value engineering, continuous improvement, investment justification, and performance measurement).

PRODUCT DESIGN

The third element of target costing is considering the impact of various cost drivers during product design. Many companies set price and performance targets in the product planning process, but detailed cost information is not available until the product's conceptual design is submitted to cost estimating for a cost buildup. Often, suppliers involved in the design process are given only design specifications or blueprints, with little indication of design cost targets.

Consideration of the impact of various cost drivers during product design can help a company create a different perspective. By using the preliminary target cost set by considering the best levels of competitive performance, engineers can develop a conceptual design that factors in the best designs from the company's own existing products as well as from competitors' products. The QFD matrix is used to guide the design effort by providing information about matches between customer requirements and technical parameters, as prioritized by customer requirements, competitor performance, and cost levels. This information allows the engineers to factor in many cost saving design features up front in the design process.

Supplier Involvement

Lack of up-front cost and quality requirements can lead to suboptimal decisions on material selection, assembly techniques, and manufacturing process design. For this reason, the sharing of competitor performance and product tear-down information should also be a key element of the process of obtaining the involvement of suppliers.

Target cost information provides suppliers with a better understanding of customer requirements and also gives them insight into the type of materials and processes that they should use in the design of their subsystems and components. Many suppliers do not have ready access to competitor information, so they depend on receiving that information from their customers to develop competitively designed components.

A Compressed Development Cycle

Accurate target cost information can also help compress the product development cycle. During the design of a product in a traditional environment, much time and significant resources are expended by the time the cost estimating department can provide engineering with a design cost estimate. Usually, the cost comes back too high, so the engineers must rethink their conceptual design.

Unfortunately, the cost estimates may not provide enough insight into the real causes of the cost overruns to guide the engineers in their redesign effort. This iterative process is repeated again and again in many companies as they work feverishly to complete an acceptable conceptual design.

Value Engineering

Once a conceptual design is complete, internal cost models can help estimate the cost of the new product. The internal cost models give value engineering teams detailed information about current production costs. They also reveal potential areas of improvement by identifying opportunities for design changes and for eliminating non-value-adding processes and activities.

In the bicycle example, the competitor cost model (see Exhibit D2.9) indicates a high scrap cost ($2.50 current cost versus $1.25 estimated competitor cost) due to the process selected for tube forming. In addition, assume that the internal cost model reveals significant inspection and downtime costs for the frame-fabricating processes. The company's value engineering team therefore brainstorms about how to change the tube-forming and frame-fabricating processes to reduce the levels of waste caused by the current design concept.

By using the cost models to develop an understanding of the cost drivers that affect new product design, the value engineering team can accomplish the following:

- Focus its efforts on the areas of greatest opportunity; and
- Use the models to fine-tune the initial target cost to more accurately reflect existing conditions (while still maintaining a reasonable target cost level that will foster further improvement).

The refined target cost guides the manufacturer during the detailed design of the product and the production processes.

The cost models continue to guide value engineering efforts during detailed design efforts. They allow engineers to test what-if scenarios based on potential differences in materials, design parameters, and production processes.

A final refinement of the target cost usually is made at the start of production. This refinement reflects lessons learned during production trials

EXHIBIT D2.10

Prioritized Cost Elements

Cost element	Cumulative percent	Value-added	Non-value-added
Material offal and trim	20%		$10.00
Reactive maintenance labor	35		7.50
Material handling labor	45		5.00
Salaried supervision	52		3.50
Purchase supplies	57	$2.50	
Finishing labor	62	2.50	
Inspection labor	66		2.00
Downtime labor	70		2.00
Value-adding labor	73	1.50	
Tooling expense	76	1.50	
Utilities	78	1.00	
Overtime premium	80		1.00
		$9.00	$31.00

and includes some level of improvement expected during the first stages of production. The standard cost during the first phase of production can be set based on the refined target cost. The cost models also help to establish continuous cost improvement targets by setting milestones for cost-improvement efforts after production begins and at various stages of the product life cycle.

CONTINUOUS IMPROVEMENT

The fourth and final element of target costing is fostering continuous improvement. Many organizations now are working to implement total quality management, of which continuous improvement is an integral part. As part of continuous improvement efforts, target costing concepts can be applied to existing products as well as to new products. Cost structure analysis and cost models that are developed for existing products can support continuous improvement by identifying and prioritizing causes of non-value-added costs and waste. Improvement teams can use this information to attack root causes of cost, thus reducing or eliminating activities and problems that cause waste.

Exhibit D2.10 shows an example of cost elements that have been categorized and prioritized as either value-adding or non-value-adding. Experience indicates that the top 20 percent of the cost elements contribute about 80 percent of the costs added to the product during the manufacturing process. The non-value-added cost elements are waste that should be eliminated. However, not all non-value-added costs can be eliminated; even the best producer incurs some non-value-added costs. Target costing techniques provide focus for improvement teams as they work to eliminate waste in all areas of the business.

Cost Driver–Based Performance Measures

The target costing process assists in prioritizing improvement efforts by linking unit costs to specific cost drivers. Workers, supervisors, and management can track improvement efforts by monitoring improvement trends in the cost driver measures. By selecting cost driver measures that are not based on dollars or cost (e.g., downtime percentage, scrap percentage, head counts, and overtime levels), the resulting trend analysis can help to provide rapid or immediate feedback to those closest to the production process.

A company can use cost models to identify those cost drivers that provide the largest opportunity for improvement. Teams of workers can focus on the high-potential cost drivers to analyze the root causes of the key cost drivers, then develop specific action plans to eliminate those root causes by improving the product design, the process, the materials used in production, or organization-related drivers such as material-handling labor or inspection.

An Organizational Agent of Change

Target costing can be more than an element of the organization's cost management strategy; it can be an agent of change. Its use of external information can redirect the company to an external perspective, which is essential to understanding customer requirements and creating competitive advantage. The credible targets yielded by target costing can help an organization understand why it needs to change, then identify and prioritize the areas where it should focus efforts to make the largest improvements.

Target cost information can help establish key performance indicators that correspond to the key cost drivers and to unit cost. Exhibit D2.11, with its four graphs, illustrates the linkage between trends in key performance indicators that are related to cost drivers and trends in unit costs.

Key performance indicators can be set as performance measures for improvement teams and for subplant, plant production, and support groups. By focusing the key performance indicators on the underlying causes of waste within the product and the production system, substantial improvements are possible that could never be realized by means of traditional cost-reduction programs that focus narrow-mindedly on material or labor targets.

EXHIBIT D2.11

Relationship Between Key Performance Indicators and Unit Costs

Source: Andersen Consulting, a division of Arthur Andersen & Co. S.C. (1991).

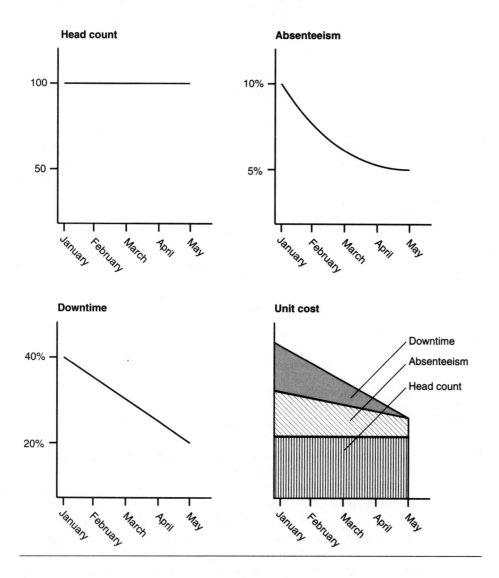

Investment Justification

Another benefit of target costing is how it supports movement toward a JIT (or "lean manufacturing") environment. The key focus of JIT is the continuous elimination of waste. Target costing provides a framework for justifying changes in the production environment. It provides a means for identifying benefits that could result from the comprehensive application of JIT and lean manufacturing techniques—benefits that are usually difficult to measure with traditional cost accounting systems.

For example, improvements that shorten lead time, improve quality, or reduce support costs typically have more impact on overhead costs than on direct labor. Traditional cost accounting systems usually only reflect changes in overhead composition on an annual basis using some assessment of relative utilization of support cost by department. By contrast, target costing models provide what-if capability to analyze the impact of changes in all cost drivers, so a company can base investment and resource allocation justifications on a broader view of the potential benefits.

A company can use cost models to make periodic updates in cost standards to achieve market-based targets. Unlike traditional performance measurement systems that compare this year's results to historical results, target costing can provide a means to set performance targets to stay ahead of the competition.

A Complex Manufacturing Environment

Today's complex manufacturing environment makes target costing a somewhat complicated exercise—one that often calls for embellishment of the four elements of target costing. While it is fairly easy to establish a target market price for a new product, target prices for individual components and subassemblies are much more difficult to determine.

Exhibit D2.12 provides an example of one company's experience in dealing with complex manufacturing issues. The exhibit shows a sample bill of material for a manufactured product. Marketing has determined that product A can sell for $100 in the marketplace. Given an expected margin of 10 percent, the maximum manufacturing cost is $90. Problems arise when target costs must be established for subsystems A and B or for components $C, D, E,$ and F.

As Exhibit D2.12 shows, market prices are usually not available for these engineered subsystems. Target costing, in a case like the one in the exhibit, thus becomes a more involved process.

The Automotive Industry: A Case Study

The automotive industry provides an apt case study of the manufacturing complexities with which target costing must deal. The automotive indus-

EXHIBIT D2.12

Target Costing in a Complex Environment: An Example

Source: Andersen Consulting, a division of Arthur Andersen & Co. S.C. (1991).

Market price	$100
Expected margin (10%)	10
Maximum manufacturing cost	$ 90

```
                              ┌──────────────┐
                              │  Product A   │
                              │    $100      │
                              └──────────────┘
  Market
  price?
              ┌──────────────┐            ┌──────────────┐
              │  Subsystem   │            │  Subsystem   │
              │      A       │            │      B       │
              └──────────────┘            └──────────────┘
  Market
  price?
     ┌───────────┐  ┌───────────┐   ┌───────────┐  ┌───────────┐
     │ Component │  │ Component │   │ Component │  │ Component │
     │     C     │  │     D     │   │     E     │  │     F     │
     └───────────┘  └───────────┘   └───────────┘  └───────────┘
```

try has used target costing in varying degrees since the early 1980s. The approach has been to outline a vehicle cost target using market studies that establish various price points and price sensitivities within a given market niche. After subtracting the desired margin, the resulting target cost is compared to the actual cost of a similar vehicle. The resulting percentage difference is then applied to the actual cost of all the various subsystems and components to establish target costs for each new subsystem and component.

Exhibit D2.13 provides a hypothetical target costing example for a vehicle. The exhibit illustrates the difference between a target cost established as a set percentage below current cost and competitive-based target costs. The difference between the current vehicle cost of $10,000 and the target cost for the new vehicle of $9,000 is 10 percent. To develop simple cost targets for each major subsystem, current component costs have been reduced by the 10 percent overall cost-reduction target to yield the "10% target cost" column (column 2) in the middle of the exhibit. The "Competitive target" column (column 3) on the right-hand side of the exhibit indicates what the actual target should have been based on competitive studies and market requirements for cost, quality, and performance.

EXHIBIT D2.13

Market-Driven Target Costing

Source: Andersen Consulting, a division of Arthur Andersen & Co. S.C. (1991).

	1990 vehicle	1994 target
Price	$10,000	$11,000
Margin	0	2,000
Cost	$10,000	$ 9,000

	(1) Current cost	(2) 10% target cost	(3) Competitive target
Transmission	$ 1,000	$ 900	$ 850
Engine	900	810	750
Sheet metal	750	675	500
Interior trim	1,675	1,500	1,400
Electrical	1,335	1,200	1,150
Other	4,340	3,915	4,350
	$10,000	$9,000	$9,000

Difficulties With Complex Products

This case study confirms the difficulties of setting target costs for complex products. In many cases, the time and effort involved in developing accurate target costs for all of the various vehicle subsystems is prohibitive.

Automobile manufacturers and their suppliers of key components must collect data continuously to establish effective target costs for the significant subsystems and components of all new vehicle programs. If they do not and inappropriate targets are set (as in the case of across-the-board percentage targets), suppliers of the subsystems and components and product development engineers will not accept the targets and will not actively work to achieve them.

Process Industry Application

While target costing has been applied widely in discrete manufacturing industries that have rapidly declining product life cycles, process industries can apply the concepts as well. Typically, process industries are not as flexible in product design and planning as their counterparts in discrete industries, especially in terms of the control the developers have over the cost structure of the end product. However, since target costing provides a way to better understand current and future cost structures, target costing can be as beneficial to process industries as it is in a discrete environment.

A BROADER CONTEXT AND APPLICATION

Although target costing in its simplest form is merely a calculation—target price minus margin—today's complex manufacturing environment can make target costing an indispensable, value-adding management technique. Specifically, target costing:

- Reduces product design cycle time;
- Increases the profitability of new products;
- Fosters continuous cost improvement by identifying differences in cost structures; and
- Helps in forecasting future cost structures.

How a Japanese Auto Maker Reduces Costs

Yasuhiro Monden

Professor of Management Accounting and Operations at the University of Tsukuba, Japan.

John Y. Lee

Schaeberle Professor of Accounting at Pace University in New York.

Source: Published by *Management Accounting,* August 1993, Institute of Management Accountants, Montvale, NJ.

The usefulness of standard cost systems, which have been used as the primary cost control vehicle by U.S. firms for the last several decades, recently has been questioned by many practitioners and academicians.

Activity-based cost management has gained a prominent status in cost management by clearly depicting the demands a firm's various activities, production as well as other corporate functions, place on the firm's resources. On another front, target costing has emerged as the system that is effective in managing costs in the new product design and development stage.[1]

Kaizen costing, a critical means of ensuring continuous improvement activities used by Japanese auto makers, supports the cost reduction process in the manufacturing phase. Employed together with target costing, Kaizen costing helps Japanese manufacturers achieve their goal of cost reduction in the entire product design development production cycle.

To illustrate this process, we look at the Kaizen costing practice used by Daihatsu Motor Company of Osaka, Japan. Daihatsu, a mini-car manufacturer owned in part by Toyota, ranks seventh of the nine Japanese automakers in terms of their domestic sales volume. In Japan, Daihatsu's mini-car sales outnumber Isuzu, Mazda, and Subaru. It has established mini-car markets in more than 120 countries. In the United States, Daihatsu began marketing Charade, its only U.S. passenger car, and Rocky, a sports truck, in 1988 from its subsidiary, Daihatsu America Inc. of Los Alamitos, Calif. In early 1992, Daihatsu announced its plan to withdraw from the U.S. market due to its strategy change. As a partner of Daihatsu, Toyota uses a similar system of Kaizen costing discussed here.

THE AIM OF KAIZEN COSTING IS DIFFERENT

Kaizen costing, functioning in a similar fashion as a budgetary control system, operates outside the standard cost system. It aims at reducing the actual costs *below* the standard costs—in distinct contrast to the focus of a standard cost system, which emphasizes meeting the cost standards. Daihatsu's Kaizen costing calls for the establishment of a cost reduction target amount and its accomplishment through Kaizen activities—continuous improvement in operations.

Daihatsu defines Kaizen costing activities as those activities that "sustain the current level of the existing car production costs, and further reduce it to the expected level based on the company plan." These cost-improvement activities are very specific with respect to each department and each accounting period.

The periodic cost-improvement process is preceded by the annual budgeting process, or short-term profit planning process, which represents the first-year segment of Daihatsu's five-year long-range plan. In the short-term profit—planning process, each department prepares the following:

Plan 1. Production, Distribution, and Sales Plan (which includes projections of contribution margins from sales).

Plan 2. Projected Parts and Materials Costs.

Plan 3. Plant Rationalization Plan (projected reductions in manufacturing variable costs).

Plan 4. Personnel Plan (for direct labor work force and service department personnel).

Plan 5. Facility Investment Plan (capital budget and depreciation).

Plan 6. Fixed Expense Plan (for prototype design costs, maintenance costs, advertising and sales promotion expenses, and general and administrative expenses).

These six projections and plans, when their costs and profits are incorporated together in the current period planning pocess, become the annual profit budget.

The production, distribution, and sales plan is the nucleus of the current period planning process. The plan establishes the planned profit contributions using a variable costing approach, based on the actual cost performance of the previous year, and the estimated volumes and prices of car models in the coming year.

In a formula,

Total planned profit contribution =

the sum of contribution margin
per unit of each car model i of $\times$ estimated sales volume of the car model i
the previous year

The actual cost performance of the previous year is used as cost standards for the coming year.

Projected parts and materials costs provide the targets to attain for the purchasing department. The plant rationalization plan, which represents projections for reductions in manufacturing variable costs, is the core component of Kaizen costing practice in a plant. It provides variable manufacturing cost reduction targets. The personnel plan provides cost reduction targets for direct and indirect labor.

The sales forecast for the year turns into budgeted operating profit through the following process, as illustrated in Figure 1. Expected variable costs, which represent standard costs, are subtracted from budgeted sales to yield budgeted contribution margin in Plan 1. Plan 2 and Plan 3 provide expected changes in variable costs, which are used to adjust the contribution margin. Expected fixed costs from Plan 4, Plan 5, and Plan 6 are deducted from the adjusted contribution margin to produce budgeted operating profit. Labor costs are treated as fixed costs because labor transfers within the company do not change the total

FIGURE 1

From Sales Forecast to Budgeted Operating Profit

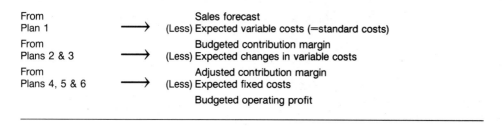

labor cost used in the profit plan for the company as a whole. At Daihatsu, the cost improvement plans (Plan 3 and Plan 4) are integrated with the profit plan. Plan 2, Plan 5, and Plan 6 also influence costs.

The annual budgeted profit for the company is broken down to budgeted profits of sales departments. The performance of each sales department is evaluated by comparing actual profits to budgeted profits, which is done for each car model. For this purpose, standard costs of sales (computed based on the actual costs of the previous year) and general administrative expenses are subtracted from actual sales revenues to yield actual profits.

KAIZEN COSTING—PLANT COST IMPROVEMENT SYSTEM

At Daihatsu plants, cost improvement through Kaizen costing, which is also called "plant total expense management," is practiced as follows:

Variable Cost Improvement. The actual production cost per car of the previous year serves as the cost base of the current year. Cost reductions will be determined from this base figure. The ratio of the target reduction amount to the cost base is called the target reduction rate. Figure 2 illustrates the relationships among them. The horizontal axis represents monthly measurements. The vertical axis denotes amounts.

Total cost base of the current month is calculated as follows:

$$\text{Total cost base of the current month} = \text{Current cost base per car} \times \text{Actual production quantity of the month}$$

The production quantity of the month, which is used in the above formula, represents the "converted quantity" for a typical car model. The converted quantity, which is measured based on labor hours, is used to determine what grade of performance has been achieved as explained below.

FIGURE 2

The Cost Base and The Target Reduction Amount

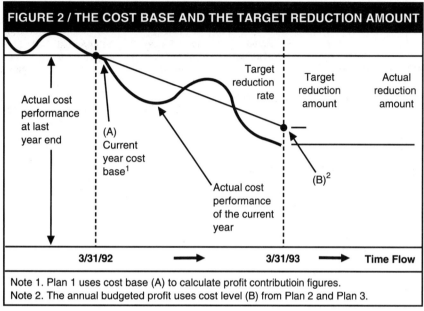

FIGURE 2 / THE COST BASE AND THE TARGET REDUCTION AMOUNT

Note 1. Plan 1 uses cost base (A) to calculate profit contributioin figures.
Note 2. The annual budgeted profit uses cost level (B) from Plan 2 and Plan 3.

Let us assume we want to measure department performance using the production quantity converted in a car model A. As presented in Table 1, target labor times of all the models—A, B, and C—are multiplied by the respective production quantities to yield total target time, which is calculated as 108,000 minutes. Total target time (108,000 minutes) divided by the cost base per car of model A (30 minutes) produces the converted quantity of 3,600 units. [108,000/30 = 3,600] The actual performance per a converted model A, 30.3 minutes, is computed by dividing total actual time (109,000 minutes) by the converted quantity of 3,600 units. [109,000/3,600 = 30.3] The achieved grade of 99.1% is calculated by dividing the target labor time for model A (30 minutes) by the actual performance per the converted model (30.3 minutes). [30/30.3 = 99.1%]

In order to evaluate the performance of each department, actual cost reduction, called actually rationalized amount, is first computed. This amount is compared to the target reduction amount, and variance is calculated as follows:

TABLE 1

Calculation of the Converted Quantity in Labor Hours Table

Models	(1) Target Labor Time (min.)	(2) Actual Production Quantity	(3) = (1) × (2) Total Target Labor Time (min.)	(4) Total Actual Labor Time (min.)	(5) = (4)/(2) Actual Performance per car (min./car)
A	30	2,000	60,000	57,000	28.5
B	50	800	40,000	40,000	50.5
C	40	200	8,000	12,000	60.5
		3,000	108,000	109,000	Achieved Grade 99.1%

NOTE: "Converted quantity" for car model A
= Total target labor time/target labor time per car of model A
= 108,000/30
= 3,600

Actually rationalized amount (A) =

$$\text{total cost base of the current month} - \text{total actual cost of the current month}$$

Variance =
actually rationalized amount (A) − target cost reduction amount

The variance calculated here is the real performance indicator for a specific department. It indicates whether an actual cost reduction that has been achieved is satisfactory compared to the target. Even a positive actually rationalized amount (A) is evaluated as "unfavorable" if the variance from the target is negative (Table 2.)

In Table 2, Plant A, as a whole, has exceeded the Kaizen target by +5 although the actually rationalized amount of indirect labor cost was −5. Plant B, with an unfavorable variance of 3, has not attained the Kaizen cost target.

Fixed Cost Improvement. The target cost reduction amount is not prepared for fixed costs in the same manner as it is done for variable costs, with the exception of energy cost. For fixed costs, the total budgeted amount of each cost element is considered a target. If the actual performance is better than the budgeted, the rationalization objective is regarded as achieved.

TABLE 2

Kaizen Costing Performance Evaluation

		Current Month			Cumulative	
	Target	Actual	Variance	Target	Actual	Variance
Plant A Costs						
Direct labor	40	35	(5)	160	165	5
Indirect labor	0	(5)	(5)	0	(35)	(35)
Material	15	25	10	60	75	15
Energy	10	15	5	40	50	10
Transportation	5	5	0	20	35	15
Total	70	75	5	280	290	10
Plant B Costs						
Direct labor	20	25	5	80	75	(5)
Indirect labor	0	5	5	0	10	10
Material	10	5	(5)	40	25	(15)
Energy	5	0	(5)	20	15	(5)
Transportation	5	2	(3)	20	15	(5)
Total	40	37	(3)	160	140	(20)

Note: Target: Target cost reduction amount
     Actual: Actually realized amount
     ( ): Loss or unattained amount

DETERMINATION OF COST REDUCTION TARGETS

Daihatsu establishes the target cost reduction rate for each cost element, relating to the cost base per car, at each year-end for the following year, as shown in Table 3. The company-wide target reduction amount is computed as follows:

Company-wide target reduction amount =

Sum of Cost base   Converted production   Target reduction rate for
per car for each $\times$ quantity of the current $\times$ each cost element j
cost element j   year

Variations in prices and wage rates are not reflected in performance evaluation. Reductions in labor hours, resource usage, and expense figures are scrutinized. The target reduction rate for each cost element is almost fixed each year. Only small changes are made, with the exception of transportation and energy costs, which undergo changes on a larger scale. The assigned target reduction rate in each plant may be higher or lower than the company-wide rate.

The company-wide cost reduction target amount is allocated to each plant based on the proportion of the following cost (C) of each plant to the combined total cost of all plants:

$$C = \begin{array}{c} \text{Total cost base of a plant per car} \\ \text{at the end of the previous year} \end{array} \times \begin{array}{c} \text{Actual converted production quantity} \\ \text{of the plant in the previous year} \end{array}$$

While the calculation formula is established, the allocation process is not rigidly set. The director in charge of all plants incorporates other factors, which are unique for each plant, into consideration also before allocations are finalized.

The decision to decompose the cost reduction target into various cost elements and departments is delegated to each plant. Within each plant the objective decomposition process proceeds downward through the hierarchical organization line:

Plant top management $\longrightarrow$ Department $\longrightarrow$ Section $\longrightarrow$ Subsection $\longrightarrow$ Process

During the decomposition process, multiple meetings are held at each hierarchical level within the plant. In such meetings the target reduction rate will be determined on the basis of how successful each unit was in the previous year in achieving the assigned Kaizen cost target. The decomposition process helps section managers become more cost conscious.

CHANGES IN TARGET RATES

The target reduction rate in Kaizen costing sometimes represents the integration of (a) the target reduction rate of the cost improvement system that functions within the annual profit planning process and (b) the target reduction rate of a cost improvement project or a cost improvement committee, which is initiated on an ad hoc basis.

The ad-hoc cost improvement project or committee is established (1) when the company faces serious external challenges, such as an oil crisis, yen currency's sudden appreciation, etc.; and/or (2) when the company faces a specific need to reduce the costs of certain car models.

Accordingly, the integrated target reduction rate of a cost element represents the combination of the rate (a) and the rate (b). The total Kaizen cost target, therefore, should reflect the integrated target reductions rates of all cost elements.

The target reduction rates shown in Table 3 are yearly rates. For actual implementation of Kaizen activities, however, the yearly rates must be translated into monthly rates. This is usually done by dividing the yearly target reduction rates by 12 months. Based on the monthly rates, the monthly Kaizen costs, target direct labor hours, and so on, are established.

Although target reduction rates are applied in a linear fashion, the rates are often revised in mid-year for the following reasons:

TABLE 3

Target Reduction Rate for Each Cost Element

Cost Elements	Evaluation Measures	Annual Target Reduction Ratio
Direct Materials Costs		
Raw material (Casting metals, sheet metals, etc.)	Monetary amount per unit of car	xx%
Purchased parts	Monetary amount per unit of car	xx%
Other direct materials (paints, thinner, etc.)	Monetary amount per unit of car	xx%
Conversion Costs		
Variable:		
Variable indirect material (supplies, etc.)	Monetary amount per unit of car	xx%
Parts transportation	Total monetary amount	xx%
Variable overhead (utilities)	Monetary amount per unit of car	xx%
Direct labor	Labor hours per unit of car	xx%
Fixed:		
Indirect labor	Number of workers and overtime	Note 1
Other fixed costs:		
Office utilities	Total monetary amount	xx%
Service department	Total monetary amount	Note 1
Depreciation	Total monetary amount	Note 1

Note 1: The target reduction rate is not established for these cost elements. The difference between the budgeted and actual total amounts is used to evaluate the rationalization (cost reduction) efforts.

A design change in the middle of the year. A design change may be caused by:

- Specification change from the viewpoint of the quality reliability counter-measures against customer claims;
- Value analysis (value engineering) based on continuous improvement (Kaizen) activities; and
- Certain demands of customers for additional options of a car.

Among all the factors that cause a mid-year design change, the first factor would certainly increase costs. This would lead to an upward revision of the cost base of direct labor hours and the target Kaizen cost. The revisions would support a fair evaluation of cost improvement activities of a plant. Such revisions are made on a monthly basis.

Currently value engineering is performed most thoroughly in the development and design phase, and target costing is applied to this phase. The role of value engineering is rather limited in the Kaizen costing process that is employed in the manufacturing phase. The coordination of target costing and Kaizen costing is done to ensure a proper implementation of the total cost management goal

FIGURE 3

Time Flow and Kaizen Costing

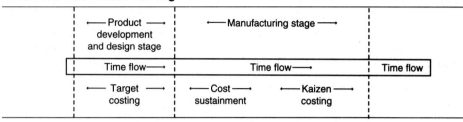

for the company. This is necessary because, when safety as a quality is emphasized in the development phase, the sheet metal, for example, could be made very thick. This could satisfy the safety criterion at the expense of other improvement activities when work-pieces flow in the line.

The alteration of mixed model production. The second reason for the change in target reduction rate is the alteration of the models in an assembly line in any month. When models change, the average assembly labor hours will change. This leads to the subsequent change in the converted quantity of a representative model. The monthly cost base G (standard) will be

$$G = \begin{array}{l}\text{Cost base of all cost elements per a} \\ \text{representative car}\end{array} \times \text{Monthly converted quantity}$$

Therefore, when the car models that flow in a line change in the middle of the year, the monthly reduction target for direct labor hours should be revised accordingly.

KAIZEN COSTING—STRENGTHS AND WEAKNESSES

When related to the stages of product development, design, and manufacturing, Kaizen costing follows target costing when time flow is considered, as illustrated in Figure 3. A substantial part of many Japanese auto makers' successful cost control is realized in the product development and design stage employing target costing.

Kaizen costing as compared to standard costing aims at reducing costs in a very aggressive manner. See Table 4. As a result, it may be overly stressful and taxing to the employees and managers. In order not to overwhelm them, Daihatsu, as well as those other Japanese auto makers who use Kaizen costing, has installed a grace period in the manufacturing stage. During this period, which

TABLE 4

Standard vs. Kaizen Costing

Standard Costing Concepts	Kaizen Costing Concepts
Cost control system concept	Cost reduction system concept
Assume current manufacturing conditions	Assume continuous improvement in manufacturing
Meet cost performance standards	Achieve cost reduction targets
Standard Costing Techniques	**Kaizen Costing Techniques**
Standards are set annually or semiannually	Cost reduction targets are set and applied monthly
	Continuous improvement (Kaizen) is implemented during the year to attain target profit or to reduce the gap between target profit and estimated profit
Cost variance analysis involving standard costs and actual costs	Cost variance analysis involving target Kaizen costs and actual costs reduction amounts
Investigate and respond when standards are not met	Investigate and respond when target Kaizen amounts are not attained

follows a new model introduction to the manufacturing area, a system of cost sustainment becomes operational.

The cost sustainment system allows for the learning process to take place before the goals of target costing and Kaizen costing are imposed upon the organizational units. This system is positioned where it is primarily because of the difficulty of attaining Kaizen targets so early in the stage. Organizational units are required to sustain the actual cost levels of the previous period rather than to improve upon them. The period of cost sustainment lasts about three months for the date of a new model introduction.

As we discussed earlier, Kaizen costing is implemented outside the standard cost accounting system and is not limited by the financial accounting focus of the standard costing system in Japanese automakers. The strength of Kaizen costing comes from its close link with the profit planning process of the whole company. This consistent connection with the overall planning and budgeting process ensures that the company can monitor its progress toward the long-term goals without being confined to the tasks of meeting cost standards and investigating variances in conventional cost control systems.

Notes

Please refer to Y. Monden and K. Hamada. "Target Costing and Kaizen Costing in Japanese Automobile Companies," *Journal of Management Accounting Research*, Fall 1991, pp. 16–34, for an overall perspective of the total cost management approach used by Japanese auto makers.

Glossary

ABC—see *activity-based costing.*

Absorption costing—A method of costing that assigns all or a portion of the manufacturing costs to products or other cost objects. The costs assigned include those that vary with the level of activity performed and also those that do not vary with the level of activity performed.

Activity—1. Work performed within an organization. 2. The aggregations of actions performed within an organization that are useful for purposes of activity-based costing.

Activity analysis—The identification and description of activities in an organization. Activity analysis involves determining what activities are done within a department, how many people perform the activities, how much time they spend performing the activities, what resources are required to perform the activities, what operational data best reflect the performance of the activities, and what value the activity has for the organization. Activity analysis is accomplished by means of interviews, questionnaires, observations, and reviews of physical records of work.

Activity attributes—Characteristics of individual activities. Attributes include cost drivers, cycle time, capacity, and performance measures. For example, a measure of the elapsed time required to complete an activity is an attribute. (See *cost driver* and *performance measures.*)

Activity capacity—The demonstrated or expected capacity of an activity under normal operating conditions, assuming a specified set of resources and over a long period of time. An example of this would be a rate of output for an activity expressed as 500 cycles per hour.

Activity cost assignment—The process in which the cost of activities are attached to cost objects using activity drivers. (See *cost object*, and *activity driver.*)

Activity cost pool—A grouping of all cost elements associated with an activity. (See *cost element.*)

Activity driver—A measure of the frequency and intensity of the demands placed on activities by cost objects. An activity driver is used to assign costs to cost objects. It

---

This glossary is based on the Computer Aided Manufactuirng-International, Inc. (CAM-I) "Glossary of Activity-Based Management," edited by Norm Raffish and Peter B.B. Turney. CAM-I is a not-for-profit membership organization with offices in Arlington, Texas, and Poole, England. Norm Raffish is a manager with Ernst & Young in Woodland Hills, California. Peter B.B. Turney is a professor of cost management at Portland State University in Portland, Oregon.

represents a line-item on the bill of activities for a product or customer. An example is the number of part numbers, which is used to measure the consumption of material-related activities by each product, material type, or component. The number of customer orders measures the consumption of order-entry activities by each customer. Sometimes an activity driver is used as an indicator of the output of an activity, such as the number of purchase orders prepared by the purchasing activity. (See *intensity, cost object,* and *bill of activities.*)

Activity driver analysis—The identification and evaluation of the activity drivers used to trace the cost of activities to cost objects. Activity driver analysis may also involve selecting activity drivers with a potential for cost reduction. (See *Pareto analysis.*)

Activity level—A description of how an activity is used by a cost object or other activity. Some activity levels describe the cost object that uses the activity and the nature of this use. These levels include activities that are traceable to the product (i.e., unit-level, batch-level, and product-level costs), to the customer (customer-level costs), to a market (market-level costs), to a distribution channel (channel-level costs), and to a project, such as a research and development project (project-level costs).

Activity-based costing—A methodology that measures the cost and performance of activities, resources, and cost objects. Resources are assigned to activities, then activities are assigned to cost objects based on their use. Activity-based costing recognizes the causal relationships of cost drivers to activities.

Activity-based cost system—A system that maintains and processes financial and operating data on a firm's resources, activities, cost objects, cost drivers, and activity performance measures. It also assigns cost to activities and cost objects.

Activity-based management—A discipline that focuses on the management of activities as the route to improving the value received by the customer and the profit achieved by providing this value. This discipline includes cost driver analysis, activity analysis, and performance measurement. Activity-based management draws on Activity-based costing as its major source of information. (See *customer value.*)

Allocation—1. An apportionment or distribution. 2. A process of assigning cost to an activity or a cost object when a direct measure does not exist. For example, assigning the cost of power to a machine activity by means of machine hours is an allocation, because machine hours is an indirect measure of power consumption. In some cases, allocations can be converted to tracing by incurring additional measurement costs. Instead of using machine hours to allocate power consumption, for example, a company can place a power meter on machines to measure actual power consumption. (See *tracing.*)

Assignment—See *cost assignment.*

Attributes—Characteristics of activities, such as cost drivers and performance measures. (See *cost driver* and *performance measure.*)

Attribution—See *tracing.*

Avoidable cost—A cost associated with an activity that would not be incurred if the activity was not required. The telephone cost associated with vendor support, for example, could be avoided if the activity were not performed.

Backflush costing—1. A costing method that applies costs based on the output of a process. The process uses a bill of material or a bill of activities explosion to draw quantities from inventory, through work-in-process, to finished goods; at any intermediate stage, using the output quantity as the basis. These quantities are generally costed using standard costs. The process assumes that the bill of material (or bill of activities) and the standard costs at the time of backflushing represent the actual quantities and resources used in the manufacture of the product. This is important, since no shop orders are usually maintained to collect costs. 2. A costing method generally associated with repetitive manufacturing. (See *repetitive manufacturing* and *standard costing*.)

Benchmarking—See *best practices*.

Best practices—A methodology that identifies an activity as the benchmark by which a similar activity will be judged. This methodology is used to assist in identifying a process or technique that can increase the effectiveness or efficiency of an activity. The source may be internal (e.g., taken from another part of the company) or external (e.g., taken from a competitor). Another term used is *competitive benchmarking*.)

Bill of activities—A listing of the activities required (and, optionally, the associated costs of the resources consumed) by a product or other cost object.

Budget—1. A projected amount of cost or revenue for an activity or organizational unit covering a specific period of time. 2. Any plan for the coordination and control of resources and expenditures.

Capital decay—1. A quantification of the lost revenues or reduction in net cash flows sustained by an entity due to obsolete technology. 2. A measure of uncompetitiveness.

Carrying cost—See *holding cost*.

Competitive benchmarking—See *best practices*.

Continuous improvement program—A program to eliminate waste, reduce response time, simplify the design of both products and processes, and improve quality.

Cost Accounting Standards—1. Rules promulgated by the Cost Accounting Standards Board of the United States Government to ensure contractor compliance in the accounting of government contracts. 2. A set of rules issued by any of several authorized organizations or agencies, such as the American Institute of Certified Public Accountants (AICPA) or the Association of Chartered Accountants (ACA), dealing with the determination of costs to be allocated, inventoried, or expensed.

Cost assignment—The tracing or allocation of resources to activities or cost objects. (See *allocation* and *tracing*.)

Cost center—The basic unit of responsibility in an organization for which costs are accumulated.

Cost driver—Any factor that causes a change in the cost of an activity. For example, the quality of parts received by an activity (e.g., the percent that are defective) is a determining factor in the work required by that activity, because the quality of parts received affects the resources required to perform the activity. An activity may have multiple cost drivers associated with it.

Cost driver analysis—The examination, quantification, and explanation of the effects of cost drivers. Management often uses the results of cost driver analyses in continuous improvement programs to help reduce throughput time, improve quality, and reduce cost. (See *cost driver* and *continuous improvement program*.)

Cost element—An amount paid for a resource consumed by an activity and included in an activity cost pool. For example, power cost, engineering cost, and depreciation may be cost elements in the activity cost pool for a machine activity. (See *activity cost pool, bill of activities,* and *resource*.)

Cost object—Any customer, product, service, contract, project, or other work unit for which a separate cost measurement is desired.

Cost of quality—All the resources expended for appraisal costs, prevention costs, and both internal and external failure costs of activities and cost objects.

Cost pool—See *activity cost pool.*

Cross-subsidy—The improper assignment of costs among cost objects such that certain cost objects are overcosted while other cost objects are undercosted relative to the activity costs assigned. For example, traditional cost accounting systems tend to overcost high-volume products and undercost low-volume products.

Customer value—The difference between customer realization and sacrifice. *Realization* is what the customer receives, which includes product features, quality, and service. This takes into account the customer's cost to use, maintain, and dispose of the product or service. *Sacrifice* is what the customer gives up, which includes the amount the customer pays for the product plus time and effort spent acquiring the product and learning how to use it. Maximizing customer value means maximizing the difference between realization and sacrifice.

Differential cost—See *incremental cost.*

Direct cost—A cost that is traced directly to an activity or a cost object. For example, the material issued to a particular work order or the engineering time devoted to a specific product are direct costs to the work orders or products. (See *tracing*.)

Direct tracing—See *tracing.*

Discounted cash flow—A technique used to evaluate the future cash flows generated by a capital investment. Discounted cash flow is computed by discounting cash flows to determine their present value.

Diversity—Conditions in which cost objects place different demands on activities or activities place different demands on resources. This situation arises, for example, when there is a difference in mix or volume of products that causes an uneven assignment of costs. Different types of diversity include: *batch-size, customer, market, product mix, distribution channel,* and *volume*.

Financial accounting—1. The accounting for assets, liabilities, equities, revenues, and expenses as a basis for reports to external parties. 2. A methodology that focuses on reporting financial information primarily for use by owners, external organizations, financial institutions. This methodology is constrained by rule-making bodies such as the Financial Accounting Standards Board (FASB), the Securities Exchange Commission (SEC), and the American Institute of Certified Public Accountants (AICPA).

First-stage allocation—See *resource cost assignment.*

Fixed cost—A cost element of an activity that does not vary with changes in the volume of cost drivers or activity drivers. The depreciation of a machine, for example, may be direct to a particular activity, but it is fixed with respect to changes in the number of units of the activity driver. The designation of a cost element as fixed or variable may vary depending on the time frame of the decision in question and the extent to which the volume of production, activity drivers, or cost drivers changes.

Flexible factory—The objective of a flexible factory is to provide a wide range of services across many product lines in a timely manner. An example is a fabrication plant with several integrated manufacturing cells that can perform many functions for unrelated product lines with relatively short lead times.

Focused factory—The objective of a focused factory is to organize around a specific set of resources to provide low cost and high throughput over a narrow range of products.

Forcing—Allocating the costs of a sustaining activity to a cost object even though that cost object may not clearly consume or causally relate to that activity. Allocating a plant-level activity (such as heating) to product units using an activity driver such as direct labor hours, for example, forces the cost of this activity to the product. (See *sustaining activity* .)

Full absorption costing—See *absorption costing.*

Functional decomposition—Identifies the activities performed in the organization. It yields a hierarchical representation of the organization and shows the relationship between the different levels of the organization and its activities. For example, a hierarchy may start with the division and move down through the plant, function, process, activity, and task levels.

Holding cost—A financial technique that calculates the cost of retaining an asset (e.g., finished goods inventory or a building). Generally, the calculation includes a cost of capital in addition to other costs such as insurance, taxes, and space.

Homogeneity—A situation in which all the cost elements in an activity's cost pool are consumed in proportion to an activity driver by all cost objects. (See *cost element, activity cost pool,* and *activity driver.*)

Incremental cost—1. The cost associated with increasing the output of an activity or project above some base level. 2. The additional cost associated with selecting one economic or business alternative over another, such as the difference between working overtime or subcontracting the work. 3. The cost associated with increasing the quantity of a cost driver. (Also known as *differential cost.*)

Indirect cost—The cost that is allocated—as opposed to being traced—to an activity or a cost object. For example, the costs of supervision or heat may be allocated to an activity on the basis of direct labor hours. (See *allocation.*)

Intensity—The cost consumed by each unit of the activity driver. It is assumed that the intensity of each unit of the activity driver for a single activity is equal. Unequal intensity means that the activity should be broken into smaller activities or that a different activity driver should be chosen. (See *diversity.*)

Life cycle—See *product life cycle.*

Net present value—A method that evaluates the difference between the present value of all cash inflows and outflows of an investment using a given rate of discount. If the discounted cash inflow exceeds the discounted outflow, the investment is considered economically feasible.

Non-value-added activity—An activity that is considered not to contribute to customer value or to the organization's needs. The designation non-value-added reflects a belief that the activity can be redesigned, reduced, or eliminated without reducing the quantity, responsiveness, or quality of the output required by the customer or the organization. (See *customer value* and *value analysis*.)

Obsolescence—A product or service that has lost its value to the customer due to changes in need or technology.

Opportunity cost—The economic value of a benefit that is sacrificed when an alternative course of action is selected.

Pareto analysis—The identification and interpretation of significant factors using Pareto's rule that 20 percent of a set of independent variables is responsible for 80 percent of the result. Pareto analysis can be used to identify cost drivers or activity drivers that are responsible for the majority of costs incurred by ranking the cost drivers in order of value. (See *cost driver analysis* and *activity driver analysis*.)

Performance measures—Indicators of the work performed and the results achieved in an activity, process, or organizational unit. Performance measures may be financial or nonfinancial. An example of a performance measure of an activity is the number of defective parts per million. An example of a performance measure of an organizational unit is return on sales.

Present value—The discounted value of a future sum or stream of cash flows.

Process—A series of activities that are linked to perform a specific objective. For example, the assembly of a television set or the paying of a bill or claim entails several linked activities.

Product family—A group of products or services that have a defined relationship because of physical and production similarities. (The term *product line* is used interchangeably.)

Product life cycle—The period that starts with the initial product specification and ends with the withdrawal of the product from the marketplace. A product life cycle is characterized by certain defined stages, including research, development, introduction, maturity, decline, and abandonment.

Product line—See *product family*.

Profit center—A segment of the business (e.g., a project, program, or business unit) that is accountable for both revenues and expenses.

Project—A planned undertaking, usually related to a specific activity, such as the research and development of a new product or the redesign of the layout of a plant.

Project costing—A cost system that collects information on activities and costs associated with a specific activity, project, or program.

Repetitive manufacturing—The manufacture of identical products (or a family of products) in a continuous flow.

Resource—An economic element that is applied or used in the performance of activities. Salaries and materials, for example, are resources used in the performance of activities. (See *cost element.*)

Resource cost assignment—The process by which cost is attached to activities. This process requires the assignment of cost from general ledger accounts to activities using resource drivers. For example, the chart of accounts may list information services at a plant level. It then becomes necessary to trace (assuming that tracing is practical) or to allocate (when tracing is not practical) the cost of information services to the activities that benefit from the information services by means of appropriate resource drivers. It may be necessary to set up intermediate activity cost pools to accumulate related costs from various resources before the assignment can be made. (See *activity cost pool* and *resource driver.*)

Resource driver—A measure of the quantity of resources consumed by an activity. An example of a resource driver is the percentage of total square feet of space occupied by an activity. This factor is used to allocate a portion of the cost of operating the facilities to the activity.

Responsibility accounting—An accounting method that focuses on identifying persons or organizational units that are accountable for the performance of revenue or expense plans.

Risk—The subjective assessment of the possible positive or negative consequences of a current or future action. In a business sense, risk is the premium asked or paid for engaging in an investment or venture. Often risk is incorporated into business decisions through such factors as hurdle rates or the interest premium paid over a prevailing base interest rate.

Second-stage allocation—See *activity cost assignment.*

Standard costing—A costing method that attaches costs to cost objects based on reasonable estimates or cost studies and by means of budgeted rates rather than according to actual costs incurred.

Sunk cost—Costs that has been invested in assets for which there is little, if any, alternative or continued value except salvage. Using sunk costs as a basis for evaluating alternatives may lead to incorrect decisions. Examples are the invested cost in a scrapped part or the cost of an obsolete machine.

Support costs—Costs of activities not directly associated with production. Examples are the costs of process engineering and purchasing.

Surrogate activity driver—An activity driver that is not descriptive of an activity, but that is closely correlated to the performance of the activity. The use of a surrogate activity driver should reduce measurement costs without significantly increasing the costing bias. The number of production runs, for example, is not descriptive of the material disbursing activity, but the number of production runs may be used as an activity driver if material disbursements coincide with production runs.

Sustaining activity—An activity that benefits an organization at some level (e.g., the company as a whole or a division, plant, or department), but not any specific cost object. Examples of such activities are preparation of financial statements, plant management, and the support of community programs.

Target cost—A cost calculated by subtracting a desired profit margin from an estimated (or a market-based) price to arrive at a desired production, engineering, or marketing cost. The target cost may not be the initial production cost, but instead the cost that is expected to be achieved during the mature production stage. (See *target costing.*)

Target costing—A method used in the analysis of product and process design that involves estimating a target cost and designing the product to meet that cost. (See *target cost.*)

Technology costs—A category of cost associated with the development, acquisition, implementation, and maintenance of technology assets. It can include costs such as the depreciation of research equipment, tooling amortization, maintenance, and software development.

Technology valuation—A nontraditional approach to valuing technology acquisitions that may incorporate such elements as purchase price, start-up costs, current market value adjustments, and the risk premium of an acquisition.

Throughput—The rate of production of a defined process over a stated period of time. Rates may be expressed in terms of units of products, batches produced, dollar turnover, or other meaningful measurements.

Traceability—The ability to assign a cost by means of a causal relationship directly to an activity or a cost object in an economically feasible way. (See *tracing.*)

Tracing—The assignment of cost to an activity or a cost object using an observable measure of the consumption of resources by the activity or cost object. Tracing is generally preferred to allocation if the data exist or can be obtained at a reasonable cost. For example, if a company's cost accounting system captures the cost of supplies according to which activity uses the supplies, the costs may be traced—as opposed to allocated—to the appropriate activities. Tracing is also called *direct tracing.*

Unit cost—The cost associated with a single unit of the product, including direct costs, indirect costs, traced costs, and allocated costs.

Value-added activity—An activity that is judged to contribute to customer value or satisfy an organizational need. The attribute "value added" reflects a belief that the activity cannot be eliminated without reducing the quantity, responsiveness, or quality of output required by a customer or organization. (See *customer value.*)

Value analysis—A cost reduction and process improvement tool that utilizes information collected about business processes and examines various attributes of the processes (e.g., diversity, capacity, and complexity) to identify candidates for improvement efforts. (See *activity attribute* and *cost driver.*)

Value chain—The set of activities required to design, procure, produce, market, distribute, and service a product or service.

Value-chain costing—An activity-based cost model that contains all activities in the value chain.

Variance—The difference between an expected and actual result.

Variable cost—A cost element of an activity that varies with changes in volume of cost drivers and activity drivers. The cost of material handling to an activity, for example,

varies according to the number of material deliveries and pickups to and
activity. (See *cost element, fixed cost,* and *activity driver.*) at

Waste—Resources consumed by unessential or ineffiicient activities.

Willie Sutton rule—Focus on the high-cost activities. The rule is named after bank
Willie Sutton, who—when asked "Why do you rob banks?"—is reputed to
replied "Because that's where the money is."

Work cell—A physical or logical grouping of resources that performs a defined jo
task. The work cell may contain more than one activity. For example, all the t
associated with the final assembly of a product may be grouped in a work cell.

Work center—A physical area of the plant or factory. It consists of one or more resour
where a particular product or process is accomplished.